Private Equity, Corporate Governance and the Dynamics of Capital Market Regulation

Private Equity, Corporate Governance and the Dynamics of Capital Market Regulation

editor

Justin O'Brien

Centre for Applied Philosophy and
Public Ethics, and Charles Sturt University, Australia

Imperial College Press

Published by

Imperial College Press
57 Shelton Street
Covent Garden
London WC2H 9HE

Distributed by

World Scientific Publishing Co. Pte. Ltd.
5 Toh Tuck Link, Singapore 596224
USA office: 27 Warren Street, Suite 401-402, Hackensack, NJ 07601
UK office: 57 Shelton Street, Covent Garden, London WC2H 9HE

Library of Congress Cataloging-in-Publication Data
Private equity, corporate governance and the dynamics of capital market regulation / edited by Justin O'Brien.
p. cm.
Includes bibliographical references.
ISBN-13: 978-1-86094-847-3
ISBN-10: 1-86094-847-2
1. Corporate governance. 2. Private equity. 3. Capital market--Law and legislation.
I. O'Brien, Justin.
HD2741.P765 2007
332'.042--dc22

2007040767

British Library Cataloguing-in-Publication Data
A catalogue record for this book is available from the British Library.

Printed in Singapore by World Scientific Printers (S) Pte Ltd

In Memory of Murray Edelman

Preface

As this book was going to press, the Federal Court of Australia handed down judgment in *Australian Securities and Investments Commission v Citigroup Global Markets Australia Pty Ltd*, one of the most significant cases involving the management of conflicts of interest within investment banking. The regulator claimed that Citigroup had engaged in unconscionable conduct by trading on its own account while performing corporate advisory services for Toll Holdings in its — eventually successful — bid for Patrick, itself one of the most important takeovers in the current boom. The Court dismissed the application, which was designed to clarify whether and to what extent investment banking owed specific fiduciary duties to its clients and, if so, whether these duties could be overridden through contract. Justice Jacobson ruled that the 'law does not prevent an investment bank from contracting out of or modifying any fiduciary obligation.'[1]

The ruling was a major setback for ASIC, which had hoped that its aggressive enforcement agenda would serve a wider demonstration purpose. ASIC had invested significant reputational capital in the litigation, only to be trumped by a literal interpretation of the law from a distinguished judge, who opined that the imposition of fiduciary responsibilities was 'a matter for the legislature, not the courts.'[2] Judicial resolution does not, however, solve the underlying problems identified in the litigation and magnified by the global boom in private equity. The range and intractability of conflicts have deepened, as the dynamics of financial capitalism reconfigure, in profound manner, institutional

[1] NSD 651 (28 June 2006) [601].
[2] Ibid [602].

timeframes, conceptions of corporate duty, and the efficacy of the shareholder-dominated corporate governance paradigm, and throw into stark relief the roles and responsibilities of financial intermediaries.

The issues that this book address are truly global in nature and the solutions advocated are based on the need to transcend narrow technical legal frameworks, irrespective of whether a rules or principles approach to governance is privileged. The book would not have been possible without the generous support of the Australian Research Council's Governance Research Network and the United Kingdom's Economic and Social Research Council World Economy and Finance Program. I wish to thank the respective directors, Charles Sampford and John Driffill, for providing the financing to hold an international workshop at the Australian National University in March 2007, at which earlier versions of these chapters were presented and critiqued. On behalf of the authors, I would like to thank Stephen Bottomley, John Braithwaite, Tom Campbell, John Coffee, Arie Freiberg, Graeme Hodge, Keith Houghton, Ian Ramsay, Paul Redmond and Sally Wheeler for their erudition and support throughout this process. In particular I am grateful to Malcolm Rodgers, Executive Director of Regulation at ASIC, for giving the keynote address to the workshop. My colleagues at the Centre for Applied Philosophy and Public Ethics provided exceptional logistical support and I thank Ian Sharpe and Andrew Long. I also want to record my appreciation to Michael Buckingham and Aparna Rao for their excellent research assistance.

The success of socio-legal research on financial regulation is predicated on access. Regulatory and practitioner sources in Australia, New York and London have been remarkably generous with their time. I wish to acknowledge my gratitude to the ESRC for funding my ongoing program of research (RES 156–22–0033). I also want to thank Seumas Miller and Ian Ramsay for making me feel so welcome professionally in Australia. To Darina, Elise, Jack and Justin, this book represents another investment of your time for which I am forever indebted.

Justin O'Brien
Canberra, July 2007

Contents

Contributors

Dr Dean Cocking is a Senior Research Fellow at the Centre for Applied Philosophy and Public Ethics (an Australian Research Council-funded Special Research Centre).

Melvin J Dubnick is Professor of Political Science at the University of New Hampshire, USA.

Lauren B Edelman is Agnes Roddy Robb Professor of Law and Director, Center for the Study of Law and Society, at the School of Law, University of California, Berkeley, USA.

Dr George Gilligan is a Senior Research Fellow with the Department of Business Law & Taxation, Monash University, Australia.

Pamela F Hanrahan is Associate Professor of Law, Melbourne Law School and Deputy Director of the Centre for Corporate Law and Securities Regulation, University of Melbourne, Australia.

Jennifer Hill is Professor of Corporate Law at the University of Sydney Law School, and Visiting Professor at Vanderbilt University School of Law, USA.

Nicholas M Hodson CA, CA•IFA was a partner at Ernst & Young and led its Canadian Investigative and Dispute Services until 2005.

Iain MacNeil is Alexander Stone Professor of Commercial Law at the University of Glasgow, UK.

Doreen McBarnet is a Professor at the Centre for Socio-Legal Studies at the University of Oxford, UK.

Seumas Miller is Professor of Philosophy at the Australian National University and Charles Sturt University (joint position), and Director of CAPPE.

Justin O'Brien is Professor of Corporate Governance at CAPPE and the Faculty of Business, Charles Sturt University. He is also Honorary Professor at the School of Law, Queen's University, Belfast.

Malcolm Rodgers is Executive Director, Regulation at the Australian Securities and Investments Commission. The opinions expressed in this chapter are the author's alone and do not necessarily reflect those of ASIC or its individual Commissioners.

Introduction

The Dynamics of Capital Market Governance

Justin O'Brien

Efficiency and integrity in contemporary financial markets do not correlate without direct intervention. Notwithstanding the rhetorical power of the 'invisible hand' metaphor, the laissez-faire contractual account of governance it ordains is, at base, a political construct. What constitutes the optimal level of intervention is contingent on the variable interaction of material and ideational factors. These include the depth, liquidity and importance of capital markets, interest group organisational power, and international regulatory trends. The extent and direction of change are further affected by the environmental impact of professional norms and behavioural mores on the formal and informal nodes supporting the structural architecture.[1] A critical mediating factor is the ideational terms of reference set by the wider political firmament. The extent to which it internalises market-derived conceptions of utility helps determine risk profile and appetite. The complex interaction of these vectors determines who is given voice, authority and legitimacy within the complex network of organisational forms in the overarching regulatory matrix.[2]

---

[1] Neil Fligstein, *The Architecture of Markets: An Economic Sociology of Twenty-First Century Capitalist Societies* (2001); Steven Vogel, 'Why Freer Markets Need More Rules' in Marc Candy, Martin Levin and Martin Shapiro (eds), *Creating Competitive Markets* (2006) 25, 27.

[2] Leigh Hancher and Michael Moran, 'Organizing Regulatory Space' in Leigh Hancher and Michael Moran (eds), *Capitalism, Culture and Economic Regulation* (1989) 271; for conception of regulatory space as network, see Albert-Laszlo Barabosi, *Linked: The New Science of Networks* (2002) ('Real networks are not static … there is a hierarchy of hubs

Key performance indicators for regulatory agencies ostensibly resolve the tension over the form and substance of market oversight.[3] They delineate duties and responsibilities. They set expectations against which the delivery of specific regulatory objectives can be measured. They offer assurance to the regulated that accountability extends to the regulator. They act as homogenising agents of remarkable strength.[4] Evaluating regulatory effectiveness through this lens can be, however, exceptionally problematic. As the 20th century's most celebrated mathematician recognised: 'not everything that counts can be counted, and not everything that can be counted counts.'[5]

Perception of what constitutes value differs among institutional actors in any given regulatory matrix. Relative ranking inevitably impacts on the design and authority of deployed indicators. Here it is important to differentiate between technical and value-driven indicators of performance. The first is relatively unproblematic. Technical improvements can — and should — ameliorate unnecessary duplication. Greater consultation can — and should — improve the cost–benefit analysis. Clearer governance and accountability structures can — and should — place the exercise of discretion within accepted and acceptable parameters. Furthermore, for the agency itself, careful design calibration can — and should — minimise the risk of privileging indicators designed for administrative convenience rather than analytic value.

The management of these conflicting imperatives becomes more difficult when accountability for maintenance of market probity requires

---

that keep these networks together, a heavily connected node closely followed by several less connected ones, trailed by dozens of even smaller nodes. No central node sits in the middle of the spider web, controlling and monitoring every link and every node. There is no single node a scale-free web is a web without a spider': at 221).

[3] What constitutes performance has mutated from simplistic financial measurement to 'balanced scorecard' approaches, which in turn require multidimensional mechanisms to evaluate competing perspectives: for review see David Bryde, 'Methods for Managing Different Perspectives of Project Success' (2005) 16 *British Journal of Management* 119.

[4] See, eg, Giandomenico Majone, 'Regulation in Comparative Perspective' (1999) 1 *Journal of Comparative Policy Analysis* 309. This process privileges self-regulation through nodal networks in which the state plays a diminished role. What is particularly striking is that the capacity of the state itself is circumscribed by acceptance of market-ordering terms of reference: see Clifford Shearing, 'A Constitutive Conception of Regulation' in John Braithwaite and Peter Grabosky (eds), *Business Regulation and Australia's Future* (1993) 67, 72; see also Cass Sunstein, *After the Rights Revolution: Re-Conceiving the Regulatory State* (1990) 42.

[5] The quotation was appended to a sign outside Albert Einstein's office at Princeton University.

ongoing credible commitments from those given delegated authority within fragmented or 'decentred' processes of self-regulation and co-regulation.[6] None of the aforementioned performance indicators can deal adequately with the measurement of integrity within this wider architecture.[7] Indeed, the focus on technocratic resolution exacerbates the problem, because associational imperatives can cut against personal integrity by situating ethics within narrowly defined legal parameters.[8] This occurs because of cognitive dissonance between institutional actors over what constitutes integrity and who should shoulder responsibility for probity.

Those providing corporate advisory services have long adopted a range of 'perfectly-legal' strategies to transact around 'soft' compliance obligations, including adherence to internally devised and policed codes of conduct.[9] This approach is often justified by reference to the corporate imperative to maximise profits within 'the rules of the game'.[10] To be effective across efficiency and integrity vectors, performance indicators

---

[6] For an account of how the fragmentation of authority gives rise to competing legitimacy problems, see Julia Black, 'Critical Reflections on Regulation' (2002) 27 *Australian Journal of Legal Philosophy* 1; for self-regulation as a specific policy process, see Tony Porter and Karsten Ronit, 'Self-Regulation as Policy Process: The Multiple and Criss-Crossing Stages of Private Rule-Making' (2006) 39 *Policy Sciences* 41.

[7] Integrity in an institutional sense refers to its completeness, wholeness or entirety. What constitutes integrity within a regulatory matrix is impacted by the interplay of associational, corporate, divisional and personal values: see Susan Babbitt, 'Personal Integrity, Politics and Moral Imagination' in Samantha Brennan et al (eds), *A Question of Values: New Canadian Perspectives on Ethics and Political Philosophy* (1997) 107, 118.

[8] See Bronwen Morgan, 'Technocratic v Convivial Accountability' in Michael Dowdle (ed), *Public Accountability, Designs, Dilemma and Experiences* (2006) 243, 253 (situating regulatory reform processes associated with cost–benefit analysis within a 'triadic logic' that is itself informed by the need to present decisions on the basis of 'ostensibly objective, relatively opaque, expert knowledge': at 253. This process 'mutes the discretionary, value-laden dimensions of those decisions': at 257). Morgan argues instead for a conceptualisation based on inculcating 'a particular *tenor* or *texture* of debate, a texture that transmits and generates implicit senses of community because of its capacity to defy rountinization and the explicit codes of expert knowledge': at 259 (emphasis in original). By acknowledging these assumptions, the debate takes on a more finely grained appreciation of underlying dynamics, which is central to an agonistic conception of political debate, see generally Chantal Mouffe, *On the Political* (2005) 18–25.

[9] See Doreen McBarnet and Christopher Whelan, 'The Elusive Spirit of the Law: Formalism and the Struggle for Legal Control' (1991) 54 *Modern Law Review* 848.

[10] Milton Friedman, 'The Social Responsibility of Business Is to Improve Its Profits', *New York Times* (New York), 13 September 1970, 32–3, 122–6.

need to be amenable to both specific and holistic analysis. They must be capable of evaluation — in isolation and in combination — against the transformative potential of the *ex ante* and *ex post* regulatory mechanisms deployed by operational directorates and cross-cutting inter- and intra-agency taskforces. Moreover, they must be viewed in terms of how performance impacts on the goals of regulation, not simply the processes by which this was achieved. And this requires embedding accountability throughout the regulatory system, not just the regulatory agency itself.

Critics of attempts to broaden the debate on corporate governance and purpose from value to values suggest exceeding formal legal requirements diverts the corporation from its core purpose.[11] Furthermore, if new standards are to be introduced, what should the benchmark be? Who should set it? When core values conflict, which should be privileged and why? Should interpretation of (non-) compliance and censure rest with the corporation itself (through shareholder activism), the market (with variations in share price signalling displeasure), the gatekeeper professions (given delegated authority), the regulator (through enforcement strategies that transcend the existing legal core by mandating particular governance forms) or wider society (through a reinterpretation of the core responsibilities owed by the firm in return for the benefits of incorporation)? Can this be done in a piecemeal manner? Alternatively, does it require a more fundamental reconstruction: a re-imagining, as it were, of the societal purpose of the market? Mapping how ideational disputes directly influence the trajectory of public policy allows for a consideration of whether it is possible to instil order under the current system of control or whether, as with Sisyphus, we are caught in a laborious yet futile struggle.[12]

---

[11] See Frank Easterbrook and Daniel Fischel, *The Economic Structure of Corporate Law* (1991); see also Michael Whincop, 'Another Side of Accountability: The Fiduciary Concept and Rent-Seeking in the Governance of Government Corporations' (2002) 25 *University of New South Wales Law Journal* 379.

[12] Sisyphus is one of the great tragic figures in Greek mythology. His persona is often associated with deception and hubris. A renowned trader and negotiator, he deceived the Queen of the Dead, Persephone, and escaped the Underworld. When eventually returned, he was sentenced to an eternity of interminable labour for thinking that he could defy the Gods. This involved pushing a boulder to the top of a hill only for it to slip down, whereupon he was destined to repeat the process. The cruelty of the punishment was frustration.

The problem ceases to be an academic puzzle when the regulator sets — or is set — a policy objective of enhancing integrity within technocratic terms of reference that simultaneously require market promotion. On the one hand, regulators are charged with ensuring that markets operate in a fair, efficient and transparent manner, if necessary by adopting a coercive enforcement agenda. On the other, prevailing economic and political orthodoxy links robustness to increased costs, reduced choice and capital flight.[13] The new dynamics of global financial capitalism raise a host of normative issues, which are made difficult to resolve because asymmetrical power relations produce restraining influences on national regulatory capabilities. [14]

This book advances an integrity-based approach to market regulation within a realist framework. The cardinal pillars of financial regulation, namely, market efficiency, contractual probity and financial stability, inform its conceptual parameters. Scholars and practitioners from across the social sciences and across the world outline the deficiencies associated with the current paradigm, and evaluate how to integrate more closely regulatory 'mission' or 'purpose' with the normative values posited by institutional actors, which are central to their own conceptions of what constitutes their professional ethos. The intention is to generate a synthesis that could reduce incommensurability problems. It will be argued that this approach offers a much more meaningful indicator of ultimate performance and has applicability beyond the narrow field examined in this study.

The aim is best illustrated through an extended example of the dynamics of a specific regulatory environment. The remainder of the chapter is structured as follows. First, the regulatory architecture in Australia is examined to assess how conceptions of 'best-practice' are arrived at and legitimated. As with other developed capital markets, a nexus of exogenous forces is buffeting the Australian market, not least of which is the rapid expansion of private equity. Second, the difficulties of enrolling professional groupings in the surveillance apparatus is presented and critiqued. Third, the contours of an alternative approach are delineated based on the interlocking relationship between ethics and

---

[13] McKinsey Report, *Sustaining New York's and the US' Global Financial Services Leadership* (2007); Committee on Capital Markets Regulation, *Interim Report of the Committee on Capital Markets Regulation* (2006).

[14] For perceptive analysis, see Martin Wolff, 'New Revolution as Unfettered Finance Reshapes the Global Economy', *The Australian* (Sydney), 25 June 2007, 33.

compliance. The chapter serves as an introduction to the ideas in the collection, which has been conceived as a deliberative approach to regulatory design, with a focus on how to secure agonistic acceptance of an integrated suite of high-level principles capable of transcending formal legal compliance.

I THE AUSTRALIAN REGULATORY ARCHITECTURE

The capital markets in Australia are regulated through a 'twin peaks' model of oversight.[15] The model is situated within a wide-ranging Corporate Law Economic Reform Program.[16] The framework is designed to promote confidence that fair, orderly, and transparent processes govern the market.[17] Within this rubric, the Australian Prudential Regulation Authority ('APRA') has responsibility for ensuring capital adequacy, banking regulation and the superannuation industry. Market integrity issues, including continuous disclosure, the regulation of directorial conduct and fiduciary obligations imposed on intermediating professions, fall within the ambit of the Australian Securities and Investments Commission ('ASIC'). The peak regulatory agencies

[15] For early references to the structure, see Ian Johnston, 'The New Financial Services Reform Disclosure Regime, Likely Impacts on our Industry' (Speech delivered at the Financial Planning Association Conference, Gold Coast, 10 May 2002); David Knott, 'Changing Dynamics of the Superannuation Industry' (Speech delivered at the Association of Superannuation Funds of Australia Ltd Luncheon, Sydney, 25 September 2002).

[16] See *Corporate Law Economic Reform Program* (1998) Commonwealth of Australia <http://www.treasury.gov.au/documents/264/PDF/clerp.pdf>. The CLERP process, which is now in its ninth incarnation, retains as a core objective 'the need to encourage free enterprise for the benefit of all Australians': at iv. This process has been accompanied by a similarly wide ranging review of regulatory policy: see Taskforce on Reducing Regulatory Burdens on Business, Parliament of Australia, *Rethinking Regulation: Report of the Taskforce on Reducing Regulatory Burdens on Business* (January 2006) ('Banks Report'); Australian Government, *Rethinking Regulation: Report of the Taskforce on Reducing Regulatory Burdens on Business: Australian Government's Interim Response* (April 2006); Australian Government, *Rethinking Regulation: Report of the Taskforce on Reducing Regulatory Burdens on Business: Australian Government's Response* (August 2006). See also Gary Banks, 'Reducing the Regulatory Burden: The Way Ahead' (Speech delivered at the Monash Centre for Regulatory Studies, Melbourne, 17 May 2006).

[17] As such, the reform process cannot be dismissed as a knee-jerk response to scandal, see Jennifer Hill, 'Evolving "Rules of the Game" in Corporate Governance Reform', in this book.

interdict with Treasury and specialist organisations, including the Reserve Bank of Australia (on macro-economic stability), the Australian Taxation Office (on the tax impact of financial engineering), the Australian Consumer and Competition Commission (on trade practices) and the Takeovers Panel (as the primary adjudicator of contractual disputes during merger and acquisition process).

This hybrid architecture contrasts with the unitary approach to market governance adopted by the Financial Services Authority ('FSA') in London.[18] In contradistinction with the multiplicity of organisational forms given authority in the United States,[19] the formal separation of prudential and disclosure regulation is conceptually neat and intellectually cogent. The separation allows for the simultaneous adoption of coercive and less intrusive forms of market surveillance within an integrated principles-driven framework.[20] However, unlike its counterparts in London and Washington, ASIC does not have the capacity to set rules. While discretion is limited to interpretation of legislative intent within public values, this is not an insubstantial power.[21] Independence is further circumscribed by specific policy guidelines, which are framed within a process explicitly

---

[18] Iain MacNeil, 'Enforcement of Capital Markets Regulation: The United Kingdom and Its International Markets', in this book.

[19] The Securities and Exchange Commission has oversight for the capital markets but regulation of banks fall within the Federal Reserve and the Office of the Comptroller of the Currency. In addition, state regulators have formal delegated authority and state Attorneys-General have emerged as increasingly important autonomous actors, see Justin O'Brien, 'Securing Corporate Accountability: The Efficacy and Pitfalls of Pre-Trial Diversion' (2006) 19 *Australian Journal of Corporate Law* 161.

[20] The formal separation has not been trouble-free: see, eg, Commonwealth of Australia, HIH Royal Commission, *The Failure of HIH Insurance* (2003). Commissioner Justice Owen observes that APRA 'was aware of its lack of general insurance experience, [yet] there was no evidence that any steps were put in place to monitor the progress of the individuals who had the front-line jobs supervising this industry': at 24.1.6. This systemic problem was exacerbated by the 'light and non-obtrusive supervisory methodologies adopted': at 24.1.7. He concludes: APRA did not give sufficient consideration to the consequences of reform and full integration. In this context, it did not give adequate consideration to creating systems to ensure it would meet its regulatory responsibilities. This resulted in systemic weakness in APRA's supervisory regime': at 24.1.12. Both agencies have worked hard to dispel the criticism through an ongoing series of civil prosecutions and banning orders.

[21] See ASIC, *Working for Australia: ASIC Annual Report 2005–06* (2006) 44 (requiring decision-making informed by impartiality, honesty, diligence and service); all ASIC staff are also subject to wider statutory-imposed values and codes of conduct: *Public Service Act 1999* (Cth) ss 10(1), 13.

predicated on the need to minimise transactional costs. All major policy revisions require an accompanying Regulatory Impact Statement ('RIS').[22] The RIS is a standard public policy response that defines the problem, sets out objectives, delineates options, evaluates cost and benefit, includes a consultation and recommendation statement, and outlines the strategy for implementation.[23]

Despite these restrictions, an independent taskforce charged with evaluating effectiveness has identified signs of 'regulatory creep' across the institutional framework.[24] According to its report, 'risk aversion' imperatives were particularly present in the financial sector.[25] Significantly, the Banks Report ruminated that enforcement strategies were in part to blame for reinforcing sensible commercial opportunities, thus having a detrimental impact on the 'overall efficiency and dynamism of the economy'.[26]

As noted above, the debate on what constitutes the optimum level of enforcement is predicated on what regulatory priorities are set, and how they are ranked and implemented. Even if these priorities have demonstrable 'whole of organisation' value, absent wider market professional buy-in to the concept, active enforcement is reduced to symbolic and potentially counterproductive intervention, as the case taken by ASIC against Citigroup in the Federal Court of Australia graphically demonstrates.

---

[22] Office of Best Practice Regulation, *Best Practice Regulation Handbook* (2006). It expresses a clear policy preference for time-limited intervention, for example through sunset clauses: at [4.7.6]).

[23] See Melvin J Dubnick, '*Sarbanes-Oxley* and the Search for Accountable Corporate Governance', in this book.

[24] [Taskforce on Reducing Regulatory Burdens on Business] *Rethinking Regulation*, above n 16, 14–15 (citing increased 'risk aversion' as a primary cause for increasing the burden and dysfunctional incentives facilitating its growth, for example, the lack of integration between cost and benefit, policy silos and heavy-handed and legalistic approach to enforcement).

[25] Ibid 89–90 (recommending development of performance indicators that speak directly to the need to enhance 'efficiency and reduce business costs': at 90).

[26] Ibid 90 (Recommendation 5.3). In addition, the Taskforce included a provocative statement from the Association of Australian Permanent Building Societies on guidance material emanating from APRA and ASIC: 'their observance has become almost mandatory and those that treat them as non-binding do so at their own peril. They are now in effect de facto law': at 91. The Taskforce implicitly agreed with this formulation in its demand that regulators refrain from overly prescriptive measures: at 91. It also appeared to reject any use of enforceable undertaking that imposes obligations to a higher standard of compliance than that mandated by law: at 93.

It is, of course, perfectly understandable that enforcement is one of the most widely used indicators of regulatory performance. It represents a visible and easily quantifiable metric. It also offers a means to delineate at surface level between form and substance of regulatory agendas.[27] Conversely, viewed in isolation, it skews policy direction, budgetary priorities, operational capacity and overarching effectiveness. More problematically, inculcating a punitive deterrence model can have a deleterious impact on agonistic engagement.[28] Undue emphasis on enforcement proclivity is, therefore, a flawed and potentially misleading indicator of performance but not necessarily for the reasons outlined by the Banks Report.

While a critical regulatory tool, enforcement is best viewed as a mezzanine-failure of specific market actors to understand or accept the value of self-restraint. Effective self-restraint requires the internalisation of a common conception of what constitutes ethical practice, which in turn requires thinking beyond technical compliance. What is particularly evident in the Australian context is the exceptionally narrow conception of regulatory purpose informing the Taskforce on Reducing Regulatory Burdens on Business.[29] The conflation between the means of regulation and the ultimate goals inevitably privileges minimalist intervention, designed only to correct 'market failure'.[30] This is exacerbated by an emphasis on the need to curtail direct costs rather than extend embedded value.[31] It is in this context that the need to evaluate ideational pressures comes into clear focus.

---

[27] See John Coffee, 'Law and Enforcement' (Paper delivered at the Dynamics of Capital Market Governance Forum, Australian National University, 14 March 2007).

[28] Robert Baldwin, 'The New Punitive Regulation' (2004) 67 *Modern Law Review* 351; see also Justin O'Brien, *Redesigning Financial Regulation: The Politics of Enforcement* (2007).

[29] George Gilligan, 'The Significance of Relative Autonomy in How Regulation of the Financial Services Sector Evolves', in this book.

[30] See Tony Prosser, 'Regulation and Social Solidarity' (2006) 33 *Journal of Law and Society* 364 (suggesting many of the conflicts centre on values rather than technicalities: at 372); for a practitioner's perspective, see William McDonough, 'Accountability in the Age of Global Markets', in Justin O'Brien (ed), *Governing the Corporation: Regulation and Corporate Governance in an Age of Scandal and Global Markets* (2005) 47.

[31] In this, the Australian framework mirrors the UK Treasury's SMART regime: see HM Treasury, *The Green Book: Appraisal and Evaluation in Central Government* (2007). 'SMART' is an acronym for 'specific, measurable, achievable, relevant and time-bound': at 13. If no market value can easily be adduced, values should be calculated based on tabulating 'willingness to pay' against willingness to accept: at 23.

As Lauren Edelman remarks, 'corporate governance is not only the subject of legal regulation; it is also constitutive of legal regulation.'[32] For Edelman, the governance of capital markets must be seen in the context of 'overlapping fields' of authority and 'multiple logics' through which law and regulation become infused with managerial values and assumptions. This nuanced conception contrasts starkly with the linear approach to regulatory design adopted by the Banks Report. The emasculating nature of the latter becomes evident when one examines guidelines for public agencies. The Australian Handbook on Regulatory Best Practice is instructive of the inhibiting logic. It mandates, absent compelling arguments, extensive consultation throughout the policy-making process.[33] This introduces multiple veto points to reform based on managerial conceptions of what constitutes intervention risk, including moral hazard, compliance costs, impact on competition and capital flight.[34]

Contrary to the formulation adopted in the Banks Report that 'government alone makes regulation',[35] the state is best described as a 'structural effect'.[36] Regulatory capacity is determined, in part, by the alignment of political opinion. In a recent speech the shadow Treasurer, Wayne Swan, noted that regulation was simply 'an unavoidable reality of

---

[32] Lauren B Edelman, 'Overlapping Fields and Constructed Legalities: The Endogeneity of Law', in this book.

[33] Office of Best Practice Regulation, above n 22, [2.4]. This approach dovetails that adopted by the FSA in the United Kingdom, see Harry McVea, 'Financial Services Regulation under the Financial Services Authority: A Reassertion of the Market Failure Thesis' (2005) 64 *Cambridge Law Journal* 413, 428.

[34] McVea, above n 33, 424 ('cost–benefit analysis reinforces the idea of markets as a naturally preferred form of social organisation and helps in providing a yardstick for limiting unwarranted state action': at 425).

[35] Banks, above n 16 ('Regulation is *made* by government, and most examples of inappropriate regulation can be sheeted home to deficiencies in the processes and institutions whereby governments respond to these demands': at 11 (emphasis in original)).

[36] See, eg, Timothy Mitchell, 'The Limits of the State: Beyond Statist Approaches and Their Critics' (1991) 85 *American Political Science Review* 77, 90, 94; for definitive treatment of 'structuration' theory, see Anthony Giddens, *The Constitution of Society: Outline of the Theory of Structuration* (1984); see also George Gilligan, 'The Significance of Relative Autonomy in How Regulation of the Financial Services Sector Evolves' in this book. For how this 'steers' policy through agenda setting, see Porter and Ronit, above n 6, 48–9.

modern markets' rather than a positive normative choice.[37] This reduction of purpose fails to deal with the externality costs incurred by privileging such emasculated conceptions of corporate and professional responsibility. Swan held out the possibility of ending the bifurcated model in favour of the FSA approach. More controversially, in the interim, both agencies were urged to set as an explicit goal the promotion of the financial services sector. No reference was made to how precisely the regulator should mediate its determination of promotion in the presence of conflict or how globalisation and the privileging of transactional imperatives over relational ones impacts negatively on the efficacy of professional norms.[38] These problems are magnified when the regulatory agency has responsibility for oversight of the professions as well as of the corporations to whom they provide advice, which is precisely the case in Australia.

II THE CONFLICTING ROLE OF THE PROFESSIONS

A critical component for longer-term market stability is the projection and maintenance of probity. The complexity of contemporary markets creates enormous oversight problems that can only be addressed through the formal enrolment of financial intermediaries into the surveillance apparatus. This is far from unproblematic.[39] By facilitating access to both products and markets, the professions act as 'gatekeepers' to an inherently conflicted space. The capacity of these communities of professionals to engage in self-dealing detrimental to the interests of individual clients or, by extension, the integrity of the wider market system, is central to the articulation of fiduciary obligation.[40] In common

[37] Wayne Swan, 'Speech to ASFA: Building Prosperity for the Next Decade' (Speech delivered at the Association of Superannuation Funds Australia Ltd Lunch, Westin Hotel, Sydney, 15 March 2007).

[38] See Porter and Kronit, above n 6, 59–61.

[39] See McBarnet, 'Compliance, Ethics and Responsibility: Emergent Governance Strategies in the US and UK' in this book; Cocking, 'Professional Norms' in this book; for a United States perspective, see John C Coffee, *Gatekeepers: The Professions and Corporate Governance* (2006).

[40] The fiduciary obligation originates in trust, see *Meinhard v Salmon* (1928) 164 NE 545, 546: 'A trustee is held to something stricter than the morals of the marketplace. Not honesty alone, but the punctillo of an honor the most sensitive is the standard of behavior'. In its most absolutist form, the fiduciary must render her own interests

with compliance, however, fiduciary obligation is itself a remarkably elastic proposition.[41] The relationship requires interlocking determinants: the binding (or perceived binding) obligation to act in the interests of another, without intermediating contractual provisions limiting the fiduciary's independence to act.[42] These overrides make it exceptionally differentiate a breach from manifestation of standard (if sharp) industry practice.[43]

The requirement that lawyers act as officers of the court, for example, can be deflected by reliance on fiduciary duty to justify a professional obligation to serve the client. Using claims of privilege to thwart regulatory investigations is an integral component of successful practice in the adversarial legal method, which in turn generates enormous transaction costs.[44] Recent legislative changes in Australia to the governance of the legal and accounting profession further stretch definitional limits. The expansion of Incorporated Legal Practices from New South Wales to the entire country generates new and complex ethical problems for the legal profession and its regulators, rendered more so by the historic public listing of Slater & Gordon in May 2007. By extending the benefits (and problems) of incorporation to the legal profession, another potential conflict emerges. The legal practitioner is not only an officer of the court and gatekeeper for wider market values; he or she is also now a representative of a corporate entity. This structural change exerts further potentially conflicting obligations and loyalties. In the presence of conflict, how does (or should) the individual lawyer or corporate entity order commitments and responsibilities?[45]

---

subservient to those of her client unless provided for by informed consent, see *Bristol & West Building Society v Mothew* [1998] Ch 1, 18 (Millett LJ).

[41] Paul Finn, *Fiduciary Obligations* (1977) 1.

[42] Ibid 9–13.

[43] See Kenneth B Davis, 'Judicial Review of Fiduciary Decision-Making — Some Theoretical Perspectives (1985) 80 *Northwestern University Law Review* 1.

[44] Robert Kagan, *Adversarial Legalism: The American Way of Law* (2003); Jeremy P Carver, 'The Role of the Lawyers: Hired Guns or Public Servants' in Justin O'Brien (ed), *Governing the Corporation: Regulation and Corporate Governance in an Age Of Scandal and Global Markets* (2005) 223. For an account that emphasises the technical nature of compliance across the professions, see Doreen McBarnet, 'After Enron: "Will Whiter than White Collar Crime" Still Wash' (2006) 46 *British Journal of Criminology* 1091. For its application in relation to private equity, see Douglas Cumming and Sofia Johan, 'Is It the Law or the Lawyers? Investment Covenants around the World' (2006) 12 *European Financial Management* 535.

[45] Slater & Gordon state explicitly that duties to the court will always trump short-term

The auditing profession faces structural problems of a similar and, arguably, more pressing, magnitude. The audit regulation framework in Australia is notable for the multiplicity of actors involved. This is exacerbated by ambiguity over the application and limits of requisite duties and responsibilities of each actor within the matrix. Responsibility for ensuring compliance with professional and ethical practice rests primarily with the audit firm itself through the Code of Ethics for Professional Accountants. External adjudication of effectiveness rests primarily (but not solely) within the disciplinary processes of the Accounting Professional and Ethical Standards Board, an industry-designed and controlled initiative. It lacks formal delegated authority, however, to ensure that the audit process is undertaken with due consideration of relevant ethical requirements. ASIC supplies this function through an inspection regime.

The extent to which this regime influences the dynamics of ethical performance is determined by four further factors. First, the conceptual rationale and scope of the inspection process itself, including the background and operating assumptions of those carrying out the review. Second, the extent of agreement between each of the institutional actors in the oversight process on what compliance means in practice. Third, the extent to which the findings are made public. Fourth, the methods that are chosen to disseminate to the wider profession the results of individual or collective firm performance. The complexity of this matrix of control makes it essential that each actor is cognisant of — and engages constructively with — overarching conceptions of compliance and fiduciary duty.

Dean Cocking suggests that one way forward is to reinvigorate the norms by which professional groups define themselves. For Cocking, integrity does not necessarily come from strengthened external oversight. Ethical change occurs by situating the inculcation of professional values within an overarching matrix, which gives due cognisance to the fact that technically legal opinion can have a detrimental impact on systemic integrity. Without this shift, technical gaming will render the framework worthless.

---

considerations: see Slater & Gordon, *Prospectus* (13 April 2007) 81–4, available at <http://www.slatergordon.com.au/docs/prospectus/Prospectus.pdf> ('There could be circumstances in which the lawyers of Slater & Gordon are required to act in accordance with these duties and contrary to other corporate responsibilities and against the interests of Shareholders and the short-term profitability of the Company': at 84).

III SETTING REGULATORY PRIORITIES

The book begins with an overview of the dynamics governing changes to capital markets in the aftermath of scandal. Malcolm Rodgers argues that is essential that regulatory agencies are armed with a clear conceptual underpinning of what drives policy implementation. Absent such a framework, he notes a danger of inconsistency, which is an all too common refrain across today's markets, in particular the United States. What should be the appropriate response is, however, exceptionally contested. Jennifer Hill finds 'significant differences' in regulatory strategies. These challenge any assumption of an orderly, seamless progression towards a uniform model of good corporate governance. Her analysis suggests that the most important causal factor impacting design and implementation is whether interest group cohesiveness can set or maintain the system's philosophical underpinnings. Hill concludes that a 'fluid, dynamic and increasingly fragmented picture of corporate governance has emerged' that partially falsifies the convergence thesis of company law and corporate governance. This suggests that it is essential to excavate more carefully what gives regulatory action (or inaction) authority and legitimacy.

As Hill points out, principles may provide more flexibility and discretion but 'their very lack of precision requires the *ex post* exercise of discretion based on a variety of specific factual and contextual matters, and embedded social values.' What this means in practice is conditioned by how market values infuse juridical interpretation, a process examined in detail by Lauren Edelman. In part, however, legitimacy also derives from the accreted weight of tradition, as George Gilligan explains in a compelling historical analysis of self-regulation. The interplay gives significant traction to the value of exploring financial regulation through a structuration lens. As Gilligan points out, 'social structures do not exist without human agency, but those same structures do shape the actions of people. Structures and agency are so interdependent that all change is influenced by earlier institutional praxis and no change can completely remove existing praxis, so that social agents make social facts, but always from existing social praxis.' For Gilligan, as with Edelman, legal rules and norms derive legitimacy and moral force through this interaction, which simultaneously justifies and reinforces the paradigm's ongoing force. The critical question is whether this legitimacy is, in fact, warranted. This has become imperative in the Australian context following the comprehensive defeat of ASIC in its controversial litigation against Citigroup. The case was designed to clarify the extent to which investment banks owe fiduciary obligations and, if so, whether these can be transacted around. As Pamela Hanrahan argues, enforcement is an inappropriate mechanism to change corporate practice in the absence of explicit fiduciary obligation, thus necessitating a greater emphasis on *ex ante* regulatory techniques. This takes to an the alternative approach adopted by the Financial Services Authority ('FSA') in the United Kingdom.

Despite the much-vaunted disclosure imperatives governing the regulation of capital markets in the United Kingdom, actual compliance with the spirit of its *Combined Code on Corporate Governance* (2003) ('*Combined Code*') is, at best, mixed. Iain MacNeil provides significant evidence to suggest that the 'explain' component of the 'comply or explain' principle 'is often ignored, casting doubt over the willingness of institutional investors to undertake the scrutiny envisaged by the *Combined Code* and the willingness of the FSA to undertake enforcement of the disclosure obligation on which investor scrutiny relies.'

This does not necessarily mean that the FSA lacks credible mechanisms to guide market behaviour. MacNeil rejects a mechanistic account of regulatory effectiveness: 'It follows that there can be no simple conclusions drawn between the low incidence of enforcement action and levels of compliance because compliance is a function of several different factors and it is difficult to separate the causal effect of each.' Critically, as MacNeil demonstrates, enforcement priorities are designed to uphold the integrity of the underpinning principles. To dates the defendants accepted the authority of the FSA rather than questioning legitimacy in the courts. If, however, the interpretation of what constituted the principle were challenged, this would open the door to a more complex and costly system of enforcement, precisely because the FSA has made clear that it would rely on expert adjudication.

This articulation of gatekeeper responsibility brings us to the problem of whether market integrity can be vouchsafed by a process that rewards 'creative compliance'. Flaws in the audit process exacerbate the problem. For Nicholas Hodson, a practitioner with 20 years experience as an auditor and forensic investigator, the audit is an exceptionally inefficient instrument to detect fraud. Through an extended hypothetical example he illustrates the danger of reliance on technical expertise: '*People* commit fraud: it is not the system, the controls, the processes, it is the people. While people at one end of the scale may be lazy, not very bright or prepossessing, at the other end they are extraordinary, do astounding things, put forth incredible effort, show unbelievable fortitude and will.'

The problem extends to issues that are ethically debatable but within the realms of the law, which informs Dean Cocking's critique of professional norms outlined above. This issue has also informed much of Doreen McBarnet's work on business ethics. For McBarnet, 'creative compliance' depends on cultural terms of reference. Part of the problem, as she conceives it, is that the flouting of underpinning principles in favour of narrow short-term advantage is deemed 'both clever and legitimate'. She criticises professional legal and accounting treatments that construct authoritative rules, transact around them and then use the transactional mechanism as a justification for following legal practice. To combat this, she argues for the inculcation of 'ethical compliance', a project that requires recalibrating the corporate social responsibility ('CSR') discourse. Rather than voluntary (and unenforceable) expression of commitment to core values, ethical compliance becomes constitutive of citizenship. Linking to the endogeneity of law themes developed by Edelman and Gilligan, McBarnet argues that the critical test is not whether an individual expression of CSR surpasses legal requirements but rather whether actual corporate practices meet the underpinning spirit.[46] To be successful, however, requires the institutionalisation of a much broader conception of what constitutes accountability. Melvin Dubnick cautions that effective accountability cannot be understood within one vector; rather it must be embedded throughout the matrix, based on an agonistic acceptance of underlying purpose.[47] Despite the ending of business quiescence over regulatory costs, the rise of private equity offers a time-limited opportunity to reconfigure the regulation of capital markets precisely because it represents a profound ideational challenge to the shareholder conception of the corporation. As O'Brien explores, disputation generates the opportunity to partially reconstruct the social contract governing the corporation and the market in which it

---

[46] Doreen McBarnet, 'After Enron: Corporate Governance, Creative Compliance and the Uses of Corporate Social Responsibility' in Justin O'Brien (ed), *Governing the Corporation: Regulation and Corporate Governance in an Age Of Scandal and Global Markets* (2005) 205; see also Doreen McBarnet, Aurora Voiculescu and Tom Campbell (ed), *The New Corporate Accountability: CSR and the Law* (2007).

[47] Melvin J Dubnick, 'Orders of Accountability' (Speech delivered at the World Ethics Forum: Leadership, Ethics and Integrity in Public Life, Oxford, 2006).

is nested. Notwithstanding the mediating effect of attempts to inculcate responsible corporate citizenship, governance is largely presented as a mechanism to ensure shareholder protection. Positing wealth maximisation for shareholders as the primary purpose of the corporation reduces the capacity of governance to deal with the ideational challenge presented by private equity.

Given that most leveraged buy-outs offer substantial premiums over underlying market prices, shareholders are rarely compromised, unless the sale process is itself fundamentally flawed. More generally, the dynamics of private equity make the efficacy of the gatekeeper function, accorded to intermediaries by law or professional norms, potentially unsustainable in the longer term. As O'Brien makes clear: 'at issue is not the legitimacy of private equity, but rather how the financial and social impact can be managed.'

For Seumas Miller, perennial market failure is inextricably linked to conceptual ambiguity. Miller argues that 'the basic normative question that needs to be asked of a business corporation, or financial market, is the same as for any other social institution, namely: What collective good(s) does it exist to provide?' The failure to reach a common understanding of 'purpose' makes Miller reach a damning conclusion: 'Without an answer to this question, an integrity system for the financial services sector — and a regulatory system insofar as it is concerned with institutional (ethical) integrity, as it surely must be — is quite literally without one of its basic purposes: it does not know what ethical ends it is seeking to embed in its target institution.' The mere establishment of key regulatory performance indicators cannot vouchsafe integrity within the rubric of financial capitalism. Taking a holistic approach to the problem, Miller suggests the need to design an overarching integrity system, which is defined as 'an assemblage of institutional entities, roles, mechanisms and procedures, the purpose of which is to ensure compliance with minimum *ethical* standards and promote the pursuit of *ethical* goals.'

This book has been designed as the first step on that process.

Chapter 1

The Conceptual Underpinnings of Australian Securities Regulation

Malcolm Rodgers

I want to organise my remarks under four broad headings: the importance of a clear conceptual framework for the regulatory process; some influences on ASIC's thinking over the last 15 years; some current challenges for ASIC; and the need to bring the academy and the regulatory community closer together.[1]

I A CLEAR CONCEPTUAL FRAMEWORK

Regulatory organisations like ASIC tend to be very transaction-focused. At any one time, most ASIC staff will be spending their working days dealing with transaction-level issues. Some of this work is a response to external transactions: an application for a licence to conduct a financial services business; an application for relief to facilitate for an IPO, or a new financial product; examination of a prospectus or takeover documents; and so on. ASIC staff might be working on a specific policy to provide guidance on how we approach the law as it applies to a given fact situation; or on our response to a particular law reform proposal.

Sometimes, the 'transaction' in question is created by the interplay between external conduct and regulatory response: we draw up

[1] The views expressed in this article are the author's alone and do not necessarily reflect the position of either the Australian Securities and Investments Commission or its individual Commissioners.

notices to seek information in response to a complaint about misconduct; we conduct 'desk-based' or on-site reviews to determine whether a financial market participant (or class of participants) is complying with their obligations, for example in how they manage conflicts of interest; or we commence a formal investigation into suspected misconduct with a view to bringing administrative, civil or criminal action against a miscreant, if the evidence supports it. But this myriad of transaction-based activities does not make sense internally or externally unless it can be accounted for in a conceptually coherent way.

The legislation that created ASIC and the laws it is ASIC's job to administer do not of themselves supply that coherence. They do supply some of the starting points: there are high-level 'mission-statement' expectations set out in s 1 of the *Australian Securities and Investments Commission Act 2001* (Cth); that Act and the other legislation we administer create obligations for us and give us extensive and sometimes intrusive powers to go about our job. I defy anyone to derive conceptual coherence by looking at the many obligations the legislation we administer creates for the regulated population. Some parts of it hang together and look like the product of a single mind; others are a patchwork of history, politics, and sometimes dubious drafting.

Above all, the legislative framework does not account for a key feature of regulatory activity: the exercise of regulatory discretion in just about everything we do. Our kind of regulatory policy is discretionary; so is most compliance and enforcement work. Even where we have a statutory obligation to do a piece of work — decide a licence application, or a request for relief — we have enormous discretion about the way we do that work and the resources we devote to it.

So in broad terms it is up to the regulator to supply conceptual coherence to the work it does. This does not necessarily mean esoteric or elaborate theories about regulation, about the behaviour of regulated populations, or about the efficacy of, for example, civil over criminal remedies. Nor am I suggesting we should be striving for a unified theory of everything-to-do-with-regulation. But a conceptual framework does, at a minimum, need to provide a clear and well understood basis for the decisions that the regulator's staff will take every day, and arm the regulator with the ability to communicate its thinking in a variety of venues. What questions will such a conceptual framework answer? Let me suggest four that seem absolutely necessary: Why are we doing what we're doing? Why is it important? What outcomes are we seeking? What regulatory tools will best produce those outcomes? In devising answers to those questions, we need a robust conceptual framework with at least the following key characteristics. It will be:

a) externally and whole-of-system focused: our job is to connect the big book of laws we administer to the real world (if you can call the world of capital markets and financial services the real world). In this country, we are seen as primarily as an economic regulator. If we succeed, we will contribute to the effectiveness of the economic system as a whole.
b) conduct focused: our job is to influence the behaviour of those we regulate — how they interact with their clients or the markets they participate in; how they behave in the boardroom; what conduct and attitudes they bring to the table when preparing disclosure documents; and so on.
c) value data and information about results: it is not what we do that counts, but what outcomes we produce. We need to be able to measure or otherwise account for outcomes in a meaningful way, and be able to tell whether we're making a difference.
d) guide the choice of regulatory tools: we are a regulatory agency with a broad range of tools at our disposal to produce results. Tools of persuasion, compliance monitoring and enforcement tools are all part of our armoury, and we need to make confident, well-informed decisions about what tool, or combination of tools, to use to produce a particular result.
e) be the basis of the regulator's accountability: a regulator needs a clear and comprehensive starting point as the basis for its own assessment of its performance, and to ground a credible account to its stakeholders of what it has achieved.

It will also need to be pragmatic — practice-focused in a real sense — and able to guide decisions about how we allocate resources, how we structure the organisation, what qualities we are looking for in our staff, and so on. In short, to guide all the decisions we make as managers of a regulatory agency.

A regulator who does not have a solid framework of this kind runs some grave risks. For example, regulatory decision-making may not be consistent, or be seen as capricious and unprincipled in a literal sense. That will undermine confidence in our ability to deliver. The regulator may be less able to account externally for our work in a persuasive way — and therefore likely to lose the confidence of key players in the system. Lack of confidence can manifest itself in any part of the system. It may be on the part of the government who funds us, or the on the part of consumers or the community more generally who help shape the political environment in which we operate.

Above all, lack of confidence on the part of the regulated population has immediate and serious consequences, and directly undermines the regulator's ability to deliver. That is because it usually means the regulator is less able to rely on persuasion as a way of delivering regulatory outcomes. And regulators of our type always need to be aware that persuasion is the cheapest of the tools available to the regulator — less costly than intensive supervision programs or enforcement actions. In short, what I have been arguing is that a clear and rigorous conceptual framework is crucial for the effectiveness of the regulatory process. Such a framework forms the basis of our ability to communicate persuasively with all our stakeholder groups, and to deliver on our underlying mandate.

II INFLUENCES ON ASIC'S THINKING

Under this heading I want to mention a few ideas, born in the academy, that have influenced in a fundamental way our approach to the regulator's task over the last 15 years. I plan only to mention a few. This is of course an invidious task. My selection is illustrative only and does not mean that we have not been open to other ideas, or that ASIC staff have not been diligent in keeping up with academic and other debates. I want to illustrate the openness of ASIC as an organisation to the rigorous and holistic analytical thinking that characterises much academic work. And I also want to provide an insight into how ideas that begin life in the academy can have a profound effect on the way a regulator goes about its job.

The work of Ian Ayres and John Braithwaite has influenced ASIC's thinking over many years.[2] Sometimes, I perhaps should add, in ways that its authors might not recognise, or would want to disclaim responsibility for. Nonetheless, ASIC's thinking about its role as a regulator owes much to the concepts of 'responsive regulation' and the

---

[2] Ian Ayres and John Braithwaite, *Responsive Regulation: Transcending the Deregulation Debate* (1992).

'regulatory pyramid'. Our understanding that being a regulator means more than being an enforcement agency, our concepts about having a 'regulatory toolbox' to choose from, the importance of choosing the right tool for the right task, and related ideas, are now so deeply embedded in ASIC's thinking that their intellectual origins have perhaps been obscured. In effect, an entire generation of regulators has absorbed these ideas, often without engaging with the original academic work. Thinking 'pyramidally' about our regulated population is also part of the way we think as an organisation and a culture. At the base of the pyramid, and — we hope — occupying a large proportion of it, is that part of the population who are naturally disposed (for whatever reason) to compliance. They need help, but most times education and persuasion will get them there. The second band is comprised of those who need the threat of detection and the occasional taste of coercive powers to keep them on the straight and narrow. In ASIC, these are colloquially known as those who 'keep playing until the referee blows the whistle'. And finally there is the apex part of the pyramid: the naturally non-compliant for whom enforcement looks like the only remedy that will work almost all the time.

For close to ten years, the work of Malcolm Sparrow from the Kennedy School of Government at Harvard has been a significant influence on many of us in ASIC. Malcolm ran a 5 residential school for senior staff from ASIC and other Australian regulators in 2000 and has been a regular visitor to Australia since then. From his work we take the fundamental notion that the job of the regulator is to 'pick important problems and fix them'; that this requires systematic collection of ex ante and ex post data, and both rigour and innovation in designing regulatory responses; that causation — especially in financial services regulation — is often hard to demonstrate; and that regulators often need to communicate through the use of 'stories' (accounts about why they think the interventions they made resulted in observable changes in the underlying data sets). We have also drawn heavily on his knowledge of and experiences in other regulatory disciplines: policing; occupational health and safety regulation; environmental regulation; taxation administration; and so on.

I could not leave out of this list of examples of work done in the academy that has influenced ASIC the empirical work done over many years at the Centre for Corporate Law & Securities Regulation under Ian Ramsay's leadership. This body of work is different in its influences from the two I have already mentioned, but is no less important. I single it out because of the close relevance of many of the topics researched to ASIC's activities and daily preoccupations. For example, in 2006 the Centre published research on corporate law reform and delisting, employee share ownership schemes and an empirical study of the operation of the takeovers panel (I also note also Emma Armson's work). All these were topics that, one way or another, came across my desk as a regulator last year. ASIC values highly access to data-rich analyses of current regulatory topics.

III Current Challenges

Now I want to turn to three current issues that are on ASIC's agenda. All arise from the recent debates about regulation in this country, and, one way or another, reflect issues raised in the report of the Government's Taskforce on Reducing Regulatory Burdens on Business, *Rethinking Regulation*.[3]

(A) *Accounting for Regulatory Performance*

One recommendation in the Banks Report was that regulatory agencies in the financial sector need to account more fully and effectively for the performance of their regulatory functions: outcomes-based reporting. This recommendation tied in with an existing Government initiative that responded to an earlier review — the Uhrig review. That review called for better accountability by regulatory agencies, and proposed that there be a formal exchange of letters between government and regulators in the form of a Statement of Expectations (government to regulator) and a Statement of Intent (regulator to government). Leaving aside the bureaucratic niceties, what this calls for is for regulators to do more in their public reporting than simply relate the activities they undertook. It asks for regulators to really think about, document and report on the community-wide and economy-wide outcomes they deliver in carrying out their mandated functions. The question is, what difference did you really make?

---

[3] Taskforce on Reducing Regulatory Burdens on Business, Parliament of Australia, *Rethinking Regulation: Report of the Taskforce on Reducing Regulatory Burdens on Business* (January 2006) ('the Banks Report').

This is a considerable challenge, and not amenable to simple solutions. As with our counterparts internationally, we spend considerable time and energy thinking about these things internally. There is no clearly established and effective methodology that has been tested in a variety of market and environmental conditions. It's hard, but it makes sense to strive to fulfill that expectation. In the work that we do in this area over the next year or so, we need all the help we can get.

(B) *Costs and Benefits of Regulation*

At the heart of much of the debate about 'over-regulation' in this country is industry concern that much regulation to which it is subject is burdensome, and more costly than it should be. In particular, neither the manufacturers of regulation nor its administrators have an adequate understanding of the costs imposed by the decisions they take, or subject their regulatory proposals to rigorous analysis, especially cost-benefit analysis. In our business, this is a hard ask. In principle, it should not be impossible to ascertain with some reliability the costs imposed by decisions to introduce new or changed regulation, or to administer it in a particular way. But there are two formidable hurdles.

First, cost information is held by regulated entities, not the regulator. How can industry be persuaded to part with reliable information that it might not be in their interest to provide? Second, accounting systems do not have a general ledger category called 'regulatory costs', let alone a category that might give an answer to the real question: what is the incremental ('dead-weight') cost to industry of that regulatory decision, especially by contrast with alternatives to achieving an equivalent quality result. And if costs are hard, benefits are even more difficult, especially if the goals are to have comparably derived measures for costs and benefits that facilitate balanced decision-making.

In the regulation of financial markets and financial services, the benefits might be the absence of things that, absent regulation, might otherwise occur (for example, large scale fraud, or distortion of efficiencies in markets). Are these invisibles amenable to quantification? Alternatively, regulatory benefits might consist of something even less tangible, for example market confidence, or the willingness of consumers to participate fully in markets for financial services and products. How can these be accounted for in a meaningful way and compared to the costs imposed by regulatory decisions? What we don't yet have — and what we need to develop — is a well-thought-through and rigorous analysis, not of the need for cost/benefit analysis, but of what methodology or combination of methodologies might, over the long term, provide reliable information to those who make decisions about regulation.

(C) *Principles versus Rules — Practical Implications for Regulators*

As a matter of policy, the Australian Commonwealth Government and ASIC support 'principles-based' regulation. In essence, this means legislative requirements should, wherever possible, mandate outcomes to be achieved, rather than prescribe detailed processes or rules. This leaves to a regulated entity the choice of working out a way to comply that is optimally efficient for it. But this approach to the legislative framework poses a number of challenges for the regulator responsible for administering legislation made in this way. For example, what is the role of the regulator in filling the gaps between high-level legislative principles and market reality? How much is it up to the regulator to deliver on market needs for certainty? Will principles-based regulation increase the risk of surprise in the administrative and enforcement decisions the regulator makes? In a practical sense, does principles-based regulation make enforcement action more difficult because of the degree of ambiguity inherent in legislation written in outcome terms rather than as specific rules of conduct? And we need to remember that, in dealing with these questions, ASIC is in an unusual position compared to many of its counterparts internationally. ASIC has no positive rulemaking power: it cannot make binding rules of conduct that are enforceable at law. Its enforcement actions will always require proof of non-compliance with the text of the legislation.

IV Partnerships between Regulator and the Academy

The list of examples of issues currently facing ASIC is the basis of my closing comments about relations between the academic and regulatory communities. In searching for ideas about how to tackle these important and challenging issues, I am often surprised to find that there is less research and academic thinking on these issues than I would hope.

Assuming my research techniques are not so woefully inadequate that I am simply not finding available material, what might explain it? And, more importantly, what might be done about it? If I am right in thinking that the kinds of issues I have mentioned today are important (as I think they are), and that they are intellectually challenging and would benefit by rigorous research, thought and analysis, how can we close the gap? We have started in some areas. We are beginning partnerships with academic economists and finance experts to help encourage broad thinking about cost-benefit issues in regulation. But we need more. That is a challenge for us as regulators and for you as the possible source of some of this work. I hope my remarks this morning have drawn attention to a need for us to come closer together in examining issues that in the end are important not just for ASIC or the academy, but for the broader community in which we are both actors.

Chapter 2

Evolving 'Rules of the Game' in Corporate Governance Reform

Jennifer Hill*

Parallels between Jean Renoir's classic film, *La Règle du Jeu* ('The Rules of the Game') and contemporary corporate governance might not be readily discernible. Renoir's film, a box office flop at the time of its release in 1939, was notable for displaying a set of strictly ordered social rules and mores of the French haute bourgeoisie, which the audience witnesses dissolve as the film progresses. Renoir himself said that his aim in making the film was to show 'a rich, complex society where ... we are dancing on a volcano'.[1]

Contemporary corporate governance has had its own seismic shift in the form of the international corporate collapses, epitomised by Enron and WorldCom in the US, and HIH and One.Tel in Australia. In the pre-scandal era at the beginning of this decade, the convergence–divergence debate in comparative corporate governance was at its height, with some scholars claiming that orderly convergence of corporate governance regimes was both inevitable and imminent.[2] A background assumption to this argument was that a cohesive Anglo-American governance model already existed and would form the point of

---

* My thanks to Alice Grey for her excellent research assistance.

[1] From Jean Renoir's 1961 interview with the Office de Radiodiffusion Télévision Française (ORTF), cited in Alexander Sesonske, *Jean Renoir: The French Films, 1924–1939* (1980) 382.

[2] Henry Hansmann and Reinier Kraakman, 'The End of History for Corporate Law' (2001) 89 *Georgetown Law Journal* 439, 469.

convergence. Even scholars on the opposite side of this debate[3] at times seemed to share the assumption of a unified common law governance model,[4] while disputing the view that civil law jurisdictions would inevitably adopt these rules.

The international corporate collapses complicated this debate. Common law jurisdictions, such as the US, UK, Australia and Canada introduced a variety of regulatory responses to the corporate scandals.[5] Similar motivations underpinned these reforms, potentially providing evidence of the convergence hypothesis at work. Nonetheless, there are several factors which challenge such a straight-forward regulatory picture. In spite of the existence of common themes in the international post-scandal reforms, significant differences emerged in terms of focus, structure and regulatory detail.

Some of the common law post-Enron reforms are interesting from the perspective of what they did *not*, rather than what they did, address. Thus, for example, there is an interesting dichotomy between strengthening of shareholder participatory rights versus protection of shareholder interests evident in the reforms. Strengthening of shareholder participatory rights was a significant theme in the Australian and the UK reforms, but not in the US reforms. The shape of these reforms has also affected subsequent corporate law debates in the US, UK and Australia that address quite different policy concerns.

Scholars have noted that, even where similar motivations underpin various reform agendas, it is unlikely that their long-term effects will coincide.[6] Another aspect of this long-term regulatory unpredictability is the impact of backlash, recently exemplified by the Report of the Committee on Capital Markets Regulation ('Paulson Committee Report').[7]

---

[3] Mark J Roe, 'Path Dependence, Political Options and Governance Systems' in Klaus Hopt and Eddy Wymeersch (eds), *Comparative Corporate Governance: Essays and Materials* (1997) 165, 165.

[4] Jeffrey N Gordon and Mark J Roe (eds), *Convergence and Persistence in Corporate Governance* (2004) pose the question: 'Is the Anglo-American model of shareholder capitalism destined to become standard or will sharp differences persist?'

[5] Jennifer G Hill, 'Regulatory Responses to Global Corporate Scandals' (2005) 23 *Wisconsin International Law Journal* 367.

[6] Donald C Langevoort, 'The Social Construction of *Sarbanes-Oxley*' (2007) 105 *Michigan Law Review* 1817.

[7] Committee on Capital Markets Regulation, Interim Report of the Committee on Capital Market Regulation (2006).

One criticism of convergence theory is that it engaged in over-generalisation, which could obscure significant differences within the common law world.[8] The post-scandal developments discussed in this chapter support the view that interesting differences in regulatory approach exist within the common law world itself, and challenge any assumption of an orderly, seamless progression towards a uniform model of good corporate governance. As in Renoir's famous film, the regulatory picture they present is a more complex, dynamic and unpredictable one.

I COMPARATIVE CORPORATE GOVERNANCE

Although in the early 1990s, a central issue in comparative corporate governance was whether the US should adopt governance mechanisms from other jurisdictions, such as Germany and Japan,[9] the comparative corporate governance debate did a u-turn later in the decade. With interest in globalisation then at its peak, the new focus of debate became the export of US style corporate governance principles internationally.[10]

Comparative corporate governance literature posits a divide between jurisdictions with dispersed ownership structures, such as the US, and those with concentrated ownership structures, traditionally found in continental Europe and Asia.[11] This formed the backdrop to the

[8] Steven Toms and Mike Wright, 'Divergence and Convergence within Anglo-American Corporate Governance Systems: Evidence from the US and UK, 1950–2000' (2005) 47 *Business History* 267, 267.

[9] Cf Mark J Roe, 'Some Differences in Corporate Structure in Germany, Japan and the United States' (1993) 102 *Yale Law Journal* 1927; Roberta Romano, 'A Cautionary Note on Drawing Lessons from Comparative Corporate Law' (1993) 102 *Yale Law Journal* 2021.

[10] Arthur R Pinto, 'Globalization and the Study of Comparative Corporate Governance' (2005) 23 *Wisconsin International Law Journal* 477; Jennifer G Hill, 'The Persistent Debate about Convergence in Comparative Corporate Governance' (2005) 27 *Sydney Law Review* 743.

[11] William W Bratton and Joseph A McCahery, 'Comparative Corporate Governance and the Theory of the Firm: The Case against Global Cross Reference' (1999) 38 *Columbia Journal of Transnational Law* 213; Brian R Cheffins, 'Does Law Matter? The Separation of Ownership and Control in the United Kingdom' (2001) 30 *Journal of Legal Studies* 459; John C Coffee, 'The Future as History: The Prospects for Global Convergence of Corporate Governance and Its Implications' (1999) 93 *Northwestern University Law Review* 641, 707; Gustavo Visentini, 'Compatibility and Competition between European and American Corporate Governance: Which Model of Capitalism?' (1998) 23 *Brooklyn Journal of International Law* 833.

convergence–divergence debate, in which the scholarship of La Porta, Lopez-de-Silanes, Shleifer and Vishny proved so influential.[12] La Porta et al argued that jurisdictions with a high level of minority shareholder protection would develop dispersed ownership structures, such as those existing in the US and UK. According to the study, law, and indeed legal origins, matter. The normative subtext was that common law legal protections were superior to those found in civil law legal systems.[13] This message provided strong support for a convergence theory of corporate governance, via a quasi-evolutionary progression towards the superior legal rules, presumed to exist in the common law world.[14]

Not all commentators were convinced of La Porta et al's hypothesis. Comparative law scholarship contains a long tradition of scepticism about the feasibility of transplanting elements of one legal system to another.[15] Within this general theoretical tradition, contemporary scholars such as Mark Roe have identified historical, political and social 'path dependence' factors, which may create, or perpetuate, differences in legal regimes.[16]

The convergence and 'law matters' hypotheses have been challenged from a range of perspectives. Some commentators, while accepting the strong homogenising influences of globalisation, challenged the view that convergence would be a continuous and steady process.[17] Indeed, it has been argued that the very concept of 'convergence' is ambiguous, in that it is sometimes unclear whether it

---

[12] Rafael La Porta, Florencio Lopez-De-Silanes and Andrei Shleifer, 'Corporate Ownership around the World' (1999) 54 *Journal of Finance* 471; Rafael La Porta et al, 'Law and Finance' (1998) 106 *Journal of Political Economy* 1113.

[13] David A Skeel, 'Corporate Anatomy Lessons' (2004) 113 *Yale Law Journal* 1519, 1544–5.

[14] Cally Jordan, 'The Conundrum of Corporate Governance' (2005) 30 *Brooklyn Journal of International Law* 983, 985–90.

[15] Otto Kahn-Freund, 'On Uses and Misuses of Comparative Law' (1974) 37 *Modern Law Review* 1; Amir N Licht, 'Legal Plug-Ins: Cultural Distance, Cross-Listing, and Corporate Governance Reform' (2004) 22 *Berkeley Journal of International Law* 195; Troy A Paredes, 'A Systems Approach to Corporate Governance Reform: Why Importing US Corporate Law Isn't the Answer' (2004) 45 *William and Mary Law Review* 1055; Gunther Teubner, 'Legal Irritants: Good Faith in British Law or How Unifying Law Ends Up in New Divergences' (1998) 61 *Modern Law Review* 11.

[16] Roe, 'Path Dependence, Political Options and Governance Systems', above n 3.

[17] Curtis J Milhaupt, 'Property Rights in Firms', in Jeffrey N Gordon and Mark J Roe (eds), *Convergence and Persistence in Corporate Governance* (2004) 210, 213.

relates to form or substance.[18] Other commentators disputed the presumed link between transplantation and efficiency gains, warning that transplantation may disrupt the internal balance and consistency of a regulatory system, creating a newly minted, but now dysfunctional, governance system.[19] Also, the intended consequences of regulation are often subverted by the underlying social environment.[20]

Finally, the methodology and background assumptions in the 'law matters' study have been criticised. One strand of criticism focuses on the broad generalisations underlying the 'law matters' hypothesis with some scholars arguing that the presumed differences between civil law and common law systems adopted by many convergence theorists are too sharply defined and often inaccurate.[21] On the other hand, regulatory differences that sometimes exist between common law countries are simply obscured or ignored.[22] Takeover law, where fundamental differences exist between, for example, US, UK and Australian law, is a good example of this problem.[23] It has also been argued that the primary focus in La Porta et al's study on 'law on the books'[24] was misguided, since it ignored or concealed important dynamic features of legal

---

[18] Ronald J Gilson, 'Globalizing Corporate Governance: Convergence of Form or Function' in Jeffrey N Gordon and Mark J Roe (eds), *Convergence and Persistence in Corporate Governance* (2004) 128, 158.

[19] Bratton and McCahery, above n 11, 219; Reinhard H Schmidt and Gerald Spindler, 'Path Dependence and Complementarity in Corporate Governance' in Jeffrey N Gordon and Mark J Roe (eds), *Convergence and Persistence in Corporate Governance* (2004) 114, 119, 122.

[20] Langevoort, above n 6; Christine Parker et al, 'Introduction' in John Braithwaite et al (eds), *Regulating Law* (2004) 1, 7.

[21] Jordan, 'The Conundrum of Corporate Governance', above n 14, 1005; Katharina Pistor et al, 'The Evolution of Corporate Law: A Cross-Country Comparison' (2002) 23 *University of Pennsylvania Journal of International Economic Law* 791, 799; Skeel, above n 13, 1546.

[22] Ruth V Aguilera et al, 'Corporate Governance and Social Responsibility: A Comparative Analysis of the UK and the US' (2006) 14 *Corporate Governance: An International Review* 147, 147–8; Paul Davies and Klaus Hopt, 'Control Transactions' in Reinier Kraakman et al (eds), *The Anatomy of Corporate Law: A Comparative and Functional Approach* (2004) 157, 172; Toms and Wright, above n 8.

[23] John Armour and David A Skeel, 'Who Writes the Rules for Hostile Takeovers, and Why? The Peculiar Divergence of US and UK Takeover Regulation' (2007) *Georgetown Law Journal* (forthcoming); Davies and Hopt, 'Control Transactions', above n 22, 172.

[24] Katharina Pistor and Chenggang Xu, 'Incomplete Law' (2003) 35 *New York University Journal of International Law and Policy* 931; Skeel, above n 13, 1543.

systems, such as the operation of social norms[25] and enforcement intensity.[26]

Alternative, and arguably more nuanced, approaches to regulatory difference than the convergence and 'law matters' hypotheses have emerged in recent times. Thus, for example, Kraakman et al's 2004 book, *The Anatomy of Corporate Law*, identifies a wide range of regulatory and governance strategies used to control opportunism and conflicts of interest between corporate participants.[27] In contrast to the approach of La Porta et al, the methodology adopted in *The Anatomy of Corporate Law* focuses on 'substantive results rather than on mere legal origin',[28] avoiding the normative subtext of the convergence debate. The vision of comparative corporate governance adopted in this book is, therefore, one in which different jurisdictions address common corporate governance problems with the aid of a diverse range of regulatory tools. It is a picture that allows us to see regulatory paradigm shifts both within, and between, common law and civil law jurisdictions.

II THE POST-SCANDAL REGULATORY RESPONSES: LAWS, PRINCIPLES AND POLITICS

The international corporate scandals elicited a range of regulatory responses in common law jurisdictions, such as the US, UK, Australia and Canada. These included legislative reforms[29] and governance changes by self-regulatory organisations.[30]

---

[25] John C Coffee, 'Do Norms Matter? A Cross-Country Evaluation' (2001) 149 *University of Pennsylvania Law Review* 2151.

[26] Gerard Hertig, 'Convergence of Substantive Law and Convergence of Enforcement: A Comparison' in Jeffrey N Gordon and Mark J Roe (eds), *Convergence and Persistence in Corporate Governance* (2004) 328, 328; John C Coffee, 'Law and the Market: The Impact of Enforcement' (Working Paper No 304, Centre for Law and Economic Studies, Columbia University School of Law, 2007).

[27] Skeel, above n 13.

[28] Paul Davis, Gerard Hertig and Klaus Hopt, 'Beyond the Anatomy' in Reinier Kraakman et al (eds), *The Anatomy of Corporate Law: A Comparative and Functional Approach* (2004) 215, 221.

[29] These legislative reforms include the *Sarbanes-Oxley Act of 2002*, Pub L No 107–204, 116 Stat 745 (2002) ('*Sarbanes-Oxley*'); the *Combined Code on Corporate Governance (2003)* (UK) ('*Combined Code*') (an updated version of the *Combined Code*, with limited amendments, was released in June 2006 and is available at

At one level, the corporate law reforms addressed similar governance concerns, particularly with respect to gatekeeper conflicts of interest,[31] and potentially provided more evidence of the convergence hypothesis at work.[32] Although similar concerns and motivations prompted the reforms, there are several matters that challenge such an ordered regulatory picture and highlight significant differences between the various regulatory responses.

First, in spite of globalising influences, many of the reforms responded specifically to local issues. In the US, *Sarbanes-Oxley* closely tracked the contours of Enron.[33] Local issues were also prominent in UK reforms[34] and, in Australia, aspects of the *CLERP 9 Act 2004* were directly linked to the failure of HIH Insurance, which was the largest collapse in Australian corporate history.[35]

Convergence sceptics have highlighted the importance of politics, and the fact that 'corporate law rules are the products of collective action', in support of the proposition that convergence is highly unlikely.[36] Localised political pressures are revealed in several aspects of the post-scandal reforms, including their timing and evolution. The most immediate legislative response to the corporate scandals

---

<http://www.frc.org.uk/corporate/combinedcode.cfm>); the *Companies Act* 2006 (UK); the *Corporate Law Economic Reform Program (Audit Reform and Corporate Disclosure) Act 2004* (Cth) ('*CLERP 9 Act*').

[30] Eg, New York Stock Exchange, Inc, *Listed Company Manual* (2003) § 303A (corporate governance rules approved by the Securities and Exchange Commission ('SEC') on 4 November 2003); ASX Corporate Governance Council, *Principles of Good Corporate Governance and Best Practice Recommendations* (2003), available at <http://www.shareholder.com/visitors/dynamicdoc/document.cfm?documentid=364&companyid=ASX>.

[31] John C Coffee, 'Understanding Enron: 'It's About the Gatekeepers, Stupid'' (2002) 57 *Business Lawyer* 1403; John C Coffee, 'Gatekeeper Failure and Reform: The Challenge of Fashioning Relevant Reforms' (2004) 84 *Boston University Law Review* 301; Jeffrey N Gordon, 'What Enron Means for the Management and Control of the Modern Business Corporation: Some Initial Reflections' (2002) 69 *University of Chicago Law Review* 1233.

[32] Paul Von Nessen, 'Corporate Governance in Australia: Converging with International Developments' (2003) 15 *Australian Journal of Corporate Law* 1.

[33] Larry E Ribstein, 'Market vs Regulatory Responses to Corporate Fraud: A Critique of the *Sarbanes-Oxley Act of 2002*' (2002) 28 *Journal of Corporation Law* 1, 4–18.

[34] Eilis Ferran, 'Company Law Reform in the UK: A Progress Report' (Working Paper No 27/2005, European Corporate Governance Institute, Cambridge, 2005) 25.

[35] Commonwealth, HIH Royal Commission, *The Failure of HIH Insurance* (2003) vol 1 ('HIH Royal Commission').

[36] David Charny, 'The Politics of Corporate Convergence' in Jeffrey N Gordon and Mark J Roe (eds), *Convergence and Persistence in Corporate Governance* (2004) 293, 296.

occurred in the US, where a full-scale regulatory overhaul was achieved in 2002.[37] The speed with which the reforms were introduced became a focal point in subsequent academic discussion. It has been argued that the real impetus for reforms emanated not from Enron, but from the US political climate that developed after the WorldCom scandal, when investor protection became a major issue in looming elections.[38] Unusual bipartisan cooperation enabled the swift passage of reforms that effectively reshaped the allocation of regulatory power between the states and federal law in the US.[39] Critics of *Sarbanes-Oxley* have linked the perceived defects of the legislation to its hasty passage, describing it as 'emergency legislation',[40] which was enacted in an overheated political environment without the benefit of careful deliberation and policy assessment.[41] Others, while acknowledging that the Act came into existence quickly as a result of political expediency, argue that it delivered real benefits and improvements in the corporate governance process.[42]

Reforms in other common law jurisdictions were enacted at a slower pace and with broad consultation. Australia's parallel legislative response, the *CLERP 9 Act*, which commenced operation in mid-2004, was the subject of extensive public debate. Furthermore, it integrated the recommendations of the HIH Royal Commission, which itself lasted for 18 months.[43] In the UK, reform processes were already underway several years prior to the corporate scandals and advanced by degrees,[44] only recently culminating in the passage of the massive *Companies Act 2006* (UK).[45]

---

[37] Via *Sarbanes-Oxley* and the NYSE Corporate Governance Rules and NASDAQ listing requirements.

[38] Langevoort, above n 6, 1821.

[39] William B Chandler and Leo E Strine, 'The New Federalism of the American Corporate Governance System: Preliminary Reflections of Two Residents of One Small State' (2003) 152 *University of Pennsylvania Law Review* 953, 973; Robert B Thompson, 'Corporate Governance after Enron' (2003) 40 *Houston Law Review* 99, 100.

[40] Roberta Romano, 'The *Sarbanes-Oxley Act* and the Making of Quack Corporate Governance' (2005) 114 *Yale Law Journal* 1521, 1528.

[41] Ibid 1549ff, 1602.

[42] J Robert Brown, 'Criticizing the Critics: *Sarbanes-Oxley* and Quack Corporate Governance' (2006) 90 *Marquette Law Review* 309.

[43] HIH Royal Commission, above n 35.

[44] Ferran, above n 34.

[45] The *Companies Act 2006* (UK) received Royal Assent on 8 November 2006. All parts of the Act will be operational by October 2008 (UK Department of Trade and Industry,

There are also philosophical differences between the US reforms and those introduced in the UK and Australia, in terms of reliance on rules and principles as regulatory techniques. Scholars have long debated the respective merits of rules and principles as regulatory mechanisms.[46] Rules are generally perceived to promote certainty — they have clear, determinate boundaries defining *ex ante* whether conduct is or is not permissible, and allow for little discretion in the decision-maker.[47] Principles (or standards), on the other hand, are often viewed as promoting substantive equality and fairness, as opposed to formal equality under rules. Their very lack of precision requires the *ex post* exercise of discretion based on a variety of specific factual and contextual matters, and embedded social values.[48] Classic criticism of rules relates to their perceived inflexibility and the increased scope for evasion of, or 'creative compliance' with, rules that have precise and determinate contours.[49] Rules are also often reactive and thereby subject to over- or under-inclusion, while principles avoid this problem by conferring greater discretion on the decision-maker.[50] It has been argued that there is a decline in the ability of rules to provide certainty, commensurate with an increase in the complexity of the matter regulated.[51] In many situations, however, the line between rules and principles may be somewhat blurred, with regulation comprising hybrids of the two.

The dynamics and interplay between rules and principles have become more complex due to greater fragmentation and internalisation

---

'Bill to Save Business Millions Receives Royal Assent' (Press Release, 8 November 2006)).

[46] Carol M Rose, 'Crystals and Mud in Property Law' (1988) 40 *Stanford Law Review* 577; Cass R Sunstein, 'Problems with Rules' (1995) 83 *California Law Review* 953; Duncan Kennedy, 'Form and Substance in Private Law Adjudication' (1976) 89 *Harvard Law Review* 1685.

[47] Christie Ford, 'New Governance, Compliance and Principles-Based Securities Regulation' (2007) *American Business Law Journal* 1, 8–9 (forthcoming), available at <http://ssrn.com/abstract=970130>; Kathleen M Sullivan, 'The Supreme Court 1991 Term — Foreword: The Justices of Rules and Standards' (1992) 106 *Harvard Law Review* 22.

[48] Kennedy, above n 46.

[49] Doreen McBarnet and Christopher Whelan, 'The Elusive Spirit of the Law: Formalism and the Struggle for Legal Control' (1991) 54 *Modern Law Review* 848, 849.

[50] Ford, above n 47, 8, footnote 26; Sullivan, above n 47, 58–9.

[51] John B Braithwaite, 'Rules and Principles: A Theory of Legal Certainty' (2002) 27 *Australian Journal of Legal Philosophy* 47.

of contemporary corporate governance practices.[52] Principles and norms, embodied in self-regulatory codes of corporate governance,[53] have become an increasingly important regulatory tool. As in the case of legal rules, enforcement of self-regulatory codes is obviously an important issue, and one that will vary depending on the relevant legal and social culture.[54]

The international scandals resulted in a hardening of norms in both Australia and the UK. There has also been a global trend for stock exchanges to be more involved in corporate governance regulation. Although the Australian Securities Exchange ('ASX') had been tangentially involved in corporate governance regulation since 1996, that involvement intensified after the corporate collapses. In 2003, following public pressure and criticism about its credibility as a regulatory body, the ASX introduced its *Principles of Good Corporate Governance and Best Practice Recommendations* ('ASX corporate governance principles'),[55] which adopted a UK-style 'comply or explain'[56] regulatory model that was more stringent than the previous disclosure requirement in Australia.[57]

Corporate governance norms were also enhanced in the United Kingdom as a result of the *Review of the Role and Effectiveness of Non-Executive Directors*.[58] The Higgs Report recommended strengthening the independence of the board from management within the pre-existing

---

[52] Christine Parker, 'Meta-Regulation: Legal Accountability for Corporate Social Responsbility' in Doreen McBarnet et al (eds) *The New Corporate Accountability: Corporate Social Responsibility and the Law* (2007).

[53] For a comprehensive guide to international corporate governance codes, see the European Corporate Governance Institute website <http://www.ecgi.org/codes/all_codes.php>.

[54] Eddy Wymeersch, 'Implementation of the Corporate Governance Codes' in Klaus Hopt et al (eds), *Corporate Governance in Context: Corporations, States and Markets in Europe, Japan, and the US* (2005) 403, 408.

[55] ASX Corporate Governance Council, *Principles of Good Corporate Governance* (2003), above n 30.

[56] The preferred terminology under the Australian model, however, appears to be an 'if not, why not' model: ASX Corporate Governance Council, *Response to the Implementation Review Group Report* (2004).

[57] Joanna Bird and Jennifer Hill, 'Regulatory Rooms in Australian Corporate Law' (1999) 25 *Brooklyn Journal of International Law* 555, 598–600. Previously, it had only been necessary for a company to disclose in the annual report its main corporate governance practices, if any.

[58] Derek Higgs, Report to the UK Department of Trade and Industry, *Review of the Role and Effectiveness of Non-Executive Directors* (2003).

'comply or explain' regulatory framework, and these recommendations were subsequently incorporated into the UK *Combined Code*.

Traditionally, the development of self-regulatory codes has tended to be either a response to the lack of specific governmental regulation in particular areas, or, in some cases, a justification for the absence of such regulation. A number of the post-scandal reforms in Australia and the UK fall into the latter category. They also reflect a strong preference for the flexibility offered via regulation by principles rather than mandatory legal rules, and recognition that inadequate enforcement of good governance practices could result in the imposition of onerous government regulation.[59]

In contrast to the reforms in Australia and the UK, the US reforms appear to reflect the process of 'juridification',[60] in their conspicuous shift towards a rules-based approach to corporate governance with a higher level of mandatory governance standards. The final NYSE corporate governance rules, for example, introduced a range of mandatory requirements concerning board structure to reflect generally accepted best practice in corporate governance,[61] the substance of which is often stricter than its counterparts in other jurisdictions, such as Australia.[62] *Sarbanes-Oxley* also imposed many new prescriptive rules, thereby affecting the balance of regulatory power between the states and federal law. However, not all of the reforms under *Sarbanes-Oxley* are of this ilk. Sections 406 and 407 respectively direct the SEC to issue rules requiring a company to disclose whether it has adopted a code of ethics for senior financial officers (and if not, why not), and whether at least one member of the audit committee is a financial expert (and if not, why not). While these provisions are framed as disclosure provisions only, they have been described as 'disguised substance', the likely contextual effect of which will be to mandate compliance.[63]

Sarbanes-Oxley has been depicted as creating a 'shadow corporation law',[64] and criticised for deviating from the traditional US model of corporate law, under which state-based law is viewed as

---

[59] Richard Humphry, 'If Not, Why Not?' (Speech delivered to the Australian Institute of Company Directors Forum, Sydney, 2 April 2003) 3.
[60] Wymeersch, 'Implementation of the Corporate Governance Codes', above n 54, 418.
[61] NYSE, above n 30, § 303A.
[62] Hill, 'Regulatory Responses to Global Corporate Scandals', above n 5, 383.
[63] Thompson, above n 39, 104.
[64] Chandler and Strine, above n 39, 973.

facilitative and competitive.[65] *Sarbanes-Oxley* also laid greater emphasis on criminal liability in corporate governance[66] than reforms in Australia and the UK. Nonetheless, some commentators have viewed the Act's criminal provisions as adding little to pre-existing US law, and unlikely to be an effective form of deterrence.[67]

While some countries in continental Europe, such France and Germany, adopted reforms based on *Sarbanes-Oxley*,[68] there was an explicit rejection in Australia and the UK of the rules-based regulatory approach to corporate governance that underpinned the Act. At the time the ASX corporate governance principles were introduced in Australia, for example, the then Managing Director and CEO of the Australian Stock Exchange stated that '[t]hrough a disclosure based approach, the ASX is keen to avoid a US style *Sarbanes-Oxley* legislative solution'.[69] The Chair of the Higgs Committee, Derek Higgs, was similarly direct in his preference for regulation by principles over rules, commenting that the 'brittleness and rigidity of legislation cannot dictate the behaviour, or foster the trust, I believe is fundamental to the effective unitary board and to superior corporate performance'.[70] The Chief Executive of the London Stock Exchange has recently confirmed this regulatory preference.[71]

The Canadian post-scandal approach to corporate governance and securities regulation, led by British Columbia, also appears to favour a principles-based approach, focusing on voluntary compliance over regulatory enforcement.[72] Canada's publicly listed corporate sector, like

---

[65] Romano, above n 40, 1523, 1528–9.

[66] See, eg, the *Sarbanes-Oxley Act*, Title VIII ('Corporate and Criminal Fraud Accountability'); Title IX ('White Collar Crime Penalty Enhancements'); Title XI ('Corporate Fraud and Accountability').

[67] Michael A Perino, 'Enron's Legislative Aftermath: Some Reflections on the Deterrence Aspects of the *Sarbanes-Oxley Act of 2002*' (2002) 76 *St John's Law Review* 671.

[68] Luca Enriques, 'Bad Apples, Bad Oranges: A Comment from Old Europe on Post-Enron Corporate Governance Reforms' (2003) 38 *Wake Forest Law Review* 911, 918ff.

[69] Humphry, above n 59, 3.

[70] Higgs, above n 58, 3.

[71] Clara Furse, 'Comment: SOX Is Not to Blame — London Is Just Better as a Market', *Financial Times* (London), 17 September 2006, 19.

[72] Ford, above n 47; Erinn B Broshko and Kai Li, 'Corporate Governance Requirements in Canada and the United States: A Legal and Empirical Comparison of the Principles-Based and the Rules-Based Approaches' (Working Paper, Sauder School of Business, University of British Columbia, 2006), available at
<http://papers.ssrn.com/sol3/papers.cfm?abstract_id=892708>.

that of Australia,[73] contains a high level of controlling blockholder ownership structures and many 'small-cap' firms, and it has been suggested that principles-based regulation may be better suited to this kind of market profile.[74]

The presumed dichotomy between rules and principles, and between rigidity and flexibility, is relevant to the issue of regulatory amendment. Romano, in her critique of *Sarbanes-Oxley*, notes that 'legislation drafted in a perceived state of emergency can be difficult to undo'.[75] By contrast, the norms embodied in the ASX corporate governance principles appear to be extremely fluid. The principles have been the subject of almost continual assessment and consultation since their introduction in 2003, including two reports by the Implementation Review Group ('IRG').[76] Following a twelve-month review, in November 2006 the ASX Corporate Governance Council released an Explanatory Paper and Consultation Paper on proposed changes to the principles.[77] A consistent message in these reviews has been the inherent flexibility and non-prescriptive nature of the ASX corporate governance principles. The reviews have stressed the fact that 'the only *compliance* required is disclosure'[78] and that corporations are free to depart from the principles, provided they explain why.[79] Reflecting this underlying philosophy, the reviews have also recommended removal of the term 'best practice' from the title of the ASX corporate governance principles, on the basis that it might imply that other practices are inferior.[80] This is

---

[73] Asjeet S Lamba and Geoffrey Stapledon, 'The Determinants of Corporate Ownership Structure: Australian Evidence' (Public Law Research Paper No 20, University of Melbourne, 2001), available at <http://ssrn.com/abstract=279015>.
[74] Ford, above n 47.
[75] Romano, above n 40, 1602.
[76] ASX Corporate Governance Council IRG, *Principles of Good Corporate Governance and Best Practice Recommendations: Report to the ASX Corporate Governance Council* (2004); ASX Corporate Governance Council IRG, *Second Report to the ASX Corporate Governance Council* (2005).
[77] ASX Corporate Governance Council, *Explanatory Paper and Consultation Paper* (2006).
[78] ASX Corporate Governance Council IRG, *Principles of Good Corporate Governance* (2004), above n 76, 1.
[79] ASX Corporate Governance Council, *Explanatory Paper*, above n 77, 6.
[80] ASX Corporate Governance Council IRG, *Principles of Good Corporate Governance* (2004), above n 76, 1; ASX Corporate Governance Council, *Explanatory Paper*, above n 77, 9.

a theme which also resonates in the Canadian securities regulation context.[81]

In its 2006 Explanatory and Consultation Paper, the ASX emphasises the evolving nature of the corporate governance debate, and the interrelation of the principles with other parts of the corporate governance ecosystem.[82] Several proposed changes to the ASX corporate governance principles are due to the need to update them in light of recent progress in related areas, such as risk management and corporate responsibility and sustainability. For example, the ASX Corporate Governance Council notes that recent developments have emphasised the broad scope of the term 'risk' and explicitly incorporates this expansive interpretation into the concept of 'material business risks' in its revised draft of the principles.[83] This new emphasis on risk represents a further point of linkage between developments in corporate governance and regulation theory more broadly, given that risk management has taken an increasingly central role in the regulation debate.[84]

In the wake of the growing popularity of principles-based regulation, some commentators have become wary of the rhetoric associated with it, and of the corresponding denigration of rules-based regulation.[85] Cunningham, for example, rejects the standard dichotomy between rules and principles-based regulation, arguing that most complex regulatory systems cannot be meaningfully characterised as falling within one or the other category.[86] He suggests that the rhetoric surrounding principles-based regulation may have flourished primarily as a form of product-differentiation.[87] A prime example of this is the post-*Sarbanes-Oxley* power struggle between US state and federal corporate law. Given that *Sarbanes-Oxley* has been widely criticised as overly-

---

[81] Ford, above n 47, 38–9.

[82] ASX Corporate Governance Council, *Explanatory Paper*, above n 77, 5.

[83] Ibid 17ff.

[84] Julia Black, 'Critical Reflections on Regulation' (2002) 27 *Australian Journal of Legal Philosophy* 1, 9–10; [Julia Black, 'The Emergence of Risk Based Regulation and the New Public Management in the UK' (2005) *Public Law* 512].

[85] Lawrence A Cunningham, 'A Prescription to Retire the Rhetoric of "Principles-Based Systems" in Corporate Law, Securities Regulation and Accounting' (2007) *Vanderbilt Law Review* (forthcoming), available at <http://papers.ssrn.com/sol3/papers.cfm?abstract_id=970646>; David Kershaw, 'Evading Enron: Taking Principles Too Seriously in Accounting Regulation' (2005) 68 *Modern Law Review* 594.

[86] Cunningham, above n 85, 13–20.

[87] Ibid 54–62.

prescriptive, Delaware judges and lawyers have sought to assert the supremacy of Delaware law by emphasising its flexible, principles-based nature.[88] Claims that the UK avoided any Enron-style financial fiascos due to its principles-based accounting system have also attracted criticism.[89]

III SHAREHOLDER INTERESTS *VERSUS* PARTICIPATORY RIGHTS — WHAT THE POST-SCANDAL REFORMS DID AND DID NOT ADDRESS

Enhancing managerial accountability for the benefit of shareholders was a common goal in various reforms adopted following the international corporate scandals. On one interpretation, gatekeepers, such as auditors, and boards of directors, bore much responsibility for the scandals,[90] with shareholders seen as innocent victims.[91] Although not all commentators accept this benign view of shareholder involvement in the scandals,[92] it is an image that underlies many of the post-scandal reforms in common law countries. However, the reforms differ in the manner in which they seek to achieve the goal of enhanced managerial accountability vis-à-vis shareholders. Specifically, there is an intriguing dichotomy between strengthening of shareholder participatory rights versus protection of shareholder interests.

Strengthening shareholder participatory rights in corporate governance was an explicit governance objective in the Australian reforms.[93] The Explanatory Memorandum to the CLERP 9 Act contains numerous references to the desirability of increasing shareholder

---

[88] Ibid 55–7.

[89] Kershaw, above n 85.

[90] Coffee, above n 31; John C Coffee, 'What Caused Enron? A Capsule Social and Economic History of the 1990s' (2004) 89 *Cornell Law Review* 269; Gordon, above n 31.

[91] John C Coffee, 'A Theory of Corporate Scandals: Why the US and Europe Differ' (Working Paper No 274, Centre for Law and Economic Studies, Columbia University School of Law, 2005) 2, 15. Although cf his statements at 9–10, where he identifies the preference of institutional investors for equity-based executive compensation as indirectly influencing the US corporate scandals.

[92] Roberta S Karmel, 'Should a Duty to the Corporation be Imposed on Institutional Shareholders?' (2004) 60 *Business Lawyer* 1, 4; Leo E Strine, 'Toward a True Corporate Republic: A Traditionalist Response to Bebchuk's Solution for Improving Corporate America' (2006) 119 *Harvard Law Review* 1759, 1764, 1772–3.

[93] James McConvill and Mirko Bagaric, 'Towards Mandatory Shareholder Committees in Australian Companies' (2004) 28 *Melbourne University Law Review* 125, 131.

activism[94] and improving shareholder participation and influence in the companies in which they invest.[95] A clear example of this is in the reforms relating to executive remuneration.[96] The CLERP 9 Act permits greater shareholder participation in remuneration issues by requiring shareholders of a listed company to pass an advisory resolution at the annual general meeting approving the directors' remuneration report.[97] Although non-binding, the explicit goals of the procedure are to provide shareholders with greater voice in relation to remuneration issues,[98] and encourage greater consultation and information flow concerning remuneration policies between directors and shareholders.[99] The reform also seeks to constrain excessive compensation by 'shaming' and censure,[100] and from this perspective may be a potentially powerful governance mechanism.[101]

Nonetheless, the Australian government's professed enthusiasm for shareholder activism is not unqualified, and in one particular respect, the government has attempted to restrict shareholder participation in corporate governance. This is in relation to the so-called '100 member rule', which permits 100 shareholders to convene a general meeting of the company.[102] The rule, which is remarkably generous to shareholders compared to many other jurisdictions, has attracted criticism as being open to possible abuse by activist shareholders with a social agenda.[103] In 2005, the federal government announced that it intended to remove the

---

[94] See, eg, Explanatory Memorandum, Corporate Law Economic Reform Program (Audit Reform and Corporate Disclosure) Bill 2003 (Cth) [1.4], [4.71].

[95] Explanatory Memorandum, Corporate Law Economic Reform Program (Audit Reform and Corporate Disclosure) Bill 2003 (Cth) [4.174], [4.271]–[4.280].

[96] Jennifer G Hill, 'Regulating Executive Remuneration: International Developments in the Post-Scandal Era' (2006) 3 *European Company Law* 64, 67–8.

[97] Larelle Chapple and Blake Christensen, 'The Non-Binding Vote on Executive Pay: A Review of the *CLERP 9* Reform' (2005) 18 *Australian Journal of Corporate Law* 263; see *Corporations Act* 2001 (Cth) ss 250R(2), 249L.

[98] Explanatory Memorandum, Corporate Law Economic Reform Program (Audit Reform and Corporate Disclosure) Bill 2003 (Cth) [5.434]–[5.435].

[99] Explanatory Memorandum, Corporate Law Economic Reform Program (Audit Reform and Corporate Disclosure) Bill 2003 (Cth) [4.353], [5.413].

[100] David A Skeel, 'Shaming in Corporate Law' (2001) 149 *University of Pennsylvania Law Review* 1811.

[101] Hill, 'Regulating Executive Remuneration', above n 96, 69–71.

[102] *Corporations Act* 2001 (Cth) s 249D.

[103] Corporations and Securities Advisory Committee, *Shareholder Participation in the Modern Listed Public Company: Final Report* (2000) 15.

100 member rule,[104] however its proposal to this effect was rejected by state leaders at a meeting of the Ministerial Council for Corporations in July 2006.[105]

Increased shareholder participation and influence was a theme in the UK reforms (which included a version of the non-binding shareholder vote on the directors' remuneration report)[106] and the UK government has issued strong rhetoric about the need to encourage greater shareholder democracy and activism.[107] This policy goal was also reflected in the UK Combined Code, which included recommendations of the Higgs Report specifically aimed at strengthening the position of both institutional investors and independent directors, through a range of techniques designed to establish a close relationship between the two groups.[108] The UK Combined Code stressed the need for the board to communicate with investors generally and to encourage their participation in the annual general meeting.[109]

The US reforms present an interesting contrast in this regard. Protection of shareholder interests was a clear priority[110] and part of the legislative intent of the reforms. The preamble to *Sarbanes-Oxley* states, for example, that the aim of the Act is '[t]o protect investors by improving the accuracy and reliability of corporate disclosures made pursuant to the securities laws, and for other purposes'. Yet, in spite of this focus on protection of shareholder interests, enhancement of shareholder participatory rights and power vis-à-vis management was conspicuously absent in the US reforms.[111]

Commentators have described the refusal of *Sarbanes-Oxley* to grant shareholders greater governance power and participatory rights in,

---

[104] Chris Pearce, 'Government Consults on Proposed Corporate Governance Reforms' (Press Release, 7 February 2005); see also Explanatory Memorandum, Exposure Draft, Corporations Amendment Bill (No 2) 2005 (Cth).

[105] Leon Gettler, 'IFSA Censures States over 100-Member Rule', *Sydney Morning Herald* (Sydney), 21 June 2006, 37; Chris Pearce, 'Key Corporate Governance Reforms in Jeopardy' (Press Release, 27 July 2006).

[106] *The Directors' Remuneration Report Regulations 2002* (SI 2002/1986). The provision requiring shareholder approval of the directors' remuneration report is now found in s 439 of the recently passed *Companies Act 2006* (UK).

[107] Ferran, above n 34, 27–8.

[108] Hill, 'Regulatory Responses to Global Corporate Scandals', above n 5, 391.

[109] See generally *Combined Code,* Principle D 2 ('Constructive Use of the AGM').

[110] Karmel, above n 92, 2.

[111] Hill, 'Regulatory Responses to Global Corporate Scandals', above n 5, 392.

for example, the director election process, as notable[112] and 'the forgotten element' of the Act.[113] Another potentially forgotten element in the US reforms was the issue of executive compensation. Executive compensation was deeply implicated in Enron and other corporate scandals. Conflicts of interest were evident in the structure of many executive compensation packages, which, rather than aligning managerial and shareholder interests, often appeared to create perverse incentives for executives to manage earnings and share price to enhance the value of options and pursue short-term goals.[114] Indeed, this misalignment of interests in executive pay is one possible interpretation of the corporate collapses.[115] Yet, in spite of its prominence in the scandals, executive compensation received virtually no attention in the US reforms.[116]

Also, US reforms on board independence arguably had quite different implications for shareholder power than parallel reforms in the UK. The UK Combined Code sought to strengthen the position not only of independent directors, but also institutional investors, by fostering active dialogue between the two groups and encouraging greater participation in governance issues by institutional investors. However, the strict definition of director 'independence' under the US 2002 reforms suggests that US directors should generally be independent, not only from management, but also from major shareholders.[117] It has been argued that this aspect of the US reforms can be seen as contributing to an emerging concept of independent directors as 'public' directors in

---

[112] Langevoort, above n 6, 1829.

[113] Chandler and Strine, above n 39, 999.

[114] Iman Anabtawi, 'Secret Compensation' (2004) 82 *North Carolina Law Review* 835, 839ff; Patrick Bolton, Jose A Scheinkman and Wei Xiong, 'Executive Compensation and Short-Termist Behavior in Speculative Markets' (2006) 73 *Review of Economic Studies* 577; Janice K McClendon, 'Bringing the Bulls to Bear: Regulating Executive Compensation to Realign Management and Shareholders' Interests and Promote Corporate Long-Term Productivity' (2004) 39 *Wake Forest Law Review* 971; Charles M Yablon and Jennifer G Hill, 'Timing Corporate Disclosures to Maximize Performance-Based Remuneration: A Case of Misaligned Incentives?' (2000) 35 *Wake Forest Law Review* 83, 86–8.

[115] Coffee, 'What Caused Enron? A Capsule Social and Economic History of the 1990s' above n 90.

[116] Hill, 'Regulatory Responses to Global Corporate Scandals', above n 5, 412.

[117] Ibid 388–90.

America, potentially shifting *Sarbanes-Oxley* towards a model of public accountability rather than its stated intent of shareholder protection.[118]

Thus, even where reforms are unified by similar goals, this is no guarantee that their ultimate effects will coincide. Langevoort has recently noted this gap between motivation and regulatory outcome, due to variability in compliance and enforcement decisions, in relation to *Sarbanes-Oxley*.[119] Unpredictability in the long-term effects of legislation is compounded in the case of an array of international legislation, where 'legal irritants' and underlying differences in regulatory ecosystems can create new divergences.[120]

IV CURRENT POLICY DEBATES AND REGULATORY BACKLASH

The shape of current academic and policy debates in the US, UK and Australia has been determined to a considerable degree by what was, and what was not, incorporated into the various post-scandal reforms. These recent policy debates, like the earlier regulatory responses themselves, have a distinctly local flavour. Thus, for example, the lacuna in the US reforms concerning shareholder participation rights has had a clear influence on the direction of subsequent academic debate on the need to enhance shareholder power in the US. Bebchuk, a leading proponent of increased shareholder power and participation, has identified two key areas of corporate governance need. First, he has argued strongly for the reform of US proxy rules to allow shareholders greater influence over the director nomination process,[121] a reform for which the SEC originally exhibited some enthusiasm.[122] Bebchuk's second set of reform proposals focuses on increasing shareholder power, by permitting shareholders to initiate and effect changes to the corporate charter.[123]

---

[118] Langevoort, above n 6, 1831; Cary Coglianese, 'Legitimacy and Corporate Governance' (2007) 32 *Delaware Journal of Corporate Law* 159, 163–4.
[119] Langevoort, above n 6.
[120] Teubner, above n 15.
[121] Lucian Bebchuk, 'The Case for Shareholder Access to the Ballot' (2003) 59 *Business Lawyer* 43.
[122] US Securities and Exchange Commission, Review of the Proxy Process Regarding the Nomination and Election of Directors (2003).
[123] Lucian Bebchuk, 'The Case for Increasing Shareholder Power' (2005) 118 *Harvard Law Review* 833; Lucian Bebchuk, 'Letting Shareholders Set the Rules' (2006) 119 *Harvard Law Review* 1784.

These reform proposals would significantly alter the current balance of power between shareholders and the board of directors in the US. It is, as yet, unclear how much traction the proposals will ultimately gain. They have provoked intense debate in academic circles.[124] While few US scholars doubt that there is plenty of scope for increasing shareholder power,[125] many doubt the wisdom of doing so, particularly when it would be at the expense of managerial autonomy and power.[126] In addition, the SEC's reformatory zeal concerning the director nomination process has waned.[127]

However, the issues raised by this academic debate are now undeniably in the US corporate ether. One example of this attitudinal shift is in relation to the issue of executive compensation. In spite of the surprising lack of attention given to executive compensation in the 2002 US reforms, regulatory momentum on this issue has gathered pace since that time. In early 2006, the SEC announced that it would conduct a significant overhaul of its disclosure rules on executive compensation[128] and political rhetoric on the topic of excessive executive pay has recently intensified.[129] Activist investors, such as the AFSCME,[130] submitted shareholder proposals seeking an advisory vote on executive pay comparable to the non-binding shareholder vote introduced in the Australian and UK post-scandal reforms. Proposals to this effect were successful at some companies, such as Blockbuster and Verizon Communications, during the 2007 proxy season.[131] The issue of an advisory vote for shareholders on executive remuneration also become

---

[124] Eg, a recent issue of the *Harvard Law Review* is devoted to the issue of shareholder empowerment: see Stephen M Bainbridge, 'Director Primacy and Shareholder Disempowerment' (2006) 119 *Harvard Law Review* 1735; Bebchuk, 'The Case for Increasing Shareholder Power', above n 123; Strine, above n 92.

[125] Iman Anabtawi, 'Some Skepticism about Increasing Shareholder Power' (2006) 53 *University of California Los Angeles Law Review* 561, 569.

[126] Ibid; Bainbridge, above n 124; Strine, above n 92.

[127] Strine, above n 92, 1776–7.

[128] US Securities and Exchange Commission, 'SEC Votes to Propose Changes to Disclosure Requirements Concerning Executive Compensation and Related Matters' (Press Release, 17 January 2006).

[129] J Rutenberg, 'Bush Tells Wall St to Rethink Pay Practices', *New York Times* (New York), 1 February 2007, 11.

[130] American Federation of State, County and Municipal Employees.

[131] Gretchen Morgenson, 'Investors Get Voice on Pay at Verizon', *New York Times* (New York), 19 May 2007, 1.

the subject of Democrat-instigated congressional consideration.[132] In April 2007, the House of Representatives overwhelmingly passed a Bill that would accord US shareholders an advisory vote on executive remuneration, however, ultimate translation of the Bill into legislation is in doubt, due to White House opposition.[133]

Another aspect of long-term regulatory unpredictability is the impact of backlash.[134] Backlash can operate in either direction on a convergence-divergence axis. A recent example of backlash is the Paulson Committee Report,[135] which lays to rest any interpretation of common law post-scandal legislation as representing a unified, homogeneous regulatory response. Rather, a central tenet of the Paulson Committee Report is that the regulatory approach of *Sarbanes-Oxley* was idiosyncratic and unduly stringent by international standards, and has reduced the competitiveness of US markets.[136] Similar concerns regarding the declining pre-eminence of New York and US financial markets are evident in another report: *Sustaining New York's and the US' Global Financial Services Leadership*.[137]

This feature of the Paulson Committee Report is interesting from the perspective of the debate on cross-listing, which emerged at the high-point of the convergence-divergence controversy in comparative corporate governance. At that time, it was often assumed that the marked trend towards cross-listing of foreign firms in the US during the 1990s constituted a desirable form of regulatory competition,[138] in which companies incorporated in jurisdictions with weak minority shareholder protection could voluntarily adopt higher standards. This trend was seen

---

[132] Erin White and Aaron O Patrick, 'Shareholders Push for Vote on Executive Pay', *Wall Street Journal* (New York), 26 February 2007, B1.

[133] Kara Scannell and Siobhan Hughes, 'House Clears an Executive-Pay Measure', *Wall Street Journal* (New York), 21 April 2007, A3.

[134] On the political role of backlash generally, see Mark J Roe, 'Backlash' (1998) 98 *Columbia Law Review* 217.

[135] Committee on Capital Markets Regulation, above n 7.

[136] Ibid xi.

[137] McKinsey & Company, Report to M R Bloomberg and C E Schumer, *Sustaining New York's and the US' Global Financial Services and Leadership* (2007), available at <http://www.senate.gov/~schumer/SchumerWebsite/pressroom/special_reports/2007/NY_REPORT%20_FINAL.pdf>; see also Jenny Anderson, 'US Financial Sector Is Losing Its Edge, Report Says', *New York Times* (New York), 22 January 2007, 3.

[138] John C Coffee, 'Racing towards the Top? The Impact of Cross-Listings and Stock Market Competition on International Corporate Governance' (2002) 102 *Columbia Law Review* 1757.

as further possible evidence for the convergence of corporate governance practices towards a US model.[139] The Paulson Committee Report, however, suggests that the stringency of *Sarbanes-Oxley* and increased associated compliance costs[140] have resulted in the opposite phenomenon, whereby foreign companies are now avoiding cross-listing on US markets.[141]

Whereas a central goal of *Sarbanes-Oxley* was to restore investor confidence via rule-based regulation,[142] the Paulson Committee Report stresses the need to protect shareholders *from* excessive regulation that may impair the competitiveness of US markets.[143] This shift in the regulatory pendulum is arguably reflected in the recent rejection of greater oversight for hedge funds in the US.[144]

However, some commentators have questioned the supposed nexus between the prescriptive tenor of the post-Enron reforms and any loss of competitiveness in US capital markets. Coffee, for example, notes that much of the decline in the listing premium associated with foreign cross-listings occurred *prior* to the introduction of *Sarbanes-Oxley*, and argues that foreign firms continue to list on US markets because of their higher regulatory standards.[145] He also observes that firms which do

---

139 Cally Jordan, 'The Chameleon Effect: Beyond the Bonding of Hypothesis for Cross-Listed Securities' (2007) *New York University Journal of Law and Business* (forthcoming), available at <http://ssrn.com/abstract=907130>; Licht, above n 15, 196–8.

140 Stephen K Asare, Lawrence A Cunningham and Arnold Wright, 'The *Sarbanes-Oxley Act*: Legal Implications and Research Opportunities' (2007) 19 *Research in Accounting Regulation* 81.

141 Nicholas Lew and Ian Ramsay, 'Corporate Law Reform and Delisting in Australia' (Research Paper No 202, Centre for Corporate Law and Securities Regulation, University of Melbourne, 2006) 9–12; Amir N Licht, 'Cross-Listing and Corporate Governance: Bonding or Avoiding?' (2003) 4 *Chicago Journal of International Law* 141; Alison Maitland, 'BT Chairman Criticises US Governance', *Financial Times* (London), 23 November 2004, 22; Joseph D Piotroski and Suraj Srinivasan, 'The *Sarbanes-Oxley Act* and the Flow of International Listings' (2007), available at <http://ssrn.com/abstract=956987>.

142 Asare, Cunningham and Wright, above n 140, 82.

143 Committee on Capital Markets Regulation, above n 7, xi.

144 Stephen Labaton, 'Officials Reject More Oversight of Hedge Funds', *New York Times* (New York), 23 February 2007, 1.

145 Coffee, 'Law and the Market', above n 26, 7–8, 57–8. Coffee acknowledges that foreign issuers have migrated from US markets, however attributes this to the development of a 'separating equilibrium'. According to this explanation, firms that wish to reap the high valuation premium available in US markets, or who require shareholder support, will accept the higher costs of regulation associated with a US listing. In contrast, those firms with a 'control group' of managers or shareholders who are

cross-list on a US exchange appear to gain a significant valuation premium.[146] Davidoff, while acknowledging the decline in foreign listings on US markets, has suggested that this decline is primarily due to 'the inevitable maturation of non-US capital markets rather than … to the *Sarbanes-Oxley Act* or any other recent change in US regulation'.[147]

The issue of shareholder empowerment, prevalent in recent US academic debate, is also a subtext in the Paulson Committee Report. The Committee suggests that increased shareholder rights could themselves achieve greater board accountability, thereby reducing the need for heavy-handed formal regulation[148] and recommends enhancement of shareholder rights across several areas.[149] While issues of efficiency and firm value underpin much of the Paulson Committee Report's discussion, the fundamental power imbalance between managers and shareholders is also a clear concern.[150]

Shareholder empowerment, now permeating the US corporate law debate, provides an interesting contrast to current policy concerns in Australia and the UK, which are strongly focused not on shareholder rights, but on the interests of stakeholders. The plight of stakeholders, such as employees, and corporate responsibility generally, were major themes of the corporate scandals.[151] Nonetheless, *Sarbanes-Oxley* in the US and the *CLERP 9 Act* in Australia were mainly concerned with protection of shareholders and their interests.[152] In the UK, however, 'a

---

interested in maintaining private access to the benefits of that control will choose to list on less-regulated markets: at 7–10.

146 Ibid 8–9.

147 Steven M Davidoff, 'Regulating Listings in a Global Market' (Research Paper No 07–02, Wayne State University Law School, 2007) 9–23.

148 Committee on Capital Markets Regulation, above n 7, xi–xii.

149 Key proposals of the Paulson Committee Report relating to enhancement of shareholder rights include: (i) the requirement that classified boards gain the approval of shareholders prior to implementing a poison pill; (ii) the adoption of majority, rather than plurality, voting for board directors; (iii) clarification of the rights of shareholders with respect to gaining access to the company proxy to nominate directors for election; and (iv) enhancing shareholders' ability to access alternative means of dispute resolution: ibid xii–xiii, 93–114).

150 According to the Committee, 'When firms have a choice of legal regime, any policy proposal should adopt as a default the option most favorable to shareholders, given the fundamental asymmetry of power between managers and shareholders': ibid 103.

151 Langevoort, above n 6, 1828.

152 Cf, however, ibid 1828, 1833, claiming that, although *Sarbanes-Oxley* was by its terms about investor protection, its long-term effects may ultimately be about public accountability.

third way', advocating a long-term, enlightened shareholder value approach to corporate governance issues, was already gaining momentum.[153] Political issues, including concern by the EU to harmonise the laws of member states, contributed to this development in the UK.[154] This enlightened shareholder value principle has been given legislative force under s 172 of the recently enacted UK *Companies Act 2006*, which imposes a new duty on directors to 'promote the success of the company', requiring them to consider stakeholder interests and the long-term effects of their decisions.[155]

Corporate social responsibility has also become a major issue in Australia, largely as a result of two high-profile local corporate scandals. The first was the James Hardie saga. This involved a corporate reconstruction whereby asbestos-related liabilities were separated from other assets in the company through the creation of a foundation,[156] which was subsequently found to have insufficient funds to meet legitimate compensation claims.[157] The second concerned the Australian Wheat Board Ltd, one of the world's largest wheat marketing and management companies, which was found to have made corrupt payments to Iraq under the Oil-for-Food Program. These scandals were responsible for generating not only heated public debate about corporate social responsibility, but also two governmental reports on the topic — reports by the Parliamentary Joint Committee ('PJC Report')[158] and the Corporations and Markets Advisory Committee ('CAMAC Report').[159]

A central issue in these reports was the scope of directors' duties, and the extent to which the current Australian legal framework permits

---

[153] Cynthia A Williams and John M Conley, 'An Emerging Third Way? The Erosion of the Anglo-American Shareholder Value Construct' (2005) 38 *Cornell International Law Journal* 493.

[154] Ibid 498–9.

[155] Robert P Austin (ed), *Company Directors and Corporate Social Responsibility: UK and Australian Perspectives* (2007).

[156] The Medical Research and Compensation Foundation.

[157] Edwina Dunn, 'James Hardie: No Soul to Be Damned and No Body to Be Kicked' (2005) 27 *Sydney Law Review* 339.

[158] The PJC announced its Inquiry into Corporate Responsibility in June 2005 and released its Report in June 2006: PJC on Corporations and Financial Services, Parliament of Australia, *Corporate Responsibility: Managing Risk and Creating Value* (2006).

[159] CAMAC received a reference in March 2005 and issued its Discussion Paper in November 2005: CAMAC, *Corporate Social Responsibility: Discussion Paper* (2005). Its Final Report was released in December 2006: CAMAC, *The Social Responsibility of Corporations: Report* (2006).

directors to consider the interests of stakeholders or the broader community. This issue arose directly from the James Hardie matter, where James Hardie executives and directors sought to justify their conduct by arguing that current law essentially required them to privilege shareholder interests 'at all costs'.[160] The PJC Report observed, however, that 'rampant corporate irresponsibility certainly decreases shareholder value'.[161] Scrutiny of the actions of the James Hardie directors will inevitably persist, with the Australian Securities and Investments Commission announcing in mid-February 2007 that it would bring civil penalty proceedings against the entire board of directors.[162]

Both the PJC Report and the CAMAC Report rejected legislative change to directors' duties in Australia to embody 'enlightened shareholder value' explicitly as in s 172 of the *Companies Act 2006* (UK). The PJC Report was critical of the UK amendment to directors' duties,[163] on the basis that it was overly prescriptive and would result in confusion, while the CAMAC Report considered that a comparable statutory amendment in Australia would provide 'no worthwhile benefit'.[164] Overall, there is a degree of overlap between the tone and ultimate conclusions of the PJC Report and the CAMAC Report, with both demonstrating a preference for industry-based regulation and initiatives, rather than formal legislative change, to address corporate social responsibility issues. The CAMAC Report, in particular, acknowledged the limits to the law's ability to control corporate decision-making by prescription, portraying corporate responsibility as a fluid part of a company's operations, not a legislative 'add-on'.[165]

Conclusion

While post-scandal reforms in the US, UK and Australia were prompted by similar motivations, interesting differences in terms of their focus and structure still resonate in current corporate governance debate. The unique contours of the various regulatory responses challenge not only

---

[160] PJC Report, above n 158, 47, 181.
[161] Ibid 19.
[162] John Durie, 'ASIC Treads Fine Line on Hardie', *Australian Financial Review* (Sydney), 16 February 2007, 84; Marcus Priest and Mark Sculley, 'ASIC Seeks Bans for Hardie Asbestos Directors', *Australian Financial Review* (Sydney), 16 February 2007, 1.
[163] PJC Report, above n 158, 54–6.
[164] CAMAC, *The Social Responsibility of Corporations: Report*, above n 159, 111.
[165] Ibid 3–4.

the traditional convergence hypothesis, but also the idea that a unified common law corporate governance model exists. Rather, a fluid, dynamic and increasingly fragmented picture of corporate governance has emerged. Within this developing corporate governance framework, various jurisdictions are able to test regulatory techniques and learn by their own trial and error, and that of other jurisdictions. If any evidence of long-term convergence can be gleaned from these developments, paradoxically, it would appear to be away from the US post-scandal regulatory model. These developments reflect a complex and interesting picture of contemporary corporate governance, worthy of *La Règle du Jeu*.

Chapter 3

Overlapping Fields and Constructed Legalities: The Endogeneity of Law

Lauren B Edelman

Corporate governance is not only the subject of legal regulation; it is also constitutive of legal regulation. The chapters in this book point to important limitations of law and legal machinery in regulating corporate governance[1] and to the complex ways in which organisations themselves interweave law, ethics, and compliance.[2] This chapter addresses the relationship between organisational forms of compliance and the limits of law by showing how organisational practices help to transform the meaning of law. I rely on neo-institutional organisation theory, which offers a framework for understanding how organisations influence the

[1] See, e.g., Justin O'Brien, 'Charting an Icarian Flightpath: The Implications of the Qantas Deal Collapse', in this book; Jennifer Hill, 'Evolving "Rules of the Game" in Corporate Governance Reform', in this book; George Gilligan, 'The Significance of Relative Autonomy in How Regulation of the Financial Service Sector Evolves', in this book; Iain MacNeil; 'Enforcement of Capital Markets Regulation: The United Kingdom and Its International Markets', in this book; Melvin J Dubnick, '*Sarbanes-Oxley* and the Search for Accountable Corporate Governance', in this book; see also Justin O'Brien, *Redesigning Financial Regulation: The Politics of Enforcement: The Politics of Enforcement* (2007); John Coffee, 'Law and the Market: The Impact of Enforcement' (Paper delivered at the Dynamics of Capital Market Governance Forum, Australian National University, 14 March 2007).

[2] See, eg, Doreen McBarnet, 'Compliance, Ethics and Responsibility: Emergent Governance Strategies in the US and UK', in this book; Seumas Miller, 'Institutions, Integrity Systems and Market Actors', in this book.

worlds around them — including the legal world that seeks to regulate them.

Institutional theory invokes the construct of organisational fields to explore the force of institutionalised logics, structures, models, and rituals within recognised areas of social life.[3] Early accounts emphasised institutional isomorphism that resulted in a dominant logic within a field.[4] More recently, scholars have emphasised that fields often include multiple, contradictory logics,[5] and that actors who transcend or span field boundaries play a role in bringing disparate field logics to bear in ways that promote institutional change.[6] Further, a number of scholars

---

[3] Paul J DiMaggio and Walter W Powell, 'The Iron Cage Revisited: Institutional Isomorphism and Collective Rationality in Organizational Fields' (1983) 48 *American Sociological Review* 147; W Richard Scott and John W Meyer, 'The Organization of Societal Sectors: Propositions and Early Evidence' in Walter W Powell and Paul J DiMaggio (eds), *The New Institutionalism in Organizational Analysis* (1991) 108; W Richard Scott, *Institutions and Organizations* (2nd ed, 2002).

[4] Pamela S Tolbert and Lynne G Zucker, 'Institutional Sources of Change in the Formal Structure Organizations: The Diffusion of Civil Service Reform, 1880–1935' (1983) 28 *Administrative Science Quarterly* 22; Lauren B Edelman, 'Legal Environments and Organizational Governance: The Expansion of Due Process in the Workplace' (1990) 95 *American Journal of Sociology* 1401.

[5] Roger Friedland and Robert R Alford, 'Bringing Society Back in: Symbols, Practices, and Institutional Contradictions' in Walter W Powell and Paul J DiMaggio (eds), *The New Institutionalism in Organizational Analysis* (1991) 232; Robin Stryker, 'Legitimacy Processes as Institutional Politics: Implications for Theory and Research in the Sociology of Organizations' (2000) 17 *Research in the Sociology of Organizations* 179; Carol Heimer, 'Competing Institutions: Law, Medicine and Family in Neonatal Intensive Care' (1999) 33 *Law and Society Review* 17; W Richard Scott et al, *Institutional Change and Health Care Organizations: From Professional Dominance to Managed Care* (2000); Marc Schneiberg, 'Organizational Heterogeneity and the Production of New Forms: Politics, Social Movements and Mutual Companies in American Fire Insurance, 1899–1930' (2002) 19 *Research in the Sociology of Organizations* 39; Mark Lounsbury, Marc Ventresca and Paul Hirsch, 'Social Movements, Field Frames, and Industry Emergence: A Cultural-Political Perspective on US Recycling' (2003) 1 *Socio-Economic Review* 71; Marc Schneiberg and Sarah Soule, 'Institutionalization as a Contested, Multi-Level Process: The Case of Rate Regulation in American Fire Insurance' in Gerald F Davis et al (eds), *Social Movements and Organization Theory: Building Bridges* (2004) 122.

[6] Huseyin Leblebici and Gerald R Salancik, 'Stability in Interorganizational Exchanges: Rulemaking Processes of the Chicago Board of Trade' (1982) 27 *Administrative Science Quarterly* 227; Elizabeth S Clemens, 'Organizational Repertoires and Institutional Change: Women's Groups and the Transformation of US Politics, 1890–1920' (1993) 98 *American Journal of Sociology* 755; Elizabeth S Clemens, *The People's Lobby: Organizational Innovation and the Rise of Interest Group Politics in the United States, 1890–1925* (1997); John L Campbell, 'Mechanisms of Evolutionary Change in Economic Governance: Interaction, Interpretation and Bricolage' in Lars Magnusson and Jan

have begun to explore the impact of social movements on institutional change within fields.[7]

This chapter elaborates on ideas of overlapping fields and multiple logics in the context of the relationship between law and organisations. Institutional theory brought law and the state to the forefront of organisational analysis. In contrast to more rational and materialist perspectives on organisations, which emphasise organisations' capacity for resisting law or for capturing state administrative agencies, institutional theorists offer a more nuanced account in which the meaning of law and compliance evolves through processes of collective construction and institutionalisation. As a central component of organisations' normative environments, and as an institutional force, law encourages organisational conformity more than resistance.

Institutional theorists have struggled, however, with the precise relation of law to organisations, and with questions of institutional change. Extant analyses of law and organisations tell us too little about how organisations (and actors within organisations) make sense of law; how organisations translate law into internal policies and procedures; whether and when organisational compliance is more symbolic than substantive; and whether and how organisations exert influence on legal institutions. A particularly vexing question in the institutional literature, given institutional theory's tendency to downplay the importance of strategic action, is how to make sense of organisations' efforts to avoid lawsuits and to reduce their exposure to legal liability.

I consider these questions by offering a theoretical framework that emphasises the blurring of organisational and legal logics as a source

---

Ottosson (eds), *Evolutionary Economics and Path Dependence* (1997) 10; Heimer, above n 5; Lauren B Edelman, Sally Riggs Fuller and Iona Mara-Drita, 'Diversity Rhetoric and the Managerialization of Law' (2001) 106 *American Journal of Sociology* 1589; Daniel Lee Kleinman and Steven Vallas, 'Science, Capitalism, and the Rise of the "Knowledge Worker": The Changing Structure of Knowledge Production in the United States' (2001) 30 *Theory and Society* 451; Schneiberg, above n 5.

[7] Doug McAdam and W Richard Scott, 'Organizations and Movements' in Gerald F Davis et al, *Social Movements and Organization Theory: Building Bridges* (2004) 4; Hayagreeva Rao, Calvin Morrill and Meyer Zald, 'Power Plays: How Social Movements and Collective Action Create New Organizational Forms' (2000) 22 *Research in Organizational Behavior* 237; Gerald F Davis and Tracy A Thompson, 'A Social Movement Perspective on Corporate Control' (1994) 39 *Administrative Science Quarterly* 141; Lounsbury, Ventresca and Hirsch, above n 5; Schneiberg and Soule, above n 5.

of institutional change. My framework introduces the construct of a legal field and calls attention to the interplay of ideas at the intersection of organisational and legal fields. Just as organisational fields are understood as the environment within which organisations interact and in which conceptions of rational organisational actions and actors evolve, 'legal fields' may be understood as the environment within which legal institutions and legal actors interact and in which conceptions of legality and compliance evolve. At the point of intersection between legal and organisational fields, differing logics of the two fields come into play and respond to one another; thus it is a critical locale for institutional change. In this arena, ideas about both legality and rationality are constructed, negotiated, tested, contested, and sometimes institutionalised.

In this chapter, I discuss the differing logics of organisational and legal fields as well as the effects of those logics on the making and institutionalisation of legal meaning. I then argue that as the logics of organisational and legal fields come together in the area in which the fields overlap, law becomes *managerialised* or infused with managerial interests, assumptions, and ideas. As conflicts arise within organisations and the law is mobilised, managerialised understandings of law can then re-enter legal fields and affect the thinking of judges and the rulings of courts. In this way, managerialised law can be incorporated into and legitimated by judicial, and even legislative, constructions of law.

The result of the blurring of organisational and legal logics is that law should not be treated as an exogenous force on organisations. Rather, law should be considered at least in part *endogenous*, constructed in and through the organisational fields that it seeks to regulate. Law, then, is not a set of fixed mandates but rather a continuously evolving institution that is shaped and given meaning through its interaction with organisations. The idea of endogenous law stands in stark contrast to most institutional (as well as rational) accounts of law and organisations, which presume that law stands above and outside of organisational fields and thus constitutes a force that is exogenous, authoritative, coercive, and unambiguous.[8]

---

[8] See, eg, DiMaggio and Powell, above n 3; W Richard Scott, 'Unpacking Institutional Arguments' in Walter W Powell and Paul J DiMaggio (eds), *The New Institutional Organizational Analysis* (1991) 164; Steven Brint and Jerome Karabel, 'Institutional Origins and Transformations: The Case of American Community Colleges' in Walter W Powell and Paul J DiMaggio (eds), *The New Institutional Organizational Analysis* (1991)

The endogenous view of law has its roots in works that combine early law and society insights with the 'old institutionalism' in organisational analysis. Willard Hurst's account of the legal history of the lumber industry in Wisconsin,[9] for example, showed how the timber industry was able to take advantage of the government's interest in economic development to achieve favourable legal policies and to alter conceptions of public good with respect to the use of property and state funds. Further, Philip Selznick's work has always called attention to the interplay between public and private normative realms. In *TVA and the Grass Roots*,[10] Selznick showed how community interests infiltrated and coopted the strategies and policies of a state agency. Also, in *Law, Society and Industrial Justice*,[11] Selznick argued that the everyday conflicts in organisational life both reflected legal change and were reflected in it. In this chapter, I seek to integrate these early institutional accounts of law and organisations, which emphasised the agency of organisational actors and societal interests in shaping the law, with the new institutionalist accounts that emphasise organisational fields as homogenising forces. I show how particular actors and interest groups help to mingle the logics of organisational and legal fields so that particular constructions of law and forms of compliance come to be understood as rational, legal, and legitimate.

337; Neil Fligstein, *The Transformation of Corporate Control* (1990); Neil Fligstein, 'The Structural Transformation of American Industry: An Institutional Account of the Causes of Diversification in the Largest Firms, 1919–1979' in Walter W Powell and Paul J DiMaggio (eds), *The New Institutional Organizational Analysis* (1991) 311. DiMaggio and Powell in 'The Iron Cage Revisited' suggest that law evokes 'coercive isomorphism'; in other words, organisations become more alike because they are also subject to the coercive force of legal mandates. Scott suggests that law directly imposes certain structures on organisations when he argues that: 'Some sectors or fields contain environmental agents that are sufficiently powerful to impose structural forms on subordinate organizational units. Nation-states do this when mandating by law changes in existing organizational forms.' Brint and Karabel, at 345, argue, in discussing the origin of institutional interests, that 'there are many instances when organizational interests are pre-given by legal decrees …'. And Fligstein in 'The Structural Transformation of American Industry' also adopts an exogenous view of law when he suggests that 'the state can actually set the rules of the game for any given organizational field. … It can, therefore, alter the environment more profoundly and systematically than other organizations.'

[9] *Law and Economic Growth: The Legal History of the Lumber Industry in Wisconsin, 1836–1915* (1964).

[10] (1949).

[11] (1969).

The remainder of this chapter is divided into three sections and a conclusion. In the next section, Legal and Organisational Fields, I argue that legal and organisational fields are structured around different logics, which exert divergent forces upon the construction and implementation of law. Then, in Organisational Fields and the Managerialisation of Law, I show how ideas about rational responses to law evolve in organisational fields in ways that infuse managerial logic into legal ideals. Third, in Legal Fields and the Rationalisation of Managerialised Law, I suggest that the construction of law can come full circle, as courts incorporate managerialised understandings of rational modes of compliance, and ultimately, of the meaning of law. Finally, in the conclusion, I discuss the implications of overlapping organisational and legal fields for understandings of the relationship between law and organisations.

Throughout this chapter, I illustrate my argument by discussing the endogenous construction of the rationality of internal grievance procedures. Once available almost exclusively to unionised employees, employers now create internal grievance procedures — formal written procedures that allow employees to challenge the actions of their superiors in the organisation — because they see them as a rational response to civil rights law. Although internal grievance procedures are not legally required, they have become increasingly institutionalised over the past third of a century. A 1995 survey conducted by the General Accounting Office found that almost 90 per cent of employers use at least one form of alternative dispute resolution ('ADR') to resolve employment discrimination complaints.[12] The increasing prevalence of internal grievance procedures is attributable in large part to the claims of management consultants that these procedures would insulate organisations from legal liability. Such claims had little foundation when they were first being made (during the 1960s, 1970s, and 1980s), but courts have in recent years begun to affirm the legality of internal grievance procedures and in fact to defer to the logic of internal

---

[12] The survey involved a stratified random sample of 2000 businesses with 100 or more employees. Internal workplace dispute resolution involved some kind of fact-finding by a personnel professional or other management representative in 81 per cent of the organisations, mediation by a management representative in 38 per cent of the organisations, and mediation by a private mediator in nine per cent of the organisations: United States General Accounting Office, *Employment Discrimination: Most Private Sector Employers Use Alternative Dispute Resolution*, Report to Congress (1995).

grievance procedures. The law, then, has to some extent incorporated and legitimated the logic of organisational fields.

I Legal and Organisational Fields

The construct of 'organisational field' is now well known in the organisational literature: it refers to the subset of the environment that is most closely relevant to a given organisation, including suppliers, customers, and competitors, as well as flows of influence, communication, and innovation.[13] Courts or regulatory agencies are often recognised as relevant, but peripheral, elements of organisational fields. Legal agencies and institutions are relevant elements of organisational fields in that they are viewed as sources of 'coercive isomorphism'; that is, they promulgate rules to which organisations within the field must orient their behaviour, through either compliance or circumvention.[14] Legal institutions may be considered peripheral to organisational fields, however, in the sense that organisations generally look first to the actors with whom they interact most directly (professionals within and around the organisation, similar organisations, and business partners).

Although legal institutions may be peripheral elements of organisational fields, they may also be understood as central to a separate, but overlapping, *legal field*.[15] Legal fields are not unlike the fields of private goods- or service-producing organisations; they consist of flows of influence, communication, and innovation among the various organisations and professions that interact with legal institutions. Principal actors in legal fields are judges, lawyers, legislators, administrative agency personnel, court clerks, and inspectors. Just as legal actors and institutions are peripheral elements in organisational fields, organisations and organisational actors are peripheral elements in legal fields.

Organisational and legal fields overlap substantially: virtually every aspect of organisational life takes place against a legal backdrop and a large proportion of legal transactions involve organisations. The legal life of organisations begins with the legal act of incorporation, which in essence 'gives birth' to the organisation, and may end with the legal acts of bankruptcy, merger, or dissolution. During their life spans,

[13] Di Maggio and Powell, above n 3; Scott et al, above n 5.
[14] Di Maggio and Powell, above n 3.
[15] Edelman, Fuller and Mara-Drita, above n 6.

organisations raise capital under securities law, hire employees under labour and anti-discrimination laws, exchange goods and services under contract law, develop public identities under trademark laws, innovate under patent and copyright laws, and engage in production under environmental, health, and safety laws. Specific bodies of legal rules define, protect, and regulate many industries and most professions. Even the basic distinctions between organisations as 'private', 'public', and 'non-profit' are in large part legal constructs.[16]

Similarly, organisations are heavily intertwined in the life of law. Much law arises out of, or is changed because of, conflicts that stem from the actions and interests of corporations, non-profit organisations, social movement organisations, and other types of organisations. Law gains meaning through its interpretation by organisational actors and its implementation within organisations. Law is mobilised by and finds force in the actions of organisational actors, and its boundaries are shaped in part by organisations' buffering and decoupling strategies. The wheels of justice usually start turning at the behest of organisational actors.[17]

What distinguishes organisational and legal fields may be found less in the elements that compose them than in the logics that drive them. Although logics within fields are themselves multiple, complicated, contested, and changing,[18] a central logic within organisational fields in the United States since the early 1900s has been efficiency and rationalisation.[19] This logic has been a particularly salient factor in the rise of administrative hierarchies within corporations, municipal and civil service reform during the Progressive Era, and the governance of employees, where the 20th century has seen the rise of models of

---

[16] Lauren B Edelman and Mark C Suchman, 'The Legal Environments of Organizations' (1997) 23 *Annual Review of Sociology* 479.

[17] Marc Galanter, 'Why the "Haves" Come Out Ahead: Speculations on the Limits of Legal Change' (1974) 9 *Law and Society Review* 95; Lauren B Edelman and Mark C Suchman, 'When the Haves Hold Court: Speculations on the Organizational Internalization of Law' (1999) 33 *Law and Society Review* 941.

[18] Fligstein, *Transformation of Corporate Control*, above n 8; Schneiberg, above n 5; Schneiberg and Soule, above n 5.

[19] Alfred D Chandler, *Strategy and Structure: Chapters in the History of the American Industrial Enterprise* (1962); Alfred D Chandler, *The Visible Hand: The Managerial Revolution in American Business* (1977); W Richard Scott, *Organizations: Rational, Natural and Open Systems* (5th ed, 2003).

management that emphasise formalisation, rationalisation, and consistency.[20] At least with respect to the governance of employees, then, the dominant logic of management in the latter half of the 20th century foregrounds rationality and efficiency.

By contrast, the primary or core logic of legal fields highlights rules and rights. The logic of rules derives from the liberal legal jurisprudence that has characterised American law since the latter part of the 19th century. Liberal legal jurisprudence holds that law is developed and enacted through adherence to rational principles, producing a set of rulings that is impartial and just. It is impartial in that it is insulated from political, religious, or other substantive influence; it is just in that rules are equally applicable across all types of situations and to all citizens. Liberal legal ideology sees the legislative and executive branches as implementing the central precepts of justice articulated in a constitution and the courts as passive institutions that *apply* determinative rights and principles to particular fact situations but do not *make* law.[21]

---

[20] See, eg, Ann Shola Orloff and Theda Skocpol, 'Why Not Equal Protection? Explaining the Politics of Public Spending in Britain, 1900–1911, and the United States, 1880s–1920' (1984) 49 *American Sociological Review* 726; Sanford M Jacoby, *Employing Bureaucracy: Managers, Unions, and the Transformation of Work in American Industry, 1900–1945* (1985); James N Baron, Frank R Dobbin and P Deveraux Jennings, 'War and Peace: The Evolution of Modern Personnel Administration in US Industry' (1986) 92 *American Journal of Sociology* 350; Selznick, *Law, Society and Industrial Justice*, above n 11.

[21] It is difficult to identify the emergence of liberal legal ideology precisely, but it is clear that American jurisprudence has moved progressively toward a liberal legal model. The increasingly important role of law schools, published legal literature, and the professionalisation of legal practitioners were particularly important in the development of liberal legalism. Christopher Columbus Langdell, who became Dean of the Harvard Law School in 1870, introduced and actively promoted the idea of law as a science. To achieve his goal of moving law into the professional realm, he raised law school admission and graduation requirements, and he introduced the case method of teaching law as a means of demonstrating the subtle rationality of law. He purged the law school curriculum of economics and politics, and largely ignored legislation, instead focusing on judges' law — but judges' law narrowed to extreme formalism and abstraction: Lawrence M Friedman, *A History of American Law* (1973). Although not well-received at first, Langdell's practices eventually revolutionised law school teaching and led to the institutionalisation of liberal legalism in law schools. The publication of case decisions at the state level was common by the mid-19th century and the National Reporter System began in 1879, providing the volumes of records necessary for lawyers to develop the art of reasoning by analogy to precedent. Judges also adopted the practice of hiding their reasoning behind a cloak of legal formalism, listing strings of precedent rather than creative social reasoning. And the birth of university law reviews, beginning with the

Although liberal legal ideology is the primary and legitimating logic of legal fields, it is important to note that it is more a legitimating ideal than it is a reality. Rights and legal principles are indeterminate, easily manipulated by those with greater clout and organisation,[22] and easily rendered symbolic through corporate culture and 'creative compliance'.[23] Rights are often ambiguous and tend to acquire meaning through the interaction of social actors and institutions. This is especially true where, as in the case of employment, rights-holders lack political clout, economic wealth, and social organisation. People with power can take advantage of a stratified legal profession,[24] and can use legal tactics such as delay, procedural manoeuvres, and institutional bias to their advantage.[25] They can influence the rulings of administrative agencies,

---

Harvard Law Review in 1887, further developed the 'science' of law and its aura of autonomy from society: see Friedman (1973) for a rich history of American law. The writings of 20th century legal philosophers such as Hart, Fuller, Dworkin, and Rawls helped to solidify and institutionalise notions of liberal legalism in American scholarship, as did the (translated) writings in sociology of Max Weber. Weber adopted the liberal legal paradigm in his portrayal of rational-legal authority, the type of legal authority that he associated with modern capitalism. Rational-legal authority is justified by reason rather than tradition or charismatic decree, and it is carried out by a specialised staff who, by virtue of their official roles, can be presumed to be impartial actors fulfilling formal roles. Law, in this vision, is presumed to have an autonomous internal logic, and it is presumed to apply universally to all citizens and across all situations. Thus Weber associated law's formal rationality with the predictability necessary for capitalist development.

[22] Mark Tushnet, 'An Essay on Rights' (1984) 62 *Texas Law Review* 1363; Duncan Kennedy, 'Toward an Historical Understanding of Legal Consciousness: The Case of the Classical Legal Thought in America, 1850–1940' (1980) 3 *Research in Law and Sociology* 3; Kristin Bumiller, *The Civil Rights Society: The Social Construction of Victims* (1988); Alan Freeman, 'Antidiscrimination Law: The View from 1989'in David Kairys (ed), *The Politics of Law: A Progressive Critique* (1990) 121; Vicki Schultz, 'Telling Stories about Women and Work: Judicial Interpretations of Sex Segregation in the Workplace in Title VII Cases Raising the Lack of Interest Argument' (1990) 103 *Harvard Law Review* 1749.

[23] Lauren B Edelman, 'Legal Ambiguity and Symbolic Structures: Organizational Mediation of Civil Rights Law' (1992) 97 *American Journal of Sociology* 1531; McBarnet, above n 2; O'Brien, *Redesigning Financial Regulation*, above n 1.

[24] Jerome E Carlin, *Lawyer's Ethics: A Survey of the New York City Bar* (1966); John P Heinz and Edward O Laumann, *Chicago Lawyers: The Social Structure of the Bar* (1977); Stephen Wexler, 'Practicing Law for Poor People' (1970) 79 *Yale Law Journal* 1049.

[25] Galanter, above n 17; Catherine Albiston, 'The Rule of Law and the Litigation Process: The Paradox of Losing by Winning' (1999) 33 *Law and Society Review* 869; Edelman and Suchman, 'When the Haves Hold Court', above n 17.

which in turn influence the courts,[26] and they can prevent the voicing of legal claims in the first place.[27] Courts' adherence to precedent is tempered, then, by a society in which the rights of those without clout are often rendered symbolic.[28]

Nonetheless, liberal legal logic is important as a legitimating ideal. Because legal institutions lose legitimacy when they appear to deviate from their rationalised roles, courts must be formally attentive to rights. The language of rights empowers those who lack clout but enjoy formal rights[29] and has deep appeal for most of the public to whom judges, juries, and attorneys have to be somewhat responsive. In the language of institutional theory, liberal legal ideology consists of a set of unwritten, taken-for-granted rules that give considerable force to arguments that are framed in terms of those rules.

In recent years, a secondary (and to some extent, competing) logic has also become prominent in legal fields. Although liberal legalism remains dominant, various forms of ADR are becoming increasingly prominent parts of the legal landscape and have had an impact on formal legal ideology.[30] The ADR movement, which began in earnest in the 1970s, developed largely as a critique of the formalism of the courts and of the liberal legal model more generally. Grounded in an ideology of community rather than liberal legal rights, ADR seeks to move away from the formal constraints of procedural rules and precedent and toward a model that empowers the parties to create their own solutions to problems.[31] The ADR movement seeks not simply to resolve

---

[26] William H Clune, 'A Political Model of Implementation and the Implications of the Model for Public Policy, Research, and the Changing Role of Lawyers' (1983) 69 *Iowa Law Review* 47.

[27] William L F Felstiner, Richard L Abel and Austin Sarat, 'The Emergence and Transformation of Disputes: Naming, Blaming, Claiming …' (1981) 15 *Law and Society Review* 631; Bumiller, *The Civil Rights Society*, above n 22; Kristin Bumiller, 'Victims in the Shadow of the Law: A Critique of the Model of Legal Protection' (1987) 12 *Signs* 421.

[28] Murray J Edelman, *The Symbolic Uses of Politics* (1964).

[29] Patricia Williams, 'Alchemical Notes: Reconstructing Ideals from Deconstructed Rights' (1987) 22 *Harvard Civil Rights — Civil Liberties Law Review* 401; Martha Minow, 'Interpreting Rights: An Essay for Robert Cover' (1987) 96 *Yale Law Journal* 1860.

[30] Edelman and Suchman, 'When the Haves Hold Court', above n 17.

[31] Roger Fisher and William Ury, *Getting to Yes: Negotiating Agreement without Giving In* (1981); Carrie Menkel-Meadow, 'Toward Another View of Legal Negotiation: The Structure of Problem-Solving' (1984) 31 *University of California Los Angeles Law Review* 754; Christopher W Moore, *The Mediation Process: Practical Strategies for*

disputes but rather to use the process of conflict resolution to identify and cure underlying psycho-social pathologies, to empower individuals to recognise and assert their needs while taking into account the needs of the other, and — most generally — to build community.[32] Because ADR stresses party participation in the dispute resolution process and sees courts as less capable of finding 'correct' solutions than the parties themselves, formal legal rules and rights are often given relatively less weight and the stated interests or wishes of the parties relatively more.[33]

Resolving Conflict (1986); Alan F Westin and Alfred G Feliu, *Resolving Employment Disputes Without Litigation* (1988); Robert A B Bush and Joseph P Folger, *The Promise of Mediation: Responding to Conflict through Empowerment and Recognition* (1994); Robert A B Bush, 'The Defining Quality of Dispute Resolution: Taxonomies and Anti-Taxonomies of Quality Arguments' (1989) 66 *Denver Law Review* 335; Gerald N Rosenberg, *The Hollow Hope: Can Courts Bring About Social Change?* (1991).

[32] There are many forms of alternative dispute resolution. Some, like arbitration, retain the general form of court adjudication but relax the rules of evidence and *stare decisis*, allowing the decision-maker far greater latitude in fashioning remedies. Arbitration decisions exhibit deference to organisational practices in that arbitrators base their decisions largely on industry norms and practices rather than on statutory mandates. Other forms of ADR, such as mediation, are far less formal and do away with third party decision-making entirely. Mediation uses a facilitator who, at least in theory, makes no decisions and simply assists the parties in reaching an agreement based on their own interests and needs.

[33] Lauren B Edelman, Howard S Erlanger and John Lande, 'Internal Dispute Resolution: The Transformation of Civil Rights in the Workplace' (1993) 27 *Law and Society Review* 497. Mediation, in particular, stresses disputant participation, party-devised solutions, and the building of community over adherence to externally-specified rules or formal legal principles. In theory these solutions are based on enriched understandings of the others' position as well as of their own needs, often producing 'win–win' situations. But many critics point out that, in practice, the removal of formal sanctions leaves parties with less economic or social clout at a considerable disadvantage and effectively undermines their legal rights: Owen M Fiss, 'Against Settlement' (1984) 93 *Yale Law Journal* 1073; Richard Delgado et al, 'Fairness and Formality: Minimizing the Risk of Prejudice in Alternative Dispute Resolution' (1985) *Wisconsin Law Review* 1359; Susan Silbey and Austin Sarat, 'Dispute Processing in Law and Legal Scholarship: From Institutional Critique to the Reconstruction of the Juridical Subject' (1989) 66 *Denver Law Review* 437; Penelope Bryan, 'Killing Us Softly: Divorce Mediation and the Politics of Power' (1992) 40 *Buffalo Law Review* 441; Penelope Bryan, 'Reclaiming Professionalism: The Lawyer's Role in Divorce Mediation' (1994) 28 *Family Law Quarterly* 177; Martha Fineman, 'Dominant Discource, Professional Language, and Legal Change in Child Custody Decision-Making' (1988) 101 *Harvard Law Review* 727; Lauren B Edelman and Mia L Cahill, 'How Law Matters in Disputing and Dispute Processing (or, the Contingency of Legal Matter in Alternative Dispute Resolution)' in Bryant Garth and Austin Sarat (eds), *How Law Matters* (1998) 15.

The differing core logics of organisational and legal fields — the emphasis on rationality and efficiency in organisational fields and on rights and justice (and to some extent community) in legal fields — drive institutional change in law.[34] Tensions between the logics of organisational and legal fields come into play every time organisational and legal actors and institutions interact. Organisational actors bring managerial logic to bear as they construct the meaning of legal rules and ideals.[35] The two logics tend to blur as business actors try to make sense of law and as legal actors consider the problems that arise out of organisational contexts. For example, organisational lobbying to restrict regulations that govern health and safety, working conditions, governance, and civil rights uses the logic of efficiency to challenge the logic of rights, whereas regulation of organisational actions and interactions uses the logic of rights to tame the logic of efficiency. Individual employees base their claims on rights in order to challenge practices that are accepted as rational and efficient, and employers cite efficiency and rationality as defences to alleged rights violations. Further, managerialised understandings of law and rights frame understandings of injustice, thus shaping the nature and types of conflict that flow back into legal fields in the form of formal complaints and litigation.

As the logics come together, legal ideals tend to shape strategic action in business and managerial ideals tend to shape the thinking of lawyers and judges. In this way, law both constrains and enables the strategic actions of organisational actors, and conversely, ideas about rationality and efficiency seep into notions of justice. In the next two sections, I discuss the process through which legal logic enters into and transforms organisational fields and the process through which managerialised forms of law then re-enter legal fields. Collectively, I refer to this process as 'the endogeneity of law' because, in contrast to the usual notion of law as a coercive force, the flow of logics between fields renders law in part endogenous to organisational fields. There are six stages to the endogeneity of law: (1) the professional construction of

---

[34] Calvin Morrill (forthcoming) makes a similar argument about change at the interstice of organizational fields. See Calvin Morrill, 'Institutional Change Through Interstitial Emergence: The Growth of Alternative Dispute Resolution in American Law, 1965-1985', in Walter Powell and Daniel Jones (eds), *How Institutions Change: Institutional Dynamics and Processes* (forthcoming).

[35] Edelman, Fuller and Mara-Drita, above n 6.

the legal environment; (2) the construction and diffusion of symbolic forms of compliance; (3) the construction of law within organisations; (4) the formation of legal consciousness; (5) the construction of legal disputes; and (6) judicial deference to organisational institutions. The first three stages involve the managerialisation of law in organisational fields; the last three stages involve the flow of organisational logic into legal fields, rendering law endogenous.[36]

II THE MANAGERIALISATION OF LAW IN ORGANISATIONAL FIELDS

Rules that regulate organisations tend to be broad and ambiguous. Rather than narrowly prescribing organisational behaviour, laws tend to articulate broad principles or ideals. Organisations, as well as administrative agencies and courts, are left to discern the meaning of these principles and the manner in which they will be realised in organisational life.[37] Title VII of the *Civil Rights Act of 1964* ('*Civil Rights Act*'), for example, makes it an unlawful employment practice for an employer

> to fail or refuse to hire or to discharge any individual, or otherwise to discriminate against any individual with respect to his compensation, terms, conditions, or privileges of employment, because of such individual's race, color, religion, sex, or national origin …

or

> to limit, segregate, or classify his employees or applicants for employment in any way which would deprive or tend to deprive any individual of employment opportunities or otherwise adversely affect his status as an employee, because of such individual's race, color, religion, sex, or national origin.[38]

Nowhere does the law specify the meaning of 'to discriminate' or what it would mean to take action 'because of' an individual's race,

---

[36] Lauren B Edelman, 'Law at Work: The Endogenous Construction of Civil Rights' in Laura Beth Nielsen and Robert L Nelson (eds), *Handbook of Employment Discrimination Research: Rights and Realities* (2005) 337.
[37] Edelman, 'Legal Ambiguity and Symbolic Structures', above n 23.
[38] 42 USC § 2000e–2 (2000).

color, religion, sex, or national origin. Although it is fairly clear from the legal language that employers may not hang out a sign specifying that 'no blacks or Hispanics will be hired', the law does not say what actions employers should or may take to be in compliance with the law. Debates over this ambiguity have generated 30 years of employer experimentation, political contest, and litigation.

Other civil rights laws are equally opaque. The *Americans with Disabilities Act of 1990*, for example, specifies that:

> No covered entity shall discriminate against a qualified individual with a disability because of the disability of such individual in regard to job application procedures, the hiring, advancement, or discharge of employees, employee compensation, job training, and other terms, conditions, and privileges of employment.[39]

As with the *Civil Rights Act*, the meaning of critical terms such as 'qualified individual' and 'disability' are left open to interpretation.

Legal ambiguity leaves organisations substantial latitude to construct the meaning of compliance.[40] Understandings of 'compliance' with law and ultimately of the meaning of law itself may be crystallised by the courts but those understandings derive in large part from the everyday lives of organisations as they struggle to give meaning to rights articulated by law and to construct the meaning of compliance. Organisational actors approach the matters of legal interpretation and construction of compliance not as persons trained in law but rather as actors squarely situated in organisational fields. Law, then, tends to become managerialised in organisational fields, that is, it tends to become infused with the logic of efficiency and rationality.

(A) *Professional Construction of the Legal Environment*

Laws become relevant parts of organisational fields only when they are made known to organisational actors. Actors within organisations generally learn about the law not by reading statutes or cases or administrative regulations but rather through the compliance professionals in and around their organisations. A myriad of professional

---

[39] 42 USC § 12112 (1990).

[40] Edelman, 'Legal Ambiguity and Symbolic Structures', above n 23.

journals, websites, workshops, and consultants provide filtered accounts of what the law is and how it is relevant to organisations. Informed by these sources, compliance professionals communicate to organisational administrators what laws are relevant, how they are relevant, and how much threat they pose. Management consultants and lawyers play a central role in interpreting the legal environment for employers. Both tend to have organisational interests in mind as they make sense of the law. Although lawyers might seem to be somewhat removed from organisational fields, they often work very closely with organisations, either as in-house counsel or through retainer arrangements. Both management consultants and lawyers tend to filter the law through a set of organisational priorities and managerial interests in a way that privileges efficiency and rationality over rights. Further, the visions of law that these professions bring to organisational fields tend to be fairly similar because the practitioners are connected through professional networks; they interact at conferences, write for and read their professional journals, participate in online forums and workshops, and exchange views at work or during professional transactions.

As lawyers and management consultants present the legal environment to the business world, they help to construct the extent to which law threatens traditional managerial prerogatives, the meaning of law for organisational policy, the likelihood of lawsuits and liability, and what actions or structures constitute reasonable means of compliance. Lawyers and management consultants emphasise and often even exaggerate the threatening aspects of legal environments, both because they see their role as 'bullet-proofing the workplace',[41] and because, by emphasising the threat and offering a solution to them, they stand to gain a larger market for their services and to gain power and stature within organisational fields.[42]

From its initial exposure in organisational fields, then, the law becomes what its interpreters make it. Stories about large jury verdicts in favour of employees are told and retold, often without evidence to back

---

[41] Susan Bisom-Rapp, 'Scripting Reality in the Legal Workplace: Women, Lawyers, Litigation Prevention Measures, and the Limits of Anti-Discrimination Law' (1996) 6 *Columbia Journal of Gender and Law* 323; Susan Bisom-Rapp, 'Bulletproofing the Workplace: Symbol and Substance in Employment Discrimination in Law Practice' (1999) 26 *Florida State University Law Review* 959.

[42] Lauren B Edelman, Steven E Abraham and Howard S Erlanger, 'Professional Construction of the Legal Environment: The Inflated Threat of Wrongful Discharge Doctrine' (1992) 26 *Law and Society Review* 47.

up the claims. In a study of organisational response to wrongful termination lawsuits based on breach of implied contract, for example, Edelman, Abraham, and Erlanger found that exaggerated accounts of huge jury verdicts in favour of employees were repeatedly cited in personnel journals.[43] Although wrongful termination is a common law doctrine that varied considerably by state, the management literature described cases almost exclusively from those states (such as California) where courts were most sympathetic to employees. Even there, exaggerations were rampant. Articles in management journals repeatedly cited the 'half million dollar' figure as a typical jury verdict, providing no authority to support this figure. Yet in a systematic survey of outcomes in implied contract wrongful discharge cases, Edelman, Abraham, and Erlanger found that even in the two states most sympathetic to the implied contract action, the figures were far lower. In California, the median jury verdict in implied contract wrongful termination cases was US$93 750 and the mean was US$188 278; in Michigan the median was US$100 000 and the mean US$168 072.[44]

Characterisations of the threat of wrongful discharge, moreover, varied both with the profession of the author and with the intended audience of the journal. Journal articles written by managers were significantly more likely to exaggerate the threat of wrongful discharge than were those written by lawyers, and journals aimed at managers were more likely to exaggerate the threat than journals aimed more at management academics. Although limited to the wrongful termination context, these findings suggest that characterisations of legal threats may become more extreme as they move out of legal fields and into organisational fields. The study exemplifies, moreover, the process by which professionals help to construct the legal environment and the threat that it poses to organisations.

(B) *The Construction and Diffusion of Symbolic Forms of Compliance*

Armed with a vision of law and legal threats provided by compliance professionals, actors within organisations seek rational solutions to those threats. Because of legal ambiguity, however, it is rarely obvious how to

---

[43] Ibid.
[44] Ibid.

comply with law. Anti-discrimination law tends to be broad, ambiguous, and procedurally oriented. Statutory proscriptions against employment decisions 'based on' race or sex give employers very little guidance about what they may or should do.

Given the murkiness of both 'the law' and 'compliance', organisations turn to the organisational fields around them for models of how to comply. Especially in the mid-1960s, when there were few models for how to comply with civil rights law, public governance served as a ready source of legitimised models for private governance, and therefore as a source of solutions to laws that challenge organisational governance. In response to the ambiguous civil rights mandates of the 1960s and 1970s, employers created rules and policies that look like statutes, offices that look like administrative agencies, compliance officers who look like administrative officers or even police, and grievance procedures that look like courts.[45] These anti-discrimination rules, civil rights offices, grievance procedures and other legal structures were visible symbols of attention to law.

The forms of compliance adopted by these trend-setting organisations in turn became ready models of legitimate compliance for other organisations. Networks of compliance professionals helped to diffuse these forms. As certain forms of compliance became increasingly prevalent, the rationality of those solutions became 'mythical' or taken-for-granted, and organisations adopted those structures at increasing rates.[46] Edelman shows,[47] for example, that the creation rates of discrimination grievance procedures were slow for the first few years following the enactment of the *Civil Rights Act*, but then increased dramatically during the mid-1970s as the form became institutionalised. Similar patterns hold for Equal Employment Opportunity ('EEO') offices

---

[45] Edelman, 'Legal Ambiguity and Symbolic Structures', above n 23; Frank Dobbin et al, 'Equal Opportunity Law and the Construction of Internal Labor Markets' (1993) 99 *American Journal of Sociology* 396; John Sutton et al, 'Legalization of the Workplace' (1994) 99 *American Journal of Sociology* 944; Lauren B Edelman, Christopher Uggen and Howard S Erlanger, 'The Endogeneity of Legal Regulation: Grievance Procedures as Rational Myth' (1999) 105 *American Journal of Sociology* 406.

[46] Edelman, 'Legal Environments and Organizational Governance', above n 4; Edelman, 'Legal Ambiguity and Symbolic Structures', above n 23; Sutton et al, above n 45.

[47] Edelman, 'Legal Ambiguity and Symbolic Structures', above n 23.

and rules[48] and for 'at will' clauses in employment contracts.[49] These diffusion patterns reflect a rationalisation and institutionalisation of symbolic structures. Over time, these structures came to be seen as evidence of compliance, even though nothing in the statutory language mandated that organisations create them.

The construction of law, then, occurs as civil rights law interacts with public legal consciousness to produce a normative environment in which fair treatment of employees becomes increasingly valued and racial or gender disparities may be challenged as violations of that value. As this value becomes increasingly accepted — or institutionalised — and as sanctions are attached to organisations that appear not to comply with it, organisations are more likely to incorporate structures that visibly demonstrate attention to it. In some cases, especially early on, organisations strategically design structures that symbolise attention to legal values in order to gain legitimacy; in other cases, especially later in the institutionalisation process, organisations may adopt these structures because they come to be seen as natural and proper and are even equated with 'compliance'.

(C) *The Construction of Law within Organisations*

Once in place, compliance structures tend to serve as vehicles for the making of legal meaning within organisations, often evolving independently of the intentions of organisational strategists. As compliance professionals confront the everyday problems of organisational life (such as hiring, job assignment, employee discipline, dispute handling, as well as federal, state, and local reporting requirements), they construct the meaning of law *within* organisations.

As compliance professionals go about making sense of the law in their daily activities, they do so not as autonomous individuals but rather as inhabitants of organisational fields. In most cases, managers and even lawyers in the arena of human relations learn about the law not through an independent reading and analysis of statutes and cases but rather through common networks, through professional journals and workshops, and through business schools. Because compliance

---

[48] Lauren B Edelman and Stephen Petterson, 'Symbols and Substance in Organizational Response to Civil Rights Law' (1999) 17 *Research in Social Stratification and Mobility* 107.

[49] Sutton et al, above n 45.

professionals inhabit common organisational fields, the institutionalised ideas of those fields influence how they interpret legal requirements, process legal paperwork, and attempt to resolve law-related problems.

The meaning of law is filtered through the lens of managerial norms and tempered by managerial concerns. This filtering process has a dual nature: on one hand, it eases the way for legal ideals to enter organisational terrain by rendering them more consistent with the logic of organisational fields, thus producing a *legalisation of organisations*. On the other hand, it means that legal ideals tend to become infused with traditional managerial ways of thinking, thus producing a *managerialisation of law*.[50] As law becomes managerialised, the logic of efficiency and rationality will often trump the logic of rights and justice.

The managerialisation of law, then, occurs as law is subtly framed by managerial logic. Law is framed by managerial logic through two processes: *the internalisation of law*, in which organisations internalise elements of legislation, adjudication, and advocacy that are otherwise handled outside the boundaries of organisations; and the *rhetorical reconstruction of legal ideals*, which occurs as managerial rhetoric reframes the goals of law in ways that conform to managerial objectives.

The internalisation of law occurs as organisations create internal rules that mimic formal legislation, create internal dispute processing mechanisms that act as a substitute for formal litigation, and create in-house counsel who take over functions formerly handled by lawyers outside of organisations. Each of these types of internalisation gives organisations greater control over the law and greater opportunities to influence the form and content of law.[51]Internal legislation involves compliance through the internalisation of legal rules. Internal rules that mimic formal legal rules have clear symbolic value. But internal legislation does not ensure replication of public law or recognition of legal ideals. Rather, organisations have significant latitude in *how* they actualise the law in internal policies. In an effort to combine legal and managerial goals, managers are likely to build discretion into rules, to replace legal standards (such as disparate treatment) with managerial standards (such as consistency), or to decouple the rules from organisational practice so that they act merely as window dressing. Edelman and Petterson found,[52] for example, that affirmative action

---

[50] Edelman, Fuller and Mara-Drita, above n 6.
[51] Edelman and Suchman, 'When the Haves Hold Court', above n 17.
[52] Edelman and Petterson, above n 48.

plans (a form of internalised legislation) had no effect on the workforce representation of minorities and are actually associated with lower workforce representation of women.[53] Similarly, organisational structures such as diversity training have been shown to have no effect on the representation of women in management.[54]

In some cases, moreover, internal legislation may even 'legislate' away some or all of the thrust of legal ideals.[55] For example, when courts began to articulate a theory under which terminated employees could sue employers for violation of an 'implied contract', employers quickly began to revise their personnel policies and employment contracts to avoid legal risk by explicitly specifying that their employees worked 'at will' and thus could be fired without reason.[56]

Internal dispute resolution is perhaps the most powerful means by which organisations internalise and transform the law. Organisations increasingly create internal forums in an effort to discourage employees from filing formal complaints with external fair employment agencies, which may evolve into lawsuits. Organisations also seek to improve employee morale and harmonious employment relations through the use of internal dispute resolution.[57] Relative to formal litigation, however, internal dispute resolution tends to depoliticise and de-legalise discrimination complaints. In an empirical study of how managers within organisations handle discrimination complaints, for example, Edelman, Erlanger and Lande found that complaint handlers tend to recast complaints of discrimination as typical managerial problems, such as poor management or interpersonal difficulties, and to resolve them in those terms.[58] Poor management may be remedied by training or through pragmatic solutions such as transferring the employee; interpersonal difficulties are handled with therapeutic solutions, such as counselling, employee assistance programs, or mediation-like exchanges. These

---

[53] Alison M Konrad and Frank Linnehan, 'Formalized HRM Structures Coordinating Equal Employment Opportunity or Concealing Organizational Practices?' (1995) 38 *Academy of Management Journal* 787.

[54] Alexandra Kaley, Frank Dobbin, and Erin Kelly, 'Best Practices or Best Gueeses? Assessing the Efficacy of Corporate Affirmative Action and Diversity Policies' (2006) 71 *American Sociological Review* 589.

[55] Edelman and Suchman, 'When the Haves Hold Court', above n 17.

[56] Edelman, Abraham and Erlanger, above n 42; Sutton et al, above n 45.

[57] Edelman, Erlanger and Lande, above n 33.

[58] Ibid.

remedies serve the organisation's purpose in ensuring smooth employment relations and often resolving the employees' complaints, but they tend to discourage attention to legal rights. In so doing, these remedies depoliticise and de-legalise issues, potentially affecting not only the particular dispute but also both employee and employer reactions to future disputes.[59] Internal dispute resolution gives rise, then, to a 'common law of the organisation' that merges legal and managerial logics.

The third important form of legal internalisation is the ascendance of the in-house counsel's office. Rather than keeping law firms on retainer, large bureaucratic organisations have been creating increasingly sophisticated internal legal staffs.[60] Although many firms still use outside lawyers, they tend to rely on in-house counsel to manage the outside law firms, deciding which issues will be handled in-house and which contracted out. In interactions with outside attorneys, in-house counsel draw strength not only from their coequal claims to legal expertise, but also from their extensive discretion over the selection of outside law firms for future business.[61] The power to control outbidding to private attorneys and to handle legal issues internally substantially expands the role and influence of staff attorneys.

As in-house counsel play a greater role in organisations' legal business, they may not make organisations more compliant, but rather more skillfully evasive. Relative to private counsel, in-house counsel tend to identify more with the interests of the organisations they serve, to see law more as barrier than as norm, and to seek loopholes through those

---

[59] Ibid; Edelman and Cahill, 'How Law Matters in Disputing and Dispute Processing', above n 33; Edelman and Suchman, 'When the Haves Hold Court', above n 17.

[60] Abram Chayes and Antonia H Chayes, 'Corporate Counsel and the Elite Law Firm' (1985) 37 *Stanford Law Review* 277; Robert E Rosen, 'The Inside Counsel Movement, Professional Judgement and the Organizational Respresentation' (1989) 64 *Indiana Law Journal* 479; Marc Galanter and Joel Rogers, 'A Transformation of American Business Disputing? Some Preliminary Observations' (Working Paper, Institute for Legal Studies, Madison, 1991) 22–5; Robert L Nelson, 'The Future of American Lawyers: A Demographic Profile of a Changing Profession in a Changing Society' (1994) 44 *Case Western Reserve Law Review* 345; Robert L Nelson and Laura Beth Nielsen 'Cops, Counsel, or Entrepreneurs: The Shifting Roles of Lawyers in Large Business Corporations' (2000) 34 *Law and Society Review* 457; Bisom-Rapp, 'Bulletproofing the Workplace', above n 41; Susan Bisom-Rapp, 'Exceeding Our Boundaries: Transnational Employment Law Practice and the Export of American Lawyering Styles to the Global Workforce' (2004) 25 *Comparative Labor Law and Policy Journal* 257.

[61] Chayes and Chayes, above n 60, 292; Nelson, above n 60, 355.

barriers. In-house counsel know more about the constraints of law, but also about know more about which constraints are somewhat flexible. They can act more as strategic advisors to organisations than as cautionary enforcers.[62] The more deeply lawyers are embedded in the organisation, the more likely they become to use their expertise to serve, rather than to question, prevailing managerial objectives.

The rhetorical reconstruction of legal ideals: Models of management — such as 't-groups', 'quality circles', 'corporate culture', 'total quality management', and 'business process re-engineering' — come and go like fashions, yet can have lasting effects on organisational structure and culture.[63] Generally designed as ways to enhance productivity by 'manufacturing consent',[64] these managerial philosophies can subtly yet powerfully infuse legal constructs with managerial ideas.[65]

Edelman, Fuller and Mara-Drita studied the managerialisation of the construct of 'diversity' during the 1980s and 1990s.[66] Managerial rhetoric about diversity appears to stem from *Workforce 2000*,[67] a 1987 study by a private consulting firm that warned that by the year 2005, the workforce would become predominantly non-white and would require dramatically different management skills. Although the prediction was based on a faulty assumption,[68] it became the rallying cry for a new model of management centred on 'valuing diversity', that is, recognising that the varying backgrounds and viewpoints of a diverse workforce could be harnessed for productive purposes.

By the early 1990s, articles on 'diversity' had largely replaced articles on 'civil rights' or 'affirmative action' in the management literature. But even though managerial rhetoric on diversity appears to buttress EEO law and to draw on the same moral ideal, the shift from equal opportunity to diversity language is much more than a change in

---

[62] Rosen, above n 60.
[63] Eric Abrahamson, 'Managerial Fashion' (1996) 21 *Academy of Management Review* 254.
[64] Michael Burawoy, *Manufacturing Consent: Changes in the Labor Process under Monopoly Capitalism* (1979).
[65] Edelman, Fuller and Mara-Drita, above n 6.
[66] Ibid.
[67] William B Johnston and Arnold E Packer, *Workforce 2000: Work and Workers for the 21st Century* (1987).
[68] Judith J Friedman and Nancy DiTomaso, 'Myths about Diversity: What Managers Need to Know about Changes in US Labor Force' (1996) 38 *California Management Review* 54.

packaging. Through a content analysis of the professional management literature, the study shows that whereas accounts of diversity initially emphasised legally protected categories such as race, sex, and national origin, the focus gradually expanded to include a wide variety of extra-legal dimensions of diversity including cultural differences, geographical differences, lifestyle differences, and even differences in communication style, dress style, and taste in food. Further, managerial rhetoric about diversity tends to portray anti-discrimination law in a negative light, asserting that whereas law imposes inefficient rules on organisations, diversity management promotes creativity, harmony, and profit. Managerial rhetoric about diversity has produced a dramatic shift in how diversity is understood in management, largely disassociating the construct from its legal context and linking it instead to traditional managerial values and goals.[69]

Through the internalisation of law and the rhetorical reconstruction of legal ideals, law tends to become managerialised, or infused with managerial values. Managerialisation is a double-edged sword. On the one hand, the managerialisation of law may hasten the legalisation of organisations in that legal values recast in managerial terms may be more easily assimilated into organisational governance. On the other hand, the managerialisation of law may also weaken, de-emphasise, and depoliticise legal ideals by subsuming them within managerial goals.

III LEGAL FIELDS AND THE RATIONALISATION OF MANAGERIALISED LAW

The managerialisation of law affects not only the form and content of law in organisational fields but also the construction of law in *legal* fields. The overlap in both actors and institutions between organisational and legal fields provides an arena in which the ideas that become institutionalised in organisational fields later seep into legal fields. In the remainder of this chapter, I explain how managerialised constructions of law enter into legal fields and why judges may unwittingly defer to these constructions of law even when they undermine legal values. The implications of my argument are that law should be understood not as a coercive force that is imposed upon organisations from above, but rather

[69] Edelman, Fuller, Mara-Drita, above n 6.

as a set of understandings that evolve, at least in part, out of the logic and institutionalised models of organisational fields.

(A) *Employees' Legal Consciousness and the Mobilisation of Law*

The stages discussed so far — the professional construction of the legal environment, the construction and diffusion of symbolic forms of compliance, and the managerialisation of law — all help to shape employees' *legal consciousness*, which may be understood as the cultural schemas that employees use to make sense of the law and of its relevance to their everyday lives.[70] 'Employees' legal consciousness' comprises how individuals within and around organisations view the ideals of law, the reach of law, the threat of law, and the fairness and legality of employers' law-related actions and structures.[71]

To the extent that symbolic forms of compliance and managerialised conceptions of law become institutionalised, employees' legal consciousness is likely to incorporate them. Variation along individual characteristics may produce some differences in the schema that individuals use to understand the law, but collective experiences and social networks among employees are likely to produce a core of institutionalised schemas that are widely shared among employees.[72] Employees' legal consciousness, then, is in part the product of managerialised conceptions of law that become institutionalised in organisational fields, but it is also in part the producer of problems that travel back into legal fields.

---

[70] Patricia Ewick and Susan S Silbey, *The Common Place of Law: Stories from Everyday Life* (1998); Laura Beth Nielsen, 'Situating Legal Consciousness: Experiences and Attitudes of Ordinary Citizens about Law and Street Harassment' (2000) 34 *Law and Society Review* 1055; Idit Kostiner, 'Evaluating Legality: Toward a Cultural Approach to the Study of Law and Social Change' (2003) 27 *Law and Society Review* 328; Catherine R Albiston, 'Bargaining in the Shadow of Social Institutions: Competing Discourses and Social Change in Workplace Mobilization of Civil Rights' (2005) 39 *Law and Society Review* 11; Anna Maria Marshall, 'Idle Rights: Employee's Legal Consciousness and the Construction of Sexual Harassment Policies' (2005) 39 *Law and Society Review* 83.

[71] Sally Riggs Fuller, Lauren B Edelman and Sharon F Matusik, 'Legal Readings: Employee Interpretation and Mobilization of Law' (2000) 25 *Academy of Management Review* 200; cf Bumiller, 'Victims in the Shadow of the Law', above n 27; Bumiller, *The Civil Rights Society*, above n 22; Felstiner, Abel and Sarat, above n 27; Ewick and Silbey, above n 70.

[72] Marshall, above n 70.

Research in the sociology of law suggests that the vast majority of people who believe that their rights have been violated take no formal action to redress those violations, especially when violations occur in the employment context. Employees' legal consciousness can significantly affect what types of behaviour employees believe are problematic, the likelihood that employees will see those types of behaviour as constituting legal violations, and the likelihood that employees will mobilise their rights by filing formal complaints either within or outside of work organisations.[73]

(B) *Professional Framing of Rights Violations*

As questions of interpretation arise in organisations, compliance professionals — both managers and lawyers — are central to framing the legal issues that travel back into the legal realm. Complaint handlers and other managers within organisations serve as gatekeepers who seek to resolve complaints internally to insulate organisations from exposure to legal liability.[74] Beyond the boundaries of organisations, officials in state and federal fair employment agencies and employees' (generally plaintiffs) lawyers play an important role in shaping which complaints become formal legal complaints and how those complaints are framed. Employers' (generally defendants') lawyers further shape the form of complaints both through their settlement behaviour and through their responses (in particular, through the affirmative defences that they offer).[75]

Both employees' and employers' lawyers, in different ways, help to reinforce and to legitimate managerialised models of compliance. Employees' lawyers act as gatekeepers to the legal system, determining

---

[73] Fuller, Edelman and Matusik, above n 71; Mia L Cahill, *The Social Construction of Sexual Harassment Law: The Role of National, Organizational, and Individual Context* (2001); Felstiner, Abel and Sarat, above n 27; Richard E Miller and Austin Sarat, 'Grievances, Claims and Disputes: Assessing the Adversary Culture' (1981) 15 *Law and Society Review* 525; Bumiller, 'Victims in the Shadow of the Law', above n 27; Bumiller, *The Civil Rights Society*, above n 22; Elizabeth A Hoffmann, 'Confrontations and Compromise: Dispute Resolution at a Worker Cooperative Coal Mine' (2001) 26 *Law and Social Inquiry* 555; Marshall, above n 70.

[74] Edelman, Erlanger and Lande, above n 33; Edelman, Uggen and Erlanger, above n 45; Elizabeth Chambliss, *Title VII as Displacement Conflict* (1996) (unpublished manuscript); Edelman and Suchman, 'When the Haves Hold Court', above n 18.

[75] Albiston, 'The Rule of Law and the Litigation Process', above n 26; Bisom-Rapp, 'Bulletproofing the Workplace', above n 41.

the scope and form of issues that enter the legal realm in the form of lawsuits. As lawyers counsel clients as to whether to file lawsuits, when they agree (or do not agree) to take cases, and when they frame employees' grievances as legal causes of actions, they consider not only the formal rules on the books but also the current legal climate — that is, understandings about what kinds of claims will pass muster with judges and juries. Lawyers base their decisions largely on what they perceive to be the feasibility of making a successful claim, and thus they are less likely to pursue actions where employers' actions appear to meet the institutionalised ideals of compliance.

In the current legal climate, for example, lawyers representing employees know that it is difficult to prevail in a case where an employer had a grievance procedure in place and the employee chose not to use it. Because of institutionalised ideas about compliance, a plaintiff-side employment lawyer is less likely to pursue a sexual harassment case if the employee chose not to use an internal procedure, even if the employee had a good very reason not to use that internal procedure (for example, it might be widely known that the procedure is a sham or that the decision maker is a close friend of the harasser). In choosing not to pursue such a case, the employee's lawyer helps to reinforce the notion that cases against employers who meet the institutionalised conceptions of compliance are not winnable.[76] Similarly, employers' lawyers act as conduits of managerialised logic to the court by framing their law-related procedures and policies *as compliance* and by defending their actions in terms of legitimised rationales such as market rates and business necessity.

To the extent that managerialised conceptions of law seep into the emergence and framing of disputes by employers, employees, and their lawyers, conceptions of compliance that become institutionalised in organisational fields have a dramatic effect on both the logic and the lexicon of disputing in legal fields.

(C) *Judicial Deference to Organisational Constructions of Law*

Because organisational and legal fields overlap, institutionalised ideas about law and compliance flow unobtrusively into the judicial realm. Judges are generally interpreting ambiguous legal language. While

---

[76] Bisom-Rapp, 'Bulletproofing the Workplace', above n 41.

liberal legal theory would have judges resolve disputes over legal meaning by looking to legal precedent, judges can only make sense of that precedent by looking to organisational customs and practices. To the extent that certain models of compliance or ideas of efficiency have become widely accepted, or institutionalised, within organisational fields, judges are likely to incorporate organisational logic into their logic and their rulings about what organisational practices are fair, rational, and *legal.* As judges tend to take their cues from norms and practices that become institutionalised in organisations, the logic of organisational fields influences the logic of legal fields. In this way, institutionalised — and managerialised — organisational practices tend to be (re)incorporated into judicial standards for EEO compliance. When courts incorporate ideas from the organisational realm into new case decisions, law becomes endogenous.[77] Judicial decision-making, then, becomes a central vehicle for the transportation of ideas from organisational fields into legal fields. The logics of organisational and legal fields merge as judicial decisions incorporate organisational logic. Because institutionalised ideas seem rational, however, courts often accept employers' symbolic indicia of compliance without recognising the extent to which employers' legal structures fail to protect legal rights, and in some cases even thwart those rights. Thus, the managerialisation of law may in some cases undermine the logic of rules and rights.

Edelman, Uggen, and Erlanger show how grievance procedures have been reincorporated into legal conceptions of what constitutes justice in organisations, an illustration of the endogeneity of law.[78] Despite the fact that organisations were creating grievance procedures at increasing rates beginning in the early 1970s,[79] and the legal and personnel professions were making broad claims about the legal value of grievance procedures in the 1970s and early 1980s, there was actually little judicial attention to grievance procedures at that time.[80]

Where the use of grievance procedures as a defence did arise, primarily in sexual harassment cases denying employer liability for the acts of an agent (usually a supervisory employee), courts were not terribly sympathetic — emphasising that employers are responsible for

---

[77] Edelman, Uggen and Erlanger, above n 45.
[78] Ibid.
[79] Edelman, 'Legal Environments and Organizational Governance', above n 4.
[80] Edelman, Uggen and Erlanger, above n 45, conducted an extensive LEXIS search for all cases that mentioned the term 'grievance procedure' and the root term 'discriminat'.

the actions regardless of what the employer knew or should have known about the employee's actions.[81] There is some evidence, moreover, that courts during the 1970s were somewhat suspicious of symbolic indices of compliance such as grievance procedures. For example, in a 1979 9th Circuit case, *Abramson v University of Hawaii*, the Court held: 'appellant's claims should be determined by reference to how the University in fact makes tenure decisions, not by reference to how their guidelines say they should.'[82] The widespread notion among employers that grievance procedures would insulate them from liability under civil rights law, then, appeared to be largely mythical through the early 1980s.

In the mid-1980s, however, changes in judicial doctrine began to reflect the idea that grievance procedures could provide a measure of legal insulation to employers. In 1986, the Supreme Court in *Meritor Savings Bank v Vinson* ('*Meritor*') suggested that an effective grievance procedure might protect an employer from liability for sexual harassment.[83] Shortly thereafter, a Federal Circuit Court of Appeals adopted a similar standard in race harassment cases.[84]

Significantly, the Court in *Meritor* recognised that grievance procedures may be ineffective and should not always insulate the employer. In that case, in fact, the Court found that the grievance procedure involved was not sufficient to allow the employer to escape liability because the employee would have had to file a complaint with the person who harassed her. And in quite a few subsequent cases, courts similarly found for plaintiffs because the grievance procedures were so

---

[81] See, eg, *Anderson v Methodist Evangelical Court Hospital, Inc*, 464 F 2d 723 (CA6, 1972); *Miller v Bank of America*, 600 F 2d 211 (1971); *Munford v Barnes and Co*, 441 F Supp 459 (1977).

[82] 594 F 2d 202, 210 (9th Cir, 1979).

[83] 106 S Ct 2399 (1989). In *Meritor*, the Court recognised a new hostile environment theory of sexual harassment in which sexual harassment did not have to consist of quid pro quo sexual demands but could arise out of a general atmosphere of harassment. The hostile environment theory invoked agency principles, in which the principal (here, the employer) may be held liable only if she or he knew or should have known about the wrongful acts of her or his agent. In Meritor, the Court suggested that where an employer has an explicit policy against sexual harassment and an effective grievance procedure calculated to encourage victims of harassment to come forward, an employer may escape liability. The Court also suggested that a court would be reluctant to accept a constructive discharge argument (meaning that the employee was forced to quit her job because of hostile working conditions) where an employee chose not to use an internal grievance procedure.

[84] *Hunter v Allis-Chalmers*, 797 F 2d 1417 (1986).

inherently flawed that they could not be viewed as providing due process.[85]

Notwithstanding the caution that courts displayed in considering the relevance of grievance procedures, the *Meritor* decision gave rise to a new defence in sexual and racial harassment cases (and to a lesser extent, in a broad range of other civil rights cases). Following the *Meritor* decision, the use of a 'grievance procedure defence' in sexual and racial harassment cases increased dramatically[86] even though the court had only indirectly suggested that a grievance procedure might help an employer to avoid liability.

As the grievance procedure defence became more common, both the structure and the defence acquired even greater legitimacy as a form of compliance with civil rights law. The grievance procedure as compliance with civil rights law had begun as a stab in the dark, an effort by employers, management consultants, and lawyers to create a visible symbol of compliance. It was a form that had gained legitimacy in the context of collective bargaining agreements in unionised firms and later became an institutionalised symbol of attention to due process. Employers adopted grievance procedures both as a strategic move to demonstrate compliance and (especially later in the process) because the institutionalisation of those procedures made governance without them seem unfair, arbitrary, and even 'illegal'. There had been no explicit legal requirement that employers adopt grievance procedures and, more

[85] See, eg, *Yates v Avco Corp*, 819 F 2d 630 (1987); *Delgado v Lehman*, 665 F Supp 460 (1987); *Waltman v International Paper Co*, 875 F 2d 468 (1989). In these cases, however, the court is rejecting grievance procedures because they do not conform to the liberal legal ideal in form: requiring the grievant to complain to the perpetrator rather than to an apparently impartial arbiter does not meet the requirements of a symbol of liberal legal justice. Further, by rejecting grievance procedures that are defective in form, courts are affirming the legality of internal grievance procedures that do meet the symbolic standard. And significantly, courts do not generally look past the form of grievance procedures to the standards of decision-making and therefore do not discover that these forums employ managerial rather than legal standards of justice: Edelman, Erlanger and Lande, above n 34. For example, in *Giordano v William Patterson College*, 804 F Supp 637 (D NJ, 1992) the Court found for the employer on the hostile environment portion of the claim based on the existence of the internal policies and procedures and the employers' 'prompt and remedial action'. Yet facts of that case show that the harassment continued for a full six months after the plaintiff filed her internal grievance.

[86] Edelman, Uggen and Erlanger, above n 45.

importantly, there was nothing about the presence of those procedures that inherently met the requirements of civil rights law.

It was quite significant, then, that the United States Supreme Court ruled in 1998 that an employee's failure to use an employer's internal grievance procedure might protect an employer from liability for harassment by its supervisory employees.[87] Grievance procedures had been irrelevant to employers' liability under the *Civil Rights Act* from 1964 until 1986, were somewhat relevant beginning with the *Meritor* decision in 1986, and then — 34 years after the passage of the *Civil Rights Act* — became part of the legal standard of compliance. Although grievance procedures may in fact do little to ensure equal employment opportunity,[88] the institutionalisation of grievance procedures in organisational fields made grievance procedures available as a natural, rational, and *legal* form of compliance. Further, when courts proclaimed that internal grievance procedures could help employers avoid liability; they reinforced the legitimacy and rationality of grievance procedures as a form of compliance with law.

As the *form* of grievance procedures gains legitimacy, courts (especially lower courts) seem less likely to consider the substance of those procedures, that is, to scrutinise whether the procedures provide any measure of protection for employees. In *Cotran v Rollins Hudig Hall International, Inc*,[89] brought before the California Supreme Court (under California law, which is generally more stringent than federal law), Cotran was fired for alleged sexual harassment but a jury found that he was wrongfully terminated. The company appealed on the grounds that an internal grievance proceeding had resulted in a finding that Cotran had engaged in sexual harassment. The California Supreme Court reversed the jury verdict, holding that the jury should never have considered the merits of the case:

> In this wrongful termination action tried solely on a breach of contract theory, we hold that the critical issue was whether the employer reasonably and in good faith believed that the terminated employee had sexually harassed other employees, not whether such harassment actually occurred.

---

[87] *Faragher v City of Boca Raton*, 118 S Ct 1115 (1998); *Burlington Industries v Ellerth*, 524 US 742 (1998).

[88] Edelman, Erlanger and Lande, above n 33.

[89] 17 Cal 4th 93 (1998).

It is notable that in this case, it was the harasser rather than the employee who was disadvantaged by judicial deference to grievance procedures. This case supports the argument that courts are deferring to institutionalised organisational practices rather than simply using grievance procedures to undercut harassment claims.

In 2000, in *Leopold v Baccarat* ('*Baccarat*'),[90] the Court considered a sexual harassment case in which the plaintiff had not used an internal grievance procedure because the procedure would have required her to complain directly to her supervisor, who was the alleged harasser, and did not provide any protections against retaliation. The Court held in favour of the employer, stating that 'the law is very clear that any reasonable policy will do.' Although not all courts would find the law as clear as did the *Baccarat* Court implies, the case exemplifies the lower courts' tendency to defer to organisational policies and procedures with very little inquiry into the adequacy or quality of those procedures.

In short, organisations initially created grievance procedures because they carried a legitimate legal form. Grievance procedures became widely accepted as a symbol of compliance with EEO law, but their symbolic value did not guarantee substantive attention to legal rights. Rather, grievance procedures tended to become infused with managerial logic in a way that substantially undercut their ability to bring legal values into organisations. Courts, impressed by the legality of grievance procedures as a form, failed to examine their substance and began to confer legal and economic benefits on organisations that had internal grievance procedures. By deferring to the institutionalised notion that grievance procedures serve to protect employees' rights, courts *rationalised* a mode of compliance that began more as a rational myth. But the rationality of grievance procedures is conditional on the institutional setting: internal grievance procedures provide these market benefits only because legal institutions incorporate, legitimate, and reify the organisations' symbolic legal structures.

Although endogeneity is perhaps clearest with respect to grievance procedures, the trend is evident in other arenas as well. One such arena concerns the mandatory arbitration clauses that are required of many independent contractors and, increasingly, of employees as well. In 1991, the United States Supreme Court held in *Gilmer v*

[90] 82 Fair Empl Prac Cas (BNA) 105, SDNY, 14 February 2000.

Interstate/Johnson Lane Corp ('*Gilmer*')[91] that arbitration clauses requiring the waiver of civil rights could be upheld under the *Federal Arbitration Act*. The Court in *Gilmer* did not explicitly overrule the 1974 case, *Alexander v Gardner-Denver Co*,[92] which held that an employee could not waive a statutory right to trial under Title VII through an arbitration agreement. Nonetheless, it appears to move the law in a very different direction and a few federal circuit courts have now upheld the validity of employer arbitration clauses that require employees to waive their rights to litigate Title VII claims.[93]

A similar process can be seen in the evolution of judicial standards in wage discrimination cases. In these cases, employers often offer a 'market defence' for wage inequality, arguing that they cannot be held responsible for paying women less than men because the pay disparities represent market rates. Nelson and Bridges show that, over time, courts have accepted and legitimised employers' reasoning.[94] Rather than looking into the many ways in which employers create and exacerbate pay inequities in their own markets, courts have accepted — and thereby legitimised — employers' market defence. In this sense, Nelson and Bridges argue that courts have 'legaliz[ed] gender inequality.'

Traditional top-down perspectives on law suggest that courts ought to serve as a corrective to organisational constructions of compliance that deviate from legal purposes. But to the extent that managerialised conceptions of law and compliance seep into legal fields, the logic of rights is no longer sufficiently distinct from the logic of efficiency to counter institutionalised notions of compliance. Judges become less likely to use the logic of rights to trump the logic of

---

[91] 111 S Ct 1647.

[92] 415 US 36.

[93] See, eg, *Mago v Shearson Lehman Hutton, Inc*, 956 F 2d 932 (9th Cir, 1992); *Cole v Burns Intern Sec Services*, 133 (DC Cir, 11 February 1997) (No 96–7042). The circuit courts are split on whether mandatory arbitration clauses that require employees to waive their rights to judicial determination of statutory rights are valid. The majority view places severe limitations on the ability of arbitration agreements to bar litigation of statutory claims: See, eg, *Brisentine v Stone and Webster Engineering* (11th Cir, 21 July 1997) (no 96–6866). But in general one of these limitations is that the arbitration agreement must be entered into voluntarily. This leaves room for employers to pressure employees to accept mandatory arbitration clauses.

[94] Robert L Nelson and William Bridges, *Legalizing Gender Inequality: Courts, Markets and Unequal Pay for Women* (1999).

efficiency because forms of compliance that evolve out of organisations' interest in efficiency take on an aura of legality.

Especially under conditions of legal ambiguity, courts are more likely to look for *symbols* of compliance but to refuse to investigate too carefully the day-to-day operations of the organisations they regulate.[95] Given the complexity and decentralisation of organisations, it is often quite difficult for courts to determine whether rules in fact affect behaviour within the firm, whether offices implement legal ideals, whether written plans are anything more than words on paper, whether grievance procedures provide effective mechanisms for appeal, and more generally, whether practices discriminate on the basis of race, sex, or another illegal criterion. Although the presence of an office or functionary or procedure is no guarantee that legal goals are being met because organisations may create structures that are decoupled from their core activities as a means of maintaining ceremonial conformity with external demands or expectations,[96] courts have neither the resources nor the expertise to uncover sham structures unless there is flagrant evidence of legal violations.

CONCLUSION: OVERLAPPING FIELDS AND ENDOGENOUS PROCESSES

The merging of logics at the boundaries of social fields has implications both for the relationship of law and organisations specifically, and for institutional theory more broadly. With respect to law and organisations, the merging of field logics means that social understandings of legality and rationality evolve in relation to one another so that each contributes to the social construction of the other. Legality shapes organisational rationality by providing legitimated models of governance that shape the form of organisational response to law. Institutionalised notions of rationality in turn shape law, as organisational forms of compliance become so taken-for-granted as to be accepted by courts not just as

[95] See Keith Hawkins, *Environment and Enforcement: Regulation and the Social Definition of Pollution* (1984); Alfred Blumrosen, *Modern Law: The Law Transmission System and Equal Employment Opportunity* (1993).

[96] John W Meyer and Brian Rowan, 'Institutional Organizations: Formal Structure and as Myth and Ceremony' in Walter W Powell and Paul J DiMaggio (eds), *The New Institutionalism in Organizational Analysis* (1977) 41; Edelman, 'Legal Environments and Organizational Governance', above n 4; Edelman 'Legal Ambiguity and Symbolic Structures', above n 23.

rational practices but also as *legal* practices. The process comes full circle when courts officially legitimate organisational practices and confer real cost savings (through reduced legal exposure) on organisational practices that had previously acquired an aura of rationality. In so doing, courts further legitimate and perpetuate organisational institutions, reinforcing the legal value of institutionalised myths and symbols. Organisational structures that were created as a locally rational response to institutionalised ideas of legality gain rationality on a global scale precisely because they were created in the image of public forms of law.

With respect to institutional theory more broadly, my analysis of the endogeneity of law has identified an important set of institutional mechanisms that are involved both in the flow of logics across field boundaries and in the transformation and crystallisation of logics within fields. As institutionalised ideas move across field boundaries, logics embedded within one field become sources of change and new taken-for-granted understandings in other fields, and those logics are themselves transformed, often inadvertently, though sense-making and problem-solving activity in the area where social fields overlap.

The endogenous construction of social logics is only one process through which social change occurs, and it operates more through constitutive processes such as cultural templates and cognitive schemas than through open contestation, overt political conflict, or direct political mobilisation. Perhaps because it operates under the political radar, the endogenous construction of social logics is likely to be an especially powerful source of field structuration and social change.

Although this chapter has focused on the civil rights context, legal endogeneity is also likely to occur in the context of capital markets governance. Laws like the *Sarbanes-Oxley Act of 2002*,[97] passed to regulate corporate finance in the wake of the Enron scandal, rely largely on financial disclosure[98] and invite organisational compliance structures such as ethics codes, monitoring and auditing systems, and a reporting system so that employees may report violations.[99] In theory, these internal compliance structures would inhibit financial fraud. A number of legal scholars support the idea of legislation that delegates enforcement

---

[97] Pub L No 107–204, 116 Stat 745 (2002) ('*Sarbanes-Oxley*').

[98] O'Brien, *Redesigning Financial Regulation*, above n 1.

[99] Kimberly Krawiec, 'Cosmetic Compliance and the Failure of Negotiated Governance' (2003) 81 *Washington University Law Quarterly* 487.

functions to organisations, allowing a more participatory form of governance.[100] Other scholars are sceptical of such delegated governance, pointing to a lack of empirical evidence that it works or organisational processes that undermine its effectiveness.[101]

In their respective articles on *Sarbanes-Oxley*, Krawiec suggests that internal compliance structures fail to deter corporate misconduct and are largely ineffective,[102] and O'Brien argues that disclosure regulation is little more than 'an exercise in political symbolism'.[103] Just as managerialisation transforms civil rights law, corporate culture and the purview of corporate accountants is likely to weaken the impact of financial regulation. My own analyses of civil rights legislation support these more sceptical accounts. Organisational compliance procedures may signal ethical conduct but provide little guarantee that financial fraud has not occurred. And government agencies, including courts, are likely to defer to the mere existence of organisational disclosure so that the meaning of financial regulation is defined largely by institutionalised organisational practices.

---

[100] See, eg, Ian Ayres and John Braithwaite, *Responsive Regulation: Transcending the Deregulation Debate* (1992); Susan Sturm, 'Second Generation Employment Discrimination: A Structural Approach' (2001) 101 *Columbia Law Review* 458; Michael Dorf, 'Legal Indeterminacy and Institutional Design' (2003) 78 *New York Law Review* 875; Jody Freeman, 'Collaborative Governance in the Administrative State' (1997) 45 *University of California Los Angeles Law Review* 1; Jody Freeman, 'Extending Public Law Norms Through Privatization' (2003) 116 *Harvard Law Review* 1285; Orly Lobel, 'The Renew Deal: The Fall of Regulation and the Rise of Governance in Contemporary Legal Thought' (2004) 89 *Minnesota Law Review* 342; Kenneth Bamberger, 'Regulation as Delegation: Private Firms, Decisionmaking, and Accountability in the Administrative State' (2006) 56 *Duke Law Journal* 377.

[101] Krawiec, above n 99; O'Brien, *Redesigning Financial Regulation*, above n 1.

[102] Krawiec, above n 99, 487.

[103] O'Brien, *Redesigning Financial Regulation*, above n 1, 28; see also Edelman, *The Symbolic Uses of Politics*, above n 28.

Chapter 4

The Significance of Relative Autonomy in How Regulation of the Financial Services Sector Evolves

George Gilligan

This chapter is based on the proposition that managing conflicts of interest and other potentially problematic regulatory issues, are, and probably always have been, integral to how individuals, groups and societies manage their trading relationships with other individuals, groups and societies. In particular, the levels of regulatory relative autonomy that market actors possess, both now and in the past, can be extremely influential in deciding a jurisdiction's regulatory agendas. How those agendas and their regulatory priorities evolve can be significant in shaping market practice and perceptions of what constitutes conflicts of interest and what should, or should not, be done in relation to them. This is true for all trading sectors, but the historical analysis of this chapter is on the financial services sector. The discussion is Anglo-centric in its focus, but will have some resonance regarding *non-Anglo* jurisdictions and how they regulate their financial markets. Financial services regulation is concerned mainly with capital resources and how those resources are raised, organised and marketed. Trade is the major motivation for capital exchange and finance is the sector that facilitates these processes. The emphasis below is on highlighting some of the important regulatory markers in British financial services (largely English in truth, focused on the City of London), that have so influenced current regulatory praxis not only in the United Kingdom, but also in Australia, the

United States and elsewhere, and situating these markers within their historical context.

However, the evolution of financial services regulation has a very long history, far pre-dating any significant activity in the City of London. Levi discusses how forgery and counterfeiting posed regulatory problems for the Roman and the Byzantine states.[1] Redfield goes further back in history to the early eighth century BC, and analyses how the Greeks began to develop their *polis*, the social and political organisation which responded to market conditions and simultaneously aimed to limit the effects of the market. The Greek polis had a clearly defined social order and the economic development of their society also brought political conflict and transformation. Redfield comments on the tension of the polis–market relationship arguing that: 'The Greeks looked upon the market as a threat to the political order. The function of the state, to a large extent, was to correct the effects of the market — not by regulation, but by creating a superordinate structure of social regulations.'[2]

This model of social organisation with its inherent ambiguities is still very influential in western society today and may be a significant explanatory variable as to why contemporary societies and regulatory actors find such difficulty with issues like the management of conflicts. It is important to consider the development of financial services regulation in tandem with the development of the market because the two are entwined. Financial services regulation, and indeed law in general, are products of, and subsequently respond to, social, political and economic phenomena. Law is not an autonomous entity and may be ambiguous and indeed contradictory at times. It needs to be studied in terms of its function and its form; its function in how law came to be given its tasks and whose interests it serves; its effect in how law does what it is supposed to, and its mode of operation and appearance. These propositions underpin how this chapter takes a specific focus on the evolution of financial regulation in England.

I THE EMERGENCE OF FINANCIAL REGULATION IN ENGLAND

The regulation of securities in Britain derives from the theories of markets, with the concept of barter markets being the earliest authority, but in

---

[1] Michael Levi, *Regulating Fraud, White Collar Crime and the Criminal Process* (1987) 1.

[2] James M Redfield, 'The Development of the Market in Archaic Greece' in B L Anderson and A J H Latham (eds), *The Market in History* (1986) 29, 52.

England from 1000AD a sophisticated form of market regulation begins to emerge. Its central purpose was to introduce more certainty into economic exchange by impacting upon the processes of supply and demand. The ancient common law offences of engrossing (buying in quantity corn, etc, to sell again at a high price), forestalling (raising the price of certain goods by holding up supplies etc), and regrating (buying corn or other grains in any market so as to raise the price, and then selling it again in the same place), were all rendered statutory offences in the 14th century.[3] It can be seen therefore that market manipulations are not exclusively modern phenomena and neither are regulatory efforts to counter their effects. Nevertheless, there is a long history of mutual self-interest (partly driven by the traditional weakness of the central state in England), between the City of London, and not only the monarchy, but also elected governments after the English Civil War, which was crucial in developing the relative autonomy of the City of London. This political significance gave City professional groups and markets enormous influence with the Crown and central government. Britain is no longer a dominant world power, but the international character of the City has allowed it to retain its status as one of the world's key financial centres. In turn this has ensured its central importance to the British economy and sustained its political influence. The key relationship that has established, nurtured and maintained the City's pre-eminence in the British economy has been its connection with the Crown and central government. It is an example of what Hancher and Moran might term a core driver in the construction of regulatory space and the deployment of resources therein,[4] as relative sets of power relations facilitate key actors in shaping regulatory discourse, and the subsequent production of regulatory structures and processes.

For example, during the 16th and 17th centuries the costs of government rose dramatically as the Crown's borrowing requirement soared and it was the City that funded that borrowing).[5] Direct taxation was unpopular and the lack of a strong central bureaucracy depleted the Crown's tax-gathering potential. As a result, collection of tax revenue was extremely difficult, and the Crown became heavily dependent upon loans from City merchants and financiers to cover expenditure. The Crown's

---

[3] *Statutes of Realm* [1363] 37 Edw III c 8.

[4] Leigh Hancher and Michael Moran, 'Organizing Regulatory Space' in Leigh Hancher and Michael Moran (eds), *Capitalism, Culture and Economic Regulation* (1989) 271.

[5] Edward V Morgan and William A Thomas, *The Stock Exchange — Its History and Functions* (1962) 17.

need for loans was instrumental in the creation of the City's most important financial institutions:

> Both the Bank of England and the Stock Exchange were the products of England's 'second revolution' in the late seventeenth century which ended Charles II's attempts to restore arbitrary royal powers in financial matters. … Over 1000 subscribers, including London's leading merchants, were incorporated as the Governor and the Bank of England in 1694. The Charter was granted in return for an initial loan of £1.2 million, and in 1708 the Bank was extended by Act of Parliament the privileged status of the country's only joint-stock bank. This early monopoly which lasted for over a century, meant that other banks could only be partnerships, which were limited in number to six persons. This legislation was the direct result of the City's power and effectively retarded the development of provincial branch banking on any scale.[6]

The private nature of both the Bank of England and the London Stock Exchange ('LSE') helped shape the self-regulatory system of the UK's financial services sector for centuries. The Bank of England was nationalised by the *Bank of England Act 1946* (UK) c 27, but the process of choosing the Governor remained unchanged and nationalisation had virtually no effect on the Bank's methods of operation.[7] The privileged market positions of the LSE and the Bank of England, and the evolution of the UK's system of financial self-regulation were a direct result of the post-medieval financial dependence of the Crown upon the City of London. It is an example of the *structuration theory* of Anthony Giddens at work,[8] as individual London merchants combine the human agency effects of their political and economic strength with the structural leverage of the financial and commercial markets, in order to prise a privileged trading and regulatory position from the central state.

Structuration theory emphasises the reflexive character of human conduct. Its key elements are: structure; agency; systems; the duality of structure; the importance of routinisation; the importance of reflexive and sometimes unintended consequences; and the influence of time and space in

---

[6] Geoffrey Ingham, *Capitalism Divided? The City and Industry in British Social Development* (1984) 17.

[7] Roger Eatwell, *The 1945–1951 Labour Governments* (1979) 54–5; Trevor O Lloyd, *Empire to Welfare State* (1970) 284–5.

[8] *The Constitution of Society: Outline of the Theory of Structuration* (1984).

the constitution of social life. They interact in such a way that social structures do not exist without human agency, but those same structures do shape the actions of people. Structures and agency are so interdependent that all change is influenced by earlier institutional praxis and no change can completely remove existing praxis, so that social agents make social facts, but always from existing social praxis.[9] This perspective can be particularly informative about the reflexive arrangements that constitute the discourse and operational realities of regulation. As such it can be useful for analysing how agents in and around the financial sector influence their own regulation, but always from established sets of social structures and practices. This approach has relevance for contemporary developments in financial regulation. For example, as 2007 unfolds it will be interesting to observe the impacts upon US regulatory praxis of the work the Committee on Capital Markets Regulation ('Committee'), which is a group of 22 US experts from the investment community, business, finance, law, accounting and academia. The Committee was formed due to concerns about US financial actors becoming less competitive, the effects of an increasing regulatory burden (especially parts of the *Sarbanes-Oxley Act of 2002*)[10] and the reductions in global financial market share suffered in recent years by US financial markets, for example only five per cent of the value of global Initial Public Offerings in 2005, compared to 50 per cent in 2000. In its Interim Report the Committee has made a series of recommendations in the areas of: shareholders rights; regulatory process; public and private enforcement; and *Sarbanes-Oxley*.[11]

Similarly, in Australia in recent times, the Business Council of Australia ('BCA') has been significant in shaping how regulatory innovation and reform are likely to progress. The BCA's report, *Business Regulation Action Plan for Future Prosperity* (2005), received substantial media exposure and became a significant driver for the federal government establishing in October 2005 a Taskforce on Reducing Regulatory Burdens on Business ('the Taskforce'). The Taskforce was chaired by Gary Banks (Chairperson of the Productivity Commission) and its other members were: Rod Halstead (a corporate lawyer); Richard Humphrey (former Managing Director of the Australian Stock Exchange); and Angela MacRae (Chairperson of the Independent

---

[9] Ibid 16.

[10] Pub L No 107–204, 116 Stat 745 (2002) ('*Sarbanes-Oxley*').

[11] Committee on Capital Markets Regulation, *Interim Report of the Committee on Capital Markets Regulation* (2006).

Contractors of Australia). The Taskforce worked swiftly, producing a report within three months.[12] The federal government issued its final response to the Taskforce Report six months later, accepting in full or in part 158 of the 178 recommendations made by the Taskforce. These more recent regulatory scenarios in Australia and the US show processes of technocratic legitimacy at work, as actors with sufficient resources and influence can help shape discourses on how to evaluate regulatory praxis and order priorities for practice and reform. I am not wishing to imply that such actors automatically pursue vested interests and/or produce negative results for society, or indeed that they may not be correct and/or just in what they recommend, but rather that it is also important to consider what their positions, affiliations and motivations may be as they engage in regulatory discourse and reform.

Returning once again to the evolution of British financial regulation, the ever-increasing government appetite for capital, coupled with the funding needs of the new joint-stock trading companies that were opening up new markets both internationally and domestically, meant that by the 1690s a sophisticated stocks and shares market had emerged, with specialist dealers offering more complex products such as time bargains and options dealings. This rise in financial capitalisation was not accompanied by prudential forms of regulation and there were many allegations of sharp practice in the marketing of stocks and shares. These criticisms became more pronounced during the boom of 1693–95 and the crisis that followed — a familiar refrain in recent decades as well perhaps? A parliamentary inquiry was appointed in November 1696, 'to look after the Trade of England', as a response to widespread public disquiet about the rapacious nature of England's early capital markets. The Royal Commissioners were alarmed by the promotion of frauds and manipulation of the market, and they complained that:

> The pernicious Art of Stock-jobbing hath, of late, … wholly perverted the End and Design of Companies and Corporations, erected for the introducing, or carrying on of Manufactures, … by selling their shares for much more than they are really worth … Thus, … the Management of that Trade and Stock comes to

[12] Taskforce on Reducing Regulatory Burdens on Business, Parliament of Australia, *Rethinking Regulation* (2006).

> fall into unskilful Hands, whereby the Manufactures … dwindle away to nothing …[13]

The damning report of the Royal Commissioners prompted Parliament in 1697 to pass an *Act to Restrain the Number and Practice of Brokers and Stock-Jobbers* ('the 1967 Act'). Some features of this legislation were that brokers and jobbers had to be licensed, and that all transactions should be recorded. These innovations were not to prove popular with finance professionals in the City of London. The 1697 Act marks the first reference point of a regulatory cycle that has been a recurring feature of the financial services sector. A depressingly repetitive pattern of economic boom accompanied by deregulation, followed by recession and attendant social regulation, has been materialising periodically over the last 300 years or so in Britain and elsewhere. From the 1693–95 boom and the 1697 Act, and the South Sea Bubble boom and the *Bubble Act 1720* in Britain, to the United States in recent times, with the Enron and WorldCom scandals spawning the hurried passage of the much-criticised *Sarbanes-Oxley*.

However, what is especially significant about the 1697 Act is that it was the first attempt by government to impose certain standards of probity and competence upon those dealing in the embryonic securities market. All broking business not with a licensed broker was considered unlawful, available penalties included imprisonment, £500 fines (a very substantial amount at that time), disqualification to act as a broker, and the pillory. The legislation was both punitive and preventive, emphasising the twin concepts of anti-fraud and due diligence, and merging administrative and criminal justice processes. The statute also recognised for the first time the value of public esteem and censure as a sanction in the financial sector.

The 1697 Act was markedly forward-looking in many of its objectives, too forward-looking for some, obviously, because it was allowed to lapse in 1707. This was in spite of a Committee of the House of Commons ruling that the Act was 'fit to be continued'.[14] The reasons for its demise are not clear, but the most likely explanation is the pressure of special interest groups (centred upon the merchant classes who needed large amounts of venture capital to fund high risk expeditions to the colonies), who felt such legislation to be contrary to the spirit and needs of the predominant 'laissez-faire' philosophy of contemporary trade. This was

---

[13] On 25 November 1696, as referred to in *House of Commons Journals* (1875).

[14] As stated in Morgan and Thomas, above n 5, 40.

the first of a long line of examples (several of which are described below), of interest groups in the City being able to emasculate legislative interventions that sought to impose higher levels of accountability upon those working in the financial services industry. It must be stated, however, that many of these legislative interventions were ad hoc and intensely reactive, usually comprising a statutory 'knee-jerk' response to public crises of confidence in financial markets. They constitute an Enlightenment counterpart, if you like, to contemporary charges of *quack corporate governance* that some commentators have fired across the bows of recent statutory initiatives such *Sarbanes-Oxley*.[15] However, regarding *Sarbanes-Oxley*, it is worth noting that not everyone is a harsh critic and that others such as Asare,[16] Cunningham,[17] and Mitchell[18] emphasise the positive capacity that *Sarbanes-Oxley* may hold for improving corporate governance.

So, at times a scandal-driven and/or crisis-induced lurch to increased regulation of financial services has featured in Britain and other jurisdictions, but in Britain this has been tempered with a careful eye on economic realities, with the result that political intervention into financial markets has been generally wary and genteel. However, the discourse upon financial services regulation can at times be far from genteel. The famous author Daniel Defoe was vitriolic in his assessment of the stock-jobbing profession of the late 17th and early 18th centuries: 'there is not a man but will own 'tis a complete System of Knavery; that 'tis a Trade in Fraud, born of Deceit and nourished by Trick, Cheat, Wheedle, Forgeries, Falsehoods and all sorts of Delusions.'[19]

There were undoubtedly some unscrupulous persons working as stock-jobbers (as indeed there still are unscrupulous people working in the City of London and other parts of the financial sector around the world), but there is a danger of *scapegoating* certain groups for the effects of social and

---

[15] Roberta Romano, 'The *Sarbanes-Oxley Act* and the Making of Quack Corporate Governance' (Working Paper No 04–37, ICF Yale University, 2004), available at <http://ssrn.com/abstract=596101>.

[16] Stephen K Asare, Lawrence A Cunningham and Arnold Wright, 'The *Sarbanes-Oxley Act*: Legal Implications and Research Opportunities' (Research Paper No 122, Boston College Law School, 2006).

[17] Lawrence A Cunningham, 'The *Sarbanes-Oxley* Yawn: Heavy Rhetoric, Light Reform (and It Might Just Work)' (2003) 36 *Connecticut Law Review* 915.

[18] Lawrence E Mitchell, 'The *Sarbanes Oxley Act* and the Reinvention of Corporate Governance?' (2003) 48 *Villanova Law Review* 1189.

[19] Daniel Defoe, *The Anatomy of Exchange Alley or a System of Stock-Jobbing* (1719) 1.

systemic pressures. For example, it is possible that there may be parallels with the vitriol directed by some in recent times towards the investment activities of hedge funds and private equity partnerships, and descriptions of the factors that led to the South Sea Bubble debacle:

> As usual 'the infamous practice of stock-jobbing' was blamed for things for which the corruption of politicians, the contrivance of unscrupulous promoters, and the avarice and gullibility of the public were really responsible … not only the traders and financiers of the City, but the King and the Prince of Wales with their Courts, the majority of members of both Houses of Parliament, army officers and senior civil servants, and a great mass of country gentry, large and small. In fact most of the people who wielded political power and influence were involved.[20]

Morgan and Thomas were commenting from the perspective of writing an official history of the LSE, whilst Defoe's particular bias is not known. The true situation was probably somewhere between the two and any critique of financial services regulation must take into account the particular tendencies of commentators of every era. This is as true for the issue of managing conflicts today as it is for other issues in the regulation of the financial sector at any given time.

The next major statutory intervention after the *Bubble Act 1720* was in 1734, when an *Act to Prevent the Infamous Practice of Stock-Jobbing*, more commonly known as *Barnard's Act*, was passed. It outlawed all short-selling (when a speculator sells stock which he or she does not own, anticipating that the price will fall and he or she can effect delivery of the agreed stock at the lower price). The legislation also initiated mandatory recording of *all* transactions in the name of the principal, with the threat of criminal penalties for failure to comply.[21] It was not strictly enforced, however. Of greater importance was a wide range of private Acts vesting jurisdiction in the City of London. These powers included: the right to admit brokers; to require proof of character and competence; to confine admission to freemen of the City of London and to make regulations governing how brokers conduct their trade. Their net effect was to largely transfer regulatory responsibility to the City and establish the tradition of

---

[20] Morgan and Thomas, above n 5, 12, 69.

[21] Barry A K Rider, Charles Abrams and Eilis Ferran, *Guide to the* Financial Services Act 1986 (2nd ed, 1989) 2–4.

self-regulation in the financial services sector which has been so influential over the years in London and elsewhere.

The famous *square mile* of the City of London is literally a village in terms of its origins and its physical confines. It still maintains many of the social and cultural events, organisations and activities that are features of a small, relatively insular community. Its insular commercial traditions were crafted over the centuries by the freemen of the City of London, who were the only persons who could trade at retail within the City and all trading arrangements were controlled through the hierarchical livery companies.[22] Entry to these great companies was through family links and apprenticeship. These arrangements created the conditions for the *dictum meum pactum* — 'my word is my bond' approach, a moral code that was unwritten, but which reflected their standing as gentlemen, and which not only has dominated the operational culture of the City, but also has influenced the development of commerce in many countries. Transgressors of that code rarely faced criminal proceedings, instead they were merely shut out of the City's social and professional life by the actions of a remarkably effective peer network. This *social ostracism* proved to be the most enduring and powerful sanction in the regulation of the City.[23] This system of honour was crucial in providing certainty for trading conditions because many common trading practices were not legal for prolonged periods, for example with regard to the widespread acceptance of the non-recording of all individual transactions. Recourse to legal processes to settle disputes would have led to commercial chaos, so the City developed internal arbitration procedures. This 'my word is my bond' approach to self-regulation delivered a stable if anti-competitive trading environment and its success is well-documented.[24]

It is interesting here to draw parallels with contemporary capital markets and actors who are influential within them. Despite the increasingly global character of the financial sector, and other factors that might emasculate the social cohesion of the industry, such as the increasing disintermediation character of many transactions in financial services as online trading has become the norm, there is still the sense of the

[22] Steve Rappaport, 'Social Structure and Mobility in Sixteenth Century London: Part I' (1983) IX *The London Journal* 107; Steve Rappaport, 'Social Structure and Mobility in Sixteenth Century London: Part II' (1984) X *The London Journal* 107.
[23] Anthony Sampson, *The Changing Anatomy of Britain* (1982).
[24] Hamish McRae and Frances Cairncross, *Capital City: London as a Financial Centre* (1985).

community about those actors who influence capital markets in London and other finance centres around the world. Despite the safety nets of due diligence and contractual obligation, sociologies of trust are still immensely important in deal-making in capital markets. The structural properties of trust relationships have always underpinned the ideology of commercial exchange, but their importance is accentuated in financial services. Symbolic proxies such as share certificates, contracts, mortgages, letters of credit and cheques are exchanged for other symbolic proxies that may or may not equate with tangible goods.[25] These structures of trust are vulnerable to violation or manipulation, and so require flexible and dynamic systems of protection. A crucial safeguard for these sociologies of trust is the sense of honour to uphold one's good name when making a deal, premised on the traditions of *dictum meum pactum*. Simultaneously, these notions of trust and moral obligation help mediate conflicts and help actors, both individually and collectively, navigate the sometimes troubled currents where operational trading traditions and contemporary regulatory protocols may meet. It is within these swirling eddies that the regulated and the regulators seek to construct sufficient levels of social, legal and commercial fixity to allow the entrepreneurial drive of financial actors to flourish within appropriate parameters of socially protective regulation.

Where these points of balance of social regulatory fixity are achieved can be open to negotiation and sometimes contestation. The single most important feature of social regulatory fixity is that social practices cannot reproduce themselves. There has to be agency, whether human and/or institutional, and in practice there is usually a combination of both. If certain social practices are imbued with sufficient legitimacy, and are practised by human agents who possess sufficient power and domination over a period of time, then those practices (including how conflicts are managed), can become the most established and powerful routines. Indeed power-holders in many systems will have a vested interest in maintaining their domination within existing social orders and routines because: 'The routine repetitions of institutionalised modes of interaction between agents is not something apart from the patterns they form; it is the very stuff of which these patterns are made.'[26]

---

[25] Susan P Shapiro, 'Collaring the Crime, Not the Criminal: Reconsidering the Concept of White-Collar Crime' (1990) 55 *American Sociological Review* 346, 353.
[26] Ira J Cohen, *Structuration Theory: Anthony Giddens and the Constitution of Social Life* (1989) 77.

Consequently, if people can influence the routinised patterns of social practice (again in the case of actors in capital markets, for example, in the management of conflicts), then they can influence how human agents interact with eacsh other and with those social practices. The production of these routinised practices is therefore not a random process, but involves 'processes of "selective information filtering" whereby strategically placed actors seek reflexively to regulate the overall conditions of system reproduction either to keep things as they are or to change them.'[27]

Once they have established a sufficient level of fixity, power relations are capable of generating the levels of evidence required for their own legitimation.[28] The regulatory history of the City of London shows that strategically placed actors in the City reflexively influenced the reproduction of their social structures and systems in order to maintain routines and resist external intervention. The objectives were to retain strategic political and economic influence, and to control their own systems of self-regulation. Constellations of interests in the City were successful in projecting their preferred model of financial regulation and routinised social and business practices as the *natural* social and economic order, thereby ensuring its hegemony. A revealing insight into this hegemony, and the power and relative autonomy of the City of London, was provided with the passage of *Leeman's Act 1867*. This Act sought to stop the widespread practice of not recording transactions individually (but instead recording them as house transactions), and also aimed to reduce speculative dealing in banking securities. The traditional arrogant disregard of the City even for existing statutory controls is clear in the evidence given in 1875 by Mr Samuel Herman de Zoete, the then chairperson of the LSE to a parliamentary committee: 'Sirs, we disregarded for years Sir John Barnard's Act and we are now disregarding in the same measure Mr Leeman's Act.'[29]

As well as being almost breathtakingly arrogant (it is difficult to imagine any other business interest group openly defying a parliamentary committee in such a manner), this quote indicates the confidence that a disparate arrangement of groups and individuals in the City of London with shared economic interests possess in being able to tailor the discourse that constructs the regulation of their activities. A key explanatory factor for this is that the City has been tremendously successful in having its own interests

---

[27] Giddens, above n 8, 27.
[28] David Beetham, *The Legitimation of Power* (1991) 60.
[29] *House of Commons Journal* (1875).

widely identified as converging with the *public interest* on matters of financial regulation. This ability to shape perceptions of what entails the public interest has interacted with broader legal developments to influence significantly London's financial markets and their regulation. Like other powerful actors, the City has been able to set goals for the general interests of society.[30] The utility that its regulatory authority has held for the diverse interests that constitute the City is the fact that its cultural norms and values have been adopted as conventional working practice in the UK financial sector:

> businesses influence regulatory policy not only through pressure on legislation and the administration of justice, but by their participation in the organizational fields that 'enact' regulatory policy through daily practice. In short, organizational policies and practices constitute and reproduce regulatory meanings and structures.[31]

Similar processes are at work today in London and in other finance centres around the world, in the management of conflicts and with regard to many other issues. The twin pressures of special interest groups and market forces remain extremely influential in shaping contemporary regulatory praxis in financial services in the UK and elsewhere, just as they have done for centuries. One should not be too surprised by this because regulation can be viewed as a commodity, a raw material which is subject to market forces and may be facilitative, inherently contradictory, manipulative and complex. However, there is differential access to regulatory resources dependent upon a person or organisation's wealth, status and power, so at times regulation may be manipulated positively or negatively by those with the power and/or wealth to do so. In a market society, much power lies with capital resources, and those involved with the raising, organisation and marketing of capital have great influence. Also, the complexity of the financial services industry excludes most people from being able to evaluate its processes specifically. Add the all-pervasive moral culture of the City and one begins to understand why the City of London was able largely regulate itself for so long. These factors combined to equip the City with sufficient regulatory authority to construct its own regulatory culture

---

[30] Beetham, above n 28, 46.

[31] Nancy Reichman, 'Moving Backstage: Uncovering the Role of Compliance in Shaping Regulatory Policy' in Kip Schlegel and David Weisburd (eds), *White-Collar Crime Reconsidered* (1992) 244, 250.

and structures. A crucial factor in this regulatory autonomy has been the international nature of the City, which has had a significant effect upon Britain's social and economic history:

> The City is unique: no other international commercial, banking and financial centre has ever enjoyed such a lengthy and continuous period of operation — over 250 years. And in this crucially important respect, Britain is also unique: no other industrialised society has ever acted as host to a centre which has undertaken such a large share of the world capitalist system's commercial, banking and financial activities. Britain was not only the 'workshop of the world,' but also its 'clearing house' and whilst the former status has been lost, the latter — despite some recent competition from other centres — has not. The consequences of this enduring economic activity for the development of the dominant classes, the state system and the economy of Britain can scarcely be over estimated.'[32]

The reflexive interactions of internal City of London structures, their social and political connections, and the lobbying efforts of City professionals have protected the City's regulatory autonomy. This allowed City interest groups to benefit from the spectacular profits of the colonial era and insulated them from the subsequent decline suffered by other sectors of the UK economy.[33] The City has also had to resist the efforts of a number of inquiries over the years that were established in response to concerns regarding various established market practices. For example, concerns about inadequate disclosure requirements, problems associated with limited liability and complaints about City market practices were repeated by many witnesses before parliamentary committees in 1867, 1875, 1877 and 1878, and in 1886 before the Royal Commission on the Depression in Trade. Despite overwhelming evidence of widespread fraud being presented to them, legislators did not impose stricter regulation because of the influence of the financial community.[34] Following a series of scandalous promotional frauds during the 1870s, Lord Penzance was

---

[32] Ingham, above n 6, 40.

[33] Harold J Leavitt, William R Dill and Henry B Eyring, 'Rulemakers and Referees' in M David Ermann and Richard J Lundman (eds), *Corporate and Governmental Deviance* (1978) 259, 271.

[34] George Robb, *White Collar Crime in Modern England, Financial Fraud and Business Morality, 1845–1929* (1992) 150.

appointed in March 1877 to inquire into the administration and operation of the LSE. His major recommendations were:

a) that enforcement against fraud relating to financial markets should be vested in some public functionary;
b) that all transactions on the Stock Exchange should be individually recorded; and
c) that the Stock Exchange should be constituted in statute and be regulated by that statute.[35]

Lord Penzance argued that only increased public accountability on an external level could justify the restrictive practices operated by the LSE regarding membership and fixed minimum commissions. Unsurprisingly, the lobbying power of the City ensured that Lord Penzance's recommendations were not put into practice by the government and it took over a century for some of them to seep into the regulatory structure of Britain's financial markets. Lord Penzance was a predictor of several of the central reforms of the *Financial Services Act 1986* (UK) c 60 ('*Financial Services Act 1986*'), and ss 1–3 of the *Criminal Justice Act 1987* (UK) c 38 that created a statutory authority in the Serious Fraud Office which has responsibility to act against major frauds. Nevertheless, regulatory structures in the UK have altered dramatically in recent years and the City has shown that it possesses Darwinian instincts for survival. As broader conditions have changed in era of instant telecommunications, globalisation, removal of exchange controls, exponential surges in the numbers and types of available financial services products and providers, and an increased emphasis on nation states as mediators of capital interest, so has the regulatory rubric of the City of London adapted to seemingly seismic regulatory change. For example, the *Big Bang* in October 1986 deregulated the LSE through a series of reforms including: abolition of minimum commissions; member firms could be owned by outside institutions (most were bought by foreign banks); the Exchange becoming a private limited company; and broker/dealers could operate in a dual capacity.

The legislative accompaniment to the *Big Bang* was the *Financial Services Act 1986*, which signalled the statutory end to the City's traditional

---

[35] Lord Penzance, London Stock Exchange Commission, *Report of Commissioners* (1878).

model of self-regulation. Generally the Act vested regulatory powers in the Secretary of State for Trade and Industry, who then under s 115 of the Act delegated regulatory powers to a lead regulator the Securities and Investment Board ('SIB'), which was a private company limited by guarantee. The SIB then delegated regulatory powers to a number of Self-Regulatory Organisations ('SROs') including: the Securities Association; the Association of Futures Brokers and Dealers; the Financial Intermediaries Managers and Brokers Regulatory Association; the Investment Managers Regulatory Organisation; and the Life Assurance and Unit Trust Regulatory Organisation. This bewildering array of SROs later condensed to the Securities and Futures Association and the Personal Investment Authority. *Big Bang* was followed in 1995 by the establishment of the Alternative Investments Market which permitted smaller companies to list under less stringent conditions than the main LSE. In 1998 the Financial Services Authority ('FSA') assumed regulatory authority for the Bank of England and in 2000 the FSA took over the LSE's role as the UK Listing Authority. The FSA is an independent non-governmental body, a company limited by guarantee and financed by the financial services industry. It is given statutory powers by the *Financial Services and Markets Act 2000* (UK) c 8, and in 2001 under the full implementation of that Act, the FSA became the single UK regulator of investment services.

The historical overview above shows that the regulation of City of London has always been an inherently political process, and it was intensely political during the 1980s and 1990s. The FSA was created by a Labour government, which took office in April 1997. Such a body as the FSA did not emerge before 1997, because successive Conservative governments maintained their close links to the City, sustaining a determined, sometimes desperate, rearguard action in defence of the existing self-regulatory system. This happened, in the view of Hutton, because:

> London's status as the least regulated of world financial markets allowed it to become the centre of global finance. … Britain's company law, offering no formal status in the company's management to either bankers or shareholders — let alone any other stakeholder — reinforces the capital markets' disengagement. In this respect the entire system — from auditing through merchant banking to the new derivatives markets —

> operates as a whole. The vested interest in the status quo was immense.[36]

As Sir Andrew Large (head of SIB in the mid-1990s) later admitted (following the election of the Labour government in 1997), this pressure for the maintenance of the status quo severely inhibited his scope for regulatory innovation:

> frankly, at times it had an *Alice in Wonderland* quality … You may wonder why I didn't say all this before. The fact is I did — in private. But it is difficult to say these things openly, and with no prospect of legislation under the last government, it seemed best to soldier on.[37]

Whether Sir Andrew Large should have been more publicly critical and proactive whilst heading the SIB is a moot point; eventually the FSA and its attendant regulatory infrastructure changes emerged, and, although they were very significant regulatory changes, the City of London has adapted well to how both trading and regulatory conditions have altered. The reason the City has been able to manage is that despite its insularity and *club culture*, its moral particularity and social identity have always had an international outlook as their primary commercial goal. London has been the *world city* of finance and this facilitated the reflexive reconstruction of its *telos*, so that it could cope with the pressures of late-modern capitalism. These characteristics have permitted its transition from an environment with restrictive trade practices to a more open trading centre with its changed regulatory infrastructures.

The purpose of engaging in this swift and necessarily selective overview of some of the significant regulatory events and character of the City of London is to emphasise the value of history and context when contemplating current and future regulatory issues. Such an approach can help in disentangling the normative orders of regulation and explaining the interdependent agency/structures relationships that operate in the financial sector, such as the systemic, structural and human agency factors that can stimulate misconduct or nurture other potentially problematic phenomena such as conflicts of interests. In particular, this

---

[36] Will Hutton, *The State We're In* (1995) 166–7.

[37] P Farrelly, 'Regulators in Wonderland', *Business Section*, *The Observer* (London), 25 May 1997, 7.

deconstructive approach to the production and practice of regulation can help to show how regulation and regulatory misconduct may be factored into securities markets by their structures and agents. The meaning of regulation is constantly constructed and deconstructed by regulators and the regulated, who themselves are a reflexive and interdependent product of their social history, as they create accepted parameters of practice under changing market conditions.

II REGULATION AS A COMPETITIVE COMMODITY?

The various elements of the financial sector, including capital markets and their constituent actors, are increasingly important strategically to the economic well-being of national economies. There are ongoing and increasingly competitive efforts by governments, regulatory agencies and financial centres such as London, New York, Frankfurt, Hong Kong and Sydney to make themselves attractive to both domestic and foreign capital actors by continuing adjustment of their regulatory environments. This economic and political reality is almost certain to be triaged into the policy strategies of relevant regulatory actors.

Protecting the stability and liquidity of their financial sector is an increasingly important priority for many jurisdictions, including the UK. However, most financial regulatory structures are organised sectorally, are multi-tiered and are nationally-oriented, whereas a great deal of business is international.[38] This can lead to tensions and dilemmas for governments and regulatory agencies, especially with regard to what should be the fundamental strategic priorities and processes, and what should be the appropriate levels of powers and resources allocated to regulatory actors. However, what should be the operational priorities and key performance indicators for financial regulators, especially when trying to compare agencies in different jurisdictions? Are they supplied with sufficient resources? How does a regulator know how well their systems are structured and functioning, especially given the rapid pace of developments in the financial services sector that inevitably mean there is a very real danger of obsolescence for some parts of the legislation, and other regulatory processes such as accounting and legal systems, that are designed to supervise this dynamic area of the economy. Allied with the transformations in the technology of finance this raises the spectre of

---

[38] Andrew M Whittaker, 'Tackling Systematic Risk on Markets: Barings and Beyond' in Fidelis Oditah (ed), *The Future for the Global Securities Market* (1996) 257, 258–9.

systemic risk in financial markets.[39] Also, it is becoming increasingly difficult for regulatory agencies that are constituted predominantly on a national basis to achieve these aims in an environment where nation states seemingly have less and less prospect of controlling their financial services sector in ways that they have done in the past. This growing emasculation of the capability of individual jurisdictions to shape their financial markets has prompted trends towards internationalisation in the regulation of financial services. One product of these trends towards internationalisation has been increasing multilateral regulatory activism in the financial sector by a number of international organisations such as the International Organisation of Securities Commissions ('IOSCO') and the Basel Committee for Central Banking Supervisors. The vast majority of the world's national securities regulators are members of IOSCO, which sets out 30 principles of regulation that are based on three core objectives:[40]

a) The protection of investors;
b) Ensuring that markets are fair, efficient and transparent; and
c) The reduction of systemic risk.

These three core objectives lie at the heart of the approach that virtually all national securities regulators adopt in respect of their home markets. However, this trend towards uniformity in this core strategic sense is more than matched in some quarters by a desire for regulatory difference. There is increasing competition between different nation states and amongst financial centres for market share in the financial sector, which is sure to become more intense as they seek to promote their individual versions of leading-edge regulation, whether in the areas of financial market structure, taxation, disclosure obligations, or matters related to legal incorporation. Within the competitive environment that is the international financial sector, substantial and regular regulatory innovation may come to be seen as normal, indeed essential, for competitive survival. It is as if the evolutionary cycle of financial regulation is stuck on the fast forward button. Regulatory models, structures and processes could be viewed as expendable commodities, with limited working life, with competing models

---

[39] James H Cheek, 'Approaches to Market Regulation' in Fidelis Oditah (ed), *The Future for the Global Securities Market* (1996) 243, 244.

[40] International Organisation of Securities Commissions, *Objectives and Principles of Securities Regulation* (2003) i.

of financial regulation touted around the global markets like soap powders in the quest for market share. This is the move towards beauty parades in financial regulation, a trend which is occurring in other sectors as well. For example, in Australia, it is manifest in initiatives such as the Corporate Law Economic Reform Program, and the recent announcement by the Treasurer that the Productivity Commission will undertake annual reviews of the regulatory burdens on business in different sectors each year. In the UK, this search for competitive advantage can be seen in the strong commitment by the FSA to emphasise principles-based regulation on an ongoing basis.[41]

These types of initiatives are largely top-down driven. The greater difficulty is gauging the effects of the more complex and subtle normative interactions of regulation, especially how regulatory actors choose to exercise their regulatory authority. Regulators are in a similar position to judicial officials, because law and regulation have an inescapable social dimension. For example, when courts make moral value judgements on managerial inefficiency or mismanagement, they are basing their decisions on commercial probity, and fiduciary duties are applied on the general principle of a company as a good citizen in business. Financial services regulators are making similar decisions on a daily basis in their efforts to balance equity concerns by protecting investors and efficiency concerns by encouraging active and competitive markets. This equity–efficiency dilemma is faced by regulators in all industries. For example, Hawkins found that efficiency was the central priority of water pollution field officers as they continually weighed up economic and social cost concerns. They only utilised formal processes if there was a perceived moral consensus between regulators and regulated.[42] Moral evaluations are inherent in the exercise of choice and discretion is the essence of the law. This means that regulators and those whom they regulate are constantly engaged in a moral balancing process about regulation. Statutes, case law, and a host of regulatory mechanisms are sometimes shells that have to be filled out by moral principles and decisions. Often these decisions are guided by moral judgements on levels of harm and fault involved. This interactive relationship between law and morality is especially pronounced within financial services, because much definition and enforcement of legal norms can be a social process of negotiation. Practical concerns shape the operational morality of regulation, both in a practical and a philosophical

---

[41] FSA, *FSA Business Plan 2006/2007* (2006) 10, available at <http://www.fsa.gov.uk>.
[42] Keith Hawkins, *Environment and Enforcement: Regulation and the Social Definition of Pollution* (1984) 198.

sense, and political factors are crucial: 'the effectiveness of policing (the financial sector) is in practice inseparable from its political legitimation … Irrespective of the "actual" best methods of control, the political impact of perceived levels of control is considerable'.[43]

Legitimacy is the sum of the moral and normative aspects of power relationships, and financial services regulators are attuned to the political realities of the industry as they strive to legitimise their regulatory authority. Consequently (and this has implication for an issue such as the management of conflicts), enforcement approach and the intensity of that approach become elements in the gaming for competitive advantage between actors, such as finance centres, and the jurisdictions in which they reside. It is an effort to explain such processes at work that have given rise to models such as the well known pyramid strategies of regulation of Ayres and Braithwaite.[44]

It is a sensible strategy for both the regulators and the regulated, and for other key stakeholders such as the state and consumers, that the vast proportion of regulatory interaction, including enforcement, should take place at the lower levels of the pyramid, especially its base. Assuming that good regulatory compliance outcomes are achievable using these strategies, it is much more cost-effective and is likely to stimulate many more win–win scenarios. The difficulties of course arise with actors who may be inclined to ignore their regulatory obligations, or, for example, are ignorant of what may constitute a serious breach of their regulatory obligations. Here a more severe regulatory response from higher up the pyramid may be appropriate. The rationale is that, depending on the circumstances of the breach and the offender, different levels of regulatory response, from persuasion, to warning letter, to civil penalty, to criminal penalty, to licence suspension and finally licence revocation, may be applied. This rationale of course reflects the working practice of much of our justice system.

Pyramid approaches to regulation not only emphasise ascending scales of sanction, but also ascending scales of regulatee autonomy and official intervention. This refers to how much regulatory autonomy may be allowed to the regulated under different models of regulation, from self-regulation moving up the pyramid to command and control regulation, and, of course, we could add intermediate tiers to take

---

[43] Levi, above n 1, 49, 50.
[44] Ian Ayres and John Braithwaite, *Responsive Regulation: Transcending the Deregulation Debate* (1992) 35, 39.

account of other models of regulation. There is extensive literature relating to the theory and practice of regulation, which takes into account the effect of pyramid approaches, which I will not review in this chapter. For example, the pyramids of Ayres and Braithwaite have inspired the production of other pyramid structures, including the one by Dellit and Fisse[45] who produced a pyramid of regulatory response designed specifically for regulatory interaction with corporations.

It might be interesting to consider whether one could utilise the triangle shape (that of course forms the regulatory pyramid), in various ways to represent features of the financial sector, and also how regulation is put into practice within the financial sector. In particular, can such an approach be used to highlight the various tipping points at which regulatory action may be activated against various behaviours? For example: the management of conflicts, seeking to portray whether action is activated within an organisation internally or by external regulatory actors, against whom it is activated, and with how much severity such action is activated. So for example, the fulcrum of Packer's crime control model,[46] could be a triangle at the base of a regulatory intervention flow chart. Packer's model focused on the criminal justice system: hence 'crime control' at one axis and 'due process' at the other. Other terms could be substituted for other regulatory contexts, such as 'rule-breaking' for 'crime control', and 'regulatory autonomy' for 'due process'. The tipping-point of regulatory response could move along the base depending upon how the choices of the regulatory actor(s) are put into action.

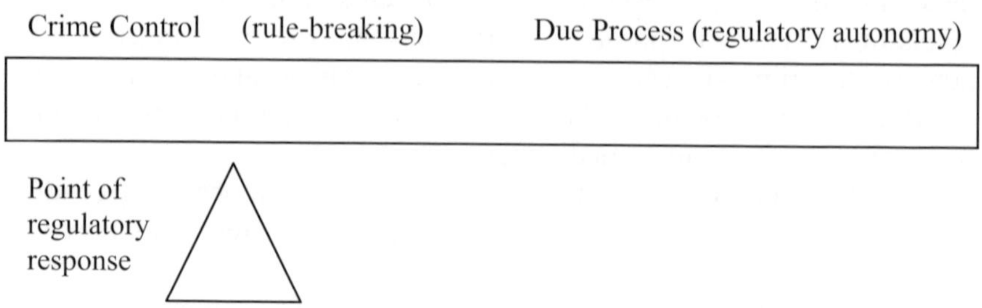

Figure 1. Model of Regulatory Tipping Points.

[45] Brent Fisse and Chris Dellit, 'Civil Liability under Australian Securities Regulation: The Possibility of Strategic Enforcement' in Gordon Walker and Brent Fisse (eds), *Securities Regulation in Australia and New Zealand* (1994) 570.

[46] Herbert L Packer, *The Limits of the Criminal Sanction* (1968).

For example, Figure 1 shows how a regulatory actor might react to a recidivist offender whose actions had caused substantial harm by employing stronger sanctions against what it perceives as persistent rule-breaking behaviour. The fulcrum of regulatory response is likely to move closer to the regulatory autonomy axis when an organisation has responded positively to a breach and instigated extensive organisational change to reduce any prospect of re-offending. The regulatory tipping point in the latter case scenario emphasizes relative autonomy and is an indicator of limited regulatory intervention. Now as we saw in the earlier sections on UK regulatory history, the City of London managed to achieve for many hundreds of years tipping points of regulatory response that were heavily weighted towards relative autonomy, when the behaviour of many in the City perhaps merited regulatory tipping points that were much closer to the rule-breaking/crime control axis. That this did not happen was due, of course, to a whole host of political, economic, historical, social, cultural and other normative factors, which allowed them to achieve relatively unfettered levels of regulatory autonomy despite a collective blatant disregard for some statutory and other regulatory obligations. There is no scope in the remainder of this chapter to do so, but it would interesting perhaps in future research to try and superimpose the above approach to a number of specific case studies in regulatory success, and/or, regulatory failure, to try and identify the tipping points of regulatory response, and the circumstances, actors and other influences which combined to create such tipping points. Similarly, there may be potential in this model for exploring specific issues such as *managing conflicts*, to see how tipping points are constructed, deconstructed and reconstructed.

III THE LEVERAGED CHARACTER OF FINANCIAL SERVICES

The financial services sector is unlikely to decrease in its strategic significance, not least because of prevailing trends towards increased leverage. That is, for example, not only in the sense of actors in the sector leveraging their capital through specific lending strategies, which is of course standard banking practice, but also more generally the leveraging effect that the financial sector overall has in relation to global GDP. The figures are stark, broad money represents 122 per cent of world GDP, but only 11 per cent of global liquidity, whereas derivative financial products represent 802 per cent of world GDP and 75 per cent of global liquidity.[47] This has been the alchemy of securitisation and other derivative trading strategies, which have transformed the global economy in recent decades, especially in relation to risk management, investment and capital management in general.

The transformations in capital trading and investment symbolised by derivatives have brought positive benefits, including a seemingly better capacity to manage sudden significant downwards movements in stock markets, which on occasion have had catastrophic effects in the past. However, there is a dark side to extreme capital leveraging as well. Hedge funds are of course often portrayed as the *bete noire* of this genre, with the spectacular near-collapse and rescue of Long Term Capital Management ('LTCM') in 1998 put forward as an example of just how disastrous the highly-leveraged strategies of some hedge funds can be. Hedge funds operate with enormous ratios of leverage in their desire to generate large profits swiftly and the intrinsic danger is that losses can multiply just as quickly as profits. Hedge funds seek out and immerse themselves in risk, building an inverse pyramid of investment capital on their relatively slender reserves base. For example, the Bank for International Settlements ('BIS') noted that LTCM's balance sheet at 31 August 1998 implied a leverage ratio of greater than 25:1.[48] Consequently, the inverted base of the LTCM capital pyramid was extremely narrow and potentially susceptible to collapse, as experience proved. Interestingly, the detailed report carried out by the US General Accounting Office placed LTCM's leverage ratio at 28:1, and noted that some of the largest US investment banks (and therefore the world's largest) were carrying comparable or greater leverage ratios at the time of LTCM's collapse. For example: Goldman Sachs Group LP (34:1); Merrill Lynch & Co, Inc (30:1); and Lehman Brothers Holdings, Inc (28:1). The major investment banks were less prone to collapse, however, because their assets were less volatile, whereas LTCM was heavily exposed to more volatile assets such as interest rate swaps.[49] Much controversy surrounded the bailout of LTCM, which involved several of the elite Wall Street investment banks including Bankers Trust, Chase Manhattan, Goldman Sachs, JP Morgan, Merrill Lynch and Morgan Stanley. Unusually, the bailout was overseen by

---

[47] Andrew Cornell, 'The Year of Easy Money', *Weekend Australian Financial Review* (Sydney), 27 December 2006, 20,

[48] Bank for International Settlements, *69th Annual Report* (1999) 100.

[49] General Accounting Office, *Long Term Capital Management — Regulators Need to Focus Greater Attention on Systematic Risk* (1999) 7.

the US Federal Reserve because it was aware that many of the largest players in the financial markets had similar positions to LTCM and there was a danger of systemic collapse. There has been criticism of the Federal Reserve's role, because it could be interpreted as *crony capitalism* and acquiescing in an abdication of moral hazard by powerful financial actors in the insular world of high-level US investment banking. Ironically the LTCM bailout occurred at a time when western bankers had been repeatedly critical of the role of *cronyism* amongst east-Asian elites in the governance of those countries devastated by that region's financial crisis.[50] It would be interesting (if sufficient access was available), to analyse from a normative perspective, and through both primary and secondary information sources, how the various tipping points of the LTCM collapse and rescue were constructed, as per the earlier discussion relating to the regulatory adaption of Packer's model. Research of this nature would contribute to developing a regulatory case study library, which in turn could contribute to better understanding and regulation of complex issues such as the management of conflicts, which of necessity demand a multidisciplinary approach in order to achieve long-term successful regulatory strategies.

CONCLUSION

The financial services sector is a complex, diffused and rapidly evolving environment, and financial services regulation can be an intrinsically political and competitive process. Conditions of late-modernity have reduced a national government's scope for ideological and policy manoeuvre, and financial services and markets have seen enormous changes in recent decades. These include: monetary reforms such as widespread relaxations of exchange controls in many countries; broader political factors such as the collapse of most centrally planned economies (most dramatically in the former Soviet Bloc), and a subsequent commitment (to a greater or lesser degree), by virtually every country in the world to an economy oriented to market principles, spectacular growth, increasing internationalisation, increasing choice, increasing flexibility, increasing competition, and technology as a driver for expansion and innovation, such as online banking, online trading, virtual

---

[50] John Plender, 'Western Crony Capitalism', *Financial Times* (London), 3–4 October 1998, 10.

exchanges, e-money and instantaneous trading in financial products. Through this maelstrom of change a constant has been the importance of normative factors, in particular regulatory autonomy, to regulatory praxis. This chapter has sought to emphasise from historical and other analytical perspectives this crucial normative character, especially in the UK context. Normative standards lie at the heart of issues such as managing conflicts and increasing regulatory competition, and should be prioritised in efforts to analyse how regulatory praxis emerges and develops in financial services and in other sectors.

Chapter 5

ASIC v Citigroup: Investment Banks, Conflicts of Interest, and Chinese Walls

Pamela F Hanrahan

In his Foreword to the 30th edition of *Snell's Equity*, Lord Millett wrote of equity that:

> It has broken through the traditional barriers which would confine its operation to the home and family and entered the business world. It brings with it obligations of loyalty, confidence and good faith, obligations higher than those imposed by the common law, which is satisfied with honesty, careful conduct and keeping one's promises. The exposure of the commercial world to equitable concepts is bringing a host of problems with which we are only now beginning to grapple.[1]

The recent decision of Jacobson J in the Federal Court of Australia in *Australian Securities and Investments Commission v Citigroup Global Markets Australia Pty Ltd (No 4)*,[2] handed down in July 2007, embodies Lord Millett's concern. In this case, the relationship between an investment bank and a client (to whom it was providing advisory services in relation to a proposed takeover bid) came under the equitable microscope. The case attracted considerable attention both in Australia and overseas. At its heart was the proposition, advanced by

---

[1] John McGhee, *Snell's Equity* (30th ed, 2000).

[2] [2007] FCA 963 ('*ASIC v Citigroup*').

Australia's financial services regulator, that proprietary trading in the target company's shares in the lead-up to the takeover (by a division of the bank separate from the advisory team) placed the bank in a situation where its personal interests conflicted with its duty to the bidder client, in breach of a fiduciary duty owed by the bank to that client.

In the event, Jacobson J found that the relationship between the bank and its client was not fiduciary in character. Accordingly, the bank was not subject to a fiduciary duty requiring it to avoid conflicts of interest and duty. His Honour went on to find that, even if the relationship had been fiduciary, the bank's proprietary trading (which took place behind a Chinese Wall separating the 'public side' proprietary traders from the 'private side' advisory team) did not, on the facts, give rise to any conflict of interest and duty that would have offended the fiduciary proscription. His Honour also went on to find that, even if the trading had given rise to a conflict, the client's fully informed consent to the existence of that conflict could have been implied from the all the circumstances of the dealing between the bank and the client.

Had the decision been otherwise, the concerns of the international investment banking community that the Australian regulator had upset a widespread (but not inevitable) practice in financial conglomerates of combining advisory businesses with equities trading businesses would have been realised. Instead the decision of Jacobson J has confirmed that this practice is not prohibited by equity, provided the relationship between the bank and the client, and the organisation of the conglomerate's business, conforms to certain conventions.

The purpose of this chapter is to unpack the conflicts element of the decision, to see what its ramifications might be for investment banks whose operations encompass both advisory and trading arms. It begins with a brief outline of the case, including a discussion of how it was that the financial services regulator came to bring an action based on (private law) fiduciary principles, and of the relationship between the conflicts elements and allegations of insider trading (which the regulator also failed to establish) that were tied up with them. It goes on to look in some more detail at Jacobson J's specific findings in relation to: firstly, the allegation that the relationship between the bank and its client was fiduciary; secondly, the allegation that the bank's proprietary trading gave rise to a conflict of interest and duty; and thirdly, the allegation that the client's informed consent had not been obtained. It then discusses briefly the role of Chinese Walls in the management of conflicts. It concludes with some observations about the broader implications of the decision for the application of fiduciary principles to advisory firms and for the (specifically Australian) regulatory landscape. In so doing it draws attention to the complex interplay in commercial relationships between the common law duties and equitable principles, and between the equitable principles *inter se*, to which Lord Millett refers. As the discussion shows, that complexity is increased by the introduction of a third element, not mentioned by Lord Millett, which is the co-opting of equitable principles into the (public) regulation of financial services firms.

I THE CASE AGAINST CITIGROUP

The defendant in the Federal Court proceedings was a company called Citigroup Global Markets Australia Pty Ltd ('Citigroup'). Citigroup is the main operating subsidiary in Australia of Citigroup Inc, the global banking and financial services company. Citigroup carries on various businesses in Australia, including a business known internally as the Corporate and Investment Bank ('CIB'). The CIB in turn includes a number of operating divisions, one of which is the Investment Banking Division ('IBD') which provides advisory services and investment banking services (including in connection with mergers and acquisitions), and another of which (known as Equities) engages in proprietary trading in securities.

(A) *The Patrick Takeover*

On 8 August 2005, Citigroup's IBD was retained by a subsidiary of an Australian listed company called Toll Holdings Limited ('Toll') to provide financial advisory and investment banking services to it in relation to a proposed takeover by Toll of another listed company, Patrick Corporation Limited ('Patrick'). Toll had been considering a takeover of Patrick for some months, as a means of entering the Australian ports logistics market. The transaction was a sizable one (valued at over A$4.5 billion on completion) and the parties were highly sophisticated. Toll appointed two investment banks to advise it in relation to the bid, of which Citigroup was one and the boutique Carnegie Wylie & Co Pty Limited ('Carnegie Wylie') was the other. Under the terms of the retainer executed on 8 August, Citigroup's IBD fees for successful completion of the takeover were likely to be in the range of A$10 to A$18 million.

Citigroup's IBD and Equities divisions were separated by formal information and other barriers known in the financial services sector as 'Chinese Walls'. Employees working in the IBD division were on the private side of the wall, because they were routinely in possession of non-public price sensitive information about securities (including, in this instance, information about Toll's intentions in relation to Patrick). Employees in the Equities division were on the public side of the wall. An important purpose of the Chinese Wall was to ensure that Citigroup did not contravene Australia's insider trading laws by trading (through the Equities division) in Patrick shares while in possession (through the IBD division) of non-public price sensitive information about Patrick.

On Friday 19 August 2005, one of the traders in Citigroup's Equities division acquired a substantial number of Patrick shares. There is no suggestion that, at the time he acquired the shares, the trader was in possession of inside information about Toll's proposed bid for Patrick. Rather the trader appears to have been responding to movements in the Patrick price, which in turn reflected broader market speculation about the likelihood of Patrick being the subject of a takeover bid (probably by Toll). By mid-afternoon on that Friday the trader had a substantial long position in Patrick, and the Patrick price had risen appreciably. At 3.30 pm, the trader's boss took him outside the office for a brief discussion in which he told the trader to stop buying Patrick shares. This is the famous 'cigarette on the pavement' discussion referred to in media reports of the case. The trader came back upstairs to the dealing room and sold down some of his position. As events unfolded, Toll's bid for Patrick was subsequently announced the following business day, on Monday 22 August 2005.

In accordance with normal practice, trading in Patrick shares in the lead-up to the bid was examined by the surveillance division of Australian Securities Exchange Limited ('ASX'), the exchange on which both Toll and Patrick were listed. ASX identified the possibility of insider trading in Patrick by Citigroup and referred the matter to the Australian Securities and Investments Commission ('ASIC') for investigation. ASIC is the financial markets and financial services regulator in Australia. Following an investigation during late 2005 and early 2006, ASIC commenced proceedings against Citigroup in March 2006.

(B) *The Allegations*

ASIC's case against Citigroup evolved between March 2006 and the beginning of the trial in April 2007; there were three substantially different iterations of ASIC's statement of claim, and a number of minor refinements to its pleadings made over that time. But in essence ASIC's allegations were two-fold.

The first was an allegation that, by reason of the proprietary trading, Citigroup had breached certain statutory provisions regulating financial services providers[3] in that it had breached a fiduciary duty owed by it to Toll to avoid conflicts of interest and duty. These allegations are referred to by Jacobson J as the conflicts claims.

The second was an allegation that Citigroup itself (rather than the individual Equities division trader) had engaged in insider trading[4] in Patrick shares. There were two allegations of insider trading; his Honour refers to them as the first and second insider trading claims. The first related to the sale of Patrick shares by the trader after the 'cigarette on the pavement' conversation. The second related to all of the trading that took place on the Friday and was based on ASIC's view that Citigroup was not entitled (for the reasons pleaded) to rely on the Chinese Wall defence to insider trading by corporations.[5] In the absence of the Chinese

---

[3] Those sections are s 912A(1)(aa) and s 1041H of the *Corporations Act 2001* (Cth) ('the *Corporations Act*') and s 12CA and s 12DA of the *Australian Securities and Investments Commission Act 2001* (Cth) ('the *ASIC Act*'). The relationship between these sections and the allegation of breach of fiduciary duty made by ASIC is explained below.

[4] Insider trading is prohibited by s 1043A of the *Corporations Act*. In essence, the section provides that a person who possesses inside information about securities, and who knows or ought to know those things that give the information the character of inside information, may not trade in those securities or procure another person to trade in those securities. Information is inside information if the information is not generally available, and, if the information were generally available, a reasonable person would expect it to have a material effect on the price or value of securities: see ss 1042A–1042D of the *Corporations Act*.

[5] The Chinese Wall defence is contained in s 1043F of the *Corporations Act*. It is to the effect that a body corporate does not contravene the insider trading prohibition by entering into a transaction at any time merely because of information in the possession of an officer or employee, if three conditions are met. The first is that the decision to enter into the transaction was made by a person other than the person in possession of the information. The second is that the body corporate 'had in operation at that time arrangements that could reasonably be expected to ensure that the information was not communicated to the person or persons who made the decision and that no advice with respect to the transaction or agreement was given to that person or any of those persons

Wall defence, the knowledge of Citigroup's IBD team would, of course, have been knowledge of Citigroup that it possessed while the Equities division was trading in Patrick shares.

This paper confines itself to a discussion of the conflicts claims. Suffice to say in relation to the insider trading claims that ASIC was unsuccessful in both.[6] In relation to the first claim, Jacobson J decided that the trader was not an 'officer' of Citigroup and accordingly that any information he might or might not have possessed following the 'cigarette on the pavement' conversation could not be attributed to Citigroup.[7] In relation to the second insider trading claim, his Honour concluded that the requirements of the insider trading defence were met, including the requirement that Citigroup have in place 'arrangements that could reasonably be expected to ensure that' information or advice did not cross from the private side to the public side.[8] In other words, his Honour found that Citigroup's Chinese Wall was adequate to repel an allegation of insider trading at the company level.

II THE CONFLICTS CLAIMS

We now turn to look in some more detail at the nature of the conflicts claims made by ASIC against Citigroup. As noted above, the essence of the conflicts claims was that Citigroup had breached certain parts of the Australian financial services laws *in that* it had breached a fiduciary duty owed by it to Toll to avoid conflicts of interest and duty. ASIC said that this alleged breach of fiduciary duty by Citigroup:

a) meant that Citigroup did not 'have in place adequate arrangements for the management of conflicts of interest that may arise wholly, or partially, in relation to activities undertaken by [Citigroup] or its

---

by a person in possession of the information': at s 1043F(b). (This is the so-called Chinese Wall requirement.) The third is that the information was not so communicated and no such advice was so given.

[6] *ASIC v Citigroup* [2007] FCA 963, [466]–[598].

[7] The effect of s 1042G(1)(a) of the *Corporations Act* is that inside information is only taken to be possessed by a body corporate if it is possessed by an 'officer' as defined in s 9. The trader was not an officer, only an employee: see *ASIC v Citigroup* [2007] FCA 963, [479]–[501]. But it is clear from his Honour's findings in relation to a range of other issues raised by the first insider trading claim (at [502]–[571]) that ASIC would have failed in this claim even if the trader had been an officer of Citigroup.

[8] *ASIC v Citigroup* [2007] FCA 963, [592]–[593].

representatives in the provision of financial services as part of [its] financial services business'. Citigroup was required to have in place such arrangements because it holds an Australian financial services ('AFS') licence issued under part 7.6 of the *Corporations Act*;[9]

b) amounted to misleading or deceptive conduct in relation to financial services, in contravention of the *Corporations Act* and the *ASIC Act*;[10]
c) amounted to unconscionable conduct in contravention of the *ASIC Act*.[11]

The relevant provisions of the financial services laws are provisions in relation to which ASIC has standing to bring civil proceedings in the Federal Court for non-compliance. ASIC sought various orders from the Court in relation to the alleged contraventions, including declarations that Citigroup's actions were in breach of the law, and injunctions requiring Citigroup to take certain steps to correct those breaches.[12]

It is important to note that, in formulating and pleading its case against Citigroup, ASIC chose to argue only that Citigroup had contravened these statutory provisions by being in breach of a fiduciary duty owed to by Citigroup to Toll. ASIC did not argue that Citigroup contravened the statutory provisions in any other way. Accordingly, as Jacobson J points out, the gravamen of ASIC's case becomes whether Citigroup owed fiduciary duties to Toll.[13] Perhaps there is an open question about whether Citigroup's conduct might have contravened these provisions in some other way, other than by being a breach of fiduciary duty (although there is nothing in Jacobson J's findings to suggest that it would). However because of the way ASIC's case was structured, if it failed to establish breach of fiduciary duty on the part of Citigroup then it also (necessarily) failed to establish the statutory contraventions that it alleged.

---

[9] The requirement on AFS licensees to have adequate arrangements for the management of conflicts of interest is contained in s 912A(1)(aa) of the *Corporations Act*.

[10] Misleading or deceptive conduct in relation to financial services is prohibited under s 1041H of the *Corporations Act* and s 12DA of the *ASIC Act*.

[11] Unconscionable conduct is prohibited by s 12CA of the *ASIC Act*.

[12] See ASIC, 'Further Amended Statement of Claim' (26 March 2007), available at <http://www.asic.gov.au/asic/asic.nsf/byheadline/ASIC+v+Citigroup?openDocument> .

[13] *ASIC v Citigroup* [2007] FCA 963, [20].

In order to establish that Citigroup's proprietary trading in Patrick shares amounted to a breach of a fiduciary duty owed by Citigroup to Toll, ASIC would have had to establish three things. They were: first, that the relationship between Citigroup and Toll was fiduciary in character and that accordingly Citigroup was required to avoid conflicts between its personal interests and its duties to Toll; secondly, that the proprietary trading undertaken by Citigroup on the Friday created a conflict of interest and duty; and thirdly, that Citigroup did not have Toll's informed consent to the existence of the conflict. In order to establish the second of these things, ASIC had (at least in respect of one part of its case) to go one step further and establish that, because it was in a fiduciary relationship with Toll, Citigroup owed Toll a positive duty to disclose all matters relevant to its mandate of which it was aware. Such a duty was said by ASIC to be derived from the observations of Brennan J in the High Court of Australia in *Daly v The Sydney Stock Exchange Limited*.[14] Jacobson J decided against ASIC on all of these issues. The reasons why, and the wider implications of his Honour's findings, are explored below.

III Issue 1: The Fiduciary Point

In order to succeed in the conflicts claims, ASIC had first to establish that the relationship between Citigroup and Toll was fiduciary in character. In this regard his Honour was referred to Dr Andrew Tuch's argument that investment banks would most likely owe fiduciary duties to their clients in the discharge of the advisory functions.[15]

The problem for ASIC was that the mandate letter, executed by Citigroup and Toll on 8 August, expressly provided that the relationship was not fiduciary. Specifically, the mandate letter included the following sentence:

> The Company acknowledges that Citigroup has been retained hereunder solely as an adviser to the Company, and not as an adviser to or agent of any other person, and that the Company's engagement of Citigroup is as an independent

---

[14] (1986) 160 CLR 371, 385 ('*Daly*').

[15] Andrew Tuch, 'Investment Banks as Fiduciaries: Implications for Conflicts of Interest' (2005) 29 *Melbourne University Law Review* 478.

> contractor and not in any other capacity including as a fiduciary.[16]

Citigroup argued that, in the face of this express contractual stipulation that its relationship with Toll was not fiduciary, it was not open to Jacobson J to find that it was. In reply, ASIC contended that the contractual stipulation would be effective to exclude the fiduciary relationship only if Citigroup had obtained Toll's informed consent to the inclusion of the provision. As Jacobson J notes:

> The gravamen of ASIC's case is that for the exclusion of the fiduciary relationship in the mandate letter to be effective, it was incumbent upon Citigroup to draw Toll's attention expressly to the effect of the exclusion, that is, that it permitted Citigroup to trade in Patrick shares on its own account, in potential conflict with the interests of Toll. …
> The substance of Citigroup's answer to the claim is that the duty of a fiduciary to obtain the informed consent of a client has no application here because it presupposes the existence of an antecedent fiduciary relationship. No such pre-existing relation is claimed to have been created.[17]

By framing its case in this way, ASIC created (essentially) two sub-issues. The first is whether, but for the contractual stipulation to the contrary, the relationship would have been fiduciary. The second is whether, and if so on what basis, the contractual stipulation is effective to prevent a fiduciary relationship arising between the parties.

(A) *The Fiduciary Character of Advisory Relationships*

Interestingly, Jacobson J concludes that 'but for the express terms of the mandate letter, the pre-contract dealings between Citigroup and Toll would have pointed strongly towards the existence of a fiduciary relationship in Citigroup's role as an adviser.'[18] In that respect his Honour comes to a similar conclusion as Dr Tuch.[19] He notes that, as is

---

[16] [2007] FCA 963, [145].
[17] *ASIC v Citigroup* [2007] FCA 963, [20]–[22].
[18] Ibid [325].
[19] Tuch, above n 15.

shown by the decisions in *Daly*, *Hadid v Lengest Communications Inc*[20] and *Aequitas v Sparad No 100 Limited*,[21] an adviser 'may have fiduciary obligations to the client.'[22] The basis upon which Jacobson J comes to this conclusion is explained at [282] to [286], which set out the orthodox bases upon which a relationship that falls outside one of the established categories may be treated by equity as fiduciary. His Honour notes that '[v]ulnerability of the client is one of the indicia of the fiduciary relationship.'[23] However that vulnerability is judged not by reference to the sophistication (or otherwise) of the client, but rather by having regard to 'the special opportunity of the adviser to abuse the expectation of loyalty'.[24]

In *Aequitas* Austin J said that:

> The fiduciary relationship between financial adviser and client arises because the financial adviser, having held itself out as an adviser on matters of investment, undertakes a particular financial advisory role for the client: *Daly v Sydney Stock Exchange Ltd*, 160 CLR at 377 per Gibbs CJ; 384–385 per Brennan J. The advisory fiduciary relationship may arise whether or not there is an anterior fiduciary relationship between the parties, such as the relationship of broker and client. The relationship can arise even where parties are dealing with one another in a transaction in which the adviser has an obvious commercial self-interest. Thus, 'a bank may be expected to act in its own interests in ensuring the security of its position as lender to its customer, but it may have created in the customer the expectation that it will nevertheless advise in the customer's interests as to the wisdom of a proposed investment': *Commonwealth Bank of Australia v Smith* (1991) 42 FCR 390, 391. But unless there is, in all the circumstances, the requisite undertaking, the adviser is under no fiduciary duty and is free to pursue its own interests: *Noranda Australia Ltd v Lachlan Resources NL* (1988) 14 NSWLR 1, 15–17.[25]

---

20 [1999] FCA 1798 ('*Hadid*').
21 (2001) 19 ACLC 1006 ('*Aequitas*').
22 *ASIC v Citigroup* [2007] FCA 963, [325].
23 Ibid [286].
24 Ibid.
25 (2001) 19 ACLC 1006, [307].

It is true that the cases to which Jacobson J refers establish a fiduciary relationship between an adviser and a client, in circumstances where 'the adviser holds itself out as an expert on financial matters and undertakes to perform a financial advisory role for the client'.[26] However, the test, expressed in those terms, is potentially very broad. The established categories of fiduciary relationship[27] all exhibit what Mason J described in *Hospital Products Limited v United States Surgical Corporation* as the 'critical feature': that the fiduciary 'undertakes or agrees to act for or on behalf of or in the interests of another person *in the exercise of a power or discretion which will affect the interests of that other person* in a legal or practical sense'.[28] Unlike a trustee, director, agent, employee or partner, an adviser does not exercise any power or discretion as part of its function. It simply advises, and the client is free to act upon or reject that advice. In the Citigroup case, Toll had retained two advisers — Citigroup and Carnegie Wylie. Presumably it did so on the basis that its own experienced mergers and acquisitions team would take into account the (perhaps differing) advice given by these advisers, and exercise its own judgment in making the final decisions relating to the Patrick bid. The case for finding that the relationship was fiduciary might be thought of as weaker in this circumstance, than in the particular circumstances in *Daly, Hadid* and *Aequitas,* to which his Honour referred.

Ultimately, though, as Jacobson J points out, 'the question of whether a fiduciary relationship exists, and the scope of any duty, will depend upon the factual circumstances and an examination of the contractual terms between the parties'.[29] His Honour goes on to point out that where (as here):

> a fiduciary relationship is said to be founded upon a contract, the ordinary rules of construction of contracts apply. Thus, whether a part is subject to fiduciary obligations, and the scope of any fiduciary duties, is to be determined by construing the contract as a whole in light of the surrounding circumstances known to the parties and the purpose and object of the transaction: see *Pacific Carriers Limited v BNP Paribas* (2004) 218 CLR 451 at [22] per Gleeson CJ, Gummow,

---

[26] *ASIC v Citigroup* [2007] FCA 963, [283].
[27] With the possible exception of the advisory aspects of the relationship between solicitor and client, which is arguably a special case: see reasons alluded to at ibid [303].
[28] (1984) 156 CLR 41, 96–7 (emphasis added) ('*Hospital Products*').
[29] *ASIC v Citigroup* [2007] FCA 963, [266].

> Hayne, Callinan and Heydon JJ; *Toll (FGCT) Pty Limited v Alphapharm Pty Limited* (2004) 219 CLR 165 at [40] per Gleeson CJ, Gummow, Hayne, Callinan and Heydon JJ; *Lion Nathan Australia Pty Limited v Coopers Brewery Limited* (2006) 156 FCR 1 at [46] per Weinberg J.[30]

In light of that conclusion, the key consideration for Jacobson J was how the contractual stipulation in the mandate letter (to the effect that the relationship was not fiduciary) should be treated in construing the contract between Citigroup and Toll.

(B) *The Effect of the Contractual Stipulation*

It is settled law that, where a person is already subject to fiduciary obligations, they must obtain the fully informed consent of the other person to the exclusion or modification of those obligations. Jacobson J confirms this general principle at [307]. Importantly, though, his Honour concludes that this principle (that fully informed consent is required to exclude the fiduciary obligations) can have no application except where the parties are in an established category of fiduciary relationship (such as trustee and beneficiary, solicitor and client, or agent and principal) or 'at very least, to those who carry fiduciary obligations before the execution of the contract'.[31] To hold otherwise 'would be to say that a person who is not a fiduciary may nevertheless owe an obligation which flows from a fiduciary relationship. That could hardly be correct.'[32] It is of the utmost significant in the context of this part of the decision that ASIC alleged that the fiduciary relationship arose out of the mandate letter,[33] and did not pre-date it.

The relationship between a financial adviser and its client, if it is fiduciary at all (see above), is not one of the established categories of fiduciary relationship.[34] Accordingly, his Honour found that the principle

---

[30] Ibid [281].

[31] Ibid [305].

[32] Ibid [346].

[33] ASIC disavowed the existence of a fiduciary relationship pre-dating the actual execution of the mandate letter: ibid [24], [306]. As his Honour points out, this distinguishes the situation from that which arose in *United Dominions Corporation Limited v Brian Pty Limited* (1985) 157 CLR 1, 11–12 (Mason, Brennan and Deane JJ).

[34] The established categories include trustee and beneficiary, agent and principal, solicitor and client, director and company, employee and employer, and partners: see *Hospital Products* (1984) 156 CLR 41, 68 (Gibbs CJ), 96 (Mason J).

that the client's fully informed consent to the exclusion or modification of the fiduciary duties was required had no application. Instead, as the mandate letter was to be interpreted in accordance with ordinary principles of contract, the contractual stipulation should be given its full effect in the absence of some contractual flaw like mistake or misrepresentation. On this basis, his Honour decided that the relationship between Citigroup and Toll was not fiduciary. He concluded that 'the exclusion of the fiduciary relationship was effective, notwithstanding the fact that Citigroup undertook to provide financial advisory services to Toll and that both parties' interests were "well aligned" in the fee structure set out in the mandate letter.'[35]

That said, it is perhaps telling that Jacobson J makes two further observations about what ASIC *did not* argue in relation to the effect of the contractual stipulation. He notes that 'ASIC did not suggest that the factual matrix, or the object or purpose of the mandate letter, could bear upon the proper construction of the acknowledgement that the relationship between the parties was not fiduciary.'[36] Nor did ASIC argue 'that the words "including as a fiduciary" should be limited or read down by anything else in the terms of the lengthy acknowledgement.'[37] In so doing his Honour is at least inviting speculation about whether the result might have been different had ASIC done so.

IV ISSUE 2: THE CONFLICTS POINT

Having concluded that the relationship between Citigroup and Toll was not fiduciary, Jacobson J was not required to go further and decide whether Citigroup's proprietary trading in Patrick shares on the Friday before the bid was announced created for it a conflict of interest and duty that would be prohibited by equity. Nevertheless his Honour goes on, at [369] to [420], to address the allegations of conflict made by ASIC in its Further Amended Statement of Claim.[38] ASIC alleged that Citigroup's proprietary trading gave rise to five separate conflicts of interest and duty. Significantly, his Honour found against ASIC on all five allegations. This bears repeating. Jacobson J found that, even if a fiduciary relationship had existed between Citigroup and Toll,

[35] *ASIC v Citigroup* [2007] FCA 963, [337].
[36] Ibid [333].
[37] Ibid [334].
[38] Above n 12.

Citigroup's proprietary trading would not, in the circumstances, have given rise to a proscribed conflict of interest and duty.[39]

(A) *The* Daly *Positive Duty of Disclosure*

The first three of ASIC's allegations of conflict rested upon its argument that, as a fiduciary, Citigroup had a positive duty to disclose to Toll all information in its possession that might be relevant to the relationship and the advice provided under it. ASIC alleged that Citigroup had a personal interest that conflicted with the performance of this duty. ASIC said that Citigroup owed a positive duty of disclosure to Toll on the basis of the observations of Brennan J in *Daly*. In this regard Jacobson J said that:

> There is force in Citigroup's submission that Australian law does not recognise a fiduciary duty to make full disclosure. The strong weight of judicial authority is that fiduciary duties are proscriptive rather than prescriptive; accordingly, a fiduciary does not have a positive duty to disclose information… It may follow that Brennan J's observations in *Daly* are to be confined in the manner discussed by Austin J in *Aequitas* at [287]. … However I do not need to consider this question because in my view the claim [relating to the first alleged conflict] fails at a factual level.[40]

In *Aequitas* Austin J said that:

> In my opinion, in light of the reasoning in *Breen v Williams* [(1996) 186 CLR 71], Brennan J's dictum [in Daly] should be taken to refer, for the most part, to the contractual aspects of the adviser-client relationship. The duty to provide 'best advice' and to disclose knowledge and information arise out of the adviser's 'undertaking' … are therefore implied terms of the contractual retainer. And disclosure may also relieve the adviser from the fundamental fiduciary duty not to 'assume a position where his self-interest might conflict with the honest and impartial giving of advice'.[41]

---

[39] *ASIC v Citigroup* [2007] FCA 963, [369].
[40] *ASIC v Citigroup* [2007] FCA 963, [375].
[41] (2001) 19 ACLC 1006, [287].

ASIC's first three allegations of conflict relied upon it establishing that Citigroup had a positive duty, under *Daly*, to disclose certain information known to particular employees of Citigroup to Toll about its position in Patrick shares, and the impact of its proprietary trading on the market for Patrick in the lead-up to the bid. Jacobson J rejected (impliedly if not expressly) the existence of such a duty. ASIC said that the interest that Citigroup had that conflicted with this duty was its interest 'in maintaining its relationship with Toll, free from a perception by Toll that Citigroup's Chinese Walls had failed'.[42] On the facts, his Honour rejected each of those claims.

(B) *The Fourth and Fifth Allegations*

The fourth allegation of conflict related to what was essentially a conflict of interests, rather than a conflict of interest and duty. ASIC alleged that it was in the interests of Toll that the price of Patrick shares not increase, because if it did it would affect the credibility of the bid.[43] This is because an increase in the price of Patrick shares would lead to an erosion of the apparent premium being offered by Toll over the pre-bid market price of Patrick shares. Citigroup's proprietary trading in Patrick shares gave it a contrary interest in the price of Patrick, that it should go up so as to produce a profit in the proprietary trader's long position.[44]

Jacobson J does not address the apparent inconsistency between his characterising all five of ASIC's claims as being based on conflict of interest and duty[45] and his treatment of the fourth claim (correctly, it is submitted) as being based on a conflict of interest and interest. In other words, the fourth claim can properly be characterised as one involving, not a conflict of interest and duty, but a situation in which one party to the arrangement has a commercial interest which diverges from that of the other. Unlike the first to third claims, and the fifth, ASIC has not here alleged any duty on the part of Citigroup with which its interest in the price of Patrick shares might conflict.

Jacobson J decided against ASIC on the fourth conflict claim, on the basis that it failed to establish the Toll had the interest alleged (that is, an interest that the price of Patrick shares should not rise during

---

[42] *ASIC v Citigroup* [2007] FCA 963, [374] and also [380], [388].
[43] Ibid [395].
[44] Ibid [396].
[45] Ibid [369].

trading on 19 August).[46] In essence, this was because an earlier date (26 July) had already been selected as the reference date for the bid — that is, as the appropriate date from which to measure the premium.[47] Accordingly ASIC failed to establish that 'noise' in the Patrick price on the last business day before the bid was material to Toll in relation to the calculation of the bid premium.

The fifth allegation of conflict seems, on the basis of his Honour's observation at [413], to be the strongest, although it ultimately failed at a factual level.[48] The allegation relates to the position in which Citigroup found itself in the afternoon and evening of 19 August, when members of its senior management and compliance teams became aware of Citigroup's substantial proprietary shareholding in Toll. The allegation made by ASIC is that Citigroup's interest in the price of Patrick shares conflicted at this point with its duty to provide disinterested and loyal advice to Toll. As his Honour goes on to note:

> The pleaded case is confined by the particulars. Two risks are asserted. The first is that Citigroup had an interest in preserving its reputation free from a perception that its Chinese Walls had failed. The second is that the senior management might be required to make a decision as to whether the bid price should be increased. It is said that this could occur if [the IBD team leader] or Toll sought senior management's view as to the issue of the bid price.[49]

The reason the claim failed was because his Honour found that there was 'no evidence to support that allegation that there was a risk that' the views of senior management on the bid price would be sought.

V ISSUE 3: INFORMED CONSENT

Having concluded that the relationship between Citigroup and Toll was not fiduciary, and that even if it was there was no conflict of interest and duty, Jacobson J was not required to decide whether Toll had given informed consent to Citigroup's proprietary trading activities. Nevertheless his Honour does go on to conclude that Toll's informed

---

46 Ibid [403].
47 Ibid [399].
48 Ibid [416].
49 Ibid [412].

consent to Citigroup's proprietary trading could be implied from the circumstances.

As noted (in relation to issue 1) above, the question of informed consent arises in relation to two separate aspects of the judgment. The first relates to whether informed consent was required and obtained to the inclusion of the contractual stipulation in the mandate letter that excluded a fiduciary relationship between the parties. His Honour held on this point that informed consent was not required because the relationship was not fiduciary at the time the mandate letter was signed (noting that ASIC pleaded that the fiduciary relationship arose out of the mandate letter and did not pre-date it). This is discussed above. The second relates to (the obiter question of) whether informed consent was obtained to Citigroup being in a position of conflict as a result of its proprietary trading in Patrick shares.

The broader context for this second consideration of the nature of informed consent is that a fiduciary is not prohibited from being in a position of conflict, or from profiting from its office, if it has the fully informed consent of the person to whom its duty is owed.[50] So in other words, even if Citigroup were in a fiduciary relationship with Toll, it would be able to overcome any potential conflict of interest and duty raised by its proprietary trading through obtaining Toll's fully informed consent.

His Honour found that

> Citigroup did not obtain Toll's express consent to trade on its own account in the context of its advisory role in the Patrick takeover, but in my view informed consent is to be implied from Toll's knowledge of Citigroup's structure and method of operations. Toll's experience and "core competency" in mergers and acquisitions must also be taken into account in determining this question: See *Farah Constructions Pty Limited v Say-Dee Pty Limited* [2007] HCA 22 at [107] per Gleeson CJ, Gummow, Callinan, Heydon and Crennan JJ.[51]

---

[50] For example, in *Consul Developments Pty Ltd v DPC Estates Ltd* (1975) 132 CLR 373, McTiernan J notes that 'if after full and frank disclosure of all material facts to the person to whom such a duty … is owed and permission has been given to make a profit for himself out of transactions which would otherwise be in breach of duty he is, of course, absolved from any obligation to account': at 377.

[51] *ASIC v Citigroup* [2007] FCA 963, [355].

The point Jacobson J makes in relation to the consent is that there must be actual consent. That consent may be express or implied — here it was implied from the dealings between the parties. His Honour expressly (and rightly, it is submitted) distinguishes this from the situation in *Kelly v Cooper*,[52] where the contract between a real estate agent and its client was held to include an implied term allowing the agent to act for other principals selling similar properties. That term was implied by Lord Browne-Wilkinson[53] because the practice is notorious and it would otherwise be impossible for real estate agents to perform their ordinary business functions. Jacobson J is at pains to point out that this is not the case here: he says that 'there is nothing in the relationship of investment banker/financial adviser and client which requires a conclusion that it is an inherent part of the business of investment banking for the banker to engage in trading in its client's target's shares.'[54] Accordingly the client's actual (albeit implied) consent is required.

VI Issue 4: Conflicts Management and Chinese Walls

The discussion of issues 1, 2 and 3, above, deals with the core fiduciary arguments on which ASIC's case was based. We now move to consider a related issue, which arises out of the statutory obligation on financial services firms to manage conflicts of interest. In essence that issue is: do Chinese Walls work as a means of managing conflicts of interest?

The answer to that broader question, at least in the context of *ASIC v Citigroup* case, is complicated by the particular statutory context in which it arises. Under Australian law, people who carry on a business of providing financial services are required to hold an AFS licence; Citigroup held such a licence. Among other things, s 912A(1)(aa) of the *Corporations Act* provides that an AFS licensee must 'have in place adequate arrangements for the management of conflicts of interest that may arise wholly, or partially, in relation to activities undertaken by the licensee or a representative of the licensee in the provision of financial services as part of the financial services business'. This is one of the statutory provisions on which ASIC's civil proceedings against Citigroup were based. ASIC's case against Citigroup was that Citigroup had breached this duty by having breached a fiduciary duty owed by it to

[52] [1993] AC 205.
[53] Ibid 214.
[54] *ASIC v Citigroup* [2007] FCA 963, [360].

Toll. Having failed to establish that the relationship was fiduciary, ASIC necessarily failed to establish a breach of s 912A(1)(aa). Jacobson J notes that:

> ASIC did not concede that as a matter of construction the obligation in s 912A(1)(aa) only applies to a licensee who occupies a fiduciary position. However, ASIC did concede that in the present case that is how the conflict is said to arise. That is, the subsection is not engaged unless Citigroup and Toll were in a fiduciary relationship.[55]

In fact, s 912A(1)(aa) did not apply to Citigroup in this context.[56] The reason for this is that investment banking is expressly excluded from being treated as the provision of a financial service for the purposes of the *Corporations Act*, by reg 7.1.29(3)(c) of the *Corporations Regulations 2001* (Cth). The conflicts management obligation in s 912A(1)(aa) only applies to conflicts that arise in relation to activities undertaken by a licensee in 'the provision of financial services'. Because Citigroup was not providing a financial service, the conflicts management obligation did not apply.

Nevertheless, Jacobson J makes some useful (although necessarily limited) comments about what might amount to the adequate management of conflicts in the contemplation of a provision like s 912A(1)(aa). First, his Honour confirmed that, on the words of the statute, the 'management' of conflicts did not require their elimination (for example, by obtaining the client's express consent).[57] Secondly, his Honour confirmed that Chinese Walls can be an effective means of managing conflicts that might arise in this context.[58] Thirdly, his Honour re-confirmed that more than formal policies are required; there must be real engagement with the business for the wall to be effective.[59]

(A) *Chinese Walls*

At [310], [318] to [319] and [448] to [452], Jacobson J adopts with approval the approach to Chinese Walls taken by the UK Law

[55] Ibid [422].
[56] Ibid [440].
[57] Ibid [443]–[445].
[58] Ibid [448]–[452].
[59] Ibid [453]–[454].

Commission in its *Consultation Paper No 124*[60] and by Lord Millett in *Prince Jefri Bolkiah v KPMG.*[61] His Honour begins by pointing out that Chinese Walls do not, of themselves, eliminate conflicts of interest and duty. He then goes on to make this important observation:

> However, as the UK Law Commission observed, a financial conglomerate may obtain protection against any allegation of breach of the duty of loyalty if the client consents to the company carrying on business using Chinese Walls as part of its organisational structure. The extent of the duty of loyalty would then be determined according to the contractual arrangements between the parties: see *Law Commission Consultation Paper* at [4.5.1].[62]

In other words, the combination of an effective Chinese Wall and the client's consent given on the basis that the wall is in place and robust should be sufficient to avoid any allegation of conflict on the part of the conglomerate.

What makes an effective Chinese Wall? His Honour expressly adopts[63] the criteria developed by the Law Commission and articulated by Lord Millett in *Bolkiah* that there should be: (i) the physical separation of departments to insulate them from each other; (ii) an educational programme, normally recurring, to emphasise the importance of not improperly or inadvertently divulging confidential information; (iii) strict and carefully defined procedures for dealing with situations where it is thought the wall should be crossed, and the maintaining of proper records where this occurs; (iv) monitoring by compliance officers of the effectiveness of the Chinese Wall; and (v) disciplinary sanctions where there has been a breach of the wall.

Jacobson J goes on to refer with approval[64] to the comments of Bryson J in *D&J Constructions Pty Limited v Head*,[65] that 'it is not realistic to place reliance on such arrangement in relation to people with

---

[60] United Kingdom Law Commission, 'Fiduciary Duties and Regulatory Rules' (Consultation Paper No 124, 1992) [4.5]. The final report is Report No 236 (1995).
[61] [1999] 2 AC 222 ('*Bolkiah*'). See also Charles Hollander and Simon Salzedo, *Conflicts of Interest and Chinese Walls* (2nd ed, 2004).
[62] *ASIC v Citigroup* [2007] FCA 963, [315].
[63] Ibid [319].
[64] Ibid [320].
[65] (1987) 9 NSWLR 118, 123.

opportunities for daily contact over long periods'. Jacobson J cautions that:

> Adequate arrangements require more than a raft of written policies and procedures. They require a thorough understanding of the procedures by all employees and a willingness and ability to apply them to a host of possible conflicts.[66]

This is an important caution.

VII IMPLICATIONS FOR ADVISERS

Jacobson J's decision in *ASIC v Citigroup* does not in any way fundamentally change our understanding of the legal position of investment banks providing advisory services to sophisticated clients. Nevertheless his Honour does make a number of findings about the application of fiduciary duties to investment banks that are of significance for them and for other corporate advisers.

The *first* is that, but for the contractual stipulation that it was not, Jacobson J would have been inclined to treat the relationship between Citigroup and Toll as fiduciary.

The *second* is that a provision in a contract to the effect that the relationship created by the contract is not, and is not understood by either party to be, fiduciary should be effective to exclude a fiduciary relationship, so long as there is no mistake or misrepresentation or other contractual flaw. The fully informed (as distinct from ordinary contractual) consent of the affected party to the inclusion of such a provision is not required where the relationship is not one of the established categories of fiduciary relationship (such as agent and principal or trustee and beneficiary) and it cannot be shown (or, as in this case, it is not alleged) that a fiduciary relationship arose from the pre-contractual dealings between the parties.

The *third* is that where the relationship between the parties is one of the accepted fiduciary relationships or their pre-contractual dealings gave rise to fiduciary obligations, the fully informed consent of the affected party to the inclusion of a provision limiting or removing the fiduciary proscriptions would be required.

---

[66] *ASIC v Citigroup* [2007] FCA 963, [454].

The *fourth* is that equity will only prohibit a fiduciary from having an interest that conflicts with a duty owed by the fiduciary to the client where the nature of the interest, the extent of the duty, and the impact of the interest on the duty can be clearly demonstrated.

The *fifth* is that, where equity requires a person's informed consent to a relaxation or exclusion of the fiduciary proscriptions, that consent can be express or implied. Actual consent (whether express or implied) is required unless the state of affairs giving rise to the alleged conflict is notorious and is inherent to the fiduciary's ordinary business, in which case courts will imply into the arrangement a term permitting that state of affairs to exist.

The *sixth* is that an effective Chinese Wall, combined with the consent of the client to a fiduciary carrying on operations behind that wall that would otherwise have contravened the fiduciary proscriptions, will protect a financial conglomerate from allegations of breach of its duties of loyalty to the client.

VIII THE NATURE OF FIDUCIARY DUTIES

More broadly, the decision invites reflection on the nature of fiduciary duties and the relationship between the fiduciary obligations of loyalty and the other equitable and common law obligations (including obligations of confidence and good faith) that are referred to by Lord Millett in his Foreword to *Snell's Equity*.[67]

The question of whether Citigroup was in a fiduciary relationship with Toll was significant not in and of itself, but because a finding that the relationship was fiduciary would have indicated the application of the fiduciary proscriptions — the no conflicts rule and the no profits rule. These are the duties of loyalty to which Lord Millett refers. Finding that Citigroup is not a fiduciary means that the duties of loyalty do not apply, but the other equitable and common law duties still do.

In the execution of the mandate, Citigroup clearly came into possession of confidential information owned by Toll that would be and is protected by equity;[68] this is not in doubt. The restrictions that apply to Citigroup in the use of that information (specifically, preventing it from

---

[67] Above n 1.
[68] See R P Meagher, J D Heydon and M J Leeming, *Meagher, Gummow & Lehane's Equity: Doctrines & Remedies* (4th ed, 2002) ch 21 ('Confidential Information').

misusing that information for its own gain) apply regardless of whether the relationship between Citigroup and Toll is fiduciary. In other words, is it not necessary to show that a fiduciary relationship exists before the sorts of protections that surround confidential information are triggered.

Similarly, a finding that a particular relationship is not fiduciary will not of itself affect the application of a (positive) duty to a person to act in the interests of another person, where such a duty otherwise arises either as a matter of contract or under (other) equitable principles. The relationship between the positive duty to act in the interests of another person, and the negative duties to avoid unauthorised conflicts and unauthorised profits, is explained by Austin J in *Aequitas*. There, his Honour concluded that:

> In the High Court's view [in *Breen v Williams* (1986) 186 CLR 71], the essential fiduciary obligations were to avoid conflicts between interest and duty or between duty and duty, and profits arising out of the fiduciary office, in the absence of fully informed consent. Obligations to act in the interests of another, or to act prudently, are not fiduciary obligations. According to Dawson and Toohey JJ (at 93), what the law extracts from a fiduciary relationship is loyalty, often of an uncompromising kind, but no more than that. Gaudron and McHugh JJ (at 113) held that a fiduciary is obliged not to obtain any unauthorised benefit from the relationship and not to be in a position of conflict, but 'the law of this country does not otherwise impose positive legal duties on the fiduciary to act in the interests of the person to whom the duty is owed'. Gummow J (at 137) said that the special position of the trustee does not provide a proper foundation for 'the imposition upon fiduciaries in general of a quasi-tortious duty to act solely in the best interests of their principals'. Fiduciary obligations often arise in cases where one person is under an obligation to act in the interests of another, but that does not mean that the obligation to act in the interests of another is a fiduciary obligation.[69]

While the existence of a duty on one person to act in the interests of another person might be a necessary pre-condition for finding that the relationship between them is fiduciary, it is not a sufficient condition on its own. Nor, as Austin J points out, is the duty itself a fiduciary duty. A

---

[69] (2001) 19 ACLC 1006, [284].

person might have undertaken to act in the interests of another person, giving rise to a duty in contract or in equity to do so. However, as Jacobson J concludes in *ASIC v Citigroup*, the relationship between them will only be fiduciary if that person 'has undertaken to act in the interests of another *and not in his or her own interests*'.[70] Even then 'all the facts and circumstances must be carefully examined to see whether the relationship is, in substance, fiduciary'.[71] So for a relationship to be fiduciary there needs to be an expectation not only that one person will act in the interests of another, but also that they will subsume or sacrifice their own interests to do so.

IX IMPLICATIONS FOR REGULATION

In addition to its implications for advisers, the decision in *ASIC v Citigroup* obviously has implications for Australia's financial services regulation.

In commencing proceedings against Citigroup, it seems that ASIC was not primarily concerned with protecting the interests of Toll. Had it wished to complain about Citigroup's proprietary trading in Patrick shares, Toll presumably had sufficient resources of its own to do so. In fact, it appears from Jacobson J's judgment that Toll had no complaint (or at least no complaint that it wished to air in court). The evidence of Toll's Chief Financial Officer indicated that Toll understood that Citigroup would engage in proprietary trading, and had no objection so long as Citigroup did not misuse Toll's confidential information.[72]

Accordingly ASIC appears to have been acting in pursuit of a broader aim, directed at the integrity of the capital markets and of the actions of those who participate in them. In its press release issued on 31 March 2006 when the proceedings were commenced, ASIC's Deputy Chairman said 'this is a significant case raising two very important issues for the securities industry: having adequate arrangements for managing

[70] *ASIC v Citigroup* [2007] FCA 963, [272] (emphasis added).
[71] Ibid.
[72] Jacobson J says: 'It is true that [the Chief Financial Officer of Toll] did not turn his mind to the question of whether Citigroup would suspend its proprietary trading during the period of the mandate, but the effect of his evidence was that he accepted Citigroup could trade for third parties or for itself, so long as it did not use Toll's confidential information. … Moreover, [he] did not believe that Citigroup had an obligation to inform Toll if it engaged in proprietary trading, so long as there was no possibility of Citigroup using Toll's confidential information': ibid [357], [358].

inside information and dealing with conflicts of interest.'[73] ASIC's intention appears to have been force some change to existing investment banking practice (with which Citigroup was complying) in relation to these areas.

As is clear from Jacobson J's judgment (from which ASIC has since indicated it will not appeal),[74] ASIC's case in these areas was weak. Indeed, in terms of a case to test important principles about conflicts of interest and inside information, it could be characterised as poorly chosen and run. In particular, the case does little to enhance our understanding of the application of s 912A(1)(aa) outside the context of fiduciary relationships, or of the correctness of ASIC's Regulatory Guide 181.[75] The author's own view is that s 912A(1)(aa) is fundamentally flawed and should be repealed. Instead a licensee's conduct ought to be measured, as it traditionally has been, by reference to what is efficient, honest and fair (see s 912A(1)(a) of the *Corporations Act*).[76]

Beyond this, the approach taken in *ASIC v Citigroup* makes plain the fundamental difficulty with co-opting fiduciary principles into a regulatory framework. Here ASIC has sought to rely on a (private) fiduciary principle to achieve a (public) regulatory aim. The reason why this does not work is that fiduciary principles are applied having regard to the particular understanding and circumstances of the parties to the relationship, not to broader considerations about market integrity. If, as in *ASIC v Citigroup*, the parties agree that the fiduciary proscriptions should not apply, or should apply in a limited way, then a court will accept this, unless a statute expressly prevents contracting out of or limiting the fiduciary duties.[77] As Professor John Langbein has observed in relation to fiduciary principles in trust law (and this is equally true of fiduciary relationships based on contracts):

> Despite decades of pulpit-thumping rhetoric about the sanctity of fiduciary obligations, fiduciary duties in trust law are

---

[73] ASIC, 'ASIC Commences Proceedings against Citigroup for Conflicts and Insider Trading Breaches' (Press Release, 31 March 2006).
[74] ASIC, 'ASIC v Citigroup' (Press Release, 17 July 2007).
[75] *Licensing: Managing Conflicts of Interest* (Issued 30 August 2004).
[76] For a detailed discussion of the relationship between an AFS licensee and its clients, see Robert Baxt, Ashley Black and Pamela Hanrahan, *Securities and Financial Services Law* (6th ed, 2003) chs 12, 13.
[77] In a sense, this is the effect of ss 182 and 183 and pt 2D.1, div 2 of the *Corporations Act* in relation to a director's fiduciary duties to his or her company.

> unambiguously contractarian. The rules of trust fiduciary law mean to capture the likely understanding of the parties to the trust deal, which is why both the duty of loyalty and the duty of prudence yield to the more particularized intentions that the parties may choose to express or imply in their trust deal.[78]

The private law, contractarian nature of fiduciary duties in a commercial context make them a poor platform for the erection of regulatory structures that have interests other than those of the parties at their heart.

---

[78] John H Langbein, 'The Contractarian Basis of the Law of Trusts' (1995) 105 *Yale Law Journal* 625, 629. American fiduciary law, unlike the Australian law, includes a duty of prudence (that is, care).

Chapter 6

Enforcement of Capital Markets Regulation: The United Kingdom and Its International Markets

Iain MacNeil

The cornerstone of the regulatory system for capital markets in the United Kingdom is the *Financial Services and Markets Act 2000* (UK) c 8 ('*FSMA 2000*'). The Act is envisaged as a framework for regulation and therefore its focus is on regulatory procedures such as rule-making and enforcement rather than substantive rules, which are to be found largely in the rulebook of the regulator, the Financial Services Authority ('FSA').[1] The regulatory objectives of the *FSMA 2000* are:

a) Market confidence

The market confidence objective is maintaining confidence in the financial system. The financial system includes financial markets and exchanges, regulated activities and other activities connected with financial markets and exchanges. Market confidence does not imply a policy of preventing all failures but involves minimising the impact of failures and providing mechanisms to protect consumers of financial services (in the broad sense).[2]

---

[1] The rulebook is hereafter referred to as the '*FSA Handbook*', see FSA Website, <http://www.fsa.gov.uk>.

[2] See FSA, *Reasonable Expectations: Regulation in a Non-Zero Failure World* (2003). All FSA publications are available at <http://www.fsa.gov.uk>.

b) Public awareness

The public awareness objective is promoting public understanding of the financial system. This includes awareness of the benefits and risks associated with different kinds of investments and the provision of appropriate information and advice.

c) The protection of consumers

The consumer protection objective is securing the appropriate degree of protection for consumers. In considering what is appropriate, the FSA must have regard to risk, expertise, the need for information and advice and the general principle that consumers should take responsibility for their decisions. 'Consumer' is defined broadly and includes: (1) past, present and potential customers of authorised persons; (2) companies and persons entering into transactions in a business capacity; and, (3) persons who derive rights from persons who are 'consumers'.[3]

d) The reduction of financial crime

The reduction of financial crime objective is to reduce the extent to which it is possible for a business carried on (1) by a regulated person or (2) in contravention of the general prohibition against carrying on regulated activity without authorisation, to be used for a purpose in connection with financial crime. Financial crime includes any offence involving fraud or dishonesty; misconduct in, or misuse of information relating to, a financial market; or handling the proceeds of crime. The FSMA 2000 itself establishes offences falling within the scope of this objective, such as making misleading statements and engaging in market manipulation.[4]

The *FSMA 2000* also refers to principles of good regulation to which the FSA must have regard in carrying out its duties.[5] They are:

a) the need to use its resources in the most efficient and economic way;

---

[3] *FSMA 2000* (UK) s 138(7).
[4] *FSMA 2000* (UK) s 397.
[5] *FSMA 2000* (UK) ss 2(3), 73 in respect of the FSA's function as the competent authority for listing in the UK.

b) the responsibilities of those who manage the affairs of authorised persons;
c) the principle that a burden or restriction which is imposed on a person, or on the carrying on of an activity, should be proportionate to the benefits, considered in general terms, which are expected to result from the imposition of that burden or restriction;
d) the desirability of facilitating innovation in connection with regulated activities;
e) the international character of financial services and markets and the desirability of maintaining the competitive position of the United Kingdom;
f) the need to minimise the adverse effects on competition that may arise from anything done in the discharge of those functions;
g) the desirability of facilitating competition between those who are subject to any form of regulation by the Authority.

The *FSMA 2000* should not, however, be viewed as a comprehensive system of regulation for capital markets, because it operates alongside other legal regimes which make an important contribution. From the perspective of listed entities, company law is of particular significance because it sets out the basic regulatory obligations applicable to all companies. For example, disclosure and statutory accounting obligations apply to most companies in one form or another. From the perspective of market participants (such as brokers, investment banks and fund managers), the *FSMA 2000* regulatory system operates in tandem with contractual and fiduciary obligations owed to customers in specific circumstances: these regulatory and private law obligations often appear quite similar but they are rarely coextensive. The Panel on Takeovers and Mergers is also a significant feature of the United Kingdom regulatory regime, reflecting the importance of takeovers as part of the corporate governance system in the UK. Viewed in its entirety, the regulatory system for capital markets in the United Kingdom is therefore much more than *FSMA 2000*: it is in reality a combination of legal sources which operate in different ways and pursue different objectives.

The regulatory objectives of *FSMA 2000* do not provide a clear roadmap towards an enforcement strategy, but they do provide an initial indication that enforcement is unlikely to be a mechanistic response to every contravention. That initial impression is borne out by the manner in which enforcement policy and practice has developed within the *FSMA 2000* regulatory regime and associated legal regimes. As discussed below, several features of the United Kingdom's regulatory system result in formal enforcement action being quite rare. That outcome is capable of many different interpretations.[6] In order to set it in context, I begin by first looking at the development of *FSMA 2000* regulation and then the role of self-regulatory rules and market discipline in the United Kingdom model. I then move on to examine the link between models of responsibility and enforcement. I conclude by examining the modes of enforcement and sanctions that are available within the *FSMA 2000* system.

I Risk-Based Regulation and Enforcement

A risk-based approach to regulation is now firmly embedded in the regulatory system established under FSMA 2000. That outcome is the result of a deliberate policy choice made by the FSA, as there is nothing in the statutory framework that explicitly or implicitly requires the FSA to adopt such an approach.[7] It does, however, reflect a broader move in regulatory systems towards a risk-based approach.[8] The meaning of risk-based regulation within the FSMA 2000 context is made clear by the following explanation given by the FSA Chairperson:

> The theory of risk management at the FSA is very close to that of risk management in a financial firm, in that there are the same elements of setting aims (in our case attaining our

---

[6] For a discussion of the possible causes and implications of the low-level of formal enforcement action in the UK by comparison with the US, see John Coffee, 'Law and the Market: The Impact of Enforcement' (Paper delivered at the Dynamics of Capital Market Governance Forum, Australian National University, 14 March 2007).

[7] See Joanna Gray and Jenny Hamilton, *Implementing Financial Regulation: Theory and Practice* (2006) 28. The Treasury-commissioned Hampton Review, *Reducing Administrative Burdens: Effective Inspection and Enforcement*, March 2005, Recommendation 1, 115, recommended that all regulatory activity should be on the basis of a clear, comprehensive risk assessment.

[8] See, eg, Better Regulation Commission, *Risk, Responsibility and Regulation, Whose Risk Is It anyway?* <http://www.brc.gov.uk> at 21 February 2007; Bridget M Hutter, 'The Attractions of Risk-Based Regulation: Accounting for the Emergence of Risk Ideas in Regulation' (Discussion Paper No 33, Centre for Analysis of Risk and Regulation, London School of Economics, 2005), available at <http://www.lse.ac.uk/collections/CARR> at 21 February 2007.

> statutory objectives rather than a financial objective), establishing our risk appetite, identifying risks to our statutory objectives, establishing an agreed measure of risk, monitoring those risks, and managing them through both those with direct responsibility and those who provide challenge. At a reasonably high level of generality, the process of risk management in the FSA and in a financial firm are the same. And at a very high level of abstraction, they are the same: a cycle of risk identification, measurement, mitigation, control and monitoring.[9]

As regards enforcement, risk-based regulation has two important implications. First, not all contraventions are necessarily the subject of enforcement action. Second, specific priority areas may be targeted for action because of the implications they carry in terms of risk to the FSA's statutory objectives.[10] The corollary, of course, is that there will be some contraventions that are ignored or fall below the regulatory radar because they occur in relatively low risk areas. Furthermore, there may well be instances in which the appropriateness of enforcement is predicated on the FSA's perception of the individual or specific firm. In that sense, there may be a perception of injustice on the part of an entity selected for enforcement action, where the purpose of that action is primarily to change the behaviour of others who are likely to have engaged in the same course of conduct. The net result is that risk-based regulation envisages from the outset that enforcement will not be an automatic response to a contravention. In the FSA's own words: 'The risk-based approach is as valid for enforcement as for the FSA's other activities. One practical consequence of this is that the FSA cannot, and does not, attempt to pursue every rule breach.'[11] Statistics on enforcement tend to reinforce this view. There have been only 49 occasions[12] on which a financial penalty has been imposed on a firm since N2,[13] and in more than half of those cases the firm was designated

---

[9] Sir Callum McCarthy, FSA Chairman, 'Risk Based Regulation: The FSA's Experience' (Speech delivered at the ASIC Summer School, Sydney, 13 February 2006).

[10] See FSA CEO John Tiner's Overview in the FSA, *FSA Business Plan 2006/2007* (2006) 14, for a re-statement of this approach to enforcement.

[11] FSA, *Enforcement Process Review: Report and Recommendations* (2005) 7, available at <http://www.fsa.gov.uk/pubs/other/enf_process_review_report.pdf>.

[12] Out of a total of 59 enforcement actions against authorised firms since N2: see FSA, *Enforcement Process Review*, above n 11.

[13] The date on which *FSMA 2000* became effective: 1 December 2001.

as 'high risk' within the FSA's risk classification system for authorised firms.[14] However, any interpretation of the low incidence of enforcement action in the UK must take into account that enforcement action is only one of the regulatory tools available to the FSA to deal with contraventions. Alternatives, which are regarded by the FSA as contributing to compliance, include supervisory action, theme work and the policy consultation process. It follows that there can be no simple conclusions drawn between the low incidence of enforcement action and levels of compliance, because compliance is a function of several different factors and it is difficult to separate the causal effect of each.

II PRINCIPLES-BASED REGULATION AND ENFORCEMENT

(A) *The Move towards More-Principles-Based Regulation*

The FSA is committed to developing principles-based regulation.[15] The rationale is that 'this can produce better outcomes for both consumers and the financial services industry by encouraging a keen focus on how best to act in a particular situation rather than simply following a more mechanistic approach.'[16] The emphasis on outcomes in principle-based regulation rather than inputs or processes has been stressed by the FSA, and so too has the flexibility offered by principles-based regulation to firms in responding to regulation in terms of the structure and conduct of their business.[17] Underlying this policy are two assumptions. The first is that principles-based regulation can be readily identified and differentiated from 'rule-based' regulation.[18] On its website, the FSA

---

[14] The FSA uses a system called ARROW (Advanced Risk Response Operating Framework) to categorise authorised firms according to their risk profile.

[15] See FSA, *FSA Simplification Plan* (2006) 3; FSA, *FSA Business Plan 2006/2007*, above n 10, 10.

[16] FSA, *FSA Simplification Plan*, above n 15, 3.

[17] See, eg, Dan Waters, FSA Director Retail Policy, 'Implementing Principles Based Regulation' (Speech delivered at the Association of British Insurers Conference, London, 7 December 2006), available at <http://www.fsa.gov.uk/pages/Library/Communication/Speeches/2006/1207_dw.shtml> at 5 February 2007.

[18] The proposition that the meaning of principles-based regulation is subject to some uncertainty in the financial world is supported by anecdotal evidence: see, eg, 'FSA Regulation Move to Cost City £50m', *Financial Times* (London), 7 February 2007, 4 (reporting that 'Some finance professionals are likely to balk at the cost [of the move to

poses the following question: 'What does the FSA mean by "principles-based regulation" rather than "rules"?' It provides the following answer:

> Our approach is underpinned by the principle that it is neither possible nor desirable to write a rule to cover every specific situation or need for decision that a regulated firm might encounter. Instead, we focus on the Principles set out in the *FSMA*. These set out in more general terms the types of behaviour that we expect of firms and individuals (for example — 'A firm must conduct its business with due skill, care and diligence').[19]

At one level, the structure of the *FSA Handbook* makes the principle–rule distinction quite straight-forward. It comprises high-level principles and detailed rules, which are often linked directly with the principles and expressed as giving more precise content to the generality of the principle. Such an approach is also evident in other aspects of the United Kingdom regulatory regime, such as the 'true and fair' override for accounts and audit,[20] and the 'comply or explain' approach of the *Combined Code on Corporate Governance* ('*Combined Code*' or '*Code*'). However, it is difficult to judge from this feature alone how far the regulatory system is based on principles as opposed to rules. Nor does it help particularly to compare the volume of rules that sit underneath principles, because that exercise does not in itself contribute to an understanding of the relationship between the principles and the rules. The critical features are (a) the extent to which the principles can, in isolation, form the basis for compliance and enforcement and (b) alternatively, the extent to which principles can override specific rules that flow from the principle. Thus, while it may be possible to identify regulatory systems that adopt some elements of a principles-based approach,[21] it is only when these two characteristics are present that a system can be regarded as being based on, rather than just influenced by,

---

principles-based regulation], especially given continued uncertainty in the City about the meaning of principles-based regulation and how it will work in practice').

[19] See FSA, *Facts and Figures* <http://www.fsa.gov.uk/Pages/About/Media/Facts/index.shtml> at 20 February 2007.

[20] See *Companies Act 1985* (UK) c 6, ss 226A, 235 respectively ('*Companies Act 1985*').

[21] For a discussion of such systems see Christie L Ford, 'New Governance, Compliance and Principles-based Securities Regulation' (2007) *American Business Law Journal* (forthcoming), available at <http://ssrn.com/abstract=970130> at 21 May 2007.

a principles-based approach. That is an issue I return to in Section B below.

The second assumption underlying the FSA policy is that principles-based regulation is superior as a regulatory technique to rule-based regulation. That is a common assertion[22] in the post-Enron and WorldCom environment, but not one that is always supported by evidence or reasoned argument.[23] The FSA's arguments in favour of the superiority assertion are that:[24]

a) detailed prescriptive standards have not in the past prevented misconduct;
b) the current volume and complexity of FSA standards acts as both a barrier to entry and a barrier to compliance;
c) prescriptive rules divert attention towards compliance with the letter rather than the spirit of the standard;
d) many issues are not dealt with adequately by prescriptive standards, or can be dealt with in that way only at the cost of making the system overly complex;
e) prescriptive standards are costly for FSA and consumer resources.

These arguments are certainly persuasive to some degree but they also reflect implicit judgments in respect of the causal influences that contribute to the success or failure of the regulatory system. There have been few attempts to subject the superiority assertion to widespread scrutiny or testing, but this process has occurred to some extent in the field of accounting standards, where the principles-versus-rules debate

---

[22] For example, FSA CEO John Tiner has said that: 'In short, the use of principles is a more grown-up approach to regulation than one that relies on rules': 'Principles Based Regulation: The EU Context' (Speech delivered at the APCIMS Annual Conference, Barcelona, 13 October 2006), available at <http://www.fsa.gov.uk/pages/Library/Communication/Speeches/2006/1013_jt.shtml>.

[23] See Andrew Hill, *Lombard Column*, *Financial Times* (London), 7 February 2007, referring to the role of the superiority assertion in the regulatory debate in the United States: 'The FSA is right to pioneer the principles-based approach, although its American fans have exaggerated the UK's progress in their own self-interest'.

[24] The most complete version seems to be in Andrew Whittaker, FSA Director General Counsel, 'Professional and Financial Regulation — Conflict or Convergence?' (Speech delivered at the Fountain Court Chambers Conference, 31 January 2006), available at <http://www.fsa.gov.uk/pages/Library/Communication/Speeches/2006/0131_aw.shtml>.

has a longer lineage.[25] In that context, recent versions of the superiority assertion have been premised on the basis that a rule-based system of accounting standards in the United States contributed to the collapse of Enron in a manner that would not have occurred had the (supposedly) more principles-based accounting standards in the UK applied.[26] However, it has been argued that it is simply wrong[27] to characterise accounting standards in the United States as more rule and less principle-based than those in the UK, and that a better explanation is that Enron was indicative of a failure to apply auditing principles in a manner which recognised the qualitative nature of accounting and instead applied rules in a mechanistic manner.[28] A variant on that argument is that the US Generally Accepted Accounting Principles do not lack a foundation of principles, but rather that auditors are unable or unwilling, because of the influence exerted over them by their clients, to interpret principles according to their spirit or to override the application of rules on the basis of principles.[29] Thus, as regards support for the superiority claim, it seems clear that much rests on the perceived status of the UK as having prospered under a version of principles-based regulation combined with the absence of a major failure on the scale of Enron.[30]

Another issue to be clarified in this context is the relationship between principles-based regulation and 'light-touch' regulation. While the former relates to the structure and formulation of rules and can in principle be applied across the entire range of FSA regulation, light-touch regulation is more limited in its scope and relates to the substance of the obligations imposed rather than their formulation. The FSA has made clear that light-touch regulation is appropriate for the wholesale (or

---

[25] See Institute of Chartered Accountants of Scotland, *Principles Not Rules: A Question of Judgement* (2006), available at <http://www.icas.org.uk> at 23 February 2007.

[26] Waters, above n 17, 3, comments: 'We need not look too far to find the sort of regime that a defensive, legalistic approach will lead to. How many years would it take before we had our very own Enron experience?'

[27] See also William W Bratton, 'Enron, *Sarbanes-Oxley* and Accounting: Rules versus Principles versus Rents' (2003) 48 *Villanova Law Review* 1023.

[28] See David Kershaw, 'Evading Enron: Taking Principles Too Seriously in Accounting Regulation' (2005) 68 *Modern Law Review* 594.

[29] See Bratton, above n 27, 1047–51.

[30] Recent comments by Federal Reserve Chairman Ben Bernanke do however make the case for a broad adoption of principles-based regulation in US based on its proven success in the US banking sector: see 'Bernanke Calls for UK-style Regulation', *Financial Times* (London), 15 May 2007 (online edition).

inter-professional) marketplace[31] and has not referred to this approach in the concept of retail markets.[32] Thus, it would be wrong to equate principles-based regulation with less onerous regulation in the sense that principles-based regulation represents an implementation choice and not a choice as regards the substance or intensity of regulation.[33] For example, few would doubt that the *Combined Code* is principles-based, but it represents an additional tier of regulation for listed companies, and regulates matters such as board structure and composition in a manner that had not occurred before its introduction.

(B) *The Enforcement Implications of Principles-Based Regulation*

As suggested earlier, there are (at least) two tests for identifying a principles-based regulatory system. The first is whether the principles can stand on their own for the purposes of compliance and enforcement.[34] The second, relevant in particular when there may be the

[31] See Thomas Huertas, FSA Director Wholesale Firms Division, 'Regulating the Relationship: Banks, Firms and the FSA' (Speech delivered at the Joint AFB and ACT Conference, 8 February 2005), available at <http://www.fsa.gov.uk/Pages/Library/Communication/Speeches/2005/sp226.shtml> at 20 February 2007.

[32] But note the comment in the Treasury-commissioned Macrory Report, *Regulatory Justice: Making Sanctions Effective* (2006) 34, available at <http://www.cabinetoffice.gov.uk/REGULATION/news/2006/060522.asp> at 20 February 2007, concurring with the view of the Better Regulation Commission that the regulatory regime (across all sectors) 'remains light touch'. It is not entirely clear if that is intended as shorthand for regulation being appropriate and proportionate or whether it means, as in the FSA context, less intense regulation.

[33] The restructuring of the anti-money laundering requirements provides an example. The FSA replaced 57 pages of detailed rules with two pages of high-level principles, deleting rules with over £250 million of administrative costs. No claim was made, however, about the intensity of regulation, which has presumably remained the same following the changes, not least because of the obligations imposed externally by the EU.

[34] For this purpose the potential complication of distinguishing clearly between principles and rules is ignored. Even within a regulatory system such as *FSMA 2000*, which distinguishes explicitly between principles and rules, the matter may become confused. The FSA, when referring to enforcement, has sometimes described principles as rules: see, eg, Clive Briault, FSA Managing Director Retail Markets, 'Treating Customers Fairly and More Principles-Based Regulation' (Speech delivered at the FSA Summer School, Cambridge, 24 July 2006), available at <http://www.fsa.gov.uk/pages/Library/Communication/Speeches/2006/0724_cb.shtml> at 5 February 2007: 'Finally, what does a more principles-based approach mean for

possibility that compliance with detailed rules in a particular instance will result in a departure from a principle, is whether principles are capable of overriding rules.[35] In both instances it seems clear that if the test is met the system can correctly be described as principles-based. These tests distinguish a true principles-based system of regulation from those in which principles may be present to some degree but do not meet the two tests.[36]

Closely linked with the issue of whether a particular principle has the capacity to be enforced independently, is the issue of predictability. This focuses on whether a principle has sufficient content to guide the regulated to compliant solutions and to provide a sufficiently clear basis for the regulator to be able to take enforcement action. The issue of predictability is important in both the formal sense of compliance with the European Convention on Human Rights[37] and also in terms of the perceived validity of the enforcement process within the regulated community.[38] Its practical relevance can now be seen in the frequent reference within FSA rules and guidance to the high-level principle from which they are derived. While such a strategy cannot cope with every possibility, it does provide a means whereby the purpose and objective of the principle becomes clearer, with the result that firms are better able to determine their own implementation of a principle in a given situation.

---

enforcement? Three points are worth noting here. *First, our Principles are rules*. We can take enforcement action on the basis of them' (emphasis added).

[35] This is the essence of the 'true and fair' override which applies both to directors in their preparation of accounts and auditors in the giving of an audit opinion: see David Flint, *A True and Fair View in Company Accounts* (1982), available at <http://www.icas.org.uk> at 20 February 2007.

[36] See, eg, Ford, above n 21, for a much broader definition of principles-based regulation. It is true (as Ford comments) that virtually all systems of securities regulation are based on principles to some degree. However, my contention is that the two enforcement tests distinguish what may be regarded as the embedding of principles within the system from the inevitable inclusion of some (usually weak) form of principles within a regulatory system.

[37] *Convention for the Protection of Human Rights and Fundamental Freedoms*, opened for signature 4 November 1950, CETS No 005 (entered into force 3 September 1953) ('*Convention for Protection of Human Rights*'), incorporated into the law in the United Kingdom by the *Human Rights Act 1998* (UK) c 42 ('*Human Rights Act 1998*').

[38] The latter point in particular has not been lost on the FSA, which has frequently referred to the need for its principles to satisfy the requirement of predictability: see, eg, Whittaker, above n 24.

It is clear from the structure of FSMA 2000 and the FSA Handbook that FSA principles are capable of being enforced independently. This was apparent even before the recent initiative to move to more principles-based regulation. For example, in 2002 the Court of Appeal upheld a decision of the Disciplinary Appeals Tribunal of the Securities and Futures Authority to apply SFA[39] Principles directly to an individual.[40] More recent examples of the independent enforcement of principles are the penalty of £13.9m imposed on Citigroup[41] for breach of FSA Principles 2[42] and 3[43] in connection with a failure to control the firm's bond trading, and the penalty of £6.3m imposed on Deutsche Bank[44] for breach of Principles 5[45] and 2 in connection with book-building and price stabilisation exercises. The significance of these cases is that enforcement action was not possible under the market abuse regime because the relevant conduct fell outside the scope of the regime in each instance: it was only through independent enforcement of principles that the FSA was able to take action. A similar approach to the independent enforcement of principles can be found in the retail financial sector.[46]

[39] The Securities and Futures Authority had regulated investment firms prior to the creation of the FSA.

[40] *R (ex parte Fleurose) v Securities & Futures Authority* [2002] IRLR 297. In that case, the individual was found to be in breach of Principles 1 and 3 and suspended from acting as a 'registered person' for two years.

[41] See 'FSA Fines Citigroup £13.9 million (€20.9mn) for Eurobond Trades' (Press Release, 28 June 2005), available at <http://www.fsa.gov.uk/pages/Library/Communication/PR/2005/072.shtml> at 26 February 2007.

[42] *FSA Handbook* PRIN 2.1.1R: 'A firm must conduct its business with due skill, care and diligence.'

[43] *FSA Handbook* PRIN 2.1.1R: 'A firm must take reasonable care to organise and control its affairs responsibly and effectively, with adequate risk management systems.'

[44] See 'FSA Fines Deutsche Bank £6.3 million and Mr David Maslen £350,000 for Market Conduct' (Press Release, 11 April 2006), available at <http://www.fsa.gov.uk/pages/Library/Communication/PR/2006/036.shtml> at 26 February 2006.

[45] *FSA Handbook* PRIN 2.1.1R: 'A firm must observe proper standards of market conduct.'

[46] See the enforcement action taken against the Nationwide Building Society <http://www.fsa.gov.uk/pubs/final/nbs.pdf>; GE Capital Bank <http://www.fsa.gov.uk/pubs/final/gecb.pdf>; and Home and County Mortgages <http://www.fsa.gov.uk/pubs/final/hcml.pdf>.

The most important implication of the independent enforceability of FSA principles is that firms and individuals cannot rely on compliance with detailed rules as an adequate compliance strategy. In that sense firms and individuals bear the risks associated with the application of principles to new developments or unforeseen circumstances,[47] with the proviso that the principle provides a sufficient degree of predictability regarding the range of appropriate responses. How extensive that risk will become as principles-based regulation expands depends to a considerable extent on (a) the reaction of the courts[48] to the challenges that are likely to be made in instances in which principles are argued not to have the required degree of predictability, and (b) the extent to which the FSA 'fleshes out' principles through rules and guidance. Rather ominously, the FSA, in observing that enforcement of principles may require a different approach to the enforcement of rules, has pointed to the possibility that greater use may have to be made of expert evidence.[49] If that is indeed the case, it suggests that principles-based enforcement may result in tension and confusion, with the ex ante benefits of principles-based regulation being offset to some extent ex post by a more complex and costly system of enforcement.

III THE ROLE OF SELF-REGULATION AND MARKET DISCIPLINE

At one level the regulatory regime for capital markets can be viewed as comprising regulatory (or public law) principles and rules that are enforced primarily by public authorities. That view, however, ignores two important influences on the regulatory regime. The first is the body of private law rules that govern transactions in the capital markets and the organisational structure of entities that engage in those transactions. Private law is relevant because the regulatory system is (largely) premised on the basis that the role of regulation is to address market

---

[47] See, for a general discussion of this transfer of risk in regulatory systems, Louis Kaplow, 'Rules versus Principles: An Economic Analysis' (1992) 42 *Duke Law Journal* 557, 559–60.

[48] The Financial Services and Markets Tribunal has a wide-ranging jurisdiction over many of the FSA's decisions, including those of a disciplinary nature. It is not an 'appeals' tribunal in the strict sense, as it determines matters de novo and is able to consider fresh evidence that was not available to the FSA. The Tribunal must determine what, if any, is the appropriate action for the FSA to take. Decisions of the Tribunal may, with permission, be appealed to the courts on a point of law.

[49] Waters, above n 17, 3.

failure, which occurs when the market mechanisms, which include private law, fail to provide adequate solutions. An example of this linkage can be seen in the FSA's current work on contract certainty in London's wholesale international insurance market. While the FSA is concerned that the absence of adequate disclosure of brokers' commissions may be harmful to London's international competitiveness, it has made clear that it will only intervene via regulation if appropriate contractual solutions cannot be reached within the marketplace.[50] The second influence is that of self-regulation, which, despite a deliberate policy shift towards statutory-based regulation in the UK since the mid-1980s, remains an important element of the regulatory regime. Indeed, such has been the success of the most prominent example of self-regulation, the *Combined Code*, that it has become one of the UK's most successful exports during the past decade. Self-regulation, and in particular its implementation in the *Combined Code*, means that the regulatory system and its enforcement has to find a means to accommodate the quite different culture of market discipline that is given effect by the *Code*. As discussed below, this gives rise to some potential difficulties. The *Combined Code*[51] does not form part of the UKLA[52] Listing Rules. This has the effect that the *Code* itself does not have the same legal status as the Listing Rules, which are made and can be enforced under statutory authority.[53] The Listing Rules[54] do, however, require that in the case of a company incorporated in the United Kingdom, the following additional items must be included in its annual report and accounts:

---

[50] John Tiner, FSA CEO, 'Principles-Based Regulation and What It Means for Insurers' (Speech delivered at the Insurance Sector Conference, 20 March 2006), available at <http://www.fsa.gov.uk/pages/Library/Communication/Speeches/2006/0320_jt.shtml> at 20 February 2007.

[51] For the current and previous version of the *Code*, see Listing Rules in the *FSA Handbook*, available at <http://www.fsa.gov.uk> at 15 April 2005.

[52] In its role as the designated 'competent authority', for the purpose of the EC Directives on listing, the FSA operates under the title of United Kingdom Listing Authority.

[53] See *FSMA 2000* Pt VI.

[54] *FSA Handbook* LR 9.8.6R. Non-compliance results in a breach of the Listing Rules, which can be sanctioned by public censure, fine or suspension from listing under the *FSMA 2000*. There are no instances in which the FSA or Financial Reporting Council ('FRC') has taken action against a company for failing to make disclosures associated with the *Combined Code*.

a) a statement of how it has applied the principles set out in s 1 of the *Combined Code*, providing explanation which enables its shareholders to evaluate how the principles have been applied;
b) a statement as to whether or not it has complied throughout the accounting period with the *Code* provisions set out in s 1 of the *Combined Code*. A company that has not complied with the *Code* provisions, or complied with only some of the *Code* provisions or (in the case of provisions whose requirements are of a continuing nature) complied for only part of an accounting period, must specify the *Code* provisions with which it has not complied, and (where relevant) for what part of the period such non-compliance continued, and give reasons for any non-compliance.

The statement required by paragraph (a) is generally referred to as the 'appliance' statement, while the statement required by paragraph (b) is termed the 'compliance' statement. It can be seen that the Listing Rules require not just disclosure that there has or has not been compliance, but a reasoned explanation of non-compliance in respect of each instance of non-compliance. This approach forms the basis of the 'comply or explain' principle, because without adequate explanation in the event of non-compliance, there can be no possibility of the market evaluating whether or not it is justified. The disclosure obligation provides a mechanism whereby outsiders such as investors and analysts can observe and monitor compliance with the *Combined Code*. This is not to say, however, that compliance is an objective matter on which all observers agree. There is, for example, considerable divergence between the percentage of companies who consider themselves to be fully compliant (47 per cent) with the *Code* and those whom Pensions Investment Research Consultants Ltd ('PIRC') regards as fully compliant (34 per cent).[55] Moreover, not all aspects of the *Code* are capable of independent verification.[56] This point carries implications for the operation of the 'comply or explain' principle. A company which believes that it complies with the *Code*, but in reality does not, will not provide a non-compliance statement, and therefore the market will not be called on to

---

[55] See PIRC, *Corporate Governance Annual Review 2004* (2004) 9.

[56] PIRC comments that interpretation is often required as to whether there has been compliance as a result of drafting ambiguities (in the *Code*) or because there are different ways of understanding a particular issue: ibid.

exercise judgment in relation to that issue, at least not immediately.[57] However, as it seems likely that the market will weed out covert non-compliance over time,[58] the main effect of differing views of compliance as between companies and outsiders is to delay, rather than to prevent, a finding of non-compliance.[59]

Non-compliance with the 'comply or explain' obligation contained in the *Code* should in principle trigger two responses. The first is that investors should demand that an adequate explanation be given. There is little evidence in the public domain that this does in fact occur.[60] However, there are two complicating factors. One is that there is some evidence to suggest that a company which is able to sustain relative out-performance in its share price will not be asked to provide a 'comply or explain' reason for its departure from the *Combined Code*.[61] A possible rationalisation of this outcome is that the board of such a company has demonstrated superior management skills and should therefore be permitted greater leeway in setting the organisational and operational framework.[62] Another is that investors may prefer to exert influence in private rather than public on the basis that public disagreements are likely to be damaging to reputation and the share price. The second response that might be triggered by contravention of the 'comply or explain' principle is enforcement action by the FSA or FRC.[63] To date, no such action has been initiated, indicating that attention has focused on

---

[57] Assuming of course that the market cannot independently discover non-compliance as it occurs. It seems likely that the market will discover covert non-compliance over time, not least because reports from organisations such as the PIRC are prepared specifically to inform institutional investors.

[58] This is likely to occur as a result of monitoring by or on behalf of institutional investors: see, eg, the PIRC surveys.

[59] This can also be evidenced in the PIRC, above n 55, where the compliance rate is increasing year-by-year.

[60] See Sridhar Arcot, Valentina Bruno and Antoine Grimaud, *Corporate Governance in the UK: Is the Comply-or-Explain Approach Working?* (2005) London School of Economics <http://fmg.lse.ac.uk/upload_file/496_1st%20Dec%20paper.pdf> at 26 February 2007, finding that one in five explanations for non-compliance is not a good explanation.

[61] See Iain MacNeil and Xiao Li, 'Comply or Explain: Market Discipline and Non-Compliance with the *Combined Code*' (2006) 14 *Corporate Governance: An International Review* 486.

[62] Of course, such an outcome raises the possibility of escalation of risk when the board is permitted such leeway on the basis of share price performance, which turns out to have been based on a false premise. Enron provides a cautionary tale in this regard.

[63] See below Part V Section A for the role of the FRC.

the formal aspect of the 'explain' obligation in instances of non-compliance rather than on whether a proper explanation has been given. An additional complication in this field is that the FSA's focus on market detriment as the driver of enforcement action suggests that it would be reluctant to act if institutional investors were satisfied with a given explanation.[64]

Rather perversely, it appears to be the case that pure self-regulation on the part of investors may work more effectively than the hybrid form of self-regulation that is represented by the *Combined Code*.[65] Some evidence for this may be found in the operation of the self-regulatory rules developed by the Association of British Insurers/National Association of Pension Funds in respect of share issues made by listed companies. The underlying objective of these rules is to add an additional layer of regulation to the statutory rules governing pre-emption rights that aim to protect the proportionate shareholding of investors when new share issues are made.[66] In contrast with the position under the *Combined Code*, there is evidence both of *ex ante* approval of new issues and *ex post* enforcement action in respect of contraventions. Perhaps it is the case that there are more direct private benefits associated with enforcement in this sphere (ie avoidance of dilution of a shareholding) than in relation to the *Combined Code*; but even so, it is somewhat surprising to find that the more formal enforcement structure under the *Combined Code* appears to be less active.

Another limitation of the 'comply or explain' obligation in the Listing Rules is that it applies only to companies incorporated in the UK.[67] This appears to link the *Code* more with company law, which

---

[64] See MacNeil and Li, above n 61, noting the link between share price performance and tolerance of non-compliance accompanied by inadequate explanation.

[65] The *Combined Code* can be regarded as a hybrid form of self-regulation because, although it developed outside the formal legal framework, it is closely linked with the listing rules and there is the potential for the FSA to enforce the 'comply or explain' disclosure obligation. An alternative description of the *Code*, favoured by the FRC, is 'market-led regulation', but that obscures rather than clarifies its legal status.

[66] See generally Iain MacNeil, 'Shareholders' Pre-Emptive Rights' (2002) *Journal of Business Law* 78.

[67] The reference to a company incorporated in the United Kingdom in *FSA Handbook* LR 9.8.6R makes clear that the *Combined Code* does not apply to overseas listed companies in the United Kingdom. In this respect, the United Kingdom differs from some other jurisdictions: see Iain MacNeil and Alex Lau, 'International Corporate Regulation: Listing Rules and Overseas Companies' (2001) 50 *International and Comparative Law Quarterly* 787, 806. However, to be included in the FTSE 100 index, foreign-listed

applies in that manner, rather than with the Listing Rules, which apply as a result of the process of admission to listing. While that is an odd outcome for a governance *Code* that in its genesis and development aimed to place itself outside the formal structure of company law, it can be rationalised on the basis that to apply the *Code* to overseas listed companies would damage the UK's competitive position in attracting foreign listings. It is nevertheless ironic that a Code, which is trumpeted as a major achievement of the UK's regulatory system,[68] should not form part of the regulatory framework for international companies when many are attracted in the first instance by the quality of the regulatory regime.[69] The UK approach stands in sharp contrast to the extension, through s 404(a) of the *Sarbanes-Oxley Act of 2002*,[70] of the 'internal controls' requirements of federal securities law in the United States to foreign companies registered with the SEC. It also opens up the possibility, when the FRC's *Internal Control: Revised Guidance for Directors on the Combined Code* ('Turnbull Guidance')[71] is adopted as a framework for *Sarbanes-Oxley* compliance, of the 'comply or explain' principle being 'trumped' by the statutory-based compliance obligation imposed by *Sarbanes-Oxley*.[72]

---

companies will in future have to adhere to the *Combined Code*: see Tony Tassell and Neil Hume, 'London Issues Guidelines for Foreign Listings', *Financial Times* (London), 9 May 2007, 43.

[68] The CEO of the London Stock Exchange, Clara Furse, commented recently that 'London's principles-based regime, rather than a more prescriptive rules-based approach, continues to prove itself as a model that facilitates pro-competitive innovation in a tough but sensible regulatory environment. All the important independent corporate governance surveys confirm that the U.K. is number one for corporate governance standards': 'Comment: SOX Is Not to Blame — London Is Just Better as a Market', *Financial Times* (London), 17 September 2006, 19.

[69] But note that overseas companies with a primary listing on the Official List must disclose significant ways in which their corporate governance practices differ from those set out in the *Combined Code*: see *FSA Handbook* LR 9.8.7R. This obligation applies to relatively few companies, as most overseas companies have a secondary listing.

[70] Pub L No 107–204, 116 Stat 745 (2002) ('*Sarbanes-Oxley*').

[71] (2005), available at <http://www.frc.org.uk/corporate/internalcontrol.cfm>. The Turnbull Guidance provides guidance on compliance with the internal control provisions of the *Combined Code*.

[72] The SEC has identified the Turnbull Guidance as a suitable framework for *Sarbanes-Oxley* s 404(a) purposes: see FRC, *The Turnbull Guidance as an Evaluation Framework for the Purposes of Section 404(a) of the* Sarbanes-Oxley Act (2004), available at <http://www.frc.org.uk/corporate>.

It seems clear therefore that the role of self-regulation in capital markets in the UK complicates the overall pattern of enforcement. Market discipline is important in any system, but the attempt in the UK to integrate it into the regulatory structure makes the regulatory and enforcement mix particularly difficult to read. On one reading, the absence of major failures in recent years and the relative success of the UK as a location for listing and capital markets transactions might suggest that the mix works well. On another reading, self-regulation might be seen as little more than the selective protection of mutual self-interest by institutional investors, with the contribution to regulation in the public interest being quite limited.

IV CORPORATE, COLLECTIVE OR INDIVIDUAL RESPONSIBILITY?

The United Kingdom regulatory system, viewed broadly so as to include company law, adopts three different models of responsibility for acts or omissions of a corporate entity.[73] In some instances it is the corporate entity itself that bears responsibility. This model forms the basis of many of the *FSMA 2000*-based obligations, which are expressed as binding on an authorised firm or a listed entity. It also operates in company law to make a company responsible for acts or omissions that it has authorised. In others instances, it is the board of directors as a collective entity that bears responsibility. The *Combined Code* reinforces that view, its first main principle being that: 'Every company should be headed by an effective board, which is collectively responsible for the success of the company'. That reference to collective responsibility is made with the framework of the concept of accountability adopted by the *Combined Code*, which focuses on the accountability of the board to the shareholders. In that sense, collective responsibility operates internally within the company. It does not encompass regulatory or other obligations owed to persons outside the company. From the perspective of outsiders (regulators or contractual counterparties), the collective

[73] For a general discussion of models of responsibility, see Mark Bovens, *The Quest for Responsibility: Accountability and Citizenship in Complex Organisations* (1998). In addition to the three models identified here, Bovens proposes a fourth, termed 'hierarchical', in which responsibility is located by reference to position within a hierarchy. While the regulatory obligations imposed on senior managers in FSA authorised firms are related to position within the firm's hierarchy, it is argued below that the requirement for personal culpability results in the responsibility of senior managers being closer to the 'individual' rather than the 'hierarchical' model of responsibility.

nature of board responsibility is a secondary matter because, from their perspective, the company generally bears responsibility for decisions and acts of the board. Finally, it is possible for individual responsibility to be allocated to directors and senior managers. This model is evident both in company law, which, particularly in respect of criminal sanctions, frequently refers to 'directors and officers', and in *FSMA 2000* regulatory rules, which are sometimes expressed as being applicable to individuals. It is also apparent in respect of the duties of directors, which apply at the level of the individual despite the collective nature of board decision-making.

The broad framework is therefore one in which, depending on the characterisation of a particular act or omission, enforcement might be targeted against the corporate entity, the board collectively, or individuals. Characterisation of the regulatory nature of particular acts or omissions is significant because they cannot always be allocated exclusively to a particular regime. For example, a single act may well involve a breach of the *Combined Code*, FSA regulatory rules, and a director's duty of care and skill. Moreover, a single lapse might even involve conduct that appeared to comply with one particular regulatory regime but to contravene another.[74] Thus, characterisation of the lapse will affect who takes enforcement against whom and on what basis.

Within the narrower framework of the *FSMA 2000* regulatory system, the focus of enforcement is simpler because the *FSMA 2000* regulatory system does not itself recognise the concept of the collective responsibility of the board. As the FSA has made clear, regulatory obligations fall either on the entity or on an individual.[75] However, that does not mean that the issue cannot be of relevance so far as FSA enforcement is concerned. The FSA recognises the importance of the

---

[74] This possibility has been recognised as being quite real: see Gray and Hamilton, above n 7, 154–6, for the discussion of scenarios in which it might occur. The main source of conflict is that corporate law regards the duties of directors as owed to each individual company within a group, whereas the *FSMA 2000* regulatory rules for senior management — Senior Management Arrangements, Systems and Controls ('SYSC') — require senior managers to manage the group as a whole.

[75] FSA, 'Senior Management Arrangements, Systems and Controls' (Consultation Paper 35, 1999) [3.12]: 'However, under the financial services and markets legislation, the board itself cannot be the bearer of regulatory obligations. Regulatory obligations fall either upon the firm itself (whose organ the board is) or upon individual Approved Persons (including individual members of the board). There is therefore no question of the board as such becoming collectively exposed to disciplinary liability.'

collective responsibility principle established by the *Combined Code*, and its handbook gives 'due credit' for compliance with the *Code* when the issue of compliance with the FSA's own rules for senior management is being considered.[76] Nevertheless, precisely what 'due credit' means when different models of responsibility bite on the same circumstances remains to be seen. An additional complication is that the *FSA Handbook* recognises that 'controlled functions' may (so long as it is appropriate) be allocated to a 'committee of management', which could presumably comprise a sub-committee of the board or even the full board.[77] In that event, it would seem to follow that the board was indeed a 'bearer of regulatory obligations', although that outcome results from an internal decision within the firm rather than from regulatory obligations imposed externally by the FSA.

In recent years the *FSMA 2000* regulatory system has placed considerable emphasis on the individual responsibility (and liability) of senior management for compliance. The process has been described as forming part of a policy of 'individualisation'[78] of responsibility. It represents a refinement of the process of 'enrolment'[79] of key actors in the process of regulation in that it allocates individual responsibility within an enterprise for specific regulatory functions. Underlying the process is the rationale that directors and senior management must be held to account for their stewardship and cannot be permitted to hide behind the façade of a corporate entity, thereby transferring the cost of their failings to shareholders and third parties. The technique has been employed not just in financial regulation but also in the broader context of corporate and insolvency law. Examples are the identification in the *Combined Code* of the specific role of non-executive directors and members of board committees (opening up the possibility of liability for specific failures), and the possibility of directors being disqualified if, following the insolvency of a company, they are found to be unfit to be a director.[80] As is the case with the adoption of risk-based regulation, there is no specific legislative requirement that the FSA should follow the

---

[76] *FSA Handbook* SYSC 3.3.1G.
[77] *FSA Handbook* SYSC 2.1.6G.
[78] See Gray and Hamilton, above n 7, 118.
[79] See Julia Black, *Mapping the Contours of Contemporary Financial Services Regulation* (CARR Discussion Paper No 17, 2003), available at <http://www.lse.ac.uk/collections/CARR> at 21 February 2007.
[80] See, in respect of disqualification, the *Company Directors Disqualification Act 1986* (UK) c 46.

'individualisation' approach, nor is there any legislative indication of the substance of senior management responsibility. The basis of the regulatory approach to this issue is the rather opaque 'principle of good regulation'[81] that the FSA should have regard to the (non-defined) responsibilities of those who manage the affairs of authorised persons.

The starting point for considering individual responsibility is Principle 3 of the Principles for Business: '*A firm must take reasonable care to organise and control its affairs responsibly and effectively, with adequate risk management systems.*'[82] The meaning of this principle is spelt out in greater detail in the rules and guidance which comprise the Senior Management Arrangements, Systems and Controls (the SYSC component of the FSA Handbook). It is also part of the purpose of SYSC to encourage firms to vest responsibility for effective and responsible organisation in specific directors and senior executives. That represents the first step in the move towards individual responsibility because it requires the implementation of management systems that provide a basis for identification of individual responsibility. The second step is the link between SYSC and the mechanisms that are available for taking enforcement action against individuals. One of the innovations of *FSMA 2000* was to introduce an 'approved person' regime ('APER' in the *FSA Handbook*) under which persons performing 'controlled functions' require the approval of the FSA.[83] Persons to whom SYSC functions are allocated are automatically included within the APER because such functions are designated as 'controlled'. This has the effect that the sanctions[84] available for breach of APER are available in respect of persons performing or failing to perform SYSC functions. Moreover, it has been noted that close linkage in rule formulation between the SYSC and APER ensures that failings in relation to SYSC can be positively identified as contraventions of the approved persons regime, thereby

[81] See Introduction for these principles.
[82] *FSA Handbook* PRIN 3 (emphasis added). These are high-level principles that bind authorised firms.
[83] Approval is subject to the FSA being satisfied that the relevant person is 'fit and proper' to perform the relevant controlled function.
[84] *FSMA 2000*. The relevant sanctions include: withdrawal of 'approved person' status (s 63); a financial penalty (s 66); or a public statement of misconduct (s 66). A prohibition order (under s 56) preventing an individual from engaging in specified regulated activities is a broader sanction that is not limited to the approved persons regime and is regarded by the FSA as a more serious penalty than withdrawal of approval.

opening up the possibility of action against an individual.[85] Furthermore, accessory liability, in circumstances in which an approved person is 'knowingly concerned' in a contravention for which a firm bears primary responsibility, represents another route for enforcement action against individuals.[86]

The possibility of enforcement against an individual under SYSC or APER does not, however, mean that it will occur as a matter of course, even if the contravention falls within areas prioritised by the risk-based approach to regulation. A specific statutory provision requires the FSA to consider whether it is appropriate to take action against individuals.[87] This approach recognises that it may not always be appropriate to take action against individuals, and is reflected in statements made by the FSA stressing that personal culpability is an essential element of a decision to take enforcement action against an individual.[88] It is this feature that distinguishes the model of individual responsibility adopted by the FSA from a purely hierarchical model of responsibility — in which position within the hierarchy, without a requirement for personal culpability, is the basis on which responsibility is allocated.[89] The low level of enforcement action against individuals under SYSC or APER tends to bear out the impression that this statutory consideration limits enforcement action.[90] On the other hand, recent enforcement action under APER against a senior manager knowingly concerned in a breach of Principle 5[91] by Deutsche Bank[92] indicates that independent enforcement of principles applies as much to individuals as to firms.[93] In that sense, individuals also bear responsibility for interpreting and implementing principles.

---

[85] Gray and Hamilton, above n 7, 75.

[86] See *FSMA 2000* s 66; see also the enforcement action against Deutsche Bank/David Maslen, above n 44.

[87] *FSMA 2000* s 66(2)(b).

[88] FSA, 'The Regulation of Approved Persons' (Consultation Paper 26, 1999) [115].

[89] See Bovens, above n 73, ch 6, arguing that this feature of the hierarchical model violates one of the basic requirements of accountability (viz blameworthiness), resulting in such systems being fundamentally flawed.

[90] Gray and Hamilton, above n 7.

[91] *FSA Handbook* PRIN 2.1.1R.

[92] See above n 44.

[93] See FSA, *Final Notice to David John Maslen* (2006) <http://www.fsa.gov.uk/pubs/final/maslen.pdf> at 26 February 2007.

Another potentially significant source of individual liability in the context of listing and share issues is the accessory liability of 'a person discharging managerial responsibilities'[94] for contraventions of the listing rules,[95] the disclosure rules[96] or the rules relating to prospectuses. However, the very low incidence of (public) enforcement action based on this section (and its predecessor under the *Financial Services Act 1986* (UK) c 60 (repealed)) suggests that there is a reluctance to pursue the senior management of listed companies on this issue. A possible rationalisation of this approach is that such action would most often be against individuals who were not already within the FSA regulatory net, and who are not therefore as familiar with the regulatory techniques and culture of the FSA as those individuals who do fall within the FSA regulatory net as a result of being senior managers of *FSMA 2000*-regulated entities.[97]

Further support for individual responsibility is provided by the prohibition on authorised firms taking out insurance to indemnify individuals against the cost of paying a penalty imposed by the FSA.[98] This follows the approach in company law that provides that a company may not provide an indemnity to a director in respect of a fine imposed in criminal proceedings or a penalty payable to a regulator as a result of contravention of a regulatory requirement.[99] While the *FSMA 2000* prohibition is wider in its scope as it applies to any person, it is of most relevance to directors and senior managers, who are the most likely target for FSA enforcement action. The overall trend in *FSMA 2000* regulation is therefore towards individual responsibility. That trend is not immediately obvious from the relatively low incidence of enforcement

---

[94] See *FSMA 2000* s 91, as amended by *The Prospectus Regulations 2005* (SI 2005/1433) (UK). Prior to the 2005 amendment, it was only directors who could be punished for such contraventions.

[95] Applicable to the Official List, a term still used in the UK to identify the segment of traded securities that are subject to the 'super-equivalent' regime, under which the UK has gone beyond the requirements imposed by the relevant EC Directives.

[96] These are rules applicable to securities admitted to trading on all regulated markets (even if they are not on the Official List): examples are the London International Financial Futures Exchange, the Professional Securities Market, and the Virt-x Exchange Ltd. The Alternative Investment Market, which has recently attracted many listings of overseas companies, made a policy choice in 2004 not to be a regulated market so as to leave itself the freedom to set its own disclosure rules.

[97] Gray and Hamilton, above n 7, 179.

[98] See *FSA Handbook* GEN 6.1, ENF 13.1.3G.

[99] See *Companies Act 1985* ss 309A, 309B.

action against individuals but, as indicated at the outset, the incidence of enforcement action is a particularly difficult variable to interpret. It is quite likely that the deterrent effect of limited high-profile enforcement against individuals is considerable, especially when combined with the possibility of independent enforcement of principles.

V THE ROLES OF PUBLIC AND PRIVATE ENFORCEMENT

The respective roles of public and private enforcement are an important characteristic of the enforcement regime for capital markets. Public enforcement tends to focus on punishment and deterrence whereas private enforcement tends to focus on restitution and compensation: but that need not always be the case and (as noted in Part VI below) the public system of enforcement in the UK now makes provision for the FSA to pursue restitution and compensation on behalf of consumers of financial services.

(A) *Public Enforcement*

Public enforcement of contraventions of *FSMA 2000* and the *FSA Handbook* is generally undertaken by the FSA, through its internal disciplinary procedure for contraventions that are not criminal offences, and through the courts for contraventions that are criminal offences. The Department of Trade and Industry ('DTI') and the Director of Public Prosecutions are also authorised to bring prosecutions for offences created by *FSMA 2000*, but have not to date exercised their powers. However, the FSA has no role in the public enforcement of offences under the Companies Acts. Such offences[100] are prosecuted either by the registrar of companies (Companies House) or the DTI.[101] Prosecution of such offences tends to attract much less media attention than the few higher-profile cases pursued by the FSA, and, while it is generally

---

[100] *Companies Act 1985* sch 24 sets out the extensive list of offences under that Act, the mode of prosecution, and the punishment. Most prosecutions in England and Wales occur in magistrates courts and result in relatively small penalties.

[101] See *Enforcement Strategy Policy Document* (2006) Companies House <http://www.companieshouse.gov.uk/about/policyDocuments/enforcementStrategy.pdf> at 9 February 2007. Companies House has responsibility for prosecuting the offences of failing to file annual reports and annual returns (*Companies Act 1985* s 242). Other offences are prosecuted by the Department of Trade and Industry. In Scotland, all prosecution decisions are made by the procurators fiscal.

assumed that such prosecutions typically involve smaller companies rather those which are publicly listed, there is no reliable data on which to base that conclusion. Moreover, given the manner in which the company law disclosure and governance provisions mesh with those of the listing rules,[102] it would be wrong to dismiss as insignificant the regulatory role played by enforcement of the company law offences simply because they often appear rather technical and sometimes arbitrary (for example, offences in respect of time limits for the lodging of documents).

In the United Kingdom (and the European Union), the close linkage of the corporate and capital markets regulatory regimes is particularly evident in relation to the financial disclosure regime for companies. The *Companies Act 1985* (UK) c 6 sets out the basic disclosure regime for all companies.[103] That approach reflects the historic linkage of limited liability with disclosure obligations. The *FSMA 2000* and the listing rules build upon that foundation to create a more advanced and onerous disclosure regime for listed companies. The resulting disclosure regime for public listed companies therefore differs from that in parts of the United States, where corporate law does not extend disclosure obligations beyond publicly listed companies. The fact that the entire disclosure regime does not fall within the regulatory jurisdiction of the FSA is reflected in the arrangements for monitoring the accounts of listed issuers and compliance with the *Combined Code*. Those matters are the responsibility of the Financial Reporting Review Panel ('FRRP'), a subsidiary body of the Financial Reporting Council,[104] which is an independent private sector body funded by the accountancy profession, the DTI, and City institutions.[105] The FRRP reviews Reports produced by issuers of listed securities for compliance with the accounting

---

[102] In contrast, for example, with the position in some parts of the United States, where disclosure rules apply only to public listed companies.

[103] Dispensations from some requirements are given to small- and medium-sized companies.

[104] The objectives of the FRC are to promote: high quality corporate reporting; high quality auditing; high quality actuarial practice; high standards of corporate governance (it is responsible for publishing and maintaining the *Combined Code*); the integrity, competence and transparency of the accountancy and actuarial professions; and its own effectiveness as a unified independent regulator.

[105] See Stella Fearnley and Tony Hines, 'The Regulatory Framework for Financial Reporting and Auditing in the United Kingdom: The Present Position and Impending Changes' (2003) 38 *International Journal of Accounting* 215.

requirements of the listing rules.[106] It cooperates with the FSA in carrying out this function and adopts a risk-based approach to the selection of Reports for scrutiny.[107] Three outcomes are possible following identification of deficiencies in accounts. The first and most common is that the FRRP agrees a correction to accounts with the relevant issuer. The second is that the FRRP can make an application to the court to require an issuer to revise defective accounts.[108] The third is that the FRRP can refer the matter to the FSA, which can impose the following penalties for breach of the listing regime: public censure; a financial penalty to be paid by the issuer and/or possibly also its senior management;[109] discontinue or suspend listing.

(B) *Private Enforcement*

Private enforcement is not a major feature of the system of capital markets regulation in the UK. This stands in sharp contrast to the US, where private enforcement, particularly in the form of class actions, represents a major part of enforcement activity.[110] While express provision is made by *FSMA 2000*[111] to permit an action in damages for losses suffered as a result of a contravention of *FSMA 2000* or rules made under it, the provision has proven in practice to be something of a dead letter. There are three main reasons for this. First, the right to bring an action in damages has been limited in most circumstances to 'private

---

[106] Its authority to do this is provided by *The Supervision of Accounts and Reports (Prescribed Body) Order 2005* (SI 2005/715) (UK), which designates the FRRP as the prescribed body for the purposes of the functions mentioned in s 14(2) of the *Companies (Audit, Investigations and Community Enterprise) Act 2004* (UK) c 27. There is no statutory basis for the FRC's role in developing and monitoring compliance with the *Combined Code*.

[107] See *Memorandum of Understanding between the Financial Reporting Review Panel and the Financial Services Authority* (2005) <http://www.frc.org.uk/images/uploaded/documents/300305%20-%20FSA-FRRP%20Memorandum%20of%20Understanding%20_Final_1.pdf> at 23 February 2007; *Financial Reporting Review Panel Operating Procedures* <http://www.frc.org.uk/frrp/how/procedures.cfm> at 23 February 2007.

[108] *Companies Act 1985* s 245B; *The Companies (Defective Accounts) (Authorised Persons) Order 2005* (SI 2005/699) (UK). The FRRP is also empowered to compel the production of documents and the giving of information.

[109] See Part IV above.

[110] See Coffee, 'Law and the Market', above n 6.

[111] Section 150.

persons',[112] thereby excluding institutional investors and market professionals who might be more inclined to take up the action. Second, the provisions that are capable of private enforcement are limited. *FSMA 2000*[113] expressly excludes private enforcement of the Listing Rules and financial resources rules and authorises the FSA to exclude other provisions in its rulebook. The FSA has exercised this power to exclude the possibility of independent enforcement of principles through private litigation.[114] Finally, there are difficult issues of causation that arise in linking a contravention with loss and these are likely to act as a deterrent to bringing an action.[115]

Private enforcement does, however, remain at the fore in legal regimes adjacent to *FSMA 2000*. Auditor and advisory liability in negligence are probably the two most prominent examples.[116] Enforcement in these cases tends to focus on duties arising in corporate finance or restructuring transactions, in which it may be possible to establish breach of a duty of care owed to a client. It has proven much more difficult to extend that form of liability to a wider group, such as investors who buy shares in the market on the strength of incorrect accounts that have been negligently audited.[117] The *Companies Act 2006* (UK) c 46 will provide further protection for auditors by permitting companies to enter into limitation of liability agreements with them.[118] Company law in the UK currently prohibits such arrangements.[119]

---

[112] As a result of *FSMA 2000* s 150(2); *FSMA 2000 (Right of Action) Regulations 2001* (SI 2001/2256) art 3.

[113] Section 150.

[114] See *FSA Handbook* PRIN 3.4.4R.

[115] For a discussion of the problems of private enforcement under *FSMA 2000's* predecessor statute see Iain MacNeil, 'FSA 1986: Does s 62 Provide an Effective Remedy for Breaches of Conduct of Business Rules?' (1994) 15 *Company Lawyer* 172.

[116] See, eg, Philip Smith, *Negligence Claims Could Reach New Height with Litigation Funding Trend* (15 February 2007) Accountancy Age <http://www.accountancyage.com/best-practice/analysis/2183554/negligence-claims-reach-heights> at 20 February 2007.

[117] The line of case law stemming from the House of Lords decision in *Caparo Industries plc v Dickman* [1990] 2 AC 605 has generally taken a restrictive view of the persons to whom auditors owe a duty of care.

[118] See ss 532–8.

[119] See *Companies Act 1985* s 310.

VI SETTLEMENT AND SANCTIONS

Viewed in the broad context of regulatory enforcement in the UK,[120] the FSA has a relatively sophisticated set of sanctions available to it. However, the risk-based approach to regulation (above) is one factor which results in resort to formal sanctions being quite rare. Another factor is the emphasis placed by the FSA on the settlement of enforcement proceedings.[121] The rationale for settlement is that it 'results in consumers obtaining compensation earlier than would otherwise be the case, the saving of FSA and industry resources, in messages getting out to the market sooner and assists in a public perception of timely and effective action'.[122]

Another issue that has an impact on sanctions and settlement is the procedural fairness of the FSA disciplinary procedure. This issue proved contentious during parliamentary debate on the FSMA Bill in the late 1990s and has continued to drive changes in FSA practice up to the present day. Each of these issues is now considered in more detail.

(A) *Sanctions: The Statutory Options*

The range of sanctions available to the FSA is as follows:

a) Public censure. This sanction is intended to cause a change in the behaviour of its recipient and act as a deterrent to others through the potential damage to reputation that may follow from publication of a contravention.
b) Unlimited financial penalties. There are a number of provisions in *FSMA 2000* that permit the FSA to impose an unlimited financial penalty for contravention.[123] While no limits are set for the penalty, the FSA is required to publish guidance as to its practice in setting penalties.[124] The FSA holds the distinction of having imposed both

[120] For a comparison of the FSA with other regulatory agencies see the Macrory Report, above n 32.
[121] Since October 2003, around 80 per cent of disciplinary cases that resulted in a financial penalty have been concluded by settlement: FSA, *Enforcement Process Review*, above n 11, 50.
[122] Ibid.
[123] See s 66 (approved persons); s 91 (listing rules); s 118 (market abuse); s 206 (authorised persons).
[124] See, eg, *FSA Handbook* ENF 13.

the single largest[125] financial penalty of any United Kingdom regulator and of imposing the largest average penalty.[126]

c) Variation or cancellation of permission to engage in regulated activity. This option effectively allows the FSA to vary or withdraw an authorised person or firm's licence to engage in regulated financial activity.[127] The power can be exercised if there is a failure to meet the threshold conditions[128] for authorisation, or if it is desirable to exercise that power in order to protect the interests of consumers or potential consumers.

d) Prohibition orders. The FSA can prohibit an individual (ie a human person) from performing any regulated activity if it considers that he is not a fit and proper person to carry on that function. The effect of such an order is to exclude an individual from either specific activities or all regulated activity. In view of the potential to deprive a person of his or her livelihood, the FSA has made clear that it will only consider making a prohibition order in the most serious cases of lack of fitness and propriety.[129] However, when an individual is not an approved person, a prohibition order may be the only effective sanction.[130] In the case of an approved person, a financial penalty is more likely in less serious cases.

e) Restitution orders. An innovation of *FSMA 2000* was the power given to the FSA to order restitution against any person in favour of the 'victims', when it is satisfied that profits have accrued or loss has been suffered as a result of a regulatory contravention.[131] While there

---

[125] The £17m penalty imposed on Shell for market abuse: see FSA, *Final Notice to the 'Shell' Transport and Trading Company plc* (2004) <http://www.fsa.gov.uk/pubs/final/shell_24aug04.pdf> at 20 February 2007.

[126] See the Macrory Report, above n 32, 21, showing that the FSA's average financial penalty for 2004–5 was £75 000 compared to £6885 for the Health and Safety Executive, the second-ranked regulator by average penalty imposed. This outcome can be rationalised by reference to the argument advanced by Coffee that the smaller the risk of detection the larger a fine must be to act as a deterrent: John Coffee '"No Soul to Damn: No Body to Kick": An Unscandalized Inquiry into the Problem of Corporate Punishment' (1981) 79 *Michigan Law Review* 386.

[127] *FSMA 2000* s 45.

[128] These are the requirements that must be met by an applicant for authorisation under *FSMA 2000*.

[129] See *FSA Handbook* ENF 8.5.2G, for the factors to be taken into account in deciding whether to make an order against an approved person.

[130] See *FSA Handbook* ENF 8.6.1AG.

[131] See *FSMA 2000* s 384. This is additional to the option available to the FSA to apply to the court for a restitution order under s 382.

have been few instances of the express exercise of this power, it has been a significant factor in enabling the FSA to negotiate large industry-wide settlements in the market for retail financial products.[132]

f) Criminal prosecutions. Although *FSMA 2000* marked a deliberate shift away from enforcement through the criminal courts in favour of administrative sanctions, *The FSMA 2000* did create a number of criminal offences. The FSA is authorised to bring prosecutions in respect of offences, but this option has not featured prominently in FSA enforcement. A relevant factor is no doubt the higher evidential standard that is required in criminal prosecutions by comparison with FSA disciplinary hearings.[133]

g) Suspension of trading in shares. In the case of entities whose securities have been admitted to trading on a regulated market, the FSA is able to instruct the market operator to suspend trading in the securities if it suspects that an applicable provision has been breached.[134]

h) Initiation of and participation in bankruptcy or insolvency proceedings. This is possible in the case of authorised persons, their appointed representative, or persons carrying on regulated activity without the required authorisation. It provides a mechanism whereby the FSA can act to safeguard the interests of the customers of an authorised person by initiating and participating in the bankruptcy/ insolvency process.

(B) *Settlements: Process and Incentives*

Settlements for the purpose of FSA enforcement are regulatory decisions taken by the FSA, the terms of which the firm or individual concerned accepts.[135] Unlike settlements in commercial out-of-court cases, they are made public through the publicity requirements attached to FSA

---

[132] See Joanna Gray, 'The Legislative Basis of Systemic Review and Compensation for the Mis-Selling of Retail Financial Services and Products' (2004) 25 *Statute Law Review* 196.

[133] See *FSA Handbook* ENF 15.5.1G and the Financial Services and Markets Tribunal decision in the case of Davidson and Tatham, holding that the FSA was not required to meet the criminal standard of proof (beyond reasonable doubt) in disciplinary hearings.

[134] *FSMA 2000* s 87L.

[135] FSA, *Enforcement Process Review*, above n 11, 50.

decision-making.[136] A settlement is possible at any stage of the enforcement process. The main incentive for firms and individuals to engage in the settlement process is that the FSA is likely to reduce a financial penalty to recognise the degree of cooperation. Under the old guidance, early settlement of a case was treated as an element of cooperation, which could form the basis for an unspecified discount. Under the new regime,[137] an explicit discount of up to 30 per cent is available for early settlement. The starting point for the calculation of the discount is the penalty, adjusted for cooperation, and, while that adjustment will remain unspecified, it will not exceed 20 per cent.[138] A variant of the FSA type of settlement just described is the form of settlement agreed between the FRRP and listed companies in respect of corrections to published accounts. As explained earlier, scrutiny of accounts is the responsibility of the FRRP and its powers to require corrections are contained in the company law rather than *FSMA 2000*. However, in common with the FSA approach, the FRRP normally agrees corrections with companies.

(C) *Procedural Complications*

Since its inception, the *FSMA 2000* disciplinary regime has raised issues of procedural fairness.[139] The FSMA Bill was amended during its passage through Parliament to reflect this concern and to shield the FSA and government from challenges based on the incompatibility of the disciplinary process with the *European Convention on Human Rights*.[140] In particular, legal aid was made available to individuals subject to disciplinary procedures, an appeal system was put in place, and the use of compelled evidence (which has been instrumental in providing evidence in other regulatory fields) was prohibited. More recently, the FSA has proposed changes that give greater effect to the requirement[141] that there should be a separation between those who investigate

---

[136] See *FSA Handbook* DEC App 1.10.3G.
[137] See *FSA Handbook* ENF 13.7.
[138] FSA, *Enforcement Process Review*, above n 11, 56.
[139] For a summary of the process and procedural fairness issues, see Iain MacNeil, *An Introduction to the Law on Financial Investment* (2005) 83–5.
[140] *Convention for the Protection of Human Rights*, opened for signature 4 November 1950, CETS No 005 (entered into force 3 September 1953), implemented into UK law by the *Human Rights Act 1998*.
[141] *FSMA 2000* s 395.

contraventions and those who decide whether the conduct in question should be sanctioned.[142] While it does remain true, as the FSA contends,[143] that the administrative nature of the disciplinary process means that it is more flexible and less costly than formal court procedures, there is nevertheless a clear impression that the degree of difference has narrowed considerably by comparison with the expectations that surrounded the introduction of *FSMA 2000*. It had been anticipated, particularly in connection with market abuse — an area in which criminal sanctions had clearly failed to punish or deter contraventions — that a move to administrative sanctions would provide much greater flexibility to bring to book individuals and organisations who had escaped the regulatory net as a result of the evidential and procedural safeguards of the criminal law. While it is difficult to state conclusively that this has not occurred, because there are many causal influences (for example the market abuse regime has itself been subject to considerable change as a result of an EC directive), it does seem fair to conclude that the move to administrative sanctions cannot, as a result of the progressive adoption of procedural safeguards, be regarded as a major contributor to the ability to sanction contraventions in the capital markets.[144]

Conclusion

Formal enforcement action is a relatively rare occurrence in the regulatory system in the UK. It is limited primarily by the regulatory and enforcement policy adopted by the FSA. Risk-based regulation means that enforcement policy does not target or pursue all contraventions. The recent move to more principles-based regulation does not carry direct implications for the incidence or pattern of enforcement action, but it does carry implications for enforceability. In particular, it raises the possibility of challenges to independent enforcement of principles, which

---

[142] See, eg, FSA, Enforcement Process Review, above n 11, 5–10; FSA, 'Review of the Enforcement and Decision Making Manuals' (Consultation Paper 07/02, 2007).

[143] FSA, *Enforcement Process Review*, above n 11.

[144] There is mixed evidence on the incidence of market abuse since the implementation of *FSMA 2000*: see FSA, 'Measuring Market Cleanliness' (Occasional Paper 23, 2006); FSA, 'Updated Measurement of Market Cleanliness' (Occasional Paper 25 2007). The revised data presented in the 2007 Paper suggests that 'informed trading' ahead of takeover announcements increased following the implementation of the *FSMA 2000* but that such trading ahead of other significant announcements declined.

lack an adequate degree of foreseeability. However, to the extent that enforcement based on principles rather than rules is already quite well established, the process is one of expansion rather than innovation and therefore the risks are correspondingly lower.

The reliance on self-regulation and market discipline in the United Kingdom regulatory system poses a potential challenge for enforcement. There is evidence to suggest that the 'explain' element of the 'comply or explain' obligation contained in the *Combined Code* is often ignored, casting doubt over the willingness of institutional investors to undertake the scrutiny envisaged by the *Code* and the willingness of the FSA to undertake enforcement of the disclosure obligation on which investor scrutiny relies. Evidence of more active enforcement of other self-regulatory rules by institutional investors suggests that collective action and 'free rider' issues may explain the more restrained approach to enforcement of the *Combined Code*.

The presence of three different models of responsibility within the regulatory system raises the possibility of acts or omissions being characterised in different ways to fit into the appropriate regime. The overall trend is towards clearer identification of individual roles and responsibilities, but it remains to be seen how effectively this will contribute towards compliance. There are certainly grounds for believing that individual responsibility combined with independent enforcement of principles should cause senior management to reflect more carefully on their business models and personal conduct.

Enforcement of the *FSMA 2000* system of regulation relies primarily on public agencies. That is the result of the policy of prohibiting private litigation in most instances on the part of institutional investors and market professionals. However, important common law causes of action (such as auditor or adviser negligence) remain available and may lead to substantial claims. Moreover, the FSA has power to require restitution and compensation in appropriate cases, and the experience of the exercise of those powers in the retail financial markets suggests that it can be a powerful tool in persuading parties to enter into negotiated settlements.

There remains the problem of estimating the impact that either the level of enforcement or its mix (as between different techniques) has on compliance. While it is clear, for example, that the FSA devotes proportionately much less resource to enforcement than does its US counterpart, the SEC, it is not entirely clear what may safely be concluded from such an observation. It would be rash to conclude, for example, that the low-level of enforcement in the UK results in a lower level of compliance. This would imply that the other regulatory activities in which the FSA engages have a lower compliance value than enforcement action, yet there is no clear evidence of that being the case. Equally, it would be wrong to conclude that a higher level of enforcement activity in the US implies a lower level of compliance: it may simply be the result of a higher ratio of enforcement action to contraventions. Differences in the regulatory structure and enforcement patterns as between different countries simply add to the wider problem of estimating the effect of enforcement on compliance in any single regulatory system.

Chapter 7

Why Auditors Don't Find Fraud

Nicholas M Hodson

In 20 years of auditing I detected one fraud. I had many colleagues who never encountered a fraud during an entire career in auditing; in fact they would constitute the significant majority. In 20 years of investigative and forensic accounting I investigated hundreds of frauds and was aware of thousands more. Was it that all but one of my audit clients was immune to fraud? Were the clients of my colleagues also immune? Or were my colleagues and I just lucky? Evidence on the incidence of fraud in corporate North America makes the likelihood of immunity remote.[1] This paper examines the impediments that militate against auditors finding fraud. It considers the changes to auditing standards that place more emphasis on auditors' responsibility to find fraud, and their potential impact. It looks at the real-world challenges that auditors face and the way the odds are stacked against them in one example, and one hypothetical composite illustration taken from my audit and forensic

[1] In 2002 the author commissioned a telephone survey of employees in North America. Employees were asked: 'Thinking specifically about your place of work and the types of fraud listed above as well as other forms of fraud, I would like you to tell me whether you are *personally* aware of any situations *involving yourself or people you know* where fraud occurred approximately in the last year? Please remember your answer is entirely confidential, and we are only asking about situations you have witnessed personally' (emphasis added). Employees had been pre-sensitised to this question. They had been previously asked about their opinions about the seriousness of different types of fraud in order to raise their focus beyond trivial thefts of stationery. One in five employees responded positively to this question. There are probably no public issuers with fewer than five employees.

experience. Finally it considers some changes to the governance model that would, in my view, lead to more effective stewardship of the risk of fraud by senior management. This analysis draws from a 40-year career in auditing and forensic accounting.

I AUTHOR'S EXPERIENCE

As this is an experienced-based analysis, some information about my background may be relevant. My career has been in public accounting. Initially, in England, I learned the ropes of auditing. In 1975, after two years in Belgium, I moved to Canada. I continued auditing for a further decade in both client service capacity and within an applied research, development and resource function. In 1985 I joined an incipient investigative and forensic accounting practice. I retired as the head of that practice in 2005. My auditing experience ranged from the granular details of junior level auditing to directing auditing services for Canadian public companies and United States Securities and Exchange Commission ('SEC') registrants. The search for audit evidence to verify assertions embodied in financial statements including compliance with generally accepted accounting principles was, for me, a technical, analytical pursuit. I found it a disciplined, detailed process, with its share of complexities and stress.

My term in our firm's National Auditing Department caused me to think about what auditors did. I was able to engage in research and technical debate, and to hear and respond to a continual flow of technical queries from my client service colleagues. During this time I also remodelled and directed the firm's audit quality review program. The last 20 years of investigative and forensic accounting presented a different perspective on the obstacles auditors faced.

II THE ESSENTIALS

In my view, auditors have had difficulty finding fraud for the following reasons:

a) Training and experience issues:
   - (i) They have had inadequate training in the nature of fraud;
   - (ii) They had inadequate training in investigative methodologies;

(iii) They generally had insufficient understanding of how hard it is to find fraud;

(iv) They had little or no experience of searching for and investigating evidence of fraud.

b) Inertia of history:

(i) They had the inertia of generations of acknowledgement that their job is to search out and examine evidence to confirm the correctness of the financial statements before them;

(ii) They had the inertia of audit documentation of prior years that may contain no evidence or suspicion of fraud;

(iii) Until recently, auditors have been entitled to presume management's good faith absent evidence to the contrary.

c) Audit design limitations:

(i) They had auditing procedures whose focus was designed around the attestation to positive assertions embodied in financial statement components — such procedures are not well-aligned with the search for indicia of fraud;

(ii) They planned audits whose scope incorporates a quantitative concept of materiality in the measurement of an entity's operating results, but were required to consider an ill-defined subjectively evaluated notion of materiality in regard to evidence of potential misstatements caused by fraud, that might be less than the quantitatively determined materiality established for audit planning purposes.

d) Service model limitations:

(i) They had a service model that required inexperienced junior staff to seek evidence and explanations of complex and possibly fraudulent schemes from senior executives with experience and in positions of authority;

(ii) The service model that placed the least experienced audit team members in the front line of contact with the most direct exposure to the client personnel and the evidence also placed the most experienced audit team members in the rear, often with the least exposure to the client personnel and evidence;

(iii) They had a service delivery model that invariably provided to clients a roadmap, and frequently a detailed roadmap, of the timing, nature and scope of the audit, and engaged client personnel, several of whom may have formerly been auditors, in the identification and presentation for audit of relevant document evidence, the location and provision of audit document evidence and the preparation of summaries and analyses to form part of the auditors working papers;

(iv) They had a service model that required inexperienced junior audit staff to bring forward to other more experienced audit staff, who in turn were required to bring forward for review by the partner, matters of consequence that may have arisen through the execution of their work. There may have been other routes available for junior staff to reach the partner if they believed their concerns were not receiving attention. While there is nothing that prevents junior staff speaking directly with the partner, except fear of embarrassment for themselves if they are wrong or for their colleagues if they are right, if these matters are not brought forward through the normal review channels they may not be identified in the audit by other means, as they would largely be dependent on the persistence and fortitude of junior staff to take the initiative.

e) Time and budget constraints:

(i) They had the imposition of inelastic time constraints that do not necessarily contemplate the time requirements for inquiries that may have been required to pursue and resolve indicia of fraud;

(ii) They had client filing deadlines that may have presented obstacles to the delay in completion of the audit that the discovery of fraud will probably require;

(iii) They had budgets and procedures planned generally in contemplation of the absence of fraud unless particular fraud risks were identified, in which case auditors are required to expand their procedures; however, given auditors' general inexperience in dealing with fraud there is a risk that such planning may have been ineffective if in fact fraud risks are identified;

(iv) The pursuit of evidence of fraud can be time-consuming and expensive. Audit fees were generally not developed in contemplation of the possibility that extensive and expensive procedures to address fraud may be required, and may therefore need to be charged to the client beyond the budgeted audit fees and there may well be resistance to such additional charges.

f) Counter incentives:
   (i) They had a performance review and related compensation and career advancement criteria that tended to reward completion of procedures on time and on budget.

g) Access to senior corporate stewards:
   (i) They have, until recently, had limited practical access to the board and its audit committee.

Most of these characteristics are developed through example, illustration and analysis in this paper. Regulators and others have perceived a potential conflict of interest in auditors generating revenues from the provision of non-attest services to corporations that they also audit. This has given rise to the proscription of certain services to audit clients, and the requirement that other non-attest services be subject to scrutiny and approval of the audit committee. This issue is absent from the above list as it has not been relevant in my personal experience or in my knowledge of the conduct of colleagues. The personal avoidance by auditors of any relationship such as investing in a client of the auditing firm or holding directorship positions or having business relationships with clients of the auditing firm, that could bring into question the independence of the auditing firm has been at the core of auditing ethics throughout my career. This also is absent from the above list as it has also not been relevant in my personal experience or in my knowledge of the conduct of colleagues.

III DECEPTION

The whole point of fraud is that you are not supposed to find it. This may seem so obvious that is hardly worth stating, but I find it central to this analysis. Fraud is a secret scheme, with purpose and goal. It is not just lying there for someone to stumble over. The plan is to deceive those who may expose the scheme, including the auditors, and to maintain the deception for as long as the fraud continues. Fraud is not easy to discover or to prove because it is not intended to be easy to discover or to prove. The perpetrators make their fraud as difficult as possible to discover and prove, and actively manage the environment and the personalities who might represent threats. The more experienced and intelligent the perpetrators are the more ingenious and Machiavellian their risk management strategies may be. The deception is achieved by presenting evidence that simulates relevant aspects of legitimate business and concealing evidence that would be indicative of fraud. One of my mantras throughout my investigative accounting career has been that there is always evidence of fraud. Fraud can look like reality at higher levels but real business activity is a series of complex multilateral interactions of more or less independent parties, each with their own agendas. It is impossible to simulate this reality at its most granular level. But most audits have not sought this type of evidence. It can be time-consuming and expensive to obtain and corroborate.

There is nothing neutral or random about fraud. It does not occur by accident. It is parasitic. It is a scheme deliberately engineered by one or more parasites for their personal benefit at the expense of the host on whose behalf they are generally engaged. Like all parasites, if they manage their scheme well enough the host will survive. If not the host may die and so may they. Fraud is not just about numbers and money. It is an egregious crime that injures, through deceit, those who granted their trust and paid for services or invested their funds along with other innocent third parties. Victims swept up in the scheme are often seriously harmed both financially and emotionally. They can risk their life savings or their pensions, some with no prospect of recovery. Some live in fear for their personal safety. Sherron Watkins, cast as the Enron whistleblower, expressed concern for her personal safety in her testimony before Congress in February 2002. And auditors, while hardly innocent bystanders, do not escape and are close enough to the financial carnage to be casualties. Arthur Andersen is the ultimate example, but any partner in charge of the audit of a public company in which fraud is disclosed other than by the audit is at risk of living in hell for years and sometimes for the rest of his or her life.

IV THE DECEIVERS

If we begin at what I think is the beginning, *people* commit fraud: it is not the system, the controls, the processes, it is the people. While people at one end of the scale may be lazy, not very bright or prepossessing, at the other end they are extraordinary, do astounding things, put forth incredible effort, show unbelievable fortitude and will. I know people at bottom and the top of the range. Senior corporate managers come, in my experience, exclusively from the top end of the range. Financial reporting fraud is perpetrated generally by smart, driven, experienced, senior members of corporate management. They did not achieve their senior positions of authority and trust by accident. They rose to those positions because of their recognised abilities to achieve better results than their peers. Access to capital and enhancement of its value is gained by achievement of returns, or milestones on the road to returns, acceptable to the capital markets. Demonstration of attainment of objectives pleasing to the capital markets is a valued measure in promoting and hiring senior executives. A career in the front line of management in the corporate world is a continual competition. Apart from a necessary degree of skill and knowledge, those who push hardest rise above those who take a more passive or balanced attitude towards their career. This tends, in my view, to concentrate similar personalities at the senior levels of public corporations: people who understand that getting results sometimes involves distasteful but necessary decisions; people who accept that successful risk-taking is, in significant measure, what brings them rewards; people who are prepared to override the decisions of others and perhaps, in some cases, to override controls that present obstacles to the realisation of objectives; and people who prevail not only through intellect and industry but through charisma and will. The people who engage in fraudulent financial reporting are drawn from this community.

(A) *Thoughts on Collusion*

In many types of fraud, the requirement for collusion is typically considered to mitigate the risk of fraud for a number of reasons. The involvement of other people increases the risk of detection. The other people who have to be involved may be rivals and less likely to engage in cooperative activity. Other people who need to be involved may have the moral development to resist.

In financial reporting fraud collusion is virtually a prerequisite. Manipulation of the data underlying the financial statements of almost any but the very smallest public company is hard, if not impossible, to do single-handedly. The frauds that have been the subject of media headlines in the last few years were all collusive endeavours. If the people surrounding the CEO neutralise common threats and enjoy premium rewards from attaining a corporate target, and if they are bound together through their collective exposure to past adversity, whether legitimate or otherwise, collusion may not be a totally foreign condition. It may simply be considered a pejorative word for 'teamwork' that requires some sharp business practice and risk-taking.

(B) *Detailed Knowledge of Audit Process*

Many senior corporate finance positions are populated by accountants, many of who are former auditors, and some who may have previously worked for their company's auditors. They know the audit process, its limitations and its weaknesses. They also know the human frailties of their former colleagues. They routinely work with the auditors in scheduling and planning the audit, in providing assistance in the form of locating and providing documents for auditors to review, and in preparing schedules specifically for audit purposes that in due course form part of the auditors' working papers.

This practice does not absolve the auditor from examination of appropriate audit evidence, but it lays out a roadmap for corporate management of the direction the audit will take, its timing, its breadth and depth. This enhances the ability to exploit the limitations of the audit and the frailties of the people who conduct the audits. War strategists would tolerate great sacrifices to acquire this level of knowledge about their enemies.

V THE DECEIVED

Around 90 per cent or more of people who join the Big Four accounting firms in North America do not make their careers there. They are and have been for generations a training ground for accountants who migrate to industry positions. It means that there is a constant and significant turnover of staff. It also means that the average age of an average audit team is probably under 30. In larger public companies the average age of the audit team may tend to be even lower as the ratio of junior to senior staff expands with larger volumes of detailed work. Junior audit staff in Canada are typically in their early to mid 20s with undergraduate commerce degrees. Senior audit staff are typically in their late 20s with a chartered accountant designation. Managers and senior managers would also be chartered accountants in their 30s. Audit partners, of whom there are perhaps one for every 15 or more staff, range from their 30s to their late 50s or perhaps early 60s.

Most senior corporate finance managers from Controller through CFO will have business administration and/or accounting degrees and be the age of the parents of the audit staff or at least the age of their older siblings. They are people in authority and used to wielding it with effect. I have interviewed executives faced with irrefutable evidence of wrongdoing, steadfastly ignoring the evidence and redirecting the interview to areas where they can control the dialogue as they try to win me over to their own version of events and their own rationalisations of their conduct. These are people who have talked their way out of threatening circumstances time and again and are astoundingly talented manipulators of people. This is not a battle of equals.

VI AUDITOR–CLIENT RELATIONSHIPS

Perhaps surprisingly, my experience was not that of a cosy relationship with senior management. In my work in the investigation of fraud I routinely dealt with CEOs, CFOs and CLOs (Chief Legal Officers) and the board and committees thereof. As an auditor, in my larger clients I seldom encountered the CEO, hardly ever met corporate general counsel and, perhaps even more surprisingly, in many client relationships, seldom dealt directly with the CFO. Auditors typically have their key relationship with whoever is the primary producer of the financial statements, frequently the controller, perhaps even an assistant controller, or sometimes a more senior finance officer who reports to the CFO. It would be true to say that of the senior management group, the CFO would be the person with whom the auditor would typically have most interaction, but in my experience it was hardly a close relationship. I believe that experience is not uncommon among auditors.

With the *Sarbanes-Oxley Act of 2002*,[2] a greater tension has come to exist in the relationship between management and auditors. More interaction occurs between auditors and audit committee, although the relationships among auditors and audit committee and management

[2] Pub L No 107–204, 116 Stat 745 (2002) ('*Sarbanes-Oxley*').

may still be in gestation as the ripples from *Sarbanes-Oxley* continue to oscillate.

VII SENTENCING

In the 17th century Jonathon Swift offered a fairly sanguine view about fraud. In *Gulliver's Travels* he noted, in speaking of the Lilliputians:

> They look upon fraud as a greater crime than theft, and therefore seldom fail to punish it with death; for they allege, that care and vigilance, with a very common understanding, may preserve a man's goods from thieves, but honesty has no defence against superior cunning.[3]

In the 21st century we have almost caught up with Lilliput. As capital punishment has been abolished in many jurisdictions, the sentence for the most extreme crimes in those jurisdictions is life imprisonment. Bernie Ebbers, former CEO of WorldCom, was effectively sentenced to life imprisonment — at 64 years old a 25-year sentence is effectively a life sentence. Jeffrey Skilling, former CEO of Enron, is serving a 24-year sentence. As I write this, Conrad Black, former Chairman of Hollinger International and Hollinger Incorporated, is facing the greatest challenge of his life in a Chicago courtroom; a legal process whose outcome, if unfavourable to him, could result in incarceration for the rest of his life. As I see it, the spectre of spending close to the rest of your life in jail is the primary guardian of corporate ethics, not auditing, not controls, not oversight by board or regulators. If, as has been argued, it is the intensity of enforcement in the United States that confers the premium on a corporation's stock, perhaps there is economic merit in the severity and intensity of the enforcement actions and their consequent sanctions.[4]

VIII A REAL EXAMPLE

In my early career I was the recently qualified senior staff accountant with a mid-sized firm in London, in charge of the audit fieldwork of a

[3] Jonathan Swift, *Gulliver's Travels* (1726) 48.
[4] John Coffee, 'Law and the Market: The Impact of Enforcement' (Paper delivered at the Dynamics of Capital Market Governance Forum, Australian National University, 14 March 2007).

public company whose business was of no consequence to what will follow. In the client's head office where I was stationed, in Mayfair just around the corner from the Dorchester in London, a clerk, as I would have called him in those days, looked after the payroll and performed a selection of other clerical tasks. My junior colleague and I were conducting the interim audit. One of the things we did back then as part of our interim audit program was to check a couple of periods of the payroll. The payroll for the head office was maintained in a handwritten ledger. One section of the payroll was devoted to a small group of people who cleaned the head office premises. At the time we asked for the ledger the clerk said he was in the middle of doing the payroll but said we could have it for an hour or two if he could have it back so he could finish the payroll.

My junior colleague picked up the ledger and went through the routine check of names to the UK government National Insurance cards that everyone held, to see there were no fictitious people on the payroll (an interesting acknowledgement of responsibility for fraud). He checked the clock cards to see that the hours worked corresponded to the hours for which pay was calculated. Among these and several other procedures, he checked the additions and verified the accuracy of the payroll totals which we would check in due course to the posting summary, which was the medium through which the payroll costs were allocated to various functional operations of the head office that were controlled by budgets. My colleague advised me that the total payable amount for the current week of the cleaning staff payroll was recorded in pencil. This did not seem odd at the time as the clerk had said he was working on the payroll. He had probably added a column of figures and noted the total in pencil until he checked that the cross addition confirmed the accuracy of the ledger page. My colleague asked if he should write over the total in ink, as we were warned in those days against accepting figures in pencil (another interesting acknowledgement of responsibility for fraud). I suggested he make a note of the number, rather than write on the client's records, and he did. He took the ledger back to the clerk and asked if he could have it back on the following day.

Later the next day the clerk brought the ledger to our room together with the posting summary allocating the payroll costs to the various departments. He also brought the cheque, which he said he his co-worker would be taking to the bank to have cashed so that he could make up the pay envelopes for the cleaning staff. My colleague thanked him and said we would like to attend the payout to check that the appropriate people received the appropriate pay envelopes (yet another interesting acknowledgement of responsibility for fraud). My colleague checked the allocation of the payroll and advised me he was finished. I asked him if the posting summary agreed with the payroll and if the additions of the posting summary were also correct. He confirmed that everything seemed to be in order, including the comparison of the cheque amount to the total net pay for the current week.

As I glanced at the ledger and the posting summary to see that we had recorded the appropriate marks on the items we had checked, it was clear that the total previously in pencil was now recorded in ink. I asked my colleague if he had checked to see that the number he had recorded in pencil the previous day was the same as the total now recorded in ink. He had not, but did so right away, and to our surprise the number was different. It was £100 more than the number my colleague had recorded. I suggested he check the addition again. He did and confirmed that the total was overstated by £100. That meant that the clerk would get cash from the bank, pay out the cleaners' wages and have £100 left over. It may seem a small amount today and, while still small then, to give some value context my charge-out rate at the time was £4 an hour. It was also large in comparison to the total of the cleaners' weekly payroll, which was around £400. Notwithstanding these value perspectives it was still immaterial in the context of the company's financial statements. We presumed he had made a mistake. We nonetheless decided to extend our work.

My colleague checked the addition of the net pay for the previous three weeks and each time found the total was overstated by £100. We extended our work to the entire ledger for the cleaner's payroll and found the same pattern throughout the year. There were no problems with the main part of the head office payroll. The head office staff, other than the cleaners, were paid by individual cheques. We spent the remainder of the day and much of the next day considering possible explanations for the anomaly and being unable to support them. In due course I spoke with the Chief Accountant who appeared unconcerned and said I should ask the clerk to explain. He presumed the clerk must have been getting additional cash for a petty cash fund or some other department cash requirement. We had in fact already considered and ruled out these possibilities. The likely explanation was right before me but somehow I did not want to face the obvious conclusion. Today I would probably have taken all of five minutes to reach presumptive conclusions that I would quickly corroborate. It amazes me, in retrospect, how much time we spent looking for reasons for it not to be what it was, and how ready we would have been to rationalise some other explanation if we could have found any evidence that supported such an explanation.

Ultimately, I asked the clerk to our room, making surrealistic small talk as we walked from his desk to the office. I then explained to him exactly what we had found. He seemed puzzled. He did not disagree with or challenge our findings but could offer no explanation. He offered to check all the additions himself saying that there had to be an explanation. I was afraid he was going to get up and take the records and disappear. This was my first interview with a suspect and it was not going well. I had expected he would offer some explanation we had not considered. We would pound our foreheads and say, 'Of course. Why did we not think of that?' There was a long pause while I was thinking what to do. I swallowed hard and asked him a question that has stood me in good stead in subsequent years. 'How long has this been going on?' I did not say what 'this' was, and avoided terms that would have meant the clerk having to acknowledge expressly that he did what he did. It generated the dialogue that led to a confession. It transpired that 'it' had been going on for around five years. He had indeed been overstating the total payroll by adding £100 to the total. He made up the pay envelopes and put the surplus £100 in his pocket. He duly allocated the total payroll costs, including the extra £100, among several cost centres where the effect of the fraud would be reduced to an amount so far below the radar that no one noticed.

The clerk was found to have a criminal record, having been previously convicted of a similar offence. He had been taken on six years previously from a temporary help agency when the company was short staffed, and when the person who did the payroll became seriously ill, he volunteered to help out as he had done that sort of work before. The lesson I took from the experience was: never be parted from the truth by what you would like to believe. I did not want to believe that the clerk had committed a fraud, I think mostly because I was afraid of accusing someone and did not know how to deal with the stress of interviewing someone who was about to be exposed as a thief. I wanted there to be a legitimate explanation. I wanted it to go away.

After the clerk's confession, I left him with my colleague and related our findings to the Chief Accountant who took off hurriedly to see the clerk. I asked if he would like to use our room to conduct his interview. I took my colleague for an early lunchtime beer to celebrate, basking in the contemplated gratitude of my client. Perhaps a bonus from my firm would have been in order or at least a commendation from my partner. I received no accolades. The Chief Accountant, our principal point of contact, was embarrassed that we had found out that he had been asleep at the switch, the partner in charge of the audit was embarrassed that the fraud had been occurring under the noses of him and his staff for the prior five years and apparently received some caustic communication from the Managing Director of the client.

Today no auditor would do what we did. Obviously technology has changed the circumstances, but apart from circumstantial changes, the entire head office payroll would be immaterial and of little relevance in the context of the financial statements. It is ironic to reflect that the fundamental purpose of the work we did, that was unconnected in any direct way to financial statement assertions, was to identify fraud.

IX A Hypothetical Illustration

For people other than those directly involved, auditing is an obscure and even secret process. The vast majority of the population never has any relevant experience of what is involved in planning and executing an audit. In addition to the above actual example (the only fraud I ever discovered as an auditor), perhaps the best way to illustrate the current challenges is to simulate the environment and ask you, the reader, to put yourself in the shoes of a junior auditor. There is risk in doing this as the facts and circumstances are hypothetical. While I may find them consistent with my experience as an auditor and subsequently as a forensic and investigative accountant, they are not independently verifiable and consequently should be taken as they are presented, as an illustration intended to open a small window on to the nature of the auditors' world. They are also specifically intended to illustrate adverse circumstances auditors can encounter and should not be interpreted as representative of all audits or the practices of any of my former firms.

You are a second year auditor assigned for the first time to the year-end audit of a small-to-mid-sized public company in the telecommunications equipment and systems businesses. You are assigned a subsection of Accounts Receivable called Other Receivables and Prepaid Accounts. Other Receivables includes refundable deposits, an insurance claim that had been approved but not received by the year-end, amounts due from two former executives whose recoverability was questioned at the audit planning meeting and several other minor non-trade receivables. Other Receivables were collectively greater in value than the $4m materiality judgment set in the audit planning. At the audit planning meeting there had been a discussion about fraud risks. The company was stable, with long-term occupants of the CEO and CFO positions, and while its stock price oscillated, it followed industry movements. It was in the middle of the pack in size in its industry. No one perceived that there were any obvious fraud risk factors that elevated the company's profile. It was in fact a somewhat boring client. There was no comment about Prepaid Accounts or Other Receivables.

During your assigned work you find included in Other Receivables a small investment and a larger related receivable. Other Receivables is not normally the financial statement location for investments but the carrying value of this particular investment was trivial so it was of no consequence. These connected items were not specifically noted in the planning meeting or documentation. You look at last year's file, and the third quarter review file. There is a note on the schedule relating to the receivable in last year's file that all amounts are guaranteed and a copy of what is noted to be a form of guarantee in Spanish is annexed. There is also a copy of a page of what is noted to be to be from an agreement involving a trust and a foreign electronics business. Again the documents are in Spanish. A note, appended presumably by your predecessor to the working papers, indicates that the investment is trivial so no audit work was done and the loan is fully guaranteed. Last year the value of the receivable at $0.2m was immaterial and noted as such on the working paper. This year it has grown to $3.8m, an amount just under your team's assessment of what would be material to the financial statements.

You note from the third quarter file that the growth in the receivable occurred in the last quarter. The person who did this work last year was reassigned to another job and has not returned your calls and is not responding to your instant messenger inquiries. A colleague tells you he had heard the person was leaving the firm. You ask one of the more senior staff for help. She is busy on another section of the audit. She does not understand what you are saying and does not have time to think about it as she has to get her inventory section finished by the end of the week. You call the audit manager back at the office who vaguely recalls the matter from last year and the quarterly reviews and suggests you ask the relevant client finance or accounting person. He reminds you that your personal self-review form is due next week. Apprehensively, fearful of appearing inexperienced and uncertain, which, of course, you are, you ask the Assistant Controller to explain the arrangement. She fires an explanation at you that you do not really grasp and says she answered the same question for your predecessor last year and is getting tired of training auditors. She suggests you should check your last year's file, as the explanations will be there.

Do you walk away and go back to the audit manager to confess that you do not understand, acknowledging your failure? Do you walk away and try again to figure it out with the clock ticking against you and no more information than you had before? Do you walk away with the growing belief that whoever did the work last year did not understand either and begin engaging in the rationalisation that it must be appropriate if it passed muster last year? But it was very small last year. Do you stand your ground and ask the Assistant Controller to explain again until you understand? The last option may require a level of maturity and fortitude that some junior auditing staff may not possess.

You have sufficient maturity and fortitude and decide to persevere with the Assistant Controller. You explain that the guarantees given last year only covered the value outstanding at the time and the amounts are larger now. She acknowledges this and undertakes to get you the guarantees for the additional funds advanced. The next morning on your desk in the audit room is a copy of a form of guarantee similar to the one on file last year, but with a different amount that now corresponds to the current amount outstanding and with a current date. You go to thank the Assistant Controller for the guarantee document and ask if she has a copy of the full agreement with the foreign electronics company. With some irritation, she finds a copy of a 35 page multi-year research agreement with an overseas business partner through a trust. She is not happy. She gave the same document or part of it to your colleague last year. She says she needs it back. You make a photocopy to incorporate in your working paper files and return it. You apologise if it seems tedious, but it would be helpful if she could go through the explanation in simple terms one more time. She sighs ponderously. In essence, your client owns a very small interest in an overseas business venture, the majority of whose shares are held in a trust, because the jurisdiction in which the business is located does not permit foreign control of particular industries such as the one in which your client is engaged. The trustee is a local person and the foreign electronics company to which the agreement refers is the beneficiary of the trust. The company has made an interest-free loan to the trust to fund research into an electronic process that has potential military and commercial applications. The account receivable is the money your client has lent to the trust. The foreign electronics company will repay the money to the trust under a scheduled repayment program commencing next year. In return for the interest-free loan the foreign company will grant an exclusive license for your client to use the technology throughout North America. The foreign electronics company has signed guarantees to support the settlement of the loans made to the trust. You ask for the address or email address of the trustee so you can confirm the amount receivable. The Assistant Controller stares hard at you. She says she does not have either. She asks why you would possibly need to confirm anything. You have the guarantees and they were satisfactory last year. She says as far as she knows the trust was set up to get around the local foreign ownership regulations, and the COO has said that any questions should be directed through him. He said the whole thing was very sensitive because of the local foreign ownership situation. That was why the company had arranged the guarantees.

While wondering how to respond to this you ask if you can review the original signed agreement and an official English translation? You also ask if there is a trust indenture. The Assistant Controller tells you she does not have anything more than she has given you. She suggests that either or both documents may be with the Legal Department. You ask the Legal Department. They do not have the documents. The clerk to whom you spoke has never heard of them. You go back to the Assistant Controller who suggests they may be with the COO. He had been involved in setting up the arrangement last year, and it was his assistant who had provided the guarantee documents. The COO is away, and his assistant says she does not have the original or translations of either the research business venture agreement or the trust indenture. She says she speaks Spanish and could help if there was something particular you needed help understanding about the document. At your request she flips though the agreement and describes for you what each section addresses, and you annotate the agreement with her comments at each section. There seems to be nothing surprising. You ask when the COO will be back, and find he is actually out of the country meeting with the senior executives of the foreign electronics company and will back next week.

You go back a further time to ask the Assistant Controller if you could talk to the R & D people about the arrangement as this is seems to be a research project. She becomes quite annoyed and unpleasant. She asks you what you know about electronics research. She asks if you think for a minute that the research eggheads will know the first thing about where the money comes from. She tells you your job is to audit the receivables, not their research projects. You have the guarantees and she has nothing else she can give you. Why, she asks, are you questioning the judgment of your own firm? If the guarantee was acceptable last year it is acceptable this year and as far as she is concerned that is the end of the discussion. You point out that the amount is larger but she has risen and is holding the door for you to leave. Smarting and wondering if you are making a mountain out of a molehill, you return to the audit room where you and your colleagues are housed.

When you check the name of the foreign electronics company on your web browser you find that it does exist and appears to be substantial, with operations in several countries in South America. It develops and markets electronic communications devices predominantly for commercial and military applications. You include the link to the company's web site in your file. You have signed guarantees for the outstanding amounts (actually photocopies of the guarantees) and a full copy of the agreement (actually a photocopy of the agreement), with a rough indication of the meaning of each section, which is more than was on the file last year.

You are supposed to have already started on the other section of the work you had been assigned on Prepaid Accounts. After your last performance review you worried about a comment by your manager, who said you have to learn to focus as you were spending too much time on things that did not matter and needed to be more aware of getting your work done within the time budget. It was just hard when you were naturally curious to stay focused sometimes but you really need to get this work done within the allocated time budget. The likelihood is that if you follow the path of last year and rely on the guarantee, the senior staff accountant who will review your work will accept it. He will not understand it any better than you and will be impressed by the guarantee and the full 35-page agreement. If you take this path, the partner and manager will still review the work. Appropriate decisions may have to be made about the need to do more work when there may be little or no time left to do it and while the amount in questions is almost material, it is just under your materiality threshold.

Do you begin to have misgivings when, on your way home, it occurs to you that if your client had spent money directly on research instead of loaning it to the trust, the expenditures would have been charged against operations rather than appearing as a receivable? What if the entire scheme was fictitious? What if all the documents were forged? How do you know there really is a trust? How do you know there is a legally enforceable agreement with the foreign company? How do you know who actually is the real beneficiary of the trust? How do you know, even if there were a real trust and a real research agreement, that there is not an overriding side agreement that protects the foreign company and provides financial incentives for its participation in parking some research expenditure? What if there was no actual cash transfer made to the trust and instead there was a fourth quarter journal entry transferring research expenditures to the trust loan account? How do you know that the foreign company has available exportable funds to meet its potential guarantee obligations? If there is substance to the arrangement, how do you know that it is not under the effective control of your client and your client's share of the results of the trust and the foreign business venture should not be consolidated in your client's operations? How do you know that the increase in the loan value was not deliberately set to just below your materiality threshold to give you an escape route? Let us assume these misgivings did not occur to you on the way home because you are young and you have a life and you were not going home but were on your way to a party for one of your friends who was about to be married. And in the morning you are not feeling too well. So you put your problem to one side even though you are not comfortable about the whole thing and start on Prepaid Accounts. You plan to get back to the trust loan account but you run out of time. Maybe the manager is right. Perhaps you are just not cut out to be an accountant. How do your colleagues seem to get their sections done within the budget? It leaves so little time for thinking.

Two weeks later, with the closing meeting with your client management and meetings with the audit committee looming, you are called in to see the partner and the senior manager and asked about the trust and the loan account. They tell you they are not comfortable with your reliance on the guarantee. Your client advanced funds to the trust so that the trust can fund the research that would be done in the business venture. The foreign company was borrowing the money from the trust so it had a legal obligation to repay the trust. The guarantee would only be of value if the trust failed to pay over the amount to your client, and as the trust is simply a conduit, why would this be problem? They are all the more suspicious because of the perception that the client had perhaps arranged the guarantees as a smokescreen to forestall further inquiry. They are worried about the collectibility of the receivable. The partner finally calls the Controller and explains the concern about the value of the loan to the trust. Yes, it is less than materiality but there are other matters on the list of issues for discussion, and while he does not want to hold things up, he will have to get original supporting documents and confirmations. We need to get it resolved before the audit committee meeting. The Controller is really angry. You can hear him yelling down the phone at the partner. He just cannot believe that issues that we have had weeks to address are being raised now at the 11th hour when he has no time to deal with them. He says it is not even material, but the partner says there are other adjustments that he believes the audit manager has discussed with him and this is one that should be easy to fix. The Controller says he needs to speak with the CFO and will call back.

Later in the day, the CFO calls, and acknowledges that the deal was not as well documented as it might be. He attributes that to the COO who had arranged the deal and was a 'big picture person'. It had somehow slipped by him that the receivable had increased so much and, while not agreeing, acknowledges our concern about the recoverability. He had spoken to the COO who had recently returned from a visit to see the foreign electronics business partner. The COO was bullish about the project and was troubled that the auditors were suggesting there was a problem with the receivable. But he wanted the matter resolved. The COO was concerned that they should not risk jeopardising the relationship that had been hard enough to negotiate, by having auditors making his business associates nervous. The CFO announces that fortuitously the company has just concluded the sale, to a used equipment broker, of a job lot of obsolete inventory, which had been completely written off in the fourth quarter. The Controller had been going to propose that the year-end inventory obsolescence provision be reduced by the value of the proceeds, as it was clearly overstated by at least that amount, but rather than take that whole adjustment into income he is proposing half of it be used as a provision against the trust loan account. The inventory sale proceeds were slightly less than half the trust loan account, thus a provision equivalent to half of the inventory sale proceeds would reduce the exposure well below materiality. He undertook to have a more comprehensive set of documentation put together in the first quarter to support the arrangement, as it was probably going to grow in significance.

The partner proposed that, given the lack of knowledge and uncertainty even within the company, it would be more prudent to apply the whole amount to the provision for the trust account receivable, subject, of course, to satisfying himself about the inventory sale. The CFO said that as far as he knew there was no uncertainty and the COO had a complete understanding of the arrangements, but if it would get the issue off the table for the year-end he would agree to allocate the whole amount to the trust receivable provision on the understanding that it would not be on any list of issues for discussion with the audit committee. He did not want to embarrass the COO. He reconfirmed that he would get chapter-and-verse on all the documents in the first quarter. He said he had all the inventory sale documents for our examination and if we wanted to send someone to his office he would give them the package. The partner sends you off to get the documents. The CFO, who you had not previously met, is engaging. You introduce yourself and shake hands and he asks how long you had been with the firm and hopes his people had been helping you find everything you needed. He gives you a large binder of documents relating to the inventory sale. He is tall with grey hair and a kind face, an impressive executive presence — a cut above the Assistant Controller. He said while you were there that you should really get the story on the trust loan from the horse's mouth, and leads you to the adjacent office and introduces you to Jose Gonzales, the COO. Jose shakes your hand and waxes long and loud about his belief that the technology developed for military purposes by the foreign electronics firm will revolutionise handheld communication devices. And the exclusive license for North America could be worth billions. It had taken over a year to set up all of the details surrounding the trust and hammer out the research agreement. Placing his hand on your shoulder he smiles and says: 'It's a good job we have smart young auditors like you to keep us out of trouble.'

As this is a hypothetical account I can invent a hypothetical epilogue. In the first quarter of the next year, the COO left to take up another position with another company. There was little fanfare. The money advanced to the trust was never repaid, and the research never produced. The loan was written off over the next three quarters by increases to the provision as the uncertainty grew. The trust and business venture were quietly dissolved. The provision at the year-end eased the impact on the following year's results and as the amounts charged in each year were immaterial, no reference was made to the matter in the annual or quarterly reports.

In fact, the arrangement was a fraud perpetrated by the CEO, the COO and the CFO. There was a foreign electronics company and there was a joint business venture, but it was an empty shell. The beneficiary of the trust was not the foreign electronics company but a lawyer who held the shares in trust for an unnamed party, in fact a holding company owned by the CEO of the foreign electronics company who was the COO's brother-in-law. The business venture, not the foreign electronics company, drew down the funds from the trust, and under a sub-contract agreement paid the entire amount to a research consulting business in a different jurisdiction. The sub-contractor went into bankruptcy and the research results were never received. The story circulated that the research failed to fulfil expectations and was scrapped. In fact the sub-contractor invested in four other research management businesses, which in turn paid management fees for the full amount received to tax haven-based management companies of independent 'researchers', who were in fact the CEO, COO, CFO and the CEO of the foreign electronics company. The researchers' management companies invested the management fees in rare postage stamps.

The CFO would not want this matter raised at the audit committee. He would have probably expected that the guarantees set up last year and accepted for immaterial amounts would not hold this year. The increase in the provision was a deliberate fourth quarter event so it would not have hit the auditors' or the board's radar screens, although there had been careful mention of the venture in passing at the second quarter board meeting so no one could say anything was being concealed from the board. It had been mentioned that there was some expectation of the possibility of it gaining traction by the third or fourth quarter or possibly the first quarter of next year. Timelines were less predictable when dealing with South America. The receivable was purposely limited to a value below the auditors' materiality threshold so that if the issue did reach the surface it could still be argued on grounds of materiality.

The next position was the one the CFO wanted to achieve — to take a provision of sufficient size that the problem would be mitigated by accounting for it and that would reduce the amount to be written off in the following year. Had the auditors not raised the issue, he would have announced his own concern that the meeting with the foreign electronics company management had not gone as well as hoped and he believed it would be prudent for them to make a provision against the receivable.

The Assistant Controller knew nothing more than she told you. She had been given instructions by the COO to keep the auditors away from the foreign business associates. The last thing he wanted was to have auditors crawling all over his associates. They were nervous enough about the deal because of the foreign ownership regulations. If the auditors asked questions she was to stall until they ran out of time. And if necessary, he or the CFO would handle the auditors. If you had asked the Controller, as the partner ultimately did, he had instructions to warn the CFO and refer the auditors to him. If the partner were to insist that the original supporting documents be provided, they would be. It would be foolish of the CFO and the rest of the team not to have hand signed authentic documents drawn up by local counsel in Spanish. It would have been possible to produce the local trustee on the phone. It would have been a local relative of the foreign company's CEO. Had the matter had been tabled with the audit committee, the CFO would have explained that this had taken him a little unawares. He would apologise for the state of the initial documentation but would explain that the relevant documents had now been provided to the auditors. He would have recorded his agreement with the auditors on a matter of judgment about the prudence of a provision given the inherent uncertainty of research and the inherent possibility that the expectations for the research might not pan out. He would tell the audit committee that he had proposed a provision that would reduce the exposure to an immaterial amount and the auditors were satisfied. In the final analysis the money was actually still in the trust at the year-end so if a confirmation had been required it could have been produced.

While this is a hypothetical account, it is drawn from practical experience. If the partner were to accept the CFO's proposal, not only will a fraud have escaped detection but the matter would not even be brought to the attention of the audit committee. As tracks had been laid to deal with the problem by providing for the receivable, the audit focus would have been on the prospective recoverability, so when additional provisions were made in succeeding quarters the auditors would have been increasingly content.

The points this hypothetical model is intended to illustrate are:

a) how much rests on the work of relatively inexperienced audit staff;
b) how much depends on the linkage between the work done in the field and the review conducted by partners and managers;
c) how hard it can be to conceive that a fraud might have occurred;
d) how easy it can be to rationalise reliance on conclusions drawn in prior periods;
e) how difficult it can be when prior years' decisions are held out as precedents to avoid reaching different conclusions or conducting different procedures;
f) how everyday time pressures and performance measures affect execution of audit procedures;
g) how even more experienced auditors may tend to think in terms of value solutions rather than a possible fraud;
h) how actively senior management can manage auditors to keep frauds from being disclosed;
i) how middle management can be used as a foil to delay and deflect the auditor's inquiries;
j) how the insertion of layers of management can protect the most senior managers by facilitating plausible deniability;
k) how easily an auditor can be misled by senior managers intent on deceit;
l) how a fraud can occur without there necessarily being advance warning signs;
m) how easily plausible practical difficulties can be presented as reasons to prevent the pursuit of more effective audit procedures;
n) how a fraud can be presented as a difference in judgment or an error rather than an intentional deception;
o) how hard it can be to prove that a member of senior management committed a fraud;
p) how difficult it can be to prove fraud and to prosecute it;
q) how the auditor can become the scapegoat;
r) how auditing, like other personal services, is subject to the imperfections of the real world.

X THE EVIDENCE OF FRAUD

In this hypothetical case, what evidence would be available to prove that a fraud had occurred? Any business venture such as that contemplated in the illustration would normally involve an appropriate level of due diligence on the part of management. In the case of a business venture to conduct research, there would normally be a research plan, specifications of what research would be done, and who would undertake the research. There would be a business case developed and an assessment of the feasibility of the technology and the possible markets. There would be review and reporting provisions for the research that would require the presence of an administrative structure. To the extent that the research was relevant to an existing product line there would normally be evidence of that relevance. There would normally be meetings and communications between the parties in arriving at the concept and drafting the agreements. There would normally be evidence that the party undertaking to do the research had the capability to do so and was in fact doing so. As the project was a sham there would be no actual need for any of these things and, while they could conceivably have been fabricated, at some point the simulation of reality becomes unsustainable. The indicia of fraud would be the absence of evidence normally associated with a legitimate research project. While the absence of anything might not in itself be sufficient to prove that a fraud had occurred, it would be sufficient to bring to the audit committee to support the initiation of an inquiry. An investigation, if required, would follow the money and search for evidence of communications in the emails and hard drives of the COO and his assistant in the first instance. In following the money, the layering of funds through shell vehicles in different jurisdictions would not be consistent with this being a legitimate project.

Evidence of the nature described would not be focused on supporting assertions that a receivable: exists; is owed to the company; is complete; is appropriately valued; and is presented in accordance with generally accepted accounting principles. Rather, it would be focused on supporting the assertion that the receivable is the product of a fraud. It would therefore be predicated on that proposition that a fraud may have taken place. If the risk of fraud is not contemplated it is unlikely that anyone will seek out or recognise relevant evidence. Would it be necessary for an auditor to search for such evidence? If the auditor is to gain reasonable assurance that the financial statements are free from material misstatement because of fraud, the answer must be: well, perhaps. It would be argued that if sufficient provision is made, the financial statements are no longer materially misstated; in fact even if a provision is not made it might still be argued to be immaterial. If senior management stole or schemed to steal from the company an amount just less than the quantitative materiality threshold used for audit testing and planning purposes, and ultimately wrote off that amount over two years, the company's earnings would be understated by the amounts written off and the financial statements would omit disclosure of a claim against the perpetrators or, more likely, the company's insurers, of the fraud for the amount they stole. The fact that the amount at issue may be below the calculated value the auditors may use in their assessments of materiality in either year in which the funds were written off ignores any subjective assessment of materiality in the case of fraud. The Public Company Accounting Oversight Board ('PCAOB') has said: 'Qualitative considerations related to indications of fraud may mean that misstatements of relatively small amounts are material.'[5] It would be hard to say, after the event, as a subjective value judgment, that a loss of millions of dollars arising from a fraudulent conspiracy by the three most senior members of management could be considered immaterial.

Of course, in this hypothetical case, no misstatement was identified, which leads to the somewhat circular proposition that, if it could be argued that appropriate auditing standards had been followed (which might be challenging), the auditors could not be responsible for failing to find the fraud as it was less than the materiality threshold, even though it would have caused a misstatement that would probably have been considered material based on subjective criteria, had it been identified as having been caused by fraud. If, however, the circumstances subsequently came to light, the absence of detailed evidence of a substantive business arrangement might lead to an accusation, perhaps with the benefit of inquisitorial hindsight, that these were circumstances that should have sounded alarm bells and the auditors should have extended their procedures. Had they heard the alarm bells and extended their procedures, perhaps other evidence might have emerged. Perhaps

---

[5] PCAOB, *Observations on Board's Implementation of PCAOB Standards Relating to Auditors' Responsibilities with Respect to Fraud* (Release No 2007–001, 22 January 2007) 4, available at <http://www.pcaobus.org/News_and_Events/News/2007/01-22.aspx>.

the auditors would have reported the circumstances to the audit committee and the audit committee might have instigated an investigation. The company might say it would have moved right away to recover the money and would probably evaluate with counsel a cause of action against the auditors.

Of course senior management would raise defences. Management would show that the funds were still actually in a lawyer's trust account at the year-end so that the financial statements were not misstated. The CEO and CFO would say they knew nothing of any improprieties and the COO would say he had been deceived by the foreign company but had been so embarrassed by having been duped and had been threatened with dismissal by the CEO that he had been obliged to resign.

The foreign company would say that they did not draw down the money from the trust so they cannot be held responsible, and the trustee would say that a well-dressed business man came and presented impeccable credentials as being the CEO of the business venture and knew all about the arrangements. The trustee honestly believed he was legitimate and released the funds to the business venture bank account. There turned out to be some ambiguity in the agreement about whether the foreign electronics company or the business venture could draw down the funds. There would be exit strategies for all parties because the entire scheme had been planned. Perhaps the auditors would be the only party without an exit strategy.

XI CHANGING AUDITING STANDARDS

Auditors approaching an annual audit of a client's financial statements are now required to consider specifically the risks of fraud and the risk factors that would elevate the likelihood of fraud occurring, and design their audits to respond to identified risk factors. It is instructive to see how the auditing profession is responding to these circumstances and how PCAOB's inspections have found auditors are dealing with these requirements. In November 2006, the Global Public Policy Symposium, comprising the CEOs of the six largest accounting firms, released a paper titled *Global Capital Markets and the Global Economy: A Vision From the CEOs of the International Audit Networks*. The paper states:

> there is a significant 'expectations gap' between what various stakeholders believe auditors do or should do in detecting fraud, and what audit networks[6] are actually *capable* of doing, at the prices that companies or investors are willing to pay for audits.[7]

Additionally, the paper states that: 'What is sorely needed is a constructive dialogue among investors, other company stakeholders, policy makers and our own professionals about what should be done to close or at least narrow the "expectations gap" relating to fraud.'[8] In January of 2007 the PCAOB felt it necessary to issue a 14 page report commenting on over 20 shortcomings it had observed in the way auditors were addressing their responsibilities with respect to fraud. A selection of the comments follows:

a) Auditors failed to expand audit procedures when addressing identified fraud risk factors.
b) Auditors were unable to demonstrate that the required fraud risk brainstorming sessions were held during audit planning process.
c) Key members of the audit team did not attend the sessions.
d) Auditors failed to respond appropriately to fraud risk factors.
e) Auditors failed to calculate planning materiality properly and/or the threshold for posting proposed audit adjustments to a summary schedule. As a result, certain uncorrected misstatements were not evaluated, or were not evaluated appropriately, both individually and in the aggregate, with other misstatements because the summary schedule was incomplete.
f) Auditors had not addressed the risk of management override of controls with respect to journal entries and accounting estimates.
g) Auditors performed tests of journal entries, but failed to demonstrate that they had appropriately assessed the completeness and integrity of the population of journal entries.
h) No evidence in the audit documentation, and no persuasive other evidence, that an appropriate examination and evaluation of journal entries was performed.

---

[6] Audit 'networks' is the term used in this document to describe the six largest global auditing organisations.
[7] (2006) 12 (emphasis in original).
[8] Ibid.

i) Auditors excluded journal entries with lower dollar amounts from the examination. Setting the scope in such a manner fails to appropriately address the risk of fraud occurring as a result of the frequent use of low dollar entries.
j) Auditors have failed to test, or failed to document their testing of, management's assumptions and other aspects of issuers' accounting estimates.
k) In using analytical procedures auditors failed to establish expectations, establish thresholds for identifying significant differences, or investigate differences from the expectations that were greater than the established thresholds.

While this is not necessarily representative of all audits by all auditors, it is also hardly a ringing endorsement. Auditors are saying they do not believe they can meet expectations under the current model and the PCAOB is saying they are falling short on execution of current standards.

XII CONSIDERATION OF CHANGES THAT MIGHT HELP

(A) *Acknowledging a Problem*

It is a truism that the first step in treating a problem is acknowledging its existence. The events that gave rise to *Sarbanes-Oxley* were collusive subversions of financial reporting controls by the most senior members of management. While it would be an overstatement to say that the tidal wave of effort in documenting, certifying and attesting to internal controls in response to s 404 of *Sarbanes-Oxley* has been without merit, its focus was directed at almost everything but the most threatening risk. The purchasing agent who takes kickbacks, the clerk who falsifies the payroll records, the project manager who sets up fictitious vendors are all defrauding the corporation and bleeding away the stakeholders' interests. While reprehensible and worthy of attention, these risks are unlikely to bring the corporation to its knees.

The overwhelming risk is that senior management will subvert the financial reporting controls and misrepresent the state of the corporation's affairs and results of operations. It is hard to see how a corporate governance structure can discharge its stewardship responsibilities effectively when the responsibility for internal control over financial reporting remains the domain of the very management whose actions have illustrated the catastrophic consequences of their collusive frauds through subversion of the internal controls over financial reporting. It is also hard to see that auditors can efficiently discharge the responsibility of protecting a corporation's stakeholders from collusive fraud by senior management. The costs required to investigate the evidence in a significant financial reporting fraud case are many multiples of the cost of the annual audits. Detection of fraud at this level is almost not an option. That means it has to be prevented. While auditors can make contributions to mitigate these risks, they are not the only party whose contribution could be improved. Another party with an opportunity to improve its contribution is the board.

(B) *Spreading the Load*

In 1992, the Committee of Sponsoring Organisations of the Treadway Commission identified the board as one of the parties responsible for giving effect to internal control. It also stated:

> Management is accountable to the board of directors, which provides governance, guidance and oversight. Effective board members are objective, capable and inquisitive. They also have knowledge of the entity's activities and environment, and commit the time necessary to fulfill their board responsibilities. Management may be in a position to override controls and ignore or stifle communications from subordinates, enabling a dishonest management, which intentionally misrepresents results to cover its tracks. A strong, active board, particularly when coupled with effective upward communications channels and capable financial, legal and internal audit functions, is often best able to identify and correct such a problem.[9]

The SEC's 9 April 2003 final rule on *Standards Relating to Listed Company Audit Committees* states, inter alia:

> The assistance of outside advisors also may be needed to independently investigate questions that may arise regarding

---

[9] *Internal Control — Integrated Framework: Executive Summary* (1992), available at <http://www.coso.org/publications/executive_summary_integrated_framework.htm>.

> financial reporting and compliance with the securities laws. Accordingly, as proposed, the final rule specifically requires an issuer's audit committee to have the authority to engage outside advisors, including counsel, as it determines necessary to carry out its duties.[10]

As much as auditors have been castigated for their ineffectiveness in dealing with fraud, the boards of directors of the corporations involved in the financial reporting scandals since the millennium have also been ineffective. While there may be defences, the boards failed in each case to protect their corporation from its management. For boards to make a more substantive contribution to the effectiveness of governance and oversight of senior management it is, in my view, time to consider the need for professional directors, along with some measure of standardisation of procedure for execution of board responsibilities, greater prescription of the time commitment required and a significantly greater investment in the funding of board activities. Before senior management fraud becomes an audit problem it is a stewardship problem. As noted in this chapter and as acknowledged by the PCAOB in its standard AS2, collusive fraud is less likely to be detected by an audit. While auditing standards have become more focused and prescriptive about auditors' responsibility for finding material fraud, I am not confident that auditors will be able to fulfil expectations of detecting or preventing fraud today any more than in the last hundred years within acceptable cost tolerances. If, as I would tender, senior management cannot be responsible for establishing and maintaining internal controls over itself, there is only the board that can rationally fill that role. If the audit committee, for example, rather than senior management, took responsibility for the management of the risk of fraudulent financial reporting by senior management and processes were established that were aligned with the risk of management subversion, such a construct would have the potential to be a plausible deterrent that would mitigate the risk for the corporation. Upgrading boards is not something that can happen overnight, but upgrading audits is also not an overnight job. It is interesting to see that a variety of business schools are offering educational programs for directors. The regulatory requirements for financial literacy and expertise on audit committees are also moving in the direction of greater relevant expertise.

---

[10] Available at <http://www.sec.gov/rules/final/33-8220.htm>.

(C) *Controls Aligned with the Risk*

The most threatening risk is that senior management will subvert financial reporting controls and manipulate the financial reports. What controls exist to mitigate the risk of such subversion? Audit committees could file reports on such controls. Auditors could make a supporting contribution by attestation to the controls established by the board to mitigate the risk that senior management could manipulate the financial reporting process. There is a traditional line, whose brightness has faded in recent years, between governance and management.

If there is no other steward but the board who can fulfil the role of guardian against ethical misfeasance by senior management, then the development of controls to mitigate the risk of collusive subversion of financial reporting by senior management must become part of the governance model. If arguments were to be made that such activity would be tantamount to the board engaging in management, then perhaps the boundary is a sacred cow that needs to be put out of its misery.

Would the Enron pensioners have cared about the division of governance and management responsibilities as between the board and management of the corporation if the consequence had been to save their pensions?

(D) *Weakening the Defences*

People do not commit fraud with the expectation of getting caught. Getting caught is not the same as evidence of fraud being discovered. Getting caught is being proved to be the perpetrator or one of the perpetrators. To the extent that popular defences can be made unavailable the chances of getting caught increase. The audit committee is, in my view, the logical agency to have this responsibility.

(E) *Plausible Deniability*

Plausible deniability — 'It wasn't me, I knew nothing about it. I was misled by my subordinates' — is a defence probably as old as fraud itself. In the mid-1970s the US Church Committee (named for its Chair, Senator Frank Church) conducted an investigation of the US intelligence agencies. It noted:

> The Committee finds that the system of Executive command and control was so inherently ambiguous that it is difficult to be certain at what level assassination activity was known and authorized. This creates the disturbing prospect that assassination activity might have been undertaken by officials of the United States Government without its having been incontrovertibly clear that there was explicit authorization from the President of the United States.[11]

It would be relevant, in my view, for the audit committee to understand the mechanics, style and protocols of communication and responsibilities within the chain of command of management of the organisation. Senior officers who neither send or receive emails, who give direction by telephone without written confirmation, or via assistants, to their subordinates and peers, who have incoming communications filtered through assistants, who use vague and euphemistic language, are offering themselves plausible deniability defences. The Church Committee also reported that: '"Plausible denial" increases the risk of misunderstanding. Subordinate officials should describe their proposals in clear, precise, and brutally frank language; superiors are entitled to, and should demand, no less'.[12] In the same vein, a board should reasonably expect its senior management to have and follow a policy of clarity in communications. As the audit committee is authorised to retain advisors this may be an area where advice might be valuable.

CONCLUSION

I do not believe, based on 20 years experience in each case as auditor and investigative and forensic accountant, that auditors can be reasonably assured that financial statements are not materially misstated due to fraud, without revolutionary changes to the audit model whose cost and intrusiveness may be hard for corporations to accept. Alternatives under current debate contemplate the incorporation of forensic audits into the routine of annual financial audits. Further definition of what a forensic audit would entail how often it might be conducted, and other relevant

---

[11] Church Committee II, section B, 11; Church Committee IV, *Findings and Conclusions*, section C subsection 1, 261.

[12] Church Committee IV, section C subsection 5, 277.

information would be relevant in assessing the efficacy of such proposals.

It is encouraging to see the CEOs of the leading auditing firms calling in unison for global standardisation of accounting, financial reporting and auditing. And perhaps the call for dialogue will indeed engage the other players, including the financial intermediaries. If the capital markets are to restore and maintain level of confidence and trust, all the parties within the governance framework have to be at the table. Auditing appears to be in the throes of a difficult metamorphosis and, under whatever model emerges, the transition will not be easy. [13]

---

[13] Since the presentation of this paper in February 2007, the SEC approved on July 25, 2007, the PCAOB's Auditing Standard No. 5, "An Audit of Internal Control Over Financial Reporting That Is Integrated with An Audit of Financial Statements". This new standard places greater emphasis on financial reporting fraud by senior management. It specifically includes reference to controls over the risk of management override of controls over financial reporting: "…the auditor should evaluate whether the company's controls sufficiently address identified risks of material misstatement due to fraud and controls intended to address the risk of management override of other controls." It is encouraging to see the express acknowledgement of the risks posed by misfeasance of senior management. It is also encouraging to witness the readiness of regulators to modify standards so substantially and so urgently. Time will tell how effective the new standard is.

Chapter 8

Compliance, Ethics and Responsibility: Emergent Governance Strategies in the US and UK

Doreen McBarnet

The governance challenge in capital markets lies not only in corporate non-compliance but in corporate creative compliance. This chapter explores current initiatives in the US and UK to address this issue through a new emphasis on ethics and corporate responsibility in the governance of business.[1]

Creative compliance, to recap briefly on a concept already noted many times, refers to the use of technical legal work to manage the legal packaging, structuring and definition of practices and transactions, such that they can claim to fall on the right side of the boundary between lawfulness and illegality. It is essentially the practice of using the letter of the law to defeat its spirit, and to do so with impunity. Practices that might be illegal, indeed criminal, if legally structured in one way, are legally repackaged and claimed to be lawful, or at least 'not illegal'. The word 'claimed' is important, since these structures might depend on questionable or aggressive interpretations of law or facts, on 'bullish' approaches or on 'sailing close to the wind', as it was put to me in interviews with lawyers, bankers and regulators. They might be found 'legally ineffective' if challenged but even then are expected to act as

[1] This chapter is based on research funded by the ESRC Professorial Fellowship program (RES 051–27–0031). Thanks to the ESRC for funding and to Vladimir Meerovitch for research assistance.

'fraud insurance' because they are based on disputed technical legal argument rather than on non-disclosure or outright breaches of law.

I have argued elsewhere[2] that creative compliance cannot be tackled through law alone. Underlying it are two factors: law, which provides the material for creative compliers to work on, and the way law is received. Ultimately creative compliance depends on a mindset in which law is seen not as policy to be fulfilled but as material to be worked with; where it is seen as the responsibility of the regulators to make the letter of the law inviolable, rather than the responsibility of the regulated to comply with its spirit; where law is looked to not to ask: 'is what I want to do allowed by law?' but: 'how can I find a way to justify it regardless?' Fundamentally, it is a mindset in which to comply with the letter but defeat the spirit of the law is deemed clever and legitimate. To tackle creative compliance one must challenge that mindset and that culture of legitimacy, and to do that means a shift in the standard of what is deemed to constitute compliance, from a positivist vision of legal compliance as a technical task, to one where compliance also involves compliance with the spirit of the law, and an injection of ethical judgement. It means a shift from technical to ethical, or responsible, compliance.

Such a suggestion might be dismissed as mere academic aspiration. However there are developments taking place in practice which might be seen as pursuing, fostering, and, indeed, enforcing just such a shift in standards. This chapter explores the strategies being brought into play, looking not only at the initiatives of regulatory authorities but at new developments in the corporate accountability agenda of civil society.

I REGULATORY DEVELOPMENTS

(A) *US Regulation and the Enron Effect*

Enron has played a key role in recent regulatory developments in the US — and for that matter elsewhere. The trials of Enron personnel themselves focussed not on creative compliance but on outright fraud —

[2] Doreen McBarnet, 'After Enron: Corporate Governance, Creative Compliance and the Uses of Corporate Social Responsibility' in Justin O'Brien (ed), *Governing the Corporation: Regulation and Corporate Governance in an Age of Scandal and Global Markets* (2005) 205.

indeed, often on illegalities incidental to, or consequential on, the accounting structuring used rather than the accounting techniques themselves.[3] The reason was simple and understandable enough. The objective was to set an example and to get senior executives behind bars. That needed fraud charges, and fraud charges simple enough to stick. However, Enron was also heavily into creative compliance, and one of the most significant effects of its collapse has been to raise questions about the social and moral acceptability of this practice, regardless of whether it is arguably within the letter of the law or not, bringing ethical considerations much more overtly into regulatory debate.

Enron raised public awareness of the significance of esoteric corporate practices that were not necessarily out and out illegal but nonetheless deceptive in both effect and intent. It was not just the sheer size of the Enron collapse that raised awareness. It was also the extensive coverage of its social and economic effects and of its corporate culture. The style Enron employed, with its humorous names for its Special Purpose Entities, such as Star Wars characters Jedi or Chewbacca, provided material for headlines, while even its logo — an 'E' tilted on its side — lent itself to presentation as the 'crooked E', all of which facilitated media reach beyond the normal business community and made the import of Enron's practices accessible to a wider public even if the practices themselves remained opaque. The trials themselves received daily media attention, and the arguments in court from Chairman Lay and CEO/CFO Skilling that they were engaging in normal business practice, only exacerbated the image of creative compliance as routine and pervasive. An unprecedented amount of information was made available through the range of Congressional investigations that followed the collapse and the press coverage around the world, and the pervasive tone was one of outrage.

Much of this outrage focused quite explicitly not just on the issue of fraud, but on the revelation that practices claimed to be perfectly legal could still mislead and distort the market. Comments at Congressional investigations drove this point home repeatedly:

---

[3] For a detailed analysis of these issues see Doreen McBarnet, 'After Enron Will "Whiter than White Collar Crime" Still Wash?' (2006) 46 *British Journal of Criminology* 1091. The discussion of US regulatory developments in this chapter draws on and develops Part III of that article: 'Wider Repercussions'.

> The real scandal here may be from not what is illegal, but what is totally permissible. If the GAAP (Generally Accepted Accounting Principles) allow the bookkeeping shenanigans that have been reported in the press then we should all go into the derivative business. It seems that all too often the name of the corporate game is to conceal the true financial situation of the company while doing the minimum amount of disclosure to avoid legal exposure.[4]

Even the prosecutors in the Enron trials talked of 'fraud *and* accounting hocus pocus', 'funny accounting', 'arcane accounting' or 'aggressive accounting' — practices they implicitly distinguished from out-and-out fraud. Harvey Pitt, the then Chairperson of the Securities and Exchange Commission ('SEC'), talked of 'gaming the system'.[5] Concern, in short, went beyond the issue of what was lawful to what was ethical.

Outrage and disbelief also permeated the reaction to the revelation that Enron could use the different rules of tax and accounting to simultaneously report huge profits in its SEC returns, and claim tax losses and huge refunds, in its tax returns. From 1995 to 2000 Enron reported US$1.8 billion in profits. How much tax did it pay? None. In fact it received US$381 million in rebates.[6] Nor was Enron alone. Citizens for Tax Justice[7] reported 41 major companies paying 'less than zero' in at least one year in the period 1996–98. These companies reported a total of US$25.8 billion profits in their financial accounts, but rather then paying tax, they received US$3.2 billion in rebates. The *New York Times* observed:

> Imagine a company that makes a practice of keeping two sets of accounts. One version is revealed to the public through periodic Securities and Exchange Commission filings and public announcements. The other is never made public and conveys a markedly different picture. Does it sound

[4] Senator Fred Thompson, Committee on Homeland Security and Governmental Affairs Hearing 107–376, United States Senate, Washington DC *The Fall of Enron: How Could It Have Happened?* (24 January 2002).

[5] Harvey Pitt, 'Remarks' (Speech delivered at the Annual Meeting of the American Bar Association's Business Law Section, Washington DC, 12 August 2002).

[6] Scott Klinger and Holly Sklar, 'Titans of the Enron Economy', *The Nation*, 5 August 2002.

[7] 'Less than Zero: Enron's Income Tax Payments, 1996–2000' (2002) <http://www.ctj.org/html/enron.htm>.

> scandalous? Actually it's common practice. It isn't as if companies are breaking the law …[8]

Enron, in short, drew attention not only to corporate fraud, but to the problem of technical or creative compliance, raising questions about the nature of corporate compliance and about corporate and professional ethics. It also provided a catalyst for demands for change, and a new focus, within regulation, on ethics.

(B) *US Regulatory Initiatives*

Alongside the new rules and structural controls of the *Sarbanes-Oxley Act of 2002*[9] and related regulatory action, there has been a new regulatory interest in the culture of business organisations, with increasing reference in regulatory debate to a 'corrupt corporate culture',[10] and calls from the SEC for change not just in corporate law but in corporate culture and ethics.[11] Stephen Cutler, SEC Director of Enforcement, has ascribed securities laws violations to both individual failings *and* 'deficient' corporate culture.[12] Indeed part of the state's response has been to try to foster changes in corporate culture through a new emphasis on corporate compliance and ethics programs. *Sarbanes-Oxley* itself imposes a requirement for companies to have Codes of Ethics for CEOs and CFOs, but other developments take this further. The US Sentencing Commission's 2004 Guidelines ('Sentencing Guidelines') encourage adoption of company-wide Codes of Ethics and Compliance by making this a mitigating factor in future sentences. Importantly, evidence of code implementation and a culture of integrity are increasingly required. The Sentencing Guidelines, 'in response to testimony that a culture of compliance cannot exist without a culture of

---

[8] Anna Bernasek, 'Why Let the IRS See What the SEC Doesn't?', *New York Times* (New York), 5 February 2006.

[9] Pub L No 107–204, 116 Stat 745 (2002) ('*Sarbanes-Oxley*').

[10] Christopher A Wray, 'Remarks' (Speech delivered at the American Bar Association White Collar Crime Luncheon, University Club, Washington DC, 25 February 2005).

[11] Mary Ann Gadziala, 'Rebuilding Ethics and Compliance in the Securities Industry' (Speech delivered at the NYSE Regulation First Annual Securities Conference, Securities and Exchange Commission, New York, 23 June 2005).

[12] 'Tone at the Top: Getting It Right' (Speech delivered at the Second Annual General Counsel Roundtable, Washington DC, 3 December 2004).

ethics',[13] require companies to 'promote an organisational culture that encourages ethical conduct and a commitment to compliance with the law', with 'high level personnel' responsible for ensuring the program is effective. They must embed their message in the corporate culture via repeated communication and 'effective training', and through appropriate incentives and disciplinary measures. The SEC and major stock exchanges all now require not just codes of conduct but effective implementation procedures, and a culture of compliance must, says the SEC, be instilled 'from the top down'.[14]

The significance of the Sentencing Guidelines lies not only in their relevance for companies seeking to mitigate any future sentence should regulators take action against them, but because of their status in state corporate law. In a 1996 case, the Delaware Courts (Delaware corporate law being of disproportionate significance because most major US companies are registered there) used the Sentencing Guidelines' requirements of that time as the benchmark for whether directors had met their fiduciary obligation to ensure legal compliance mechanisms had been set up.[15] Directors could therefore find themselves directly in the firing line on the basis of the new Sentencing Guidelines' requirements.

One interviewee, Deputy General Counsel of a major US corporation, described the new Guidelines as 'the most significant thing that has happened because it now makes the ethical mandatory.' He spoke of *Sarbanes-Oxley*, and the 'plethora of regulations that came along with it', as having

> not that great an impact on our Codes of Conduct and on our reporting. What is having a much greater impact is the effort to move to a more values driven corporate culture, which is I think the real sleeper story of the response to the disasters … You're required not only to have a company that is compliant with legal requirements but also behaves ethically.[16]

---

[13] John F Sherman, 'Human Rights Implications of the 2004 Amendments to the US Sentencing Guidelines for Organizational Defendants' (2007) *International Commission of Jurists* (forthcoming).
[14] Gadziala, above n 11.
[15] *Re Caremark International Inc* Derivative Litig, 698 A 2d 959, 970 (Del Ch, 1996), discussed in Sherman, above n 13.
[16] Interview with Deputy General Counsel of a US corporation, May 2007.

Of course, calling for a new ethical culture and a commitment to compliance does not of itself challenge *creative* compliance, even in aspiration. To do that would mean calling for a new approach to compliance itself that focussed on a need for compliance with the spirit and not just the letter of the law. However, regulatory discourse is now setting standards for companies and professionals that go beyond mere literal compliance to compliance with the spirit of the law.

The former SEC Chairman, William Donaldson, pressed the importance of investors being able 'to see for themselves that companies are living up to their obligations and embracing the spirit underpinning all securities laws', 'beyond just conforming to the letter'.[17] His predecessor, Pitt, drove home to lawyers the point that: 'Helping a company satisfy literal legal prescriptions, even if doing so is contrary to what those legal prescriptions were intended to accomplish, doesn't satisfy a corporate lawyer's duties.'[18] The role of lawyers in driving compliance with the spirit of the law is also emphasised by SEC Commissioner Cynthia Glassman: 'In particular, I want to emphasize the importance of complying not just with the letter — but also with the spirit — of our rules and highlight the role that you as corporate counsel can play in this process.'[19]

In the accounting context, there is a new drive for principle-based regulation, with rules presented, for example, by the US Chief Accountant, Conrad Hewitt, as leading 'to an emphasis on form over substance. I think that accountants should focus more on the economic substance of a transaction rather than its form — to prevent situations such as Enron'.[20] Principle-based regulation, he argues (echoing, as we shall see, UK accounting policy of some years earlier) might foster this approach. However, any shift to principle-based regulation, he warns, must be accompanied by a new mindset on the part of business: 'I must ask you to do your part and refrain from entering into accounting-

---

[17] 'US Capital Markets in the Post-*Sarbanes-Oxley* World: Why Our Markets Should Matter to Foreign Issuers' (Speech delivered at the London School of Economics, London, 25 January 2005).

[18] Pitt, above n 5.

[19] 'Remarks: Priorities and Concerns at the SEC' (Speech delivered at the 10th Annual Corporate Counsel Compliance Institute, Washington DC, 9 March 2006).

[20] 'Remarks' (Speech delivered at the Practising Law Institute's SEC Speaks Series, Washington DC, 9 February 2007).

motivated transactions'.[21] Likewise, Deputy Chief Accountant, James Kroeker, talks of the need in principle-based accounting for judgment to be exercised 'appropriately and honestly' with a shift away from 'engineering around accounting objectives' and 'asking questions like, "can you show me where it says that I can't do this?".'[22]

There has, then, been a growing articulation in US regulatory circles of the need for an express shift in the standard of compliance required from compliance with the letter to compliance with the spirit of the law, and recognition that this needs not just new law but a new culture of ethical compliance. There have also been some regulatory initiatives, and a good deal of regulatory discourse, seeking to foster this approach. Indeed, the discourse has attained sufficient currency that US Treasury Secretary Hank Paulson, in his November 2006 speech calling for a shift to principle-based regulation for the primary purpose of retrieving US capital market competitiveness vis-à-vis principle-based London regulation,[23] could use these arguments as part of his rationale.

He noted the need to consider whether a rule-based system 'gives too much latitude to unscrupulous lawyers', called for the US to 'rise above a rules-based mindset that asks, "Is this legal?" and adopt a more principles-based approach that asks, "Is this right?"',[24] and argued for 'compliance with the spirit of regulatory principles'.[25]

(C) *Enforcement Policy*

These calls for a new standard of compliance are matched by declarations of enforcement policy and indeed by some very specific examples of enforcement practice: namely the deferred prosecution

---

[21] Conrad Hewitt, 'Remarks' (Speech delivered at Baruch College, New York, 3 May 2007).

[22] 'Remarks' (Speech delivered at the Conference on Principles-Based Accounting and the Challenges of Implementation, New York, 4 April 2007).

[23] Sir Callum McCarthy, the FSA Chairman, has referred to London's approach as a 'light touch, sometimes mistranslated into soft touch', 'Financial Regulation: Myth and Reality' (Speech delivered at the British American Business London Insight Series and Financial Services Forum, 13 February 2007).

[24] 'Opening Remarks' (Speech delivered at the Treasury's Capital Markets Competitive Conference, Georgetown University, 13 March 2007).

[25] Henry Paulson, 'Remarks: Competitiveness of US Capital Markets' (Speech delivered at the Economic Club of New York, New York, 20 November 2006).

strategy employed vis-à-vis a number of banks and accountancy firms in the aftermath of Enron.

In several key cases related to, and following on, from Enron — notably the cases against the firm of Merrill Lynch (as opposed to the prosecution of specific Merrill Lynch executives), the Canadian Imperial Bank of Commerce (another participant in Enron deals), and KPMG (pursued in knock-on investigations into tax shelters) — the state adopted a strategy of deferred prosecution agreements rather than outright prosecution. These deals set up a prosecution but defer it in return for a range of obligations being undertaken by the firm. So long as the terms of the agreement are complied with, after a specified time, the prosecution is dropped.

The agreements negotiated, or imposed, demonstrated significant leverage exerted by the prosecutors to set up new constraints on the firms in question. Typically the firm was required to admit guilt and to pay significant sums in fines, restitution and disgorgement of fees. But the terms also included governance constraints that went well beyond narrow issues of fraud prevention, targeting the prevention of not just fraud but creative compliance, addressing corporate culture and imposing direct responsibility on senior management.

One common requirement was to set up committees comprising senior executives ('head of group or experienced designee') from all the 'disciplines' in the firm, to review and approve transactions, with the need for agreement of all heads before a transaction structure was approved. This review obligation extended, for example, in the Merrill Lynch agreement to include 'all complex structured finance transactions effected by a third party with Merrill Lynch.'[26] The concerns of Congress and the press were echoed in the prohibition from engagement in any transaction intended to 'achieve a misleading earnings, revenue or balance sheet effect'[27] — note the use of 'misleading' rather than just 'fraudulent'. There was also a demand that in assessing these structures, there should be a shift of focus from technical compliance to a concern with the 'objectives' of the structuring, objectives characteristic of routine creative compliance in 'normal' transaction work. There was an express requirement too to take into account not just legal risk but 'reputational risk', extending the gamut of control beyond potential fraud

[26] US Department of Justice, *Enron Task Force Agreement with Merrill Lynch on Deferred Prosecution* (2003) 2.
[27] Ibid, see 'Exhibit A' attached to that Agreement, 1, 3.

and civil liability to what is simply not approved, and to pay attention to both 'illegal and unethical' elements'. 'Elevated standards' beyond specific legal obligations were required, and there was emphasis on the setting up of 'effective' and monitored compliance and ethics programs.[28]

More generally, beyond the deferred prosecutions, declared enforcement policy presses home the relevance of a company's implementation of an ethical compliance culture to its enforcement decisions. The SEC reports it is looking beyond procedures to culture in its examinations,[29] while the Department of Justice has declared its intention to take 'unethical' as well as 'illegal' conduct into account in its enforcement: 'A company's history of repeated unethical conduct, followed by an employee's criminal act might well be viewed quite differently from the same criminal conduct coming instead on the heels of a long history of responsible, ethical conduct.'[30]

The deferred prosecution agreements have also had a wider knock-on effect with companies and their advisers scrutinising them as guidance for what regulators will look for in assessing whether companies' new compliance and ethics programs meet regulatory standards of 'effectiveness'. Likewise regulatory pronouncements on ethical and reputational risk, and on compliance with the spirit of the law are being taken on board as criteria for setting up 'state of the art ethics and compliance programs'.[31] Our own research shows a number of companies are undertaking, in either their *Sarbanes-Oxley*-required codes of ethics or in their general corporate codes of conduct, to abide not just by the letter but by the spirit of the law. Pilot research on the top 50 corporations in the Fortune 500 shows almost half, 24 of the 50, commit themselves expressly in their codes of conduct to compliance with the spirit of law, 18 committing to the spirit of the law in general, and another 6 committing to compliance with spirit in the context of core areas of law. In the UK, some 23 companies in the FTSE 100 commit to

[28] US Department of Justice, *Re KPMG: Deferred Prosecution Agreement* (2005).
[29] Gadziala, above n 11.
[30] Interview with Christopher Wray, 'The Justice Department's Rational Approach to Deterring Corporate Crime', *The Metropolitan Corporate Counsel* (New Jersey), July 2005, 35, 53, available at <http://www.metrocorpcounsel.com/pdf/2005/July/35,53.pdf>.
[31] Theodore N Mirvis, John F Savarese and Carol Miller, 'The New Regulatory and Enforcement Environment' (2005) *Securities Reporter* 10.

the spirit of the law, 9 in general, 14 in specific areas. What that means in practice is a matter of ongoing research.[32]

(D) *Regulatory Initiatives: The UK*

There are clear parallels with this regulatory drive for a new standard of compliance, and a new ethical corporate culture, in countries other than the US. In the UK, for example, although the context and regulatory history are different from the US, making for differences in approach, emphasis and language, there is nonetheless also a clear drive in the same direction, a drive indeed with a longer history and deeper roots.

UK regulation did not need Enron to raise awareness of creative compliance, the UK having had its own crises. UK regulators had diagnosed and begun to tackle the issue of creative compliance in accounting and corporate governance long before Enron, in the late 1980s and 1990s, using the strategy of a shift from rules (which were seen as facilitating claims to technical compliance) to principles, in the format of regulations. The Accounting Standards Board ('ASB') was a particular leader in this strategy under David Tweedie (now chair of the International Accounting Standards Board), while the Financial Services Authority ('FSA') also brought in an approach based on principles to financial services regulation, and especially from the late 1990s the Inland Revenue, now Her Majesty's Revenue and Customs ('HMRC') was following through in its strategies on earlier judicial attacks[33] on creative compliance in the form of tax avoidance.[34]

There has undoubtedly been an Enron effect in the UK too, however. Enron helped licence a new focus on corporate ethics and corporate cultures including a company's attitude to law and compliance. For example, Patricia Hewitt, Secretary for Trade and Industry talked, post-Enron, of the issues of corporate governance *and* 'loose ethics'.[35] Dan Waters criticised a 'legalistic approach' to rules and compliance

---

[32] Doreen McBarnet and Vladimir Meerovitch, ESRC Professorial Fellowship research project on commitment to the spirit of the law.

[33] Especially the series of cases beginning with *Ramsay (WT) Ltd v IRC* [1982] AC 300; *Furniss v Dawson* [1984] AC 474.

[34] Inland Revenue, *A General Anti-Avoidance Rule for Direct Taxes* (1998); see also Interview with David Hartnett, Director General HMRC, *Accountancy Age*, October 2005.

[35] 'Strengthening Corporate Governance', UK, *Parliamentary Debates*, House of Commons, 29 January 2003 (Patricia Hewitt).

suggesting it would lead to 'our very own Enron experience'.[36] Margaret Cole, Director of Enforcement at the FSA, described herself in a 2007 speech as disturbed, to

> still see a blind spot when it comes to associating market misconduct with financial crime. Some people, it seems, don't believe that market manipulation, market abuse and insider dealing is as serious an issue as fraud. There is still a way to go in bringing about a cultural shift in this area.[37]

It is also perceived that, as one financial regulator put it to me: 'The prosecutions of Enron individuals have led to a re-evaluation by the industry generally as to what is acceptable behaviour.'[38]

Recent regulatory developments have seen an increased focus on changing corporate culture and compliance mindsets, increased emphasis on ethics and more overt calls for compliance with the spirit of the law. The language used is both that of ethics and of 'responsibility', a reflection of the stronger development of the Corporate Social Responsibility movement in the UK and Europe, discussed in more detail later.

Regulatory standards are being described increasingly as not just legal but ethical. The FSA in 2002 overtly described its principles, its 'high level standards' as 'based on ethical values'. The FSA's first principle simply requires firms to 'act with integrity'.[39] The ASB has also underlined the ethical nature of its principles by republishing a paper influential 25 years ago on the meaning of the principle of 'true and fair' accounting — a standard which the new president of the influential Institute of Chartered Accountants of Scotland, Isobel Sharp, describes as related to 'societal perception of truth and fairness, which is ultimately a matter of ethics and morality'.[40] The FSA has included in its key points on why insider dealing is unacceptable not just that it damages the

---

[36] Dan Waters, FSA Director Retail Policy, 'Implementing Principles-Based Regulation' (Speech delivered at the Association of British Insurers Conference, London, 7 December 2006).

[37] Margaret Cole, 'FSA Investigations & Enforcement 2007: A Practitioner's Guide for Regulated Firms' (Speech delivered at the City and Financial Conference, 24 January 2007).

[38] Research interview with regulator, May 2007.

[39] *FSA Handbook* PRIN 2.1.

[40] Robert Bruce, 'Transatlantic Squabbles over "True and Fair"', *Financial Times* (London), 1 March 2007.

market but that it is 'immoral' and 'contrary to good business ethics'.[41] To meet the demands of its new initiative on 'more principles-based regulation', boards of directors, and especially their executive managers will, says the FSA, need 'ethical integrity'.[42] The emergence of a conceptualisation of compliance as an ethical and not just a technical issue has also become part of a wider debate, with the newly-formed Financial Services Lawyers Association, for example, setting up a decision forum on 'Ethics in Financial Services Law'.[43]

Calls for a standard of compliance that focuses on the spirit of the law are becoming commonplace. The FSA's April 2007 initiative on 'more principles-based regulation' makes very clear the link between the more principle-based policy and the tackling of compliance with the letter but not the spirit of the law. Echoing David Tweedie and the Accounting Standards Board in the late 1980s and early 1990s, the FSA drives home the need for principles-based regulation not just for flexibility and dynamism but because '[i]t is also our experience … that a mass of detailed rules can … encourage a legalistic and tactical attitude to compliance.'[44] Principles, in contrast, do not allow firms to 'mine the rule book for what some lawyers call "statutory opportunities" and what the man in the street calls a loophole.'[45] Or again: 'Principles (which address the spirit of regulation) are much more difficult to avoid than rules (which feed armies of lawyers, accountants and bankers in order to meet the letter of the law but not the spirit of the outcome).'[46] Sarah Wilson, Director Retail Firms Division, argues that: 'Overly prescriptive rules divert industry attention towards complying with the letter rather than the spirit of the standard, making it less rather than more likely to

---

[41] Margaret Cole, 'Insider Dealing in the City' (Speech delivered at the London School of Economics, 17 March 2007).
[42] FSA, *Principles-Based Regulation: Focusing on the Outcomes that Matter* (2007) 18.
[43] Financial Services Lawyers Association, 'Principles-Based Regulation: Can It Work?' (Inauguration Forum, 7 June 2007), available at <http://www.fsla.org.uk>.
[44] John Tiner, FSA CEO, 'Keynote Address' (Speech delivered at the FSA Conference on More Principles-Based Regulation, 23 April 2007).
[45] Thomas F Huertas, FSA Director Wholesale Firms Division and Banking Sector Leader, 'Counting on Compliance: The Implications of More Principles-Based Regulation' (Speech delivered at the Fourth Annual Complinet Compliance Conference, 31 January 2007).
[46] John Tiner, 'Harnessing the Market through Principles and Disclosure' (Speech delivered at the Association of Corporate Treasurers, 24 April 2007).

achieve its goal.'[47] The message is repeated over and over again in the FSA's policy frameworks, discussions and speeches — all of which are presented by the FSA as not merely peripheral debate but part of the material that should guide business in its application of FSA principles.

How regulation is applied by business, and the mindset with which it is approached, is being given increasing attention, with the language of ethics and responsibility increasingly brought into play. David Tweedie, for example, recognising even principle-based regulation of the kind introduced by the ASB in the 1990s can provide material for creative compliance,[48] now emphasises the need for companies to apply even accounting principles 'responsibly and with integrity', an approach endorsed by the Department of Trade and Industry and the Treasury.[49] In 2002 the FSA issued a discussion paper on 'An ethical framework for financial services', criticising mere compliance with the letter of the law and the mindset that asks 'show me where it says we can't … ?' rather than 'how can we improve our standards and conduct our business with integrity … ?'[50] It called for a value-based corporate culture, concerned among other things with compliance with the spirit not just the letter of the law. This focus on corporate culture was further developed in its April 2007 initiative for more principles-based regulation, with its particular emphasis on the outcomes of business behaviour. Outcomes oriented behaviour, says the FSA, is 'far more likely to succeed in creating a culture of compliance'.[51] 'Cultural change' is what is required.

Implicit in these initiatives is a subtle but significant shift in the attribution of responsibility. The emphasis on culture and application demonstrates recognition that a shift to principles alone is not enough, and that there also has to be a change in the mindset of the regulated. Rather than seeing it as the responsibility of the regulators to make the words of law encompass everything the regulated might come up with by way of avoidance techniques, responsibility is being placed on the regulated to apply the law with an eye to its spirit. Margaret Cole has

---

[47] Sarah Wilson, 'Supervision in a Principles-Based World' (Speech delivered at the FSA Retail Firms Division Conference, London, 27 February, 2007).

[48] Doreen McBarnet and Christopher Whelan, *Creative Accounting and the Cross-Eyed Javelin Thrower* (1999).

[49] *Coordinating Group on Audit and Accounting Issues, Final Report* (2003).

[50] FSA, *An Ethical Framework for Financial Services* (Discussion Paper No 18, 2002) 4.

[51] Dan Waters, FSA Director Retail Policy Division, 'NEWCOB and More Principles-Based Regulation' (Speech delivered at NEWCOB Briefings, January/February 2007).

declared the dual nature of responsibility and its ethical aspect: 'Although we [regulators] have a statutory responsibility, we consider that there is a moral responsibility on market participants to work proactively to preserve the integrity of the markets'.[52]

There is a strong ethical tone underlying the approach, and an expectation of an enforcement of ethics or integrity within the firm. The role of compliance officers, for example, is presented by the FSA not just as providing technical advice but as acting as 'the conscience of the firm: make sure that people get strong signals about what is right and what is wrong, and over time, weed out wrong-doing, and if necessary, wrong-doers'.[53] What is more, 'if compliance does not act in this way, we would have serious concerns about whether senior management is fulfilling its responsibilities to establish and maintain effective systems and controls. If compliance does act this way, the firm is, we believe, well on the way to fulfilling the requirements of more principles-based regulation'.[54] The description of the compliance function as 'the conscience of the firm' is a very clear call for the elision of ethics and compliance.

(E) *Enforcement Policy: UK*

As in US policy, a change in corporate culture, pushing more responsibility onto senior management, and mitigation of enforcement on demonstration of appropriate corporate controls and culture are all elements of enforcement strategy in the UK.

Although the FSA's core eleven Principles have been in place for some time, it is only as a matter of relatively recent policy that they have been clearly declared the basis for regulatory supervision.[55] They are also clearly presented not just as ethical standards but as law that will be enforced: 'Violating the principles puts a firm on the wrong side of the law'.[56] The FSA has noted its determination to enforce its principles even if a specific rule as such has not been broken,[57] pointing to two major cases in 2006, Citigroup and Deutsche Bank.

---

[52] Cole, 'FSA Investigations & Enforcement 2007', above n 37.
[53] Huertas, above n 45.
[54] Ibid.
[55] Wilson, above n 47.
[56] Huertas, above n 45.
[57] McCarthy, above n 23.

Citigroup was fined £13.9 million, being the profit it made from the disputed dealing, plus another £4 million. Deutsche was fined £6.3 million. Both actions were for breach of principles not specific rules. Indeed when it occurred, the Citigroup activity was hailed in the press as clever rather than deviant: 'Citigroup's brazen bond bet pays off. But sooner or later there will be a casualty'.[58] Even though the action was seen to be 'brazen' and ultimately damaging to the market, it was also declared that 'the buccaneering Citigroup trade was clearly well-designed and executed', and the point was made that: 'Of course Citigroup did nothing illegal here. It legitimately filed orders that had been placed by willing counterparties, all of whom were used to dealing in large numbers. The novel aspect was to trade in such size across a range of debt at such speed. It looks to have been a clever, if controversial, piece of market trading.'[59] The longer term response was not so laudatory. There was something of an ethical backlash and the FSA took the line of enforcing its principles — those high ethical standards — rather than standing back because no specific rule breach had occurred. Lack of due regard to the risks and consequences for the market of its action, lack of adequate internal controls and senior overview, and lack of sufficient training in standards of market conduct were pointed to as constituting a breach of Principles.[60]

FSA policy is that corporate culture should be expressly targeted in assessing compliance in supervision and enforcement. 'The first step for judging compliance is to determine whether the firm has embedded the Principles and other rules into the way it does business. The second is determining that the firm's processes are in fact effective'.[61] The culture of a company is 'evidenced in its approach to training [as noted in the Citigroup case], remuneration etc — as these are key levers for senior management in getting their good intentions translated into appropriate action at the coalface …'.[62]

Pushing responsibility and accountability up the chain to senior management, is, as one regulator put it, 'an important element in [the FSA's] strategy of deterrence. This is distinct from prosecuting those

[58] 'Citigroup's Brazen Bond Bet Pays Off: But Sooner or Later There Will Be a Casualty', *Guardian Unlimited* (London), 11 August 2004.
[59] Ibid.
[60] FSA, 'FSA Fines Citigroup £13.9 million (€20.9mn) for Eurobond Trades' (Press Release, 28 June 2005).
[61] Huertas, above n 45.
[62] Wilson, above n 47.

who commit fraud (in the widest sense of the word), but relates to ensuring that senior managers are held to account where their firms do not meet the appropriate standards of compliance and thus encourage 'good behaviour' generally. This reflects the commonly held view among regulators and financial services industry practitioners, that a recognition by senior managers of their personal liability for regulatory breaches, is the biggest incentive to compliance.'[63]

There are also parallels with US mitigation strategy in the FSA's policy. Indeed there is a promise of immunity for firms as opposed to individuals. Where there is a breach, and the company self-reports, the FSA, it says, will not pursue a company that can demonstrate it has set up appropriate internal controls and culture, 'if an employee recklessly circumvents them. Instead we will pursue the individual'.[64] Of course this might foster a practice of gaining brownie points by reporting the 'vice president responsible for going to jail',[65] though an experienced regulator to whom I put this point responded that the FSA was alert to this possibility and indeed that there had been cases where such tactics had backfired prompting deeper investigations than had been expected and requirements for systemic change.[66] More generally, 'in deciding on the appropriate regulatory outcome' the FSA has stated that its approach to 'firms that consistently behave well … can and should be different to those where we do not see that behaviour'. There will be a 'regulatory dividend for good behaviour'.[67]

In 2006 HMRC, the enforcers of tax law, issued a consultation paper on which they too addressed the issue of encouraging corporate cultures of compliance by taking compliance history into account when dealing with 'apparent compliance failure' and in penalty mitigation. The kind of compliance they have in mind is 'responsible compliance'. They are exploring 'whether there could be a way of helping businesses to demonstrate "corporate responsibility" in company reports or other business plans by giving some visible evidence of 'responsible compliance.'[68]

---

[63] Correspondence with interviewee, November 2006.
[64] Cole, 'Insider Dealing', above n 41.
[65] John Braithwaite, *Corporate Crime in the Pharmaceutical Industry* (1984) 308.
[66] Research interview with regulator, May 2007.
[67] Cole, 'FSA Investigations & Enforcement 2007', above n 37.
[68] *Modernising Powers, Deterrents and Safeguards: A Consultation on the Developing Programme of Work* (2006) 13.

II ALTERNATIVE STANDARD SETTING AND ENFORCEMENT: SOCIAL AND MARKET DEMANDS FOR RESPONSIBLE COMPLIANCE

This reference to 'corporate responsibility' brings us to another set of relevant developments, the extra-legal social and market forces driving demand for a new standard of 'ethical' or 'responsible' compliance. These forces are important because there may well be limits in the potential effectiveness of legal regulation and a need for alternative sources of governance.

(A) *Potential Limitations in the Regulatory Bid for Ethical Compliance*

While at the level of legal regulation there is clearly a good deal of discourse, policy and aspiration on fostering business ethics and enforcing compliance with the spirit of the law, regulators may in fact meet difficulties in putting this into practice. The calls by the FSA for a new non-rule-oriented mindset has not prevented the same arguments and concerns emerging as always have when regulation through anything but specific rules is mooted — how are FSA principles to be applied without retrospectivity or too much regulator subjectivity? The UK's principle-based regime in accounting, as well as anti-tax avoidance strategies have all come in for such critique in the recent past.

The FSA promises 'predictability' as a means of handling this: 'In order for consequences legitimately to be attached to the breach of a principle, it must be possible to predict, at the time of the action concerned, whether or not it would be in breach of a principle'.[69] However it remains to be seen whether predictability can be achieved through guidance without retaining a rule-oriented mindset, with the guidance being treated as rules and those 'rules' rather than principles or outcomes becoming the benchmark for compliance. There are many other ways in which potential new material for rule-compliance will emerge. Likewise, there are concerns that the US Sentencing Guidelines require companies to foster an ethical culture but 'didn't provide a whole lot of guidance', as one interviewee put it, and 'nobody quite knows what

[69] Wilson, above n 47.

ethics means'.[70] Since, as noted above, the Sentencing Guidelines' requirements may well be treated as impacting on directors' fiduciary duty and liability, he foresees directors pressing for quite precise rule guidance: 'I think you will not see it in the reported case decisions. It will happen more quietly.'[71] But the implication is, as has occurred in the past, the likelihood of a seeking after rules with the usual rule compliance mindset.

The US's deferred prosecutions occurred at a moment of unusual regulatory leverage on the wave of immediate post-Enron outrage. It remains to be seen how far the kind of terms they imposed could be enforced in the future. There have already been questions raised about their fairness on rule of law grounds.[72] In the UK, the Citigroup and Deutsche cases clearly demonstrate the intention to enforce principles not just rules. However, both cases occurred in the context of an absence of rules to invoke as the basis for enforcement.[73] It is less clear whether enforcement of principles would be as readily undertaken if a company claimed to be in compliance with a rule, which the FSA sought to override with a principle. The new regime is to be *more* principle-based. But there are still plenty of specific rules in play too. It is clearly the intention that principles should prevail — the outcomes being what matter — and there are plenty of instances in law where rules have been looked through or overridden. Yet in a parallel context, the principle-based financial reporting regime of the late 1990s, research showed there was reluctance on the part of enforcers to use a principle to overrule an instance of compliance with rules. The legal principle requiring companies to provide a true and fair view in their accounts was frequently discussed as a means of overriding compliance in form rather than substance. Yet in practice it was never used for this purpose.[74]

It remains to be seen, too, how successful the FSA or SEC can be in holding senior individuals to account for the corporate culture of a firm. In the past, holding senior management to account has proved difficult. One interviewee saw the FSA as having had real problems in

---

[70] Research interview with corporate counsel, May 2007.

[71] Research interview with regulator, May 2007.

[72] Justin O'Brien, 'Securing Corporate Accountability or Bypassing Justice: The Efficacy and Pitfalls of Pre-Trial Diversion' (2006) 19 *Australian Journal of Corporate Law* 161.

[73] In the case of Citigroup there is no suggestion that a specific rule was infringed. In the case of Deutsche Bank the infringements occurred in foreign markets not regulated by the FSA, so that the FSA's specific rules did not apply.

[74] McBarnet and Whelan, above n 48.

successfully taking disciplinary action against senior individuals in firms or corporates. There has, he said, been some success where a person has been specifically tasked with carrying out a function, which he has failed properly to do. On the other hand investigations have often just had to be dropped, as in the investigations into former senior management at Shell in relation to their personal culpability for the company's misstatements of its oil reserves, 'notwithstanding the material referred to in the press, which appeared to implicate those at the top of the organisation'.[75] In the context of sales of financial products to consumers, though there have been many cases of mis-selling, and a number of companies have been found to be in breach of regulations, no senior manager has ever been penalised. Likewise, where individuals have been convicted for market abuse, it was in a case 'more readily categorised as a fraud case rather than a case of holding senior management to account in the way envisaged [by the FSA].'[76]

Of course the whole point of the new strategies is to try to overcome these limitations; it simply remains to be seen if this can be achieved. However, these regulatory strategies are not, in any case, occurring in a vacuum, but in the context of a changing social climate. In the UK in particular there is evidence of a shift in societal expectations of business behaviour and business ethics, bound up in the guise of the movement for Corporate Social Responsibility ('CSR'). What is more, the CSR movement not only provides a backdrop for the regulatory enforcement of ethics but also has in the market forces it harnesses, its own mechanisms of enforcement. And, importantly, a demand for ethical compliance is emerging on the CSR agenda.

(B) *Corporate Social Responsibility*

CSR is a term that has entered into routine usage in debates both about business and within business.[77] Post-Enron, and in a world in which the role of business in human rights and the environment is a matter of standard debate, the social and ethical responsibilities of business have

---

[75] Correspondence with interviewee, November 2006.

[76] Ibid.

[77] This section draws on Doreen McBarnet, 'Corporate Social Responsibility Beyond Law, Through Law, For Law: The New Corporate Accountability' in Doreen McBarnet, Aurora Voiculescu and Tom Campbell (eds), *The New Corporate Accountability: Corporate Social Responsibility and the Law* (2007) 9.

become key issues, and CSR has become a much talked about element in corporate governance in its widest sense. CSR essentially involves a shift in the focus of corporate responsibility from profit maximisation for shareholders within the obligations of law,[78] to responsibility to a broader range of *stake*holders, including communal concerns such as protection of the environment, and accountability on ethical as well as legal obligations.

Typically CSR policies involve a commitment by corporations, usually expressed in their Statements of Business Principles or corporate-specific Codes of Conduct, to enhanced concern for the environment, human rights, fairness to suppliers and customers, and opposition to bribery and corruption, with the range of issues involved constantly expanding. Importantly, for our concerns here, after Enron, CSR is also regarded as not only involving social and environmental issues but as going to the heart of core business operations such as accounting and even tax policies, and has become an issue for corporate governance in the narrower sense of the term. The language of business ethics is also frequently brought into play, with environmental and social impact seen as part of a new business ethics. The trend to a shift of language in business from CSR to simply CR, Corporate Responsibility, reflects this. CSR has indeed become something of a portmanteau concept that incorporates a broad sweep of concerns from saving the planet to demanding ethics in business dealings.

CSR is generally presented by business and governments alike as voluntary. In reality this is misleading. The 'voluntary' adoption of CSR policies by business has received a very firm push from external social and market forces. From the start, 'voluntary' CSR has been socially and economically driven. NGO campaigns, ethical trading initiatives, SRI (or Socially Responsible Investment) and a range of other social and market factors have put the pressure on for a new approach to corporate responsibility in big business.[79] Indeed, social and legal enforcement are beginning to overlap, with non-state organisations increasingly using private law to legally enforce what had been seen by

---

[78] Milton Friedman, 'The Social Responsibility of Business Is to Increase Its Profits', *New York Times Magazine* (New York), 13 September 1970.

[79] McBarnet, 'Corporate Social Responsibility', above n 77; David Vogel, *The Market for Virtue: The Potential and Limits of Corporate Social Responsibility* (2005).

both business and governments as voluntary or legally unenforceable commitments.[80]

CSR is a new point of pressure for ethical compliance. Indeed business has, in the very way it presents its adoption of CSR policies, laid itself open to this pressure. The voluntary image is encapsulated in the idea of CSR as 'what companies are going to do beyond mere compliance with the law',[81] the notion of going 'beyond legal compliance' being key to the image of *social* responsibility. That view of CSR, however, assumes a baseline of compliance that is in fact problematic, not only because of the significant amount of non-compliance that takes place in business, but because of the routine practice of creative compliance. In some contexts this would be, and has been, seen as not only legitimate but admirably astute. But in the context of a new business environment in which companies are keen to present themselves as socially responsible and ethical, the practice of creative compliance may raise some uncomfortable questions. How socially responsible or ethical is it to deliberately structure the legal form of activities to circumvent social and legal policy and indeed to distort capital markets themselves? Is it socially responsible or ethical to circumvent legal control through legal arguments that even the companies and lawyers employing them see as 'sailing close to the wind'?

Such questions imply a misfit between CSR claims and compliance practices, and indicate potential for CSR to become a source of leverage in getting companies to reassess their attitudes to law and compliance. As I have argued elsewhere, though CSR is generally presented as going beyond legal obligations, it may be that business could best 'demonstrate a new attitude to corporate social responsibility not so much by *surpassing* law's requirements, but by meeting those requirements *in spirit* at last'.[82]

---

[80] For detailed analysis see Doreen McBarnet, Aurora Voiculescu and Tom Campbell (eds), *The New Corporate Accountability: Corporate Social Responsibility and the Law* (2007).

[81] BT, *Social Report* (1999).

[82] McBarnet, 'After Enron: Corporate Governance, Creative Compliance and the Uses of Corporate Social Responsibility', above n 2, 221.

(C) *Legal Compliance on the CSR Agenda*

The issue of compliance is beginning to appear on the CSR agenda as a result of growing interest among NGOs, consultancies and investment funds, particularly in relation to tax avoidance — tax avoidance is indeed being seen increasingly as an issue of corporate governance. New, dedicated NGOs have emerged, using classic strategies of naming and shaming campaigns. The Tax Justice Network ('TJN'), an international NGO launched in the UK in 2003, has taken a key role in stirring up publicity and provoking responses. While its interests extend more widely to poverty in developing countries and the role in that of tax lobbying, evasion, corruption, and international tax competition, TJN has also embraced tax avoidance in general as a CSR issue. The Davos World Economic Forum ('WEF') in January 2005 was seized by NGOs[83] with a CSR agenda as an opportunity to make Corporate Social *Irresponsibility* awards, and tax avoidance joined more conventional CSR issues as one of the award categories. The two NGOs organising the ceremony described it as a reminder 'to members of the WEF and other large corporate groups that the public expects them to be responsible stewards of the environment; insists on their respect for human rights and labour rights; and does not tolerate tax avoidance.'[84] The TJN nominated the 'winner' on tax avoidance, accountancy firm KPMG, for its marketing of 'abusive' tax avoidance schemes as revealed in the post-Enron US Senate investigations.[85]

Not far behind NGOs have been consultancies advising a rethink of attitudes to tax in particular and in some cases to compliance more generally. Ironically, given its brush with infamy over 'abusive' tax avoidance,[86] or indeed because of it, KPMG has taken a lead role here. In 'Tax in the Boardroom', it acknowledges tax strategy now carries reputational risk, due not only to changing governmental attitudes but to the role of the CSR movement.[87] Tax planning is seen as key in this.

---

[83] The Berne Declaration and Pro-Natura-Friends of the Earth Switzerland.

[84] The Berne Declaration, *First 'Public Eye Awards' for Irresponsible Corporate Behaviour* (11 January 2005) <http://www.evb.ch/en/p25003365.html> at 27 June 2007.

[85] TJN, (2005) 1(1) *Tax Justice Focus Newsletter* 8.

[86] Committee on Finance Hearing 108–371, United States Senate, Washington DC *Tax Shelters: Who's Buying, Who's Selling, and What's the Government Doing About It?* (21 October 2007).

[87] KPMG, *Tax in the Boardroom* (Discussion Paper, 2004).

Corporate tax planning, KPMG notes, can range from the 'social duty' end of the spectrum to the 'shareholder duty' end. While conventionally corporate duty was seen to fall on the shareholder duty end of the spectrum, requiring minimisation of tax by all legal means, KPMG warn that the balance may be less clear now because of reputational damage and the risk that poses — despite the legality of the techniques involved — to long term shareholder value:

> Boards should recognise, when overseeing the design and monitoring of tax strategies and policies, that contemporary debates about governance, corporate social responsibility and ethics mean that even legal tax-minimisation activity can generate reputational liabilities that can destroy shareholder value.[88]

Investment organisations have entered into the debate, with Henderson Global Investors producing an influential report based on a survey of the Chairmen of FTSE 350 companies. This was explicitly presented as a response to the fact that tax, including what some view as 'inappropriate tax avoidance' is coming under greater scrutiny and that commentators are suggesting that 'approaches to tax should be seen as a matter of corporate social responsibility.'[89] Conferences, workshops and internet debates on the subject are also springing up in rapid succession.

The Organisation for Economic Cooperation and Development ('OECD') has taken up the call for compliance with the spirit of the law, in the particular context of tax, and referring directly to the impact of Enron. It urges companies to 'exert every effort to act in accordance with both the letter and spirit of those laws and regulations',[90] and it sees tax avoidance as firmly on the CSR agenda: 'Tax is where environment was ten years ago.'[91] In a multiplicity of ways, tax avoidance has emerged as an issue for the CSR agenda, and as an ethical rather than just a legal concern. To some managers, and indeed lawyers, this is entirely inappropriate, there being, in traditional legal thinking, no place

---

[88] Ibid 7.

[89] Henderson Global Investors, *Tax, Risk and Corporate Governance: Findings from a Survey of the FTSE350* (2005) 2.

[90] *The OECD Guidelines for Multinational Enterprises* (2000) 27.

[91] Vanessa Houlder, 'Tax Avoidance as a Morality Tale', *Financial Times* (London), 22 November 2004, quoting Jeffrey Owens, Director, OECD Center for Tax Policy and Administration.

for ethical judgment in tax law. But CSR is, as business keeps telling us, beyond law, and it is in the courts of public opinion and the market rather than the courts of law that business practice is being judged. Creative compliance in areas such as tax avoidance may pass the test of technical legality but fail on the test of social and ethical responsibility.

It is not surprising that tax avoidance has caught the eye of critics geared to CSR. In terms of its consequences it is clearly a social welfare and social policy issue. It is also of course a challenge for business in that it goes to the heart of the issue of profit maximisation and provides a real test of whether companies adopting CSR policies embed them throughout the organisation — including the core departments of tax and accounting — seeing them as relevant to financial and legal issues as well as the more established agenda of environment, human rights et al. But there are also indications that this is no more than the thin end of the wedge, with a more general concern with creative compliance per se, as a CSR and reputational risk, emerging. Part of the tax debate and of wider relevance for legal compliance more generally is the increasing discussion in CSR debate of compliance with the spirit of the law. A report by Business in the Community, Insight Investment and the FTSE Group looked more generally to the issue of compliance with the spirit and not just the letter of the law,[92] as did SustainAbility's report on tax.[93]

(D) *CSR as an Enforcement Mechanism*

In adopting CSR policies and holding themselves accountable to standards beyond legal compliance, companies may not have anticipated CSR reaching from calls for social responsibility on such issues as environmental concerns to calls for social responsibility in relation to legal compliance itself. But CSR has its own momentum, and the potential is there for the market to exercise judgment, and flex its muscle, in the arena of legal compliance too.

And CSR has muscle — in the form of leveraging reputation risk and deploying the market. Reputation risk is now discussed as a key issue for big business. With some 60 per cent of FTSE 100 companies'

---

[92] *Rewarding Virtue: Effective Board Action on Corporate Responsibility* (2005).
[93] SustainAbility, *Taxing Issues — Responsible Business and Tax* (2006).

market value,[94] and 53 per cent of the US Fortune 500's[95] attributed to intangibles — much of that brand value — reputation has become an important market asset, and a target for the CSR agenda of NGOs and their naming and shaming strategies. The ethical consumer market is growing and being harnessed. A survey by the Co-operative Bank in November 2006 put the UK ethical consumption market at £29 billion, an 11.4 per cent rise on the previous year compared to a 1.4 per cent rise in household expenditure more generally.[96]

SRI is also growing. UK pension funds have been spurred into taking on SRI partly as the result of legislation which required them to disclose whether or not they took into account in their investments the social environmental and ethical policies and practices of the companies in which they invested. Suddenly this became the norm. Some of the largest investment funds in the world such as CalPERS, the Californian Public Employees Retirement Fund, or the Norwegian government pension fund (with spending power of US$230 billion) take a highly activist SRI stance, with the Norwegian government fund, for example, in 2006, withdrawing investment from Wal-Mart and Freeport McMoRan Copper and Gold on human rights and environmental grounds.[97] Nor does the CSR movement limit itself to campaigning and harnessing the market. Increasingly, law is being deployed, often private law and often in highly creative ways, to bring legal sanctions to bear, as for example in the *Alien Tort Claims Act* [98] cases in the US, where US companies have been held to account for complicity in human rights abuses outside the US, through creative NGO enforcement. [99]

CSR is a much stronger and more developed force in the UK and Europe than in the US. Yet, interestingly, overt connections are beginning to be drawn in the US between regulation, ethics and corporate responsibility in the wider European sense. In Spring 2007, a conference held by the influential US Conference Board on Business Ethics and

---

[94] Vivien Beattie and Sarah Jane Thomson, 'Intangibles and the OFR' (2005) *Financial Management* 29.
[95] See Corporate Watch, *The Business Case for CSR* <http://www.corporatewatch.org/?lid=2680> at 27 June 2007.
[96] Co-operative Bank, *Ethical Consumerism Report* (2006), available at <http://www.co-operativebank.co.uk> at 27 June 2007.
[97] Social Funds, *Newsroom* <http://www.socialfunds.com/news> at 16 June 2006.
[98] 28 USC 1350.
[99] For more detailed analysis of all of these issues see McBarnet, 'Corporate Social Responsibility', above n 77.

Compliance included a session addressing the issue of integrating corporate responsibility, ethics and compliance, recognising that the European concept of business ethics typically encompasses a broader concept of corporate responsibility, and exploring the drivers for convergence in the US.[100]

One Deputy Chief Counsel for a US corporation talked in interview of the wider importance of regulatory developments such as the Sentencing Guidelines 'mak[ing] the ethical mandatory'. Effectively, he said, it has

> ended lots of disputes in US law, over what corporate responsibilities are, whether they end with the shareholders or go beyond, it's a huge thing. Now it allows us to link, I think for the first time, our standards of ethical business conduct and corporate responsibility … There is now a link that is compelled by law between ethics with a small 'e' [focussing on integrity, honesty, lack of corruption etc in how business is done] (which is the way most US companies tend to look at it), and ethics with a big 'E' which includes corporate responsibility.[101]

Legal regulation, intentionally or otherwise, is fostering not just traditional ethics but a wider CSR, and CSR in turn is reinforcing demands for a new approach to legal compliance.

CONCLUSION

There are, then, a number of emergent developments in the governance of business, both in the conventional sense of legal regulation and in the wider exercise of control by civil society through social and market factors. Both strands are focusing in on the issue of creative compliance and calling for a different standard of ethical or responsible compliance whose benchmark is not the letter but the spirit of the law. Regulators are striving for new ways to cut through the rule-oriented compliance

---

[100] Business Ethics and Compliance Conference: Creating (and Measuring) a Culture of Integrity (San Diego, 15–16 March 2007).

[101] Research interview, May 2007; see also the argument by John Sherman that the requirement for companies to promote ethical conduct could be read as requiring compliance with human rights standards: Sherman, above n 13.

mindset and to both foster a more ethical compliance culture in business and find ways to penalise those who fall short.

The bid to enforce ethics in the arena of legal regulation may not go unchallenged, and that is why there is real value in the supplementary forms of governance flourishing today, examples of what is sometimes seen as the 'new governance'. There are plenty of limitations in these alternative mechanisms of standard setting and enforcement, not least questions of legitimacy and effectiveness. Nonetheless extra-legal factors such as the CSR movement can bring an added dimension to the enforcement of ethical compliance by supplementing legal powers with the forces of public opinion and the market. Indeed in the current confluence of compliance, ethics and responsibility in both regulatory and civil society sectors we can see the new governance being brought to bear in capital markets.

Chapter 9

Professional Norms

Dean Cocking

The notion of professionals who are significantly guided by professional norms, in particular ethical and social norms of service to the community, has come under sustained assault over the years. Sociological criticisms have long characterised professional associations and professionalisation as self-serving in ways that come at the expense of the public.[1] And in recent times the settings of occupational practice have changed for a number of 'traditional' professions in ways that have been thought to pose special problems. Both lawyers and engineers, for instance, now work increasingly in large multidisciplinary firms dominated by commercial and managerial imperatives rather than the professional norms specific to practice as a lawyer or engineer. Indeed, just what the territory of work is in these cases has changed and

---

[1] See Part I ahead for those I have in mind. Of course, criticism of this sort has also long come from others. Adam Smith famously characterised the professions in this way: 'People of the same trade seldom meet together, even for merriment and diversion, but the conversation ends in a conspiracy against the publick, or in some contrivance to raise prices. It is impossible indeed to prevent such meetings, by any law which could be executed, or would be consistent with liberty and justice. But though the law cannot hinder people of the same trade from sometimes assembling together, it ought to do nothing to facilitate such assemblies; much less to render them necessary': Adam Smith, *The Wealth of Nations* (1776) book I, ch X, 129. And Shaw put Smith's point more bluntly: 'All Professions are conspiracies against the laity': George Bernard Shaw, *The Doctor's Dilemma* (1911) Act 1. I thank Mathew Ward and Tom Campbell for these references.

introduced uncertainties about the nature, limits and scope of such roles.[2] Moreover, ethico-professional[3] misconduct and, thus, the apparent failure or absence of relevant ethico-professional norms, has been highlighted in, for instance, the auditing and accounting professions by some spectacular recent corporate collapses (as widely discussed in this book).

However, it is necessary that such norms properly operate as guiding regulative psychological influences[4] in occupational actors. And this is true quite generally across occupations, although it is not *just* as true. There are important differences of kind and degree concerning how ethico-professional norms apply. Concern for public safety is, for instance, appropriately at centre stage for engineers, but not for lawyers. And more general ethico-professional norms may also vary across different occupational groups. So, for instance, professional autonomy may cover more territory and be greater in degree for lawyers or medical practitioners than for real estate agents. On the other hand, ethico-professional commitments driven by market concerns (such as fair competition or honest and transparent dealings with consumers), while

---

[2] For a discussion of such problems, see Andrew Alexandra et al, *Professionalisation, Ethics and Integrity Systems: The Promotion of Professional Ethical Standards, and the Protection of Clients and Consumers*, Report for the Professional Standards Council ('PSC') (2006), especially the empirical studies of occupations presented in chs 4 and 5.

[3] I use the term 'ethico-professional' to address the ethical dimensions of professional life. Obviously, technical dimensions are significant, and are in everyday practice commonly the primary and direct considerations with which professionals are engaged. And many technical aspects of one's professional life do not have ethical dimensions, or not primarily, but many also do, eg, technical standards for accountants in accurate and honest reporting are also obviously ethical standards.

[4] The term 'regulative' here refers to the regulation of our attitudes and conduct due to psychological guidance by norms, and these norms may be specific or general, and the guidance may be direct or indirect. It is thus a moral psychological notion referring to internal regulative influence and therefore has a different sense than does the term 'regulation', where the latter features in, eg, discussions concerning the regulation of markets or occupations, including of ethical standards. Here, the sort of guiding force imagined to attach to regulation is more specific, ie principally about how rules and laws backed by sanctions 'regulate' the conduct of individuals. The sort of regulation imagined is also thereby about external guiding factors, in particular, rules and laws, rather than internal psychological guidance by the norms that may (or may not) be expressed by those rules or laws. I have adapted the idea (to norms) of a 'regulative ideal' (coined by Justin Oakley) which is introduced in Dean Cocking and Justin Oakley, 'Indirect Consequentialism, Friendship, and the Problem of Alienation' (1995) 105 *Ethics* 86, 106. For a more developed treatment of the idea, see Justin Oakley and Dean Cocking, *Virtue Ethics and Professional Roles* (2001), especially the Introduction and chs 1 and 2.

relevant across occupations, may be much more at centre stage for the ethico-professionalisation of real estate agents than, say, for engineers or lawyers.

Nevertheless, that there are relevant ethico-professional norms, both general and specific, properly operating as guiding regulative influences in the psychologies of occupational actors is a generally significant, indispensable feature of professional life. The idea that we could somehow regulate ethico-professional standards into existence, ie, through laws and rules, has significant limitations. At least, this is what I argue in this chapter.

First, I present two general models of ethico-professional norms: the *commercial occupation/consumer protection* model and the *professional autonomy/client trust* model. I then set out some key criticisms and problems (as sketched above) concerning the legitimacy or relevance of these models. In light of these criticisms and problems, in Part II I move from this general picture of the territory of ethico-professional norms to focus more particularly on the sort of norms identified by the professional autonomy/client trust model. In this Part I put the case for the necessity and importance (albeit different in kind and degree across occupations) of professional autonomy. I focus on professional autonomy since it is central to effective guidance by ethico-professional norms in key cases, and it is also the focus of much of the criticisms of, and problems for, effective guidance by ethico-professional norms. In Part III I present the case for the correlative of the sort of professional autonomy I defend, namely, a duty of care to clients. In conclusion, I recommend the rehabilitation of professional autonomy and duties of care to clients, particularly where, as with the 'traditional' professions (although this need not be exclusively so), the occupational area is properly characterised as primarily involving expert use of a substantial, complex and largely discrete body of knowledge and skill in pursuit of the legitimate, and indeed typically significant, ethical and social interests of individuals and the community.

I Two Models of Ethico-Professional Norms

I want to defend the idea that ethico-professional norms, functioning as guiding regulative psychological influences on professional attitude and conduct, have a proper, indeed indispensable, place in professional life. I therefore introduce a general conceptual contrast that I think helpfully frames the ethico-professional territory, and so the sort of ethico-professional norms that apply both generally and more specifically across occupational groups. This will also be helpful for locating and setting out some of the criticisms of, and problems for, professionalisation, professional associations, and, in particular, their claim to guidance by norms and ideals of social or ethical note to the community.

A key contrast across occupational groups can be put in terms of two models of ethico-professional conduct and relations between 'professionals' and the public: the *commercial occupation/consumer protection* model and the *professional autonomy/client trust* model.[5] The former model applies to cover much of the ethico-professional territory of those occupational groups that are properly characterised as primarily commercial groups, such as real estate agents. Here ethico-professional considerations are dominated by concerns about their ethical status as market actors, in particular, the general commitments to norms of fair competition and consumer protection and empowerment. Other ethico-professional norms will also be operative in relation to these, for example, that real estate agents be honest and accurate in the information they present to consumers.

The second model applies to cover much of the ethico-professional territory of those occupational groups, which, while also commercial groups (meaning that market standards and norms apply), are not properly characterised as *primarily* commercial groups. Rather, their primary function or purpose is one of service to the community concerning some significant social or ethical good, as found in the 'traditional' professions. Here, then, ethico-professional considerations are *not* dominated by market considerations. In particular, ethico-professional norms also, and more significantly, attach to one's professional role responsibilities to exercise substantial, complex and largely discrete expertise in the pursuit of the legitimate, indeed typically key, social and ethical interests of individuals and the community.

In this chapter I focus on professional autonomy (in Part II) and correlative duty of care to clients (in Part III). More specific ethico-

[5] I developed these models for Alexandra et al, above n 2. I draw on my work there for this chapter and I am indebted to my co-authors, Seumas Miller, Tom Campbell, Andrew Alexandra and Mathew Ward for their contributions to this work. In particular, I thank Seumas Miller who originally helped me frame the two models above, and for guidance and contributions to their development.

professional regulative norms on account of the non-commercial or self-interested primary functions of such groups are, for instance: the promotion of human health in medicine; providing due process before the law in the legal profession; public safety for engineers; and accurate reporting and monitoring for auditors and accountants.

Setting the scene this way helpfully locates some standing criticisms concerning professionalisation. On the one hand, if we think of professions as primarily about service ideals and guidance by related standards, norms and ideals, then one may be inclined to think of the application of the category of 'professional' to commercial occupations and their associations — where the moral imperative is not so clear — as something of a mistake. Accordingly, one will also likely think of this broadened application as deforming or minimising the value dimensions that ought to characterise the ethico-professional norms of professions.

While the traditional professions of, say, medicine or law, may be said to have 'gone off the rails' or 'lost their way' by moving away from a clear focus on the moral and social goods of human health and justice that it is largely their institutional purpose to serve, these professions are nevertheless properly conceived of as 'professions', largely on account of their service to these central goods — and may be criticised against the criteria represented by these goods. It is precisely against such criteria that they have been claimed to have lost their way.[6] On the other hand, various other occupations, such as real estate agents, do not in any central or direct way serve such notable goods as human health or justice, and so are neither capable of being lauded or criticised against an ethical standard presented by such goods. Thus, broadening the application of ethico-professionalism to accommodate the primarily commercial groups may seem a category mistake that deforms the nature and value of ethico-professionalism.

As I have indicated, however, primarily commercial groups are governed by ethico-professional standards, norms and purposes, both general and specific, related to their status as primarily commercial market actors. So, for instance, while a primarily commercial group such as real estate agents would, in their everyday dealings with consumers or

[6] There is now some considerable literature concerning how various professionals have become alienated from their roles on account of their working in settings of practice that work against the ethico-professional regulative norms and ideals that properly apply to their roles. See, for instance, Oakley and Cocking, *Virtue Ethics*, above n 4, especially ch 6.

the public, be primarily and directly concerned with making financial deals regarding real estate, this everyday direct pursuit should nevertheless be governed, and so guided indirectly, by the general, overarching ethico-professional commitment to efficiently provide affordable and decent housing to the public.

Guidance by this commitment is most plausibly thought of as operating mostly *indirectly* in the psyche of occupational actors in the primarily commercial groups. We need not imagine, for instance, that real estate agents must be *directly* motivated by a commitment to efficiently provide affordable and decent housing to the public. Nevertheless, their conduct may be *governed* by this goal insofar as it is undertaken within an overall integrity system including, for instance, prescriptive laws and adherence to codes of conduct and ethics aimed at empowering consumers.[7] And, insofar as real estate associations and individuals show commitment to practice within such a system — and to develop their practice in light of it — they may be thought of as being indirectly guided by the relevant governing goals of the system.[8]

Further, in addition to the relevant ethical goals that apply to the particular occupational area, ethical occupational practice is also marked by the specific sorts of ethical commitments that properly form much of the substantial ethical content involved in the pursuit of these ethical goals — such as the commitment to honest and fair dealings with the public. Nevertheless, the concern with a hijacking of the concept of ethico-professionalism and a devaluing of its currency has particular significance due to the observation of commercial and financial imperatives that have been central to the increasing adoption of, and compliance with, codes of conduct or professional standards schemes under the monitoring and meta-regulatory control of state agencies.[9] In fact, the influence of commercial drivers upon the adoption of professional status might lead to general concerns about the fate of

---

[7] See Alexandra et al, above n 2; Seumas Miller, 'Institutions, Integrity Systems and Market Actors' in this book, for an account of integrity systems for occupations.

[8] The distinction between being guided directly or indirectly by a consideration has general application. I may, for example, be guided indirectly by the concern to relax to take up gardening. In turn I may then be directly guided by concerns specific and proper to gardening. Nevertheless, I may give up gardening if it turns out I do not find it relaxing. So the latter consideration may indirectly guide those with which I am more directly concerned. For discussion of the distinction in theoretical ethics and moral psychology, see Cocking and Oakley, 'Indirect Consequentialism', above n 4.

[9] Such as, in Australia, the PSC.

professionalism, even for traditional professions, under such a regime.[10] The general concern for the fate of professionalism here is whether guidance, either direct or indirect, by ethico-professional norms, is behind the work regarding compliance with ethico-professional standards, or whether it is simply a consequence of profit motives or, more generally, prudential concerns. One has reason to be concerned for at least four reasons. First, one may worry that there is some instability or fragility with respect to ethical compliance if the reasons for compliance are purely, or primarily, prudential, since circumstances may well be such that prudence dictates that one does not expend one's resources on compliance. It may, for instance, be less financially onerous to flout compliance and go to court, since the latter cases are rare and difficult for the complainant to win. Second, however well-targeted and comprehensive one's laws, regulations and rules may be, there will always be cases that 'fall between the cracks' and so — if one is to achieve ethical or 'best' practice — require compliance mechanisms in the form of relevant professional, including ethico-professional, norms. Third, interpretation of laws, regulations and rules is often unavoidable and open to compliance to the letter of the law that nevertheless enables unethical practice to flourish. And fourth, insofar as the misconduct of one member of an occupational group affects the reputation of the group, the group has self-interested reason to ignore or cover up the misconduct so that it does not do damage in the public arena.

On the other hand, if one thinks of professions as primarily commercial and self-interested enterprises anyway, and so one rejects or is cynical about claims concerning norms and ideals of service to the community, then these concerns — in particular, points one, three and four — are just what you would expect. The main criticisms against

---

[10] The Labor Senators sitting on the Senate Economics Legislation Committee review of the Treasury Legislation Amendment (Professional Standards) Bill 2003 (Cth) put these concerns this way:

'Most fundamentally, we are disturbed by the fact that some need an incentive in the form of capping in order to lift professional standards. Labor Senators endorse the view expressed in the Government's CLERP 9 paper in September 2002 which stated: "While the objective of improving professionals standards, including the introduction of compulsory professional indemnity insurance and risk management programs is admirable, professional bodies should be implementing such measures as a matter of best practice and should not require the incentive of a capping regime to achieve them"': Senate Economics Legislation Committee, Parliament of Australia, *Provisions of the Treasury Legislation Amendment (Professional Standards) Bill 2003* (2004) 39.

professions, their associations, and the drive to professionalise have been made by sociologists.[11] The key general concerns are: the anti-competitive effects; the anti-consumer or public interest effects; and the sophistry and obfuscation claimed of the so-called ethical service ideals of the professions in the face of their apparent practices to the contrary.[12] On such views, professionalisation has been characterised as a means to attain market power or social privilege,[13] or as a way of legitimising inequalities in social status or raising prices for services.[14] Appeals to ethico-professional norms in this context have been thought of as an abuse of moral language,[15] and much of this has been thought to provide a means to undermine the market economy ideal of informed, sovereign consumers, and thereby the efficiency of markets; that is, to provide goods and services efficiently and at reasonable prices.

A key focus of this line of attack is the claim by professional groups and individuals to special expertise in a body of knowledge and skill. This is then claimed to license some notable professional autonomy in setting the standards and norms that apply in the area, monitoring that those standards and norms are effectively operating in the area, and in determining how to best comply with and advance those standards and norms. The real purposes, or most significant purposes, of such claims, so the attack goes, are about monopolising a knowledge base to legitimate the professionals' claim to prestige, income and the right to administer themselves.

---

[11] Mathew Ward worked as a research assistant on the Report for the PSC, Alexandra et al, above n 2. I thank him for the references to the views of the sociologists I mention and for his helpful comments on their views.

[12] Of course, not all sociological views have been critical. Notable here is Emile Durkheim, *Professional Ethics and Civic Morals* (Cornelia Brookfield trans, 1992). Durkheim expressed deep concern about the general indifference that he felt the public displayed towards the morality of life in the economic sphere by comparison with morality in the private sphere: 'this amoral character of economic life amounts to a public danger … If we live amorally for a good part of the day, how can we keep the springs of morality from going slack in us? … It is therefore extremely important that economic life should be regulated, should have its moral standards raised, so that the conflicts that disturb it have an end, and further, that individuals should cease to live thus in a moral vacuum where the life-blood drains away even from individual morality': at 12.

[13] Notable here is Margali Sarfatti Larson, *The Rise of Professionalism: A Sociological Analysis* (1977).

[14] See Smith, above n 1.

[15] Such as by making a scapegoat of an offender in blatant/extreme cases, or by claiming consumer protection (say, against charlatans) when one is really about monopolising the market, or by 'playing' the technicality/indeterminacy ratio.

The attack on the claim of professional groups to a substantial, complex and discrete knowledge base targets what is called the 'technicality/indeterminacy ratio'. Jamous and Pelloile[16] have indicated how 'playing' this ratio utilises the discrete knowledge base of the group as a means of protecting and advancing their social and economic power and 'self-regulation'. Professions prevent their knowledge base from becoming routine, or from being seen as merely 'technical', since otherwise their claim to discrete and expert understanding would be undermined, and so too their claims to autonomy and power over their practise of this expertise. Instead, the professions have to assert the need for interpretation and the tailoring of their knowledge to the specific case at hand. Successful professional groups are then characterised as being able to play this ratio out in their favour. When attacked because their practice is not based on science — that is, it is too indeterminate — they may claim that they are the practitioners of an esoteric body of knowledge — that is, that it is too technical for others outside the profession to understand. When charged that their work is simply a technical set of procedures, they may assert their clinical, or legal skill in *interpreting* each case. So construed, knowledge in a profession operates to protect the profession and serves to make it extremely difficult for those outside the profession to challenge it. It also makes charges of malfeasance or unethical behaviour difficult to sustain. And this will be especially exacerbated insofar as another common characteristic of professions, namely their solidarity, is operative.

In addition to these criticisms of professional associations, professionalisation, and related claims to guidance by ethico-professional norms — in particular professional autonomy — problems have emerged with the new settings in which many professionals now find themselves working. So, for instance, engineering is a well-established profession, in particular with a history of guidance by goals that are not primarily commercial but which are primarily oriented toward serving a significant public good, namely the good of public safety. However, one important development over the past few decades in Australia has been the privatisation of major government instrumentalities such as electricity commissions, which employed large numbers of engineers, and were largely dominated by engineers. Nowadays engineers most commonly work in organisations whose prime purpose is not engineering: for

---

[16] Haroun Jamous and Bernard Pelloile, 'Changes in the French University Hospital System' in John Archer Jackson (ed), *Professions and Professionalization* (1970) 111.

instance mining companies or manufacturers. Another significant change has been the increasingly multidisciplinary nature of the work and therefore of the skills required of engineers to do such work.[17]

And, of course, some spectacular cases of apparent ethico-professional misconduct or failure have also put pressure of the idea of professional autonomy. Auditing and accountancy, for instance, are also well-established traditional professions and are notably characterised by an important economic function and significant ethical norm, namely to provide honest and accurate financial reporting. Accountants, and particularly auditors, however, have come under intense pressure with respect to their standards, competence and integrity primarily due to their perceived role in failing to prevent or predict the catastrophic corporate collapses discussed in this book.[18]

However, these negative views and problems should not lead us to 'throw the baby out with the bathwater'. While professional associations may (often) have been guilty of self-serving practices that come at the expense of the interests of the public, scope for professional autonomy is an important, necessary feature of effective occupational practice in various areas. To help better see this importance, I now put the case for professional autonomy.

II THE NECESSITY AND IMPORTANCE OF PROFESSIONAL AUTONOMY

The cluster of criticisms noted above characterise professionalisation and professional associations in terms of their self-serving tendencies, principally for greater economic and social power. Thus, the claims of certain occupational groups to a discrete body of knowledge are cast as a means to economic or social power, as are claims of technicality and indeterminacy concerning this body of knowledge.

But, of course, quite apart from such self-serving advantages attached to laying a claim to a discrete body of knowledge, the fact is that certain groups can rightly lay claim to such knowledge. Thus, doctors can rightly claim discrete knowledge, skill and expertise concerning medical health, lawyers may do so concerning the law and

[17] See Alexandra et al, above n 2, ch 4. Andrew Alexandra provided the points I use here about the current state of play in engineering.

[18] Ibid. Tom Campbell provided the points I use here about the current state of play for auditors and accountants.

just legal process, and teachers concerning education. It is not as if the self-serving practices of, say, doctors, should lead us to imagine that their claim to a body of discrete knowledge, skill and so on is *itself* simply self-serving.

Indeed, not only are the bodies of knowledge, skill and expertise in the areas of these traditional professions *genuine* bodies of knowledge, skill and expertise, they have been developed to deliver fundamental human and ethical goods, namely human health, justice and education. Accordingly, groups of individuals who may effectively use this knowledge and develop this skill or expertise play central, socially valuable, *institutional* roles.[19] Obviously, for instance, on account of our basic needs and interest in human health, society very much needs a medical profession and medical practitioners. Thus, we have institutions whose purpose is to meet such needs and provide such key human and ethical goods.

Moreover, a central aspect of the institutional role individual practitioners play here is professional autonomy. Autonomy is, of course, a fundamental notion in discussions of what it is to be a person and what it is to lead a worthwhile life for a person. Literally, autonomy means self-governance or self-rule. But what is it to be self-governing or to have self-rule? At the heart of the notion is the idea that a person can make judgments and choices about how they will act or lead their life, and they have the capacity to act and lead their life in accord with these judgments and choices. In these ways, most people can make judgments and choices about what is worth pursuing and have sufficient control over themselves and their external circumstances to act out such judgments and choices. Thus, persons may be self-governing, rather than being driven by impulse or dependent upon (or under the command of) others. Professional autonomy, broadly speaking, concerns the ability of professionals to be self-governing through the exercise of judgments, choices and control with respect to the proper territory of their professional life. The domain of professional autonomy is, therefore, narrower than that of ordinary autonomy, since it is circumscribed by the specific territory of the work, including the specific standards, norms and goals of the work. Accordingly, the sorts of choice and control relevant to professional autonomy are similarly more narrowly framed.

---

[19] Thanks to Seumas Miller for characterising these professional roles to me as 'institutional'.

Furthermore, since professional autonomy is an *institutional* notion attached to aspects of the practice of certain professional *roles*, it is, unlike autonomy generally, not something one possesses as a result, or in virtue of, one's status as a self-governing person. Professional autonomy is a narrower notion attaching to certain institutional requirements and functions of the proper performance of certain professional roles. Individuals and their collectives then, may have a claim to (some significant degree and kinds) of professional autonomy where such institutional requirements and functions are part of the proper performance of their professional role.

What then, is the rationale for thinking that there is such a claim to be laid regarding professional autonomy attaching to certain occupational roles (albeit in degrees and varying across roles)? The particular rationale I defend in this Part is where it is plausibly thought necessary for the effective use of the sorts of knowledge, skills and expertise required for the delivery of the (legitimate or valuable) goods and services it is the purpose of the occupational roles in question to deliver. Crucial here is the question of how substantial and complex the territory and related body of knowledge and expertise is, for as the territory gets more complex and less routine, it will require the exercise of judgment in a range of different and often less predictable specific situations.[20] Indeed, if one thinks generally of what it is to become skilful and effective an area involving substantial and complex considerations, it is (typically) very difficult to imagine how one could become so without regular use of interpretive and creative judgment. For example, do rules or standards of procedure apply in a given case, do they need revision or augmenting, are there conflicts in applicable rules and how might these be balanced? Thus, the criticisms based on self-serving uses of the 'technicality/indeterminacy' ratio also need to be balanced with a reality check: substantial and complex bodies of knowledge *are* typically *both* highly technical and indeterminate, as, for instance, in both medicine and law. We need practitioners who can make such judgments, both technical and indeterminate, so that the body of knowledge and expertise in respect of which they make them is effectively employed and expands and improves. Accordingly, when we train practitioners in an area, an important part of what we are concerned to do is to train and develop their capacities to make accurate and creative judgments where required.

---

[20] I thank Andrew Alexandra for: 'less routine, it will require the exercise of judgment in a range of different and often less predictable specific situations.'

Moreover, for individual professional autonomy to be effective there will also (typically) need to be relevant degrees and kinds of professional autonomy at the collective level. If the standards and norms, for instance, of medical or legal practise, were not largely set by medicos or legal experts it is hard to imagine that these standards and norms could be appropriate and desirable ones. So while in such circumstances a doctor or lawyer might have some individual professional autonomy in choosing how to conform to these standards and norms, it would be a very limited form of professional autonomy. The standards and norms need to be the right ones, and, in many cases, such as medicine and law, this would require significant professional autonomy at the collective level.[21] The self-serving considerations we have seen against professional 'self-regulation' suggest, on the most plausible reading, that we should not leave *accountability* within the exclusive control of the professional collective. So if one imagined that professional autonomy implied that the collective had exclusive control over accountability in the field, then the notion of professional autonomy would be in serious trouble. However, one need not imagine that professional autonomy implies such things. On the contrary, it implies the taking of responsibility for one's judgments and conduct, either individually or as a collective, and so implies accountability. Nevertheless, this does not suggest *at all* that such control need *not* be accountable to independent parties or standards. Thus, while recommending the rehabilitation of professional autonomy where appropriate, one must also recommend a suite of mechanisms

[21] This need not be (so much) the case. In Alexandra et al, above n 2, Andrew Alexandra distinguished between professional self-regulation (autonomy at the collective level in setting standards and norms in an area), and professional independence (autonomy at the individual level in choosing how one complies to these standards and norms), using the case of the police officer to highlight how these may come apart. For while police officers (either as individuals or as a collective) largely do not set the standards and norms that govern them (since we the community, notably through our government, do), they do exercise quite considerable individual professional autonomy in determining how they best comply with these standards and norms. The role of the police officer and the contrast here, however, seems something of a special case. As I explain above, it is, for example, part of the role of doctors, lawyers, and engineers, or their collectives, to largely determine the standards and norms in their area. Their 'individual' autonomy to comply with standards will not be worth much if the standards are misguided, and it is hard to see how they could be otherwise, if they are not significantly determined by those with the relevant expertise in these areas of substantial and largely discrete bodies of knowledge and skill.

aimed at ensuring accountability to independent parties and standards, such as the standard of fair competition.

The worry about professional autonomy seems primarily driven by the worry of abuse that it is thought to allow. If one has significant professional autonomy, then this may open the door to abuse as well as effective and proper use. To counter this it is appropriate that accountability to independent parties and standards are retained and strengthened. Nevertheless, if professional autonomy is retained and strengthened as appropriate, then it may well remain true that the vulnerability to abuse that it allows cannot be *altogether* prevented by regulation, ie, in terms of specifiable laws or rules of conduct backed by appropriate positive and negative incentives. Suppose this is true (as I think it is). Would this mean we should give up on the idea of professional autonomy, or of the relevance of ethico-professional norms as providing effective guidance for occupational actors? If we could get the goods that these occupational roles are supposed to deliver without the need for guiding ethico-professional norms, in particular professional autonomy, then we might be tempted.[22] However, this is not the case. Indeed, the fact that we cannot do without professional autonomy is not just an empirical matter. As argued above, it does not even make sense to suppose that one could become expert in an area of substance and complexity in knowledge and skill, without the exercise of interpretation and creative judgment in many cases.[23] And it is clear that this applies to the areas of expertise, such as medicine and law, which we need for the delivery of the significant social and ethical goods it is the purpose of these occupational areas to deliver.

Vulnerability to abuse is the other side of the coin of allowing professional autonomy (where needed or desirable). Indeed, it is the other side of the coin of allowing autonomy generally, ie, the individual

---

[22] One might reject the idea that we should eradicate professional autonomy *even if we could and were still able to get much of what we need out of occupational actors*. Insofar as we are persons capable of (some) autonomy, this may generally be a good thing to encourage, and discouraging it would be a bad thing. Why would autonomous people want to work where they are allowed no autonomy? And why would you want to leave the area of work undeveloped by the interpretive judgment 'calls' of persons doing the work? No doubt some reasons may be given in either case. Nevertheless, it would generally seem undesirable both for persons and their work if people were not encouraged to make choices and judgments and to take responsibility for them.

[23] As I have indicated, more specific ethico-professional norms, such as 'be honest', also unavoidably involve interpretation.

autonomy that all of us who are capable of it share. As an autonomous person I may make bad choices or choose bad things, such as to pursue my own self-interest at the expense of the legitimate claims of others. Accordingly, we have a range of informal and formal, and negative and positive incentives aimed at discouraging such choices and conduct and encouraging ethical ones. However, while we seek to eradicate such abuses, we do not suppose we should do so by eradicating individual autonomy generally. While this would do the trick, the price is not only far too high, it is also self-defeating. We can hardly respect the claims of persons not to be abused by others who choose to do so if we address the problem by removing the autonomy of people generally to choose how they conduct themselves. I might not now be vulnerable to abuse due to the unethical choices of others, but since I cannot make choices myself now, I am, in too fundamental a way, no longer a person. The respect for my status as a person grounds the need to address my abuse, and therefore we would be advised to preserve this respect. Of course, as noted above, professional autonomy and personal autonomy are very different things. In particular, unlike personal autonomy, one does not have professional autonomy on account of one's status as a person. So the removal of professional autonomy as a means to avoid the problems of abuse would not be self-defeating in the way that removal of individual autonomy would be. Nevertheless, the necessity and desirability of professional autonomy for the effective employment of expertise required for the delivery of key social and ethical goods would be undermined. It would be self-defeating then to remove professional autonomy as a way to address the problem of the vulnerability of the public to abuses of professional autonomy. Again, it may do the trick, but since the legitimate and significant interests of the public in the effective delivery of these goods would now be fundamentally undermined, it would be 'by our own lights' self-defeating.

III CORRELATIVE DUTIES OF CARE TO CLIENTS

As I have indicated, consumer protection and the need for it in relation to market and professionalisation issues is central to the ethico-professional norms of primarily commercial occupations, and remain relevant to all commercial occupations, even if not primarily so. So, for instance, and largely on account of concern with consumer protection, a professionalising group would have a commitment to, and be developing, effective processes in respect of fair competition, accountability through transparency, and reactive and preventative ethico-professional risk management strategies. However, conceptualising service users simply as *consumers* in regard to their relations with professionals is a mistake. Correspondingly, conceptualising professionals just as market actors, and ethico-professional norms as exclusively driven by market concerns, has been a mistake. These are common views — indeed, the overriding views — found in both the practical mechanisms, such as in the laws of the 'new regulatory state' (for example, the *Trade Practices Act 1974* (Cth)), and academic and governmental discussions of professionalisation, market and regulation issues. Nevertheless, these views significantly misunderstand the professions and the promotion of the interests of the public. In particular, they misunderstand the sort of ethico-professional norms that attach, not on account of one's status as a consumer, but on account of one's being a *client* of professional services.

As sketched above, a basic, general contrast that can be applied across occupational groups concerns the ultimate purposes that govern the groups. For the primarily commercial occupations, commercial imperatives are at the forefront. It is appropriate, then, that ethico-professional standards and norms and the concern to promote the interests of the public will focus on market and consumer protection issues. However, a significant marker of professions — perhaps most notably and widely recognised in the traditional professions such as law and medicine — is that members of the public are not just consumers of their services but are also their *clients*. Of course, even as a client, one does consume these services — so what is the distinction? Firstly, as I have indicated, the 'traditional professions' require the inculcation of a body of expert knowledge and skill, together with a high degree of professional autonomy for the effective use and development of this body of expert knowledge and skill. In consequence, there is a high degree of accountability and liability associated with the use of such knowledge and skill. Secondly, this expertise and professional autonomy is put in the service of, and guided by, the promotion of some (often significant) human or ethical good — such as the delivery of just process for the legal profession, or human health for medicine. Finally, this service is (typically) undertaken by the professional role occupant in *advocacy of the* (legitimate, and often significant) *interests of their client*, that is, a particular individual or organisation.

On account of the *advocacy* role played by a professional in regard to your interests, you are their client, and not simply their customer or the consumer of their services — as you are when, for example, you go to the shop or bank. Of course, your bank offers services such as financial advice and, as a consumer of these services the bank would advocate your (financial) interests. To this extent then, they might also be thought to treat you as a client. Moreover, as, say, with your General Practitioner, you might well have an ongoing relationship with your bank as their client. Indeed, albeit in a weaker, more limited way, you might perhaps be the client of your local shopkeeper and not just their customer, and so they may be careful to stock the sort of bread you regularly buy. Certainly, it has become quite common for occupational groups and businesses generally to promote themselves as providing *client* services and as regarding their customers as clients. And they may be thought to do so either in respect of how they 'look after' and so advocate the relevant interests of their customers *over time*, or by how they do especially well — that is, comprehensively — at a *particular time*. Thus, for instance, you might get your car serviced by a particular mechanic with whom you are in a client relationship over time, or at a particular time, on account of their comprehensive advocacy of your interests with regard to your car — say, by giving more investigation and long-term advice. In the case of the traditional professions however, advocating the interests of their customers as 'clients' is not a grab for a larger share of the market. Rather, it is because it is the primary institutional purpose of these occupational areas to provide expert advocacy of their clients' legitimate interests: in the case of medicine and law, to promote significant individual, social and ethical goods, ie, health and just legal process respectively.

In contrast, there has also been a significant shift by certain occupational groups, such as those involved in the human service industries, including health and welfare (and significant aspects of the legal profession), toward conceiving relations with the public on the model of customers or consumers. The central point of this shift has been to empower the *choice* of the public as consumers of these services.[24] For instance, in the case of the medical profession, as a norm of best practice nowadays, your medical practitioner (whether treating you as a 'one-off' exchange in a public hospital or as your General Practitioner) will

[24] Thanks to Kylie Cocking for developing, in discussion, the relevance of choice as crucial to the contrast between consumer–client.

typically take a good deal more time than was typical a few decades ago to explain your situation and, where appropriate, offer the information required for making certain choices.[25]

To some extent we may be *both* client, in the sense of advocacy of our (legitimate) interests, and consumer, in the sense of empowerment of one's choices regarding services offered, whether in the case of the traditional professional (such as medical practitioners), and the 'emerging' professional (such as real estate agents), or other occupational groups generally (such as motor car mechanics). However, unlike the motor mechanic or shopkeeper, the traditional professions are primarily a *cooperative* enterprise within their occupational community, with respect to the establishment and development of the discrete and substantial expertise and skills it is their institutional role to apply in the advocacy of the public interest. Such cooperation is obviously necessary to the continuing development of such bodies of expertise and skill and, so, intrinsic to their institutional role.[26]

As set out above, a key aspect of both the long-standing sociological criticisms and of the ethico-professional focus on empowering consumers, in particular their choices, is the asymmetry of knowledge (and associated power) between professionals, or many occupational actors generally, and the public. As a client of a professional, one typically stands in a relatively weak position compared to the professional: say, one's doctor or lawyer in relation to the knowledge, skill and power relevant to promoting one's medical health or justice before the law. However, that there are these asymmetries between clients and professionals is a proper feature — indeed, largely the raison d'être — of such professional–client relationships. Short of extraordinary efforts (including undertaking many years of study and training), one could not put oneself in the position of being able to make informed choices and judgments, and attaining the skill, expertise and so power to carry these out in relation to one's medical, legal, and similar needs — at least, not with any comprehensive or deep understanding and authority. Certainly, few of us could put ourselves in a position of commanding knowledge and skill across a number of areas involving

[25] For a philosophical treatment of the professional role morality of the medical (and legal) professions, see Oakley and Cocking, *Virtue Ethics*, above n 4, especially ch 4 in regard to the shift from the perceived paternalism of the traditional professional–client model prevalent in medicine decades ago.

[26] I thank Andrew Alexandra for this point.

substantial expertise. Moreover, one might not want to spend a significant part of one's life gaining the expertise of a medical doctor, or an engineer, and it is hard to see how there could be any generally applicable imperative that one ought to do so.[27] Thus, we have significant social institutions the purpose of which is to meet these significant social and ethical needs we all share. It is an entirely appropriate feature therefore, of certain relationships between the public and professionals that there is an asymmetry of knowledge, skill and expertise. Correspondingly, it is entirely appropriate that the consumer becomes a *client* of the professional in such cases, in the sense that client becomes the professional's responsibility to provide understandings and choices based upon their discrete expertise, on behalf of, and in promotion of, their client's legitimate, often significant, interests. Since promoting consumer choice here is limited — both practically and in terms of what is desirable or worthwhile — promoting ethico-professionalism here is not about promoting consumer choice.

On account of the asymmetry, the vulnerability of the public that must be addressed is not a lack of knowledge or skill the public expects, wants or should have in pursuing their interests as the client of professionals. The solution is not, therefore, to ratchet up consumer choice and so limit or eradicate the asymmetry. Rather, the overall integrity system for professional standards would here focus on promoting conditions for the proper (and improving) exercise of a professional's duty of care[28] and special responsibility to act in their client's interests *on account of the asymmetry*.

---

[27] While one might agree that we cannot reasonably be expected to have the expert professional knowledge and skills of, say, our doctor, one might argue that this does not show the limits of the consumer protection/choice model of ethico-professional relations with the public. We can, for example, solicit the expert advice of third parties, upon which we may then give informed consent concerning a particular professional's advice. Nevertheless, the key contrast remains: we are still not able to deliberate comprehensively on the specialised information and, on this basis, make our own choices about what we should do (and what should be done to, or on behalf of, us). We remain dependent upon the expertise of others whose advice and choices we may then 'authorise'. However, our authorisations remain dependent upon an effective role for professional responsibility in regard to empowering trust in our authorisation. Professional responsibility and client trust are not made redundant.

[28] 'Duty of care' is commonly a legal notion and there refers to specific duties of care — typically based on the concern to not do harm — enshrined in black letter law. Such legally binding specified duties of care are part of the picture I have in mind. However, such duties of care may cut across the consumer–client distinction, eg, that a seller not

It is, of course, important to promote one's capacity to make informed choices — including with respect to occupational areas involving a substantial, complex or discrete body of knowledge or skill. Thus, for instance, it is important that our lawyer or doctor provides us with understandings of our legal or medical situation and its related options and costs, upon which *we* can then make decisions. A good recent example of the recognition of the value of promoting informed choices in such areas in the US, Europe, and now in Australia, is the advent of surgeon report cards: that is, providing accessible data to 'consumers' that reports on the performance of surgeons across relevant surgical procedures.[29]

Nevertheless, we also need to be able to put ourselves in the hands of professionals who are experts in a body of knowledge and skill we could not reasonably be expected to share or possess ourselves. The focus here is not to empower our choices as consumers, but to promote good professional–client relationships where professionals have a special responsibility in regard to the discharge of their discrete expertise in advocacy of their client's relevant (legitimate, and typically significant) interests.

Identifying and contrasting the empowerment of consumer choice and client trust articulates different approaches to the promotion of ethico-professional standards, norms and ideals. In particular, it articulates the need to focus such efforts towards *both* the empowerment of consumer choice *and* the professional responsibility associated with professional–client relations. In the case of real estate agents, as discussed, the development of ethico-professional standards and norms would be primarily directed by a consumer protection model, rather than a client trust model. On the other hand, ethico-professional norms directed by a client trust model would be a significant focus for, say, lawyers.

A good example of an ethico-professional norm that is important for lawyer–client relationships is the well-recognised problem of an 'expectation gap' regarding what the lawyer can offer their client. In

---

pass on faulty goods to a consumer. And the duties of care I have in mind might go beyond what is, or even could be, enshrined in black letter law. As I argue, standards of ethical conduct, including ethico-professional conduct, often cannot be codified in rules or laws, or at any rate cannot be codified easily or well.

[29] For a very recent collection of essays on the advent of surgeon's report cards and their ethical implications, see Steve Clarke and Justin Oakley (eds), *Informed Consent and Clinician Accountability: The Ethics of Report Cards on Surgeon Performance* (2007).

particular, while they can be expected to provide due or just process for their client, they cannot guarantee the outcome desired by the client, even if this is the just outcome. Thus, the appropriate ethico-professional norm for lawyers is the former, not the latter. While a clarification of this sort addresses the limits of the professional services on offer, it does not serve to empower consumer choice. It is not as if on account of understanding the limits on my lawyer's services, I am in a better position to make relevant choices in the pursuit of my interests — such as to choose another lawyer's services that are not so limited. It is therefore not an ethico-professional norm that can be grounded in the consumer protection model concerned with the promotion of consumer choice. It is rather a clarification of the nature and limits of the discrete expertise that the professional may be expected to put into the service of a client's interest, where the client is unequipped to make, or act on, the relevant sort of informed choices. It is thus an ethico-professional norm that is driven by the client protection model since it is concerned to facilitate a proper and specific duty of care in relation to this 'expectation gap'. That is, to clarify both the sort of expertise the professional can put in service of their clients' interests and the sort of interests this expertise can be expected to serve.

Moreover, while some such duties of care may be amenable to reasonably comprehensive specification in terms of laws or rules, for example, in codes of conduct, many are not. Sometimes this is because the duties of care are simply quite open-ended. Consider, for example, how a professional will need to exercise professional judgment or discretion where the existing rules don't provide guidance. For example, the *Property, Stock and Business Agents Act 2002* (NSW) requires that real estate agents *be honest* in their dealings with the public. However, what this means is sometimes unclear and inevitably subject to interpretation. For instance, an industry representative I interviewed asked me the following question: does an agent have to tell a buyer that someone was murdered in the house he is selling?[30] The general prescription to 'be honest' requires some further clarity concerning what it is that one must be honest about. On the other hand, it is doubtful that one could provide an exhaustive list of such considerations. In the example given, one should presumably be guided by those considerations it would be reasonable to think may be material to a person's decision to

---

[30] This, along with other interviews by myself and others on the team, was undertaken as part of: Alexandra et al, above n 2.

buy the house — and the fact that a murder is known to have taken place in the house could count as such a consideration. But if an occupational actor is to be guided in this way, given that an exhaustive list of such considerations could not be provided to cover all such possibilities, it would seem to require that *ethico-professional conscience* be the driver for compliance with the dictum 'be honest'. That is, the professional's approach is guided by genuine commitments to be honest and transparent about considerations it would be reasonable to think may be material to their client's decision.[31]

A key implication of the client protection model is to strengthen the accountability and general integrity roles played by occupational associations and professional oversight bodies in regard to the proper discharge of the professional's duty of care to their clients. Accountability for those groups for which the market concerns of fair competition and consumer protection are at centre stage — such as real estate agents — is primarily market driven. The market, properly conceived and effectively operating,[32] where commercial integrity is about consumers and suppliers being restored to relative equals in power, knowledge, and so on, would thereby provide a proper guide for shaping the ethico-professional standards and norms for these groups — including accountability to their consumers. However, as indicated, the market cannot provide the sort of accountability required for the professional's duty of care to their clients. This duty of care is clearly not about making profit in fair ways and commitment to consumer choice. So the effective delivery of this duty of care across an area will require a significant governance role for professional oversight bodies and associations.

CONCLUSION

The legitimacy or relevance of guidance by ethico-professional norms has long been under fire on a few fronts. The self-interested tendencies of individuals and groups undermines proper guidance, and is not likely

---

[31] One of the points made by Seumas Miller in this book is how the preventative aspects of integrity systems, such as ethical and professional development programs, seek to immerse professionals in the relevant ethical issues and problems in their field and thus develop such commitments.

[32] Of course, ideal markets do not exist. However, even if they did, this would not provide a comprehensive, accurate frame for ethico-professional considerations.

to go away. A key way to work towards accommodating self-interest and guidance by ethico-professional norms is by developing the integrity mechanisms aimed at delivering *deserved* reputation in an occupational area. Reputation is important across occupational groups, both the primarily commercial and competitive groups and those groups that are primarily cooperative enterprises concerned with service to significant social and ethical institutional purposes. Insofar as deserved reputation can be established through relevant integrity mechanisms, it would work to align self-interest with relevant ethico-professional concerns, particularly those concerned with the legitimate interests of others.[33]

My concern in this chapter, however, has been to provide some characterisation of ethico-professional norms generally, and show why the ethico-professional norms attached to the professional autonomy/client trust model in particular are an indispensable and valuable feature of professional life. Problems of abuse will remain and accordingly call for a strengthening of, in particular, accountability mechanisms, including to independent parties and standards. But the idea that we might 'regulate' ethico-professional practice and do away with guidance by the ethico-professional norms fundamentally misunderstands professional ethics. Such guidance is a generally necessary and valuable feature across occupations, including for instance, real estate agents. In the case of the 'traditional' professions, however, the occupational area is properly characterised as primarily involving expert use of a substantial, complex, and largely discrete body of knowledge and skill in pursuit of significant ethical and social interests and goods. Here I have argued that effectively operating guiding ethico-professional norms, in particular robust forms of autonomy and a correlative duty of care to clients, are central to the exercise of this expertise and the pursuit of these significant individual and community interests that are the primary purposes of these groups.

---

[33] For a more developed account of ethico-professional reputation, see Alexandra et al, above n 2, especially ch 6.

Chapter 10

Sarbanes-Oxley and the Search for Accountable Corporate Governance

Melvin J Dubnick

Use the word 'corporation' in mixed company — that is, any group comprised of more than accountants, MBAs, attorneys or economists — and the image you are likely to evoke will be that of a large, impersonal business enterprise headed by a board of directors, managed by a team of executives headed by a well-paid CEO, with millions of customers, thousands of employees, offices throughout the world, and perhaps tens of thousands of big and small investors who claim some stake in the company. Say the name of a particular corporation — for example, Microsoft, Enron, Toyota, WorldCom, Sony, Tyco, or Apple — in that same group and the conjured up images are likely to be as diverse and opined as the group itself.

Taken out of mixed company and placed in context, the modern corporation's image becomes clearer in purpose if not in form or reputation. At least within the jurisdictional sphere, where Anglo-American norms and interests predominate,[1] a consensus view has emerged among those whose livelihood depends on these salient social-cultural-economic-political actors. This consensus holds that the raison d'être of corporations — their very existence and success — is tied to

[1] Despite the awkwardness of the label 'Anglo-American', I intend for it to encompass those nations and cultures (social, legal, political and economic) associated with the British governance tradition. Alternative labels (eg, 'Commonwealth', 'Anglican', etc) might have been used, so the choice is offered arbitrarily and with apologies to readers.

their pursuit of value on behalf of shareholders. That is the *pervasive* and *defining* view among students and practitioners of the modern corporate arts and sciences. Moreover, that consensus is as strongly held by corporate critics as it is by its defenders.[2] While this consensus view of corporate purpose is not without its historical and intellectual challengers, the practical result of its dominance has been to focus and set parameters around debates about corporate behaviour and possible solutions to corporate governance problems in the Anglo-American context. As that context has become both increasingly more complex and globally hegemonic, however, that consensus has become more problematic both within and outside its formal jurisdictions. This has been made especially clear with the passage and implementation of the *Sarbanes-Oxley Act of 2002*.[3]

While designed as a politically expedient response to a moral panic fed by media frenzy,[4] *Sarbanes-Oxley* has brought to the fore fundamental issues about the nature of the modern corporate form that have lain fallow for nearly a century among Anglo-American scholars. The debate about the nature of the corporation was pre-emptively dismissed as mere scholastic banter by no less an authority than John Dewey in 1926,[5] and has only intermittently been revisited.[6] The argument presented here attempts to reopen those discussions with the intent of reasserting a perspective on the purpose of corporations that allows us to assess corporate governance reforms such as *Sarbanes-Oxley*. The perspective I put forward is anchored in the contention that

---

[2] See, eg, Edward S Herman, *Corporate Control, Corporate Power* (1981); Christopher D Stone, *Where the Law Ends: The Social Control of Corporate Behavior* (1975).

[3] Pub L No 107–204, 116 Stat 745 (2002) ('*Sarbanes-Oxley*').

[4] Jose Gabilondo, 'Financial Moral Panic! *Sarbanes-Oxley*, Financier Folk Devils, and Off-Balance-Sheet Arrangements' (2006) 36 *Seton Hall Law Review* 781.

[5] See John Dewey, 'The Historic Background of Corporate Legal Personality' (1926) 35 *Yale Law Journal* 655; Bryant Smith, 'Legal Personality' (1928) 37 *Yale Law Journal* 283.

[6] See Reuven S Avi-Yonah, 'The Cynical Transformations of the Corporate Form: A Historical Perspective on Corporate Social Responsibility' (2005) 30 *Delaware Journal of Corporate Law* 767; Phillip I Blumberg, 'The Corporate Personality in American Law: A Summary Review' (1990) 38 *American Journal of Comparative Law* 49; Tokusuke Kitagawa, 'Some Reflections on the Corporate Theory, Including a Japanese Perspective' (1960) *Duke Law Journal* 535; Janet McLean, 'Personality and Public Law Doctrine' (1999) 49 *University of Toronto Law Journal* 123; William W Bratton, 'The New Economic Theory of the Firm: Critical Perspectives from History' (1989) 41 *Stanford Law Review* 1471.

modern governance — public as well as private — is at its core based on some form of accountability. Accountability-based governance, in this view, emerged historically as an effective response to the central dilemma facing secular rulers of the embryonic nation-state in the late medieval period — that is, how to maintain and sustain authority over autonomous subjects who were becoming increasingly aware of their capacity for discretionary action. The modern corporate form, I will argue, developed as part of that solution in Anglo-Norman England, and it is in light of those historical roots that contemporary corporate governance and corporate governance reforms efforts should be assessed.

I 'PURPOSE' AND THE ASSESSMENT OF CORPORATE GOVERNANCE REFORM

The assessment of a law or public policy can be approached in three ways: prospectively, retrospectively or perspectively. The prospective approach, common to many professional policy analysis efforts, is to assess the potential or possibility of a proposal. It reflects the role of assessment as part of the policy design process. Retrospective approaches, in contrast, are generally associated with technical or critical evaluations of past performance of the program or its implementers. In seeking to uncover the underlying logic or ontological context of a policy, perspective assessments are most helpful for analytic and critical tasks.

In this chapter I undertake a perspective assessment of *Sarbanes-Oxley* with the objective of measuring the law and its implementation against a model of the 'historical purpose' for which corporate governance regulation and reform legislation has been developed over the past millennium. As sweeping and daunting as that task might seem, it proves feasible because in Anglo-American law the corporate form is historically and inherently linked to the primary purpose of modern governance: accountability. As a first step in this (or any) assessment, we must distinguish among the various foci that might draw our attention. There are several candidate focal points for a policy assessment. In theory, at least, all formalised laws and policies are expected to have an explicit statement of *intent* — the goals or objectives its authors sought to address — and where these are clear they provide the grounds for assessment of programs associated with those intentions. This seems simple enough, except for the practical matter that (preamble rhetoric notwithstanding) intent is rarely so clear, especially in matters of law and policy.[7] A second focus for assessments could be the *functional* role played by a set of policies or laws beyond their expressed intentions. Among political scientists, for example, public policies and programs are evaluated as much for their symbolic value as for their intended impacts,[8] while others approach policies as both functional reflections and perpetuations of politically dominant notions of human nature.[9] Third, a more familiar focus for policy analysts are the *impacts* that a policy or other government action has on various segments of the environment.[10] Benefit–cost analyses are at their core measurements of the projected impacts (positive and negative) of a proposal, and studies of the implications of a given regulation or tax code change or interest rate increase on a segment of the population also fit this category. A fourth focal point of assessment is the unintended, secondary or delayed *consequences* derived from the laws, policies or programs.[11]

One focus rarely considered is that of *purpose*, and here we look beyond immediate intent and function (which are the most closely related) to the underlying — and yet overarching — rationale of the policy effort. This assessment standard is best explained by example. The *intent* of a government campaign to deal with a national AIDS epidemic in a developing country is to prevent it spread and treat the infected, but in the process it *functions* as a means for improving the capacity of health and social services at the community level. Its *impact* on specific population segments — for example, children under the age of six, members of a certain ethnic community — is also a subject of assessment, as is the program's long-term *consequential* impact on government legitimacy. The *purpose* of the program, however, is the meta-goal of improving the quality of life for all, and the question becomes: how does this particular anti-AIDS campaign measure up against that objective? In a comparable way, the purpose of any

[7] Jeremy Waldron, *Law and Disagreement* (1999).
[8] Murray J Edelman, *The Symbolic Uses of Politics* (1964); Murray Edelman, *Politics as Symbolic Action: Mass Arousal and Quiesence* (1971).
[9] Julian Le Grand, 'Knights, Knaves or Pawns? Human Behaviour and Social Policy' (1997) 26 *Journal of Social Policy* 149.
[10] Hidehiko Ichimura and Christopher R Taber, 'Direct Estimation of Policy Impacts' (Working Paper, National Bureau of Economic Research, Cambridge, Massachusetts, 2000).
[11] Steven M Gillon, *That's Not What We Meant to Do: Reform and Its Unintended Consequences in Twentieth-Century America* (2000).

contemporary US national security policy (assuming the conventional perspective) is maintaining world order, and a particular government decision (eg, the invasion of Iraq in 2003) can be assessed against that higher standard as well as evaluated according to its intent (eg, to depose Saddam Hussein), function (what it contributes to stabilising — or not — the Middle East), impact (the number of Iraqi civilians killed as a result), and consequence (the bolstering of anti-American sentiment throughout the world). The seeming indifference to purpose by most analysts is, in part, a result of consensus that is typically associated with meta-goals within a dominant political ontology at any particular time and place. That is the case with any anti-AIDS program under globalised conditions across populations where previous experience with the epidemic generates as much empathy as sympathy for the afflicted. Where that consensus has broken down — as in the case of US policy in Iraq — the issue of purpose comes to the fore and becomes part of the overall assessment and debate over the situation.

The relevance of all this to the subject of this chapter, *Sarbanes-Oxley*, emerges as we approach the fifth anniversary of the law and face a growing number of assessments that raise a range of issues. Some of the studies, many published immediately after passage of the Act, focus on the intentions of *Sarbanes-Oxley*. Characterised as 'legislated ethics'[12] and 'legislated risk-management',[13] it was generally assessed as a means for improving corporate governance through tougher disclosure requirements and other mechanisms.[14] As the law was implemented,

---

[12] Howard Rockness and Joanne Rockness, 'Legislated Ethics: From Enron to Sarbanes-Oxley, the Impact on Corporate America' (2005) 57 *Journal of Business Ethics* 31; Margaret L Gagne, Joanne H Gavin and Gregory J Tully, 'Assessing the Costs and Benefits of Ethics: Exploring a Framework' (2005) 110 *Business and Society Review* 181.

[13] Colin Linsley, 'Auditing, Risk Management and a Post *Sarbanes-Oxley* World' (2003) 24 *Review of Business* 21.

[14] Leonard M Baynes, 'Just Pucker and Blow? An Analysis of Corporate Whistleblowers, the Duty of Care, the Duty of Loyalty, and the *Sarbanes-Oxley Act*' (2002) 76 *St John's Law Review* 875; Michael A Perino, 'Enron's Legislative Aftermath: Some Reflections on the Deterrence Aspects of the *Sarbanes-Oxley Act of 2002*' (2002) 76 *St John's Law Review* 671; Larry E Ribstein, 'Market Vs Regulatory Responses to Corporate Fraud: A Critique of the *Sarbanes-Oxley Act of 2002*' (2002) 28 *Journal of Corporation Law* 1; William W Bratton, 'Enron, Sarbanes-Oxley and Accounting: Rules Versus Principles Versus Rents' (2003) 48 *Villanova Law Review* 1023; John C Coffee, 'The Attorney as Gatekeeper: An Agenda for the SEC' (2003) 103 *Columbia Law Review* 1293; Lawrence A Cunningham, 'The *Sarbanes-Oxley* Yawn: Heavy Rhetoric, Light Reform (and It Just Might Work)'(2003) 35 *Connecticut Law Review* 915; Megan N Gates, 'The *Sarbanes-*

more attention was given to the functional implications of *Sarbanes-Oxley*. Some focused on how it became a vehicle for extending the global reach of US market regulation,[15] while others considered its role in promoting the nationalisation of US corporate governance policy.[16] Whether intended or not, *Sarbanes-Oxley* also has begun to function as the standard for best practices in non-public firms.[17] Impact studies of *Sarbanes-Oxley* have also proliferated, covering the obvious targets such as CEOs, CFOs and corporate directors,[18] to its influence on management in general,[19] as well as accountancy, record keeping practices and auditing within the firm.[20] Among the consequences of

---

Oxley Act and Non-US Issuers: Considerations for International Companies' (2003) 10 *Journal of Commercial Biotechnology* 40; Marshall N Geiger and Porcher L Taylor, 'CEO and CFO Certifications of Financial Information' (2003) 17 *Accounting Horizons* 357.

[15] Gates, above n 14; Detlev F Vagts, 'Extraterritoriality and the Corporate Governance Law' (2003) 97 *American Journal of International Law* 289; Huddson T Hollister, '"Shock Therapy" for *Aktiengesellschaften*: Can the *Sarbanes-Oxley* Certification Requirements Transform German Corporate Culture, Practice and Prospects?' (2005) 25 *Northwestern Journal of International Law and Business* 453; Lori V Ryan, 'Corporate Governance and Business Ethics in North America: The State of the Art' (2005) 44 *Business and Society* 40.

[16] Michael E Clark, 'Hamstrung or Properly Calibrated? Federalism and the Appropriate Role of Government in the Post-*Sarbanes-Oxley* World' (2004) 1 *International Journal of Disclosure and Governance* 385; Roberta Romano, 'The *Sarbanes-Oxley Act* and the Making of Quack Corporate Governance' (2005) 114 *Yale Law Journal* 1521; Roberta Romano, 'Quack Corporate Governance' (2005) 28 *Regulation* 36.

[17] Dan R Dalton and Catherine M Dalton, '*Sarbanes-Oxley* Legislation and the Private Company: If Not a Marriage, Then Certainly an Engagement' (2005) 26 *Journal of Business Strategy* 8.

[18] Geiger and Taylor, above n 14; Ruth V Aguilera, 'Corporate Governance and Director Accountability: An Institutional Comparative Perspective' (2005) 16 *British Journal of Management* S39; Jack Keenan, 'Corporate Governance in UK/USA Boardrooms' (2004) 12 *Corporate Governance* 172; James S Linck, Jeffry M Netter and Tina Yang, 'The Effects and Unintended Consequences of the *Sarbanes-Oxley Act*, and Its Era, on the Supply and Demand for Directors' (2007), available at <http://papers.ssrn.com/sol3/papers.cfm?abstract_id=902665>.

[19] Harvey Coustan et al, '*Sarbanes-Oxley*: What It Means to the Marketplace' (2004) 197 *Journal of Accountancy* 43.

[20] Bratton, 'Enron, Sarbanes-Oxley and Accounting', above n 14; David L Schwarzkopf and Hugh M Miller, 'Early Evidence of How *Sarbanes-Oxley* Implementation Affects Individuals and their Workplace Relationships' (2005) 110 *Business and Society Review* 21; David O Stephens, 'The *Sarbanes-Oxley Act*: Records Management Implications' (2005) 15 *Records Management Journal* 98; James A Tackett, Fran Wolf and Gregory A Claypool, '*Sarbanes-Oxley* and Audit Failure: A Critical Examination' (2004) 19 *Managerial Auditing Journal* 340; James A Tackett, Fran Wolf and Gregory A Claypool,

Sarbanes-Oxley, the policy's role in raising the cost of doing business,[21] as well as reshaping the very nature of the corporate culture,[22] are starting to be scrutinised.

What has not been examined as yet is how *Sarbanes-Oxley* measures up to the historical purpose of corporate governance policy. This is in large part due to the general indifference to historical purpose inherent in the consensus discussed earlier. To remedy this I make explicit what that purpose was through an examination of its diverse historical roots as well as the millennium long development of corporate governance policies. Of special note are the ties to a particular political ontology, which highlights the modern need for accountability. My goal is to take the measure of *Sarbanes-Oxley* by applying a framework that focuses on the historical foundations of corporate accountability.[23]

II UNCOVERING THE HISTORICAL PURPOSE OF CORPORATE GOVERNANCE

> Origins are always obscure. If we endeavour to explain the genesis of any event that happens in our own days and seemingly before our very eyes, a scientific discovery, a new religion, a war, a revolution, we never get back to the simple fountain-head, the initial impulse whence it is derived. The stream we follow upwards brings us at length to difficult marshes and underground pools, never to a clear spring. If that is true of near events, how much harder is the task to trace the origins of social phenomena in the unknown and ever receding past.[24]

In seeking a historical foundation for the purpose of corporate governance policy we are heading into murky waters.

'Internal Control under *Sarbanes-Oxley*: A Critical Examination' (2006) 21 *Managerial Auditing Journal* 317.

[21] William J Carney, 'The Costs of Being Public after *Sarbanes-Oxley*: The Irony of "Going Private"' (2006) 55 *Emory Law Journal* 141; Larry E Ribstein, '*Sarbanes-Oxley* after Three Years' (University of Illinois Law and Economics Research Paper, University of Illinois College of Law, 2005).

[22] Michael Power, 'Organizations and Auditability: A Theory' (Paper presented at the SCORE Conference, Stockholm, 2005).

[23] Cf Ian Hacking, 'Two Kinds of "New Historicism" for Philosophers' (1990) *New Literary History* 343.

[24] Robert M MacIver, *The Modern State* (1926) 25.

(A) *The Modern Corporate Form as Hybrid*

The first thing to note is that there are three major claims to the parentage of the modern corporate form, one ecclesiastic,[25] one Italian, and another English.[26] Each reflects a distinct view of that form as a legal actor. An early corporate form, with roots in Roman law,[27] is found in medieval canon law as a means for dealing with the status of church property that was *held* in perpetuity but *used* by individuals in their ecclesiastic roles. Thus, an artificial and passive entity was necessary as a legal instrument representing a collectivity (the church or an order) that would transcend the actions of its membership.[28] This canonical form is manifest today in approaches that stress that the corporation is nothing more than a 'legal fiction' (*persona ficta*)[29] with an existence (ie, legal standing) independent of its members.

The Italian — actually Genoan — claim regards the modern corporation as an outgrowth of a particular joint-stock company form, developed by debt holders to handle privately-assumed public debts that spread from 15th century Genoa northward throughout the continent and then England. Unlike the passive canonical form, this corporate form is an active contractual association of individual shareholders with a common interest in the actions of the fiduciary agent.[30]

Alternatively, a case is made that the modern corporate form evolved from partnerships and chartered guilds and related entities of 10th and 11th century England. What evolved was the corporate form perceived as a distinct autonomous ('rights-and-duty-bearing') entity with 'real' interests, such as proving charitable services or the pursuit of

---

[25] Harold J Berman, *Law and Revolution: The Formation of the Western Legal Tradition* (1983).

[26] M Schmitthoff, 'The Origin of the Joint-Stock Company' (1939) 3 *University of Toronto Law Journal* 74. Each of these forms corresponds with a corporate 'personality' type in American law: see Blumberg, above n 6. Blumberg also discusses the recent emergence of a fourth corporate personality that regards it as a composite of corporate entities. See also Stone, above n 2.

[27] F R W I Maitland, 'Corporation Sole' (1900) 16 *Law Quarterly Review* 335.

[28] Berman, above n 24; Stone, above n 2, 11–13.

[29] See George F Deiser, 'The Juristic Person — I' (1908) 57 *University of Pennsylvania Law Review and American Law Register* 131.

[30] George F Deiser, 'The Juristic Person — II' (1909) 57 *University of Pennsylvania Law Review and American Law Register* 216.

profits in an open market where it competes with other 'real' persons (corporate and otherwise).[31]

The modern business corporation that is the subject of *Sarbanes-Oxley* and related laws is perhaps best seen as a hybrid of all three forms, for while it has legal standing as an artificial person and displays the structural characteristics of the joint-stock form, its existence is closely tied to the same 'realist' logic that forms the foundation of municipalities, associations and other collectivities recognised as active persons under law.[32] The development of that hybrid genre was nowhere more advanced than in England and its colonial offspring, and for that reason the 'stream we follow upwards' (in MacIver's terms) is located in the British Isles. That 'genre' was most clearly defined by US Supreme Court Chief Justice John Marshall in *Dartmouth College v Woodward* in passages worth quoting at length:

> A corporation is an artificial being, invisible, intangible, and existing only in contemplation of law. Being the mere creature of law, it possesses only those properties which the charter of its creation confers upon it, either expressly, or as incidental to its very existence. These are such as are supposed best calculated to effect the object for which it was created. Among the most important are immortality, and, if the expression may be allowed, individuality; properties, by which a perpetual succession of many persons are considered as the same, and may act as a single individual. They enable a corporation to manage its own affairs, and to hold property, without the perplexing intricacies, the hazardous and endless necessity, of perpetual conveyances for the purpose of transmitting it from hand to hand. It is chiefly for the purpose of clothing bodies of men, in succession, with these qualities and capacities, that corporations were invented, and are in use. By these means, a perpetual succession of individuals are capable of acting for the promotion of the particular object, like one immortal being. But this being does not share in the civil government of

---

[31] While I use a narrative that focuses on Anglo-Norman England, for reasons that become clear below, the theory behind this view is associated with the German political theorist and historian Gierke: see Otto F V Gierke, *Political Theories of the Middle Age* (1958). For an effective attempt at outlining Gierke's theory as it relates to corporate forms: see George F Deiser, 'The Juristic Person — III' (1909) 57 *University of Pennsylvania Law Review and American Law Register* 300.

[32] Leonard W Hein, 'The British Business Company: Its Origins and Its Control' (1963) 15 *University of Toronto Law Journal* 134.

> the country, unless that be the purpose for which it was created. Its immortality no more confers on it political power, or a political character, than immortality would confer such power or character on a natural person. It is no more a state instrument, than a natural person exercising the same powers would be. … The objects for which a corporation is created are universally such as the government wishes to promote. They are deemed beneficial to the country; and this benefit constitutes the consideration, and in most cases, the sole consideration of the grant.[33]

Two important points about Chief Justice Marshall's definition need highlighting. First, the corporation in question, Dartmouth College, was a specific type of corporation — an 'eleemosynary institution' engaged in the charitable work of providing education. Second, although business corporations do exist at the time of the decision (1819), it would be 25 more years before the British Parliament passes the *Joint Stock Companies Act 1844*[34] ('*Companies Act*') that provides for incorporation through a registration process rather than through royal charters or acts of legislation.[35] Thus, despite strong associations with business enterprises, the 'purpose' of a corporation is not found in its type (for example, charitable, proprietary, etc). Nevertheless, at the time of Chief Justice Marshall's decision there were already well-known business enterprises with corporate forms, mainly in Britain where royal or parliamentary charters were required to deal in lucrative ventures involving exploration or foreign trade, or in activities that involved charging tolls and fees for the provision of public roads, water and sewer systems, etc. For most of the 17th and 18th centuries outside these arenas there were few advantages for business enterprises in seeking corporate status (which were costly to procure and often restrictive) and a good

[33] 17 US 518, 637–8 (1819).

[34] See John Micklethwait and Adrian Wooldridge, *The Company: A Short History of a Revolutionary Idea* (2003).

[35] There are two other means for an entity to assume corporate status. One is through a finding in common law court where a non-corporate entity might be given de facto standing as a corporation to facilitate judgment (see Maitland, above n 26); and the other is through 'implication' via legislation or other government action that treats an organisational form (for example, a voluntary association or a labour union) as a distinct corporate entity: see Editorial, 'Incorporation by Implication under the *Sherman Act*' (1917) 30 *Harvard Law Review* 263.

many non-corporate enterprises, operating along the lines of the joint-stock company model emerging out of Italy, thrived.

A turning point came in 1719 when the British Parliament passed the infamous *Bubble Act*,[36] which required enterprises that 'presumed to act as a corporation' to either seek a charter, or face legal action as 'public nuisances'.[37] That Act was terminated in 1735, and during the period between the 1730s and 1844 a number of changes took place that would eventually result in the *Companies Act* of that year as well as related legislation applicable to banking.[38] At that point the benefits of incorporation — especially the cover it provided shareholders through limited liability — became extremely attractive and the rush was on in the United Kingdom, and eventually in the US where several states enacted favourable laws of incorporation.

Despite the transformation of the corporation into a form most often associated with business enterprises today, in terms of 'purpose' it retains its association with its historical roots reflected in Chief Justice Marshall's definition. But where do those roots lead?

(B) *Inventing the Corporate Form*

While no less an authority than Blackstone had attributed the invention of the corporation to the Romans,[39] our corporate (canonical-Italian-English) hybrid has comparatively modern (or at least late medieval) connections. In tracing the genesis of the corporation a century ago, Robert L Raymond offered an evolutionary narrative that highlighted the emergence of collectivities in both secular and ecclesiastic realms. While initially not recognised in law or by any generalised form of governance, these 'natural' collectivities[40] (for example, towns, convents, villages, monasteries, boroughs, guilds) developed into important economic and

---

[36] Formally the *Royal Exchange and London Assurance Corporation Act of 1719*. The law went into effect in 1720, a few weeks before the 'South Sea Bubble' fiasco that it is associated with took place.

[37] Margaret Patterson and David Reiffen, 'The Effect of the *Bubble Act* on the Market for Joint Stock Shares' (1990) 50 *The Journal of Economic History* 163, 167–71.

[38] Frank Evans, 'The Evolution of the English Joint Stock Limited Trading Company' (1908) 8 *Columbia Law Review* 339; Frank Evans, 'The Evolution of the Joint-Stock Limited Trading Company: VII Trading Companies Incorporated under General Act of Parliament' (1908) 8 *Columbia Law Review* 461.

[39] Maitland, above n 27, 336.

[40] Raymond terms them 'unit interest or oneness'.

social (religious) actors and key factors in the political dramas that played out in 11th and 12th century Europe, and especially in England. Their very existence outside the dominant legal arrangements of the time, argued Raymond, called for a 'new legal theory' that would provide a common approach to all the various forms that these many-bodies-acting-as-one entities. 'The oneness had to be given a place in business and in law as something definite.' What eventually emerged was the idea (taken from the developing body of canon law) of a 'fictitious' or 'artificial' person,[41] one that took an identity in law and governance distinct from the non-fictitious bodies (*corpi*) it included. And thus, as formally recognised through charters and other legal actions, the 'incorporated' entity was born.

Raymond places so much stress on the natural evolution of the corporate form that he overlooks the implications of the early acts of formal recognition, which are central to our understanding of the purpose of corporate governance, ie the issuance of the first known royal charters to a corporate-like entities (boroughs, towns, guilds), particularly by William I and William Rufus, his successor. In a fashion similar to the rush to incorporation by businesses in the 19th century, the early charters were sought by those collectivities for the protections and rights they bestowed. But it is critical to our understanding of 'purpose' to note that these charters were granted in name of the sovereign within the context of newly emerging form of governance. In fact, if there was a watershed event that punctuated the evolution of the modern corporation in its early stages, it was the form of accountable governance created in 1086 at Salisbury, when William I convened a meeting of representatives from all segments of his English realm and required of them an oath of fealty.

The historical importance and distinctiveness of that event must be understood in context. The 11th century was a time of considerable political turmoil. The collapse of the Holy Roman Empire had created a political void, and the Papal State in Rome had yet to consolidate its hold on power. Authority over both ecclesiastic and temporal matters throughout Europe had ontologically and practically devolved to the level of feudal lords, rendering the old political order weakened and leaving open opportunities for expansion and conquest by the strongest among the lesser nobility. This was the setting in which William, Duke of Normandy, pursued his claim to the throne of England based on a

---

[41] Robert L Raymond, 'The Genesis of the Corporation' (1906) 19 *Harvard Law Review* 350, 359–62.

promise made by Edward the Confessor and the support of the papal order. Having succeeded at Hastings, he faced the task of: (1) subduing (and often replacing) the defeated but still powerful Anglo-Saxon lords; (2) making good on his promise to Rome that he would regain control of ecclesiastic affairs in England; (3) satisfying the desires of his Norman supporters for the spoils of war; and (4) legitimising his rule in a land where the foundations and traditions of governance ran counter to his interests. Unless he succeeded in dealing with these pressures, he would go down in history as just another invader from northern Europe who had landed, conquered and left a minor mark on the British Isles. William I effectively had three options for dealing with these problems: extended conquest (force of arms); oaths; and charters. He put all three approaches to use. After 20 years of consolidating his rule of England mainly through force of arms that extracted pledges of fidelity from the most recalcitrant among his new subjects, he turned to a different type of oath in 1086, just a year before his death. In English law,[42] the tradition of fealty oaths was long standing[43] and there was a requirement that all 'free men' pledge to a lord.

What was controversial about William I's approach was the claim for such a pledge directly to the king. Moreover, as significant was that the Salisbury Oath was pledged immediately after the completion of the Domesday census, which had effectively given legible form[44] to the size and content of the English realm that William I had conquered and ruled. Thus this oath involved more than a pledge of fidelity; it also included an acknowledgment of the Norman king's claim to sovereignty over everything within his realm.[45] To an important degree, the oath taken at Salisbury established a reciprocal relationship between the modern central secular ruler and the ruled. In seeking the oath, William I was effectively acknowledging the reality that his rule depended on the deference and cooperation of his subjects, many of whom could (and

---

[42] William I and his successors made a point in their own coronation oaths and other known statements that they planned to honour the 'law of King Edward' the Confessor, and thus explicitly adopted the pledge requirement and similar practices.

[43] Patrick Wormald, 'Engla Lond: The Making of an Allegiance' (1994) 7 *Journal of Historical Sociology* 1.

[44] On the significance of 'legibility' in governance, see James C Scott, *Seeing Like a State: How Certain Schemes to Improve the Human Condition Have Failed* (1998).

[45] On the nature and use of oaths in late medieval and early modern times, see John Spurr, 'A Profane History of Early Modern Oaths' (2001) 11 *Transactions of the Royal Historical Society* 37.

sometimes did) operate as autonomous 'free men'.[46] As de facto autonomous agents pledging fealty to the king, the subjects accepted the responsibility granted by the crown for those parts of the realm with which they had been entrusted and, in turn, obligated themselves to giving an account of those holdings when called upon to do so. They became what Maitland (following Gierke) termed 'right-and-duty-bearing' subjects,[47] and the acceptance by autonomous agents of responsibility and obligation to the governing principal marked the birth of accountable governance.

That unique approach carried over into the extended issuance of charters, a practice that became increasingly common throughout medieval Europe, especially in regards to the legal creation of urban centres as pockets of 'liberties' within feudal realms.[48] Among the examples cited by Berman, the Anglo-Norman charters initiated by William I and his successors stood out for the explicit connection to the crown, and this approach characterised charters granted to individuals,[49] guilds,[50] and other collectivities. Accountability to the crown was thus a pervasive characteristic of the English charters that formed the instrumental foundation for the modern corporate form.

This connection between the birth of accountable governance and the embryonic corporate form found in those charters is critical to

---

[46] The evidence to support this is found in this history of royal charters granted to markets and guilds which indicates quite clearly that the chartering process did not *create* those entities but rather acknowledged and gave them protection and support as ongoing enterprises that could not be ordered into or out of existence nor controlled by royal edict or oversight. Markets and other collective activities thrived in England and elsewhere despite the attempts of local lords to control them, and they would thrive underground or aboveground despite any actions by the even powerful monarchs. Chartering was therefore a means for co-opting and gaining some degree of control over autonomous agents that would otherwise operate outside the law and pose constant threats to emerging regimes. Supporting this view is the fact that early charters were given to ongoing enterprises and more often than not contained provisions that were facilitating nurturing rather than controlling and restrictive: R H Britnell, 'English Markets and Royal Administration before 1200' (1978) 31 *Economic History Review* 183; Gary Richardson, 'Guilds, Laws, and Markets for Manufactured Merchandise in Late-Medieval England' (2004) 41 *Explorations in Economic History* 1.

[47] The phrase is cited in Dewey, above n 5, 565 and throughout.

[48] Berman, above n 25, 363–90.

[49] David C Douglas, 'A Charter of Enfeoffment under William the Conqueror' (1927) 42 *English Historical Review* 245.

[50] Cyril O'Donnell, 'Origins of the Corporate Executive' (1952) 26 *Bulletin of the Business Historical Society* 55.

understanding the 'purpose' that forms our standard for assessing policies and laws related to corporate governance. The corporation is more than a mere artificial person or an association of shareholders. In the Anglo-Norman tradition it exists as an 'accountable' institution, in the sense of it being an autonomous agent defined by its responsibilities and obligations to the sovereign entity that is its principal.[51]

III CLARIFYING THE STANDARD

Viewing the creation of the corporate form in this way — that is, as an accountable institution — adds a core, defining dimension to the traditional definition of the modern business corporation, and establishes a perspectively useful standard of purpose for the assessment of corporate governance reform. Typically characterised for analytic purposes as *an artificial or fictional legal entity* (reflecting the ecclesiastic roots) *comprised of shareholding owners* (the Genoan tradition) and *committed to some collective goal* (in the English tradition of making a profit for its owners, providing public conveyance for its constituents/customers, etc), we can now add its inherent condition as an *accountable* (rights-and-duties-bearing) institution.

Put in direct terms, by granting a corporate charter to an enterprise, the state has effectively determined (or at least declared) that the entity is 'fit to be held responsible' (for example, to be called to account) for its actions and activities.[52] The 'purpose' of corporate governance, therefore, is to maintain and sustain that fitness for accountability, and it is credible to regard the purpose of corporate governance reform — what we regard as 'assessable' for the present task — to be the protection and enhancement of that fitness.

Seen in this light, we are able to demarcate and differentiate the view of corporate governance that emerges from the English 'accountability' tradition and those of its historical alternatives. For present purposes we will label those alternatives the 'stakeholder' and 'fiduciary' models.

---

[51] This view of accountable governance is further developed in Melvin J Dubnick, *Situating Accountability* (2007).

[52] See Philip Pettit, *A Theory of Freedom: From the Psychology to the Politics of Agency* (2001), for the philosophical basis of my approach.

(A) *The Stakeholder Model*

Today's consensus view of corporate governance in the business and finance literature (especially in the US) takes its cue from the narrow conceptualisation of 'principals' derived from the Genoan joint-stock company tradition, and has been expressed by one source as the 'ways in which suppliers of finance to corporations assure themselves of getting a return on their investment'.[53] The problem of corporate governance, in this view, is how owners and others who provide capital for the corporate entity shape, direct, regulate, etc the operations of the agency or firm to enhance the probability that they will receive some value from their financial effort.[54] It is governance by investors and financiers and for investors and financiers.

At the heart of many discussions of corporate governance based on the stakeholder model was the controversy initiated in 1932 with the publication of Berle and Means' *The Modern Corporation and Private Property*.[55] Observing a growing problem of distance between ownership and management, their analysis helped define the central issues of corporate governance in terms of how to get the management/agents to follow the wishes of the owner/principals.[56] One result is a myopic approach to corporate governance that has turned into conventional wisdom among students of business enterprises.[57] That this myopia afflicts the model's critics as well is evident in the many reform efforts that seek to make the corporation more 'responsible', by either

---

[53] Andrei Shleifer and Robert W Vishny, 'A Survey of Corporate Governance' (1997) 52 *Journal of Finance* 737, 737.

[54] Oliver Hart, 'Corporate Governance: Some Theory and Implications' (1995) 105 *The Economic Journal* 678.

[55] (1932).

[56] Cf Rafael La Porta, Florencio Lopez-De-Silanes and Andrei Shleifer, 'Corporate Ownership around the World' (1999) 54 *Journal of Finance* 471.

[57] The book led a charmed and influential life for nearly half a century, with only scattered and intermittent studies to counter its major claims and dominance. However that changed with publication of a special symposium on the book published in 1983: see, eg, Robert Hessen, 'The Modern Corporation and Private Property: A Reappraisal' (1983) 26 *Journal of Law and Economics* 273; Douglass C North, 'Comment on Stigler and Friedland, "The Literature of Economics: The Case of Berle and Means"' (1983) 26 *Journal of Law and Economics* 269; George J Stigler and Claire Friedland, 'The Literature of Economics: The Case of Berle and Means' (1983) 26 *Journal of Law and Economics* 237.

broadening the definition of relevant stakeholders, or modifying corporate decision rules to include socially responsible actions.[58]

(B) *The Fiduciary Model*

For those following the canonical law tradition, the focus shifts from stakeholders (narrowly defined by their financial stake) to the corporate entity itself. Governance in this model is driven by fiduciary responsibilities for the current and future well-being of the artificial entity that has legal status as a corporate person. In contrast to governance *by* and *for* financial stakeholders, those who govern in this model are required to put aside personal interests and concerns — those of the shareholders as well as their own — in order to act on behalf of the well-being of the collectivity (the 'oneness') itself.[59]

The importance of this distinction from the financial stakeholder model is exemplified in the case of the proposed 'Hershey Company' sale in 2002. The fiduciary obligations of the corporate entity that held controlling interest in the firm (the Hershey School Trust, a charitable enterprise established by the founder of the Company) required it (or at least those making decisions for the Trust) to offer its 30+ per cent stake in the Company for sale. In response to severe criticism from other Company shareholders and other stakeholders, the Trust's managers held that, despite their own personal sympathies and views, their hands were effectively tied by the legal (fiduciary) responsibility; they had to do what was best for the Trust itself. Only the successful issuance of a legal injunction requested by the State of Pennsylvania halted the sale, but this episode highlighted the difference between the governance models derived from the two traditions.[60]

---

[58] Archie B Carroll, 'Corporate Social Responsibility: Evolution of a Definitional Construct' (1999) 38 *Business and Society* 268; Archie B Carroll, 'The Pyramid of Corporate Social Responsibility: Toward the Moral Management or Organizational Stakeholders' (1991) 34 *Business Horizons* 39; Richard J Klonoski, 'Foundational Considerations in the Corporate Social Responsibility Debate' (1991) 34 *Business Horizons* 9.

[59] Cf Katsuhito Iwai, 'The Nature of the Business Corporation: Its Legal Structure and Economic Functions' (2002) 53 *Japanese Economic Review* 243.

[60] For details, see Jennifer L Komoroski, 'The Hershey Trust's Quest to Diversify: Redefining the State Attorney General's Role When Charitable Trusts Wish to Diversify' (2004) 45 *William and Mary Law Review* 1769; another interesting case — also involving a Pennsylvania trust — involves the Barnes Foundation: see Ilana H Eisenstein, 'Keeping Charity in Charitable Trust Law: The Barnes Foundation and the Case for

(C) *The Accountability Model*

Corporate governance in the accountability tradition of the English model stands simultaneously separate to and 'above' (in the inclusive sense) that of the stakeholder and fiduciary forms. It is distinct from the joint-stock company form in putting the interests of stakeholders (financial and otherwise) in a secondary (albeit, not unimportant) position to that of a 'higher principal' (for example, the sovereign, public interest, public good). What distinguishes it from the legalistic canonical (fiduciary) model is the status it gives the corporate entity as an *active* 'rights-and-duty-bearing' (albeit artificial) person.[61] The English model corporation, in other words, has more than passive legal standing; it possesses a 'franchise' to take action, in the classic sense of that term, as:

> a right, privilege, or power, of public concern, which cannot be exercised by private individuals at their will, but must be secured by grant, in some form, from the sovereign power of the territory in which it is to be exercised. It carries with it an assurance of right of user, similar in character to grants of other rights and things, and there is a reciprocal agreement on the part of the grantee to use it in accord with public policy.[62]

The often-cited James Kent *Commentaries* on law is even more explicit on the obligation of the incorporated franchisee to actively pursue its authorised tasks. The grant of a franchise in the form of corporate standing contains 'an implied covenant on the part of the government not to invade the rights vested, and on the part of the grantees to execute the conditions and duties prescribed in the grant'.[63]

The governance of such a franchise requires at minimum a process that assures the entity's ongoing commitment to chartered functions and tasks, as well as the capacity to give an account to those among it principals who seek such. From this view, concerns for stakeholder interests and/or fiduciary responsibilities to the collective well-being can be added, but *in its most fundamental form corporate*

Consideration of Public Interest in Administration of Charitable Trusts' (2003) 151 *Pennsylvania Law Review* 1747.

[61] The French term for such a corporate entity — *personne morale* — captures, or at least implies, the core sense of the model.

[62] Charles W Needham, 'Franchises' (1915) 15 *Columbia Law Review* 97, 98.

[63] James Kent, *Commentaries*, quoted in Needham, above n 62, 98.

governance must meet the standard of accountability. It follows that any effort at corporate governance reform should be assessed in light of the accountability-purpose standard, if for no other reason than to determine how far the corporate form has become distanced from its historical purpose. No doubt, most contemporary attempts to regulate or change corporate governance reflect an indifference to the accountability standard. The preoccupation with shareholder and stakeholder rights and control, for example, has driven much of the intermittent reform focused on corporate management practices in the US and elsewhere.[64] A concern with traditional fiduciary responsibility (that is, to the interests of the corporate entity itself rather than its 'owners' or creditors) had faded somewhat with the elevation of shareholders to sole role of principal,[65] but it has made a comeback in recent years in calls for a shift away from shareholder value and toward increasing corporate value[66] and enhancing corporate trust and integrity.[67] While these reform efforts and proposals can be assessed on their own terms, what we are seeking here is to apply the accountability standard.

When assessing pre-*Sarbanes-Oxley* reform efforts, therefore, the issues could be put retrospectively in positive or negative terms. In a positive sense, the question to be asked is whether (and how) the reform efforts enhance or strengthen the accountability aspect of governance; in the negative, the assessment would focus on whether and how the reform efforts weaken accountability. *Sarbanes-Oxley*, however, offers a distinct opportunity to assess corporate governance reforms that were intended to enhance the reputation of corporate enterprises as accountable institutions in the historical sense. The crises that emerged from the

---

[64] Rafael La Porta et al, 'Investor Protection: Origins, Consequences and Reform' (Financial Sector Discussion Paper, World Bank, 1999); Rafael La Porta at al, 'Investor Protection and Corporate Governance' (2000) 58 *Journal of Financial Economics* 3; Rafael La Porta et al, 'Investor Protection and Corporate Valuation' (2002) 57 *Journal of Finance* 1147.

[65] Austin W Scott, 'The Fiduciary Principle' (1949) 37 *California Law Review* 539; Lawrence E Mitchell, 'The Death of Fiduciary Duty in Close Corporations' (1990) 138 *University of Pennsylvania Law Review* 1675; Lawrence E Mitchell, 'Fairness and Trust in Corporate Law' (1993) 43 *Duke Law Journal* 425.

[66] Thomas A Smith, 'The Efficient Norm for Corporate Law: A Neotraditional Interpretation of Fiduciary Duty' (1999) 98 *Michigan Law Review* 214.

[67] David B Farber, 'Restoring Trust after Fraud: Does Corporate Governance Matter?' (2005) 80 *Accounting Review* 539; John Roberts, 'Trust and Control in Anglo-American Systems of Corporate Governance: The Individualizing and Socializing Effects of Processes of Accountability' (2001) 54 *Human Relations* 1547.

scandals at Enron and other enterprises required some action — symbolic or otherwise[68] — to counter their delegitimising impact. But the circumstances surrounding this flurry of corporate difficulties called for more than readjustments in how firms would handle stakeholder or fiduciary issues. For the first time since at least the Great Depression it was the *accountable nature of the corporate form* that was at issue. How well did *Sarbanes-Oxley* measure up to that challenge?

IV ASSESSING ACCOUNTABLE GOVERNANCE: A FRAMEWORK

Despite its popular association with performance measures, there is no known metric for accountable governance.[69] Nevertheless, it is possible to identify various forms of accountability-relevant relationships that can provide the basis for comparison and assessment of governance mechanisms and proposals for reform. To accomplish this I apply a framework developed in an earlier paper[70] that allows us to categorise policies and their implementation into four types or relationships involving account-giving. The four types range from those impacting directly on the behaviour of account-giver, to those that operate at the level of moral suasion. They are presented here as four distinct 'orders' of accountability.

---

[68] Charles Conrad, 'The Illusion of Reform: Corporate Discourse and Agenda Denial in the 2002 "Corporate Meltdown"' (2004) 7 *Rhetoric and Public Affairs* 311; Justin O'Brien, 'The Politics of Symbolism: *Sarbanes-Oxley* in Context' in Paul U Ali and Greg N Gregoriou (eds), *International Corporate Governance after* Sarbanes-Oxley (2006).

[69] There have been efforts to assess the quality of performance measures and measurement systems (see, eg, D L Poole et al, 'Evaluating Performance Measurement Systems in Nonprofit Agencies: The Program Accountability Quality Scale (PAQS)' (2000) 21 *American Journal of Evaluation* 15) and some attempts to establish indicators for types of accountability mechanisms (see, eg, Stephen Page, 'Measuring Accountability for Results in Interagency Collaboratives' (2004) 64 *Public Administration Review* 591), but these fall short of measures of accountability per se. Part of the problem is the lack of a clear conceptualisation or theory of accountability: see Dubnick, *Situating Accountability*, above n 51; Melvin J Dubnick, 'Accountability and the Promise of Performance: In Search of the Mechanisms' (2005) 27 *Public Performance and Management Review* 376; Melvin J Dubnick, *Seeking Salvation for Accountability* (2002).

[70] Melvin J Dubnick, 'Orders of Accountability' (Speech delivered at the World Ethics Forum: Leadership, Ethics and Integrity in Public Life, Oxford, 2006).

First order ('performative') accountability entails a situation requiring explicit and direct acts of account-giving. Such 'speech acts'[71] typically require at least two parties — an account-giver who is *doing* the account-giving, and an account-receiver who is the intended target of that act. The fact that account-giving is an action unto itself — not merely a statement about something, but a 'doing' per se — makes it what linguists and philosophers call a performative act;[72] hence the appellation *performative accountability*. To designate it as such does not imply that it is a meaningless or vacuous act — on the contrary, as is the case with other performatives such as 'I promise' or 'I bid' or 'I bet', the awkward 'I account for' has some force and meaning within a given context.

At its most basic and informal, performative account-giving can overlap with the social act of 'reason giving' recently highlighted in the work of Charles Tilly. Humans are reason seeking/giving animals, Tilly asserts, and we engage in various forms of reason giving in a range of social relationships from the most mundane (eg, practices of etiquette) to the unfathomable (eg, attempting to comprehend the events of 9/11 as they occurred).[73] But despite a fundamental similarity in form as well as a degree of overlap, the defining line between reason giving and account-giving is crossed where the account-giver is assumed/perceived to be 'responsible' to the account-receiver for the condition, action, or event that is the focus on the relationship.

In most scholarly examinations of first order account-giving, stress is placed on its role as a functional and appropriate reaction to some error or faux pas, and thus most analyses concentrate on the social conventions for making excuses or offering justifications.[74] Although such mitigatory and explanatory first order acts of account-giving are common place, they often overshadow equally important purposes for engaging in them, as found in information-generating (monitoring,

---

[71] On the social nature of speech acts, see John L Austin, *How to Do Things with Words* (1975); John R Searle, 'Meaning and Speech Acts' (1962) 71 *Philosophical Review* 423; P F Strawson, 'Intention and Convention in Speech Acts' (1964) 73 *Philosophical Review* 439; John R Searle, *Speech Acts: An Essay in the Philosophy of Language* (1969).

[72] John R Seale, 'How Performatives Work' (1989) 12 *Linguistics and Philosophy* 535; Austin, above n 70.

[73] Charles Tilly, *Why?* (2006); Charles Tilly, 'Reasons Why' (2004) 22 *Sociological Theory* 445.

[74] Marvin B Scott and Stanford M Lyman, 'Accounts' (1968) 33 *American Sociological Review* 46.

surveilling) forms such as bookkeeping, reporting, responding to audits, subjecting oneself to inspection, etc.[75] In all these instances, the acts of account-giving — whether in the form of publishing an annual or quarterly report, issuing a press release, giving testimony at a trial or before a legislative committee, offering a public apology, providing a written elaboration of reasons for taking actions, releasing or posting of transcripts — are responses to a direct (although sometimes implied or perceived) solicitation from real or potential account-receivers. The solicitation can take the form of a speeding ticket issued by a police officer, a reporter's microphone placed in front of one's mouth, a demand by an auditor to see one's books, a phone call from one's supervisor seeking an explanation for some action, a public accusation, etc. In each case the effort is to generate a performative response from the account-giver. But not all accountability is performative. Most forms of accountability in fact occur in anticipation (sometimes anxious anticipation) of the need or requirement to engage in performative accountability. They relate, in other words, to a 'presumptive account-giver'.

Second order ('regulatory') accountability, for example, does not involve direct and explicit account-giving, but is instead manifest in following the guidance, rules and operating standards of the presumptive account-giver's task environment. This is *regulatory accountability* and it makes use of the potential 'threat' of being called to performative account to establish and maintain restrictive and directive control over the account-giver.

In a widely discussed work on the nature of cyberspace, Lessig takes note of four major mechanisms that society relies on to constrain or limit behaviour, including law, social norms, the marketplace and the 'architecture' of the operating environment.[76] Of those four,[77] law and architecture generate second order accountability by creating operating environments in which the possibility of some form performative

---

[75] Herbert Kaufman, *The Forest Ranger: A Study in Administrative Behavior* (1967); Herbert Kaufman, *Administrative Feedback: Monitoring Subordinates' Behavior* (1973).

[76] Lawrence Lessig, *Code and Other Laws of Cyberspace* (1999).

[77] Challenges or violations to social norms would more likely call for reliance on what Tilly calls 'reason giving' (Tilly, *Why?*, above n 73), and the price mechanisms of the marketplace operate within the context of law to deal with any problems. On the latter point, it is relevant that Lessig did not include the marketplace in his first examination of such mechanisms: see Lawrence Lessig, 'Open Code and Open Societies: Values and Internet Governance' (1998–2000) 74 *Chicago–Kent Law Review* 1405.

account-giving plays a significant role in shaping and directing the behaviour of agents. The use of law as a basis for regulatory accountability is well-documented both historically[78] and in contemporary analyses of requirements related to rule of law standards.[79] Lessig's major contribution has been to highlight the role of task environment 'architecture' in the regulatory endeavour. This architecture — which Lessig notes is manifest in the 'code' of everything from computer programs to constitutions — determines such things as access and the range of discretion/autonomy an individual has while operating in the constructed environment. It obviously places various checks on the range of choices or decisions that an accountable individual can make, but it also functions as a rationale for constrained or directed behaviour. Thus, if called upon to provide an account for his or her behaviour (that is, to engage in first order accountability), the person who operates within the architecture would refer to its rules, parameters, SOPs, etc.[80] Underlying all this is the belief that first order, performative accountability would be triggered if an individual was found to be challenging or violating the code.

In contrast, rather than focusing on the control of conduct, **third order ('managerial') accountability** relies on account-giving as a means of eliciting purposive behaviour. Accountability in this sense is intended to be motivational rather than regulatory, and in that sense the term *managerial accountability*[81] seems most appropriate.[82] The logic is

---

[78] Deirdre D von Dornum, 'The Straight and the Crooked: Legal Accountability in Ancient Greece' (1997) 97 *Columbia Law Review* 1483.

[79] David H Rosenbloom, *Administrative Law for Public Managers* (2003); Joseph Sanders, V Lee Hamilton and Toshikyuki Yuasa, 'The Institutionalization of Sanctions for Wrongdoing inside Organizations: Public Judgements in Japan, Russia, and the United States' (1998) 32 *Law and Society Review* 871; Arthur L Stinchcombe, *When Formality Works: Authority and Abstraction in Law and Organizations* (2001).

[80] See also the discussion of codes in reason-giving in Tilly, *Why?*, above n 73, ch 4.

[81] Not long ago the concept of 'managerial accountability' would have been more closely associated with regulation and control: see E S Mason, 'The Apologetics of "Managerialism"' (1958) 31 *Journal of Business* 1; Lee E Preston and James E Post, 'The Third Managerial Revolution' (1974) 17 *Academy of Management Journal* 476.

[82] John Dixon, Alexander Kouzmin and Nada Korac-Kakabadse, 'Managerialism — Something Old, Something Borrowed, Little New: Economic Prescription versus Effective Organizational Change in Public Agencies' (1998) 11 *International Journal of Public Sector Management* 164; A J Fowles, 'Changing Notions of Accountability: A Social Policy View' (1993) 6 *Accounting, Auditing and Accountability Journal* 97; Mark Lyons, 'The Impact of Managerialism on Social Policy: The Case of Social Services' (1998) 21 *Public Productivity and Management Review* 419; Heinz-Dieter Meyer, 'The

simple: the measure or assessment of an action or condition for which the account-giver is assumed 'responsible' is, *under the right conditions*, regarded as an effective means for motivating that individual to improve that action or condition in the future. Under third order accountability, the focus is on designing task environment conditions (again, architectures) that facilitate those motivations rather than control or constrain them. Thus, we see the extensive use of incentives and sanctions in third order accountability.[83]

While second order (regulatory) and third order (managerial) accountability operates primarily through the architecture and machinations of task environments, **fourth order ('embedded') accountability** operates through the norms and values of the account-giver — through what Foucauldians designate as 'governmentality'.[84] We will use the label *embedded accountability* to stress the internalisation of the sense of 'moral responsibility' characteristic of this form, and take special note at this point of its association with professionalism and high levels of commitment to living up to perceived expectations.

V ASSESSING *SARBANES-OXLEY*

Fourth order accountability stands as both foundational and aspirational in the present situation. On the one hand, once in place as the values and

New Managerialism in Education Management: Corporatization or Organizational Learning?' (2002) 40 *Journal of Educational Administration* 534; Stephen Page, 'The Web of Managerial Accountability: The Impact of Reinventing Government' (2006) 38 *Administration and Society* 166.

[83] Third order accountability is central to what I have called the 'promises of accountability' in other papers: see, eg, Melvin J Dubnick, 'Accountability and Ethics: Reconsidering the Relationships' (2003) 6 *International Journal of Organization Theory and Behaviour* 405; Dubnick, 'Accountability and the Promise of Performance', above n 68. These promises relate to a number of socially desirable ends, ranging from justice and democracy to ethical behaviour and enhanced performance in the production of goods and service. Despite its simple logic, however, the value and validity of managerial accountability remains an empirical question.

[84] Michel Foucault, 'Governmentality' in Graham Burchell, Colin Gordon and Peter Miller (eds), *The Foucault Effect: Studies of Governmentality: With Two Lectures by and an Interview with Michael Foucault* (1991) 87; Nikolas Rose and Peter Miller, 'Political Power beyond the State: Problematics of Government' (1992) 43 *British Journal of Sociology* 173; Nikolas S Rose, *Powers and Freedom: Reframing Political Thought* (1999); Nikolas Rose, 'Government and Control' (2000) 40 *British Journal of Criminology* 321.

norms of corporate governance — that is, once embedded in the corporate culture of a firm — it can shape and direct the use of performative, regulatory and managerial accountabilities. On the other hand, establishing an embedded fourth order accountability is an extremely challenging task, perhaps on par with Plato's strategy for creating his *Republic*. Optimistically, one can imagine policies that reward corporations for developing and fostering corporate cultures that give priority to accountable governance standards.[85] But others would argue that the effort would require not merely changes in policies related to corporate governance, but a wholesale (and unlikely) transformation of legal ontology under which the Anglo-American system operates.[86]

As it happens, the agendas for most corporate governance reform efforts are aimed at lower aspirations than creating corporate forms that are in sync with the accountability model. Requiring automobile manufacturers to meet set standards for average fuel economy on their vehicles reflects a first order (performative) solution to the problem of having those firms act responsibly. Often reform policies aim at improving performance by modifying the regulatory regime in which they have to operate. Deregulation of the airlines, buses and other forms of interstate public transportation can be regarded as shifting the second order accountability (regulatory) regime toward the open market, with the unfettered firms having to deal with a different set of account-giving relationships. Modifications in policies regarding the taxation and reporting of executive compensation and benefits can and have had impacts on third order (managerial) accountability decisions. In each of these cases, the different orders of accountability have modified some aspect of corporate decision-making.

But in the wake of the corporate scandals at Enron, WorldCom, etc, the agenda for corporate reform expanded and rose to the level of the goals implied in the accountable governance model. However, short of a miraculous transformation in the legal ontology of Anglo-American corporate operations through fourth order reforms that alter the existing 'governmentality', reforms would have to come through policies based on the lower order approaches. In that sense, there is a need for a *Sarbanes-Oxley*-like initiative that contains provisions that at least push

---

[85] See, eg, Stone, above n 2.

[86] See the interesting analysis offered in Kitagawa, above n 6. Japan's experience with modern corporate law speaks to many of the issues now raised about globalisation and its impact, particularly in light of the hegemony of the Anglo-American legal cultures.

in that direction. The immediate question is whether *Sarbanes-Oxley* is such an initiative. The answer is clearly no.

(A) *The Performative Provisions*

Sarbanes-Oxley contains 69 sections, with about two-thirds having some provisions that relate to a type of accountability relationship. Due to the necessary formalisms required of such a statute, some sections were definitional, others were redundant in regard to the substance of their accountability provisions (for example, Title XI sections contained authorisations for actions to enforce previous sections), and still others contained provisions that were not related to our task.

Of what remained, there were 17 provisions for what can be termed first order accountability mandates; that is, they detailed an action (for example, a filing of a disclosure, the development of an ethics code) that had to be taken by some actor. Of those, nine were aimed at external actors whose activities impacted (directly or indirectly) on the corporation. Of these nine, seven related to accounting firms hired to serve as auditors of the company (ss 102, 103, 109, 203, 204). The other two required actions by outside attorneys (s 307) and the securities analysis industry (s 501). The remaining eight first order provisions involved mostly disclosure and reporting requirements. Two of the disclosure requirements were general in nature, requiring complete (s 401) and quick (s 409) reporting. An additional two were targeted at specific officers, with s 302 requiring CEO and CFO certification of annual financial reports and s 1001 (which was a sense of the Senate provision) strongly suggesting that the CEO sign the corporate income tax filings.

Four additional disclosure provisions were actually indirect mandates that would clearly have third order effects. Section 407, for example, requires a report that confirms that at least one member of the audit committee is a financial expert, with the obvious implication for recruiting such an individual. Section 406 requires a similar disclosure about a corporate code of ethics for financial offices, again impacting on managerial operations. Section 403, seeking disclosure of personal financial transactions by corporate officers and major shareholders, would require the development of relevant tracking and reporting mechanisms. But perhaps the most significant provisions with secondary consequences among the disclosure requirement are found in s 404, which mandates reports on the operations and effectiveness of the firm's 'internal control structure and procedures for … financial reporting.' The development and operations of such mechanisms (if they did not already exist) have recently been noted as the most costly and problematic of the *Sarbanes-Oxley* requirements.[87]

Regarding these various first order provisions, there seems only the faintest relationship between them and objective of re-establishing accountable governance. Implied in some provisions (for example, the CEO/CFO signoffs; the code of ethics for financial managers; the development of effective internal control systems) is the assumption that such *legal* requirements will make it clear to the affected officials that they have *moral* obligations that go beyond their own self-interest or even those of the firm's shareholders and stakeholders. Whether there are connections between these requirements and fourth order (embedded accountability) effects involves empirical questions that might prove difficult to answer in the short term.

(B) *The Regulatory Provisions*

Sarbanes-Oxley also contains 21 provisions that can be categorised as second order accountability actions. Six are found in Title I of the Act which relates to the establishment and authority of the Public Company Accounting Oversight Board, a non-profit entity that deals directly with the outside accounting firms the serve that audit needs of the corporations. In addition, three other sections (201, 202, 906) contain regulatory provisions related to the outside auditors. In fact, in Title II of the Act, only s 206 relates directly to the firm by prohibiting the hiring of officers who had worked for those outside auditors during the previous year.

The remaining 11 second order provisions are scattered among the other Titles and range from determining the composition of corporate audit committees (s 301), to prohibiting the extension of credit to firm officers, or direct (s 402) to protections for whistle blowers and informants (ss 806 and 1007). Among the most important of these second order accountability provisions are those that extend and enhance the criminalisation of malfeasant behaviour of corporate officers (see, eg, ss 807, 906).

---

[87] Tackett, Wolf and Claypool, 'Internal Control under *Sarbanes-Oxley*: A Critical Examination', above n 20; Carney, above n 21.

Once again we are confronted with questions about the assumed link between these second order provisions and the objective of developing an embedded sense of moral obligation among corporate agents. Given the details of these sections, the desire for retribution and restoration may have taken priority over any intent to change the moral commitments and behaviour of corporate officials. But assuming that long-term moral and behavioural change was part of the design, there seems little in the law that addresses the potential for the hazards (moral and cognitive) associated with regulatory actions.[88]

(C) *Managerial Provisions and the Absence of Fourth Order Provisions*

In addition to the third order actions implied in the disclosure provisions of ss 404, 406 and 407 (noted above), *Sarbanes-Oxley* contains only one accountability-relevant provision that is somewhat managerial. According to s 304, if the firm's reports to the Securities and Exchange Commission are determined to be non-compliant, the firm's major officers (CEO, CFO) must forfeit bonuses and other compensation rewards. It should be noted that at various points in the deliberative process, members of Congress offered a number of management-relevant ideas for consideration. But opposition to overly intrusive policies won the day, and only s 304 remained as an explicit managerial provision when *Sarbanes-Oxley* was finally passed.

The irony is that, short of some fourth order expression of substantive standards to guide corporate decisions, third order managerial provisions might have enhanced the Act's promise as a stimulant for accountable governance. As it is, the s 404 requirements for reporting on the design and effectiveness of internal control of financial records has drawn the most reaction from corporations who complain about the ambiguities and costs associated with its implementation.

Finally and most notably, there is no single provision in the legislation that can be classified as a fourth order accountability action. There is nothing in *Sarbanes-Oxley* to deal *directly* with the assumed objective of establishing or improving the corporation's purpose as an accountable ('rights-and-duties-bearing') institution.

---

[88] Jonathon Klick and Gregory Mitchell, 'Government Regulation of Irrationality: Moral and Cognitive Hazards' (2006) 90 *Minnesota Law Review* 1620.

CONCLUSION

Of the many efforts at corporate governance reforms that have emerged in recent decades,[89] *Sarbanes-Oxley* stands out as a watershed event in several respects. It has clearly been a force in both the nationalisation of US regulation of corporate governance[90] and the Americanisation of global regulatory regimes.[91] And its impact on the daily relationships within business environment have certainly been notable, as anyone who works in the accounting or securities field can attest to.

But, because it was drawn up in haste, *Sarbanes-Oxley* can be seen as a missed opportunity in one important respect. It is probably the case that the political circumstances of the moment generated as good an effort as might have otherwise been expected in a political system that seems addicted to a policymaking-by-crisis mode. But a more thoughtful and informed debate might have led to considerations about the nature of corporate accountability that have been off the reform agenda for at least a century in the US.[92] As it now stands, the provisions of *Sarbanes-Oxley* and their enforcement have generated their own problems,[93] and the long postponed debate over the role of corporate entities as accountable institutions is likely to be extended.

---

[89] Rockness and Rockness, above n 12.

[90] Curtis Alva, 'Delaware and the Market for Corporate Charters: History and Agency' (1990) 15 *Delaware Journal of Corporate Law* 885; William L Cary, 'Federalism and Corporate Law: Reflections upon Delaware' (1974) 83 *Yale Law Journal* 663; Mark J Roe, 'Delaware's Competition' (2003) 117 *Harvard Law Review* 588.

[91] Gates, above n 14; Vagts, above n 15; Hollister, above n 15.

[92] However, additional time and deliberation might not have made a difference. In the United Kingdom the consideration of corporate governance issues has been taking place for at least a decade, with the 1992 Cadbury Report often cited as the start of an ongoing debate that has generated a number of reports over the past 15 years. Despite this extended debate, the focus remains on stakeholder reform, transparency and oversight: see Jill Solomon and Aris Solomon, *Corporate Governance and Accountability* (2004) ch 1.

[93] Justin O'Brien, 'Securing Corporate Accountability or Bypassing Justice? The Efficiency and Pitfalls of Pre-Trial Diversion' (2006) 19 *Australian Journal of Corporate Law* 161; Justin O'Brien, *Redesigning Financial Regulation: The Politics of Enforcement* (2007).

Chapter 11

Charting an Icarian Flightpath: The Implications of the Qantas Deal Collapse

Justin O'Brien

Leveraged Buy-Outs of publicly listed corporations resolve (ostensibly, partially and temporarily) a central corporate governance conundrum.[1] While the recombination of equity and control unquestionably limits managerial discretion, governance arbitrage through market exit raises a series of critical oversight questions. These exist and play out across multiple levels of the corporate governance matrix.[2] Concern radiates from the micro level of individual transactions to the mezzanine impact on particular industrial and financial sectors. The identified threats encompass potential (or actual) conflicts of interest among managers involved in market exit proposals. At market governance level they involve potential (or actual) abuse of fiduciary duty by those providing

---

[1] Michael Jensen, 'Eclipse of the Public Corporation' (1989) 67 *Harvard Business Review* 61; for original conceptual formulation, see Adolph A Berles and Gardiner C Means, *The Modern Corporation and Private Property* (1932).

[2] The asset class disperses technical and material capital at all stages of the investment process. The provision of venture capital is relatively unproblematic. Facilitating start-ups and job creation underpin the industry's normative claims, see British Venture Capital Association, *The Economic Impact of Private Equity in the UK* (2006). The focus of the present article is on the main mechanism used to exit the market, the Leveraged Buy-Out ('LBO') or Management Buy-Out ('MBO'). Within this chapter the terms private equity and LBO/MBO are used interchangeably and refer to market exit unless otherwise specified.

corporate advisory services.[3] The industry thrives at times of high liquidity, cheap debt and low levels of corporate default, conditions that pertain on global markets until the sub-prime crisis in the United States led to a sudden evaporation of credit.[4] The increasingly erratic behaviour of debt markets has prompted, however, fears of wider supranational systemic risk.[5]

Across the globe, the clearly expressed policy preference is for the market to exercise self-restraint when interdicting with LBOs. The Takeovers Panel in Australia has articulated a series of protocols to be adopted by the boards of target corporations.[6] A similar dynamic informs recent Delaware Court of Chancery jurisprudence.[7] At the mezzanine level, warnings of the increased risk of insider trading and market manipulation are designed, primarily, to trigger an industry-led calibration of internal compliance programs.[8] This has been accompanied

---

[3] The problem is a symptom of all mergers and acquisition booms. For review of recent cases in the United States, see Gretchen Morgenson, 'Whispers of Mergers Set Off Suspicious Trading', *New York Times* (New York), 27 August 2006, A1; Kara Scannell, 'Insider Trading: It's Back with a Vengeance', *Wall Street Journal* (New York), 5 May 2007, B1.

[4] William Rhodes, 'A Market Correction Is Coming, This Time for Real', *Financial Times* (London), 29 March 2007, 11 (arguing that 'pockets of excess are becoming harder to ignore'). The predicted credit crunch appeared to emerge as this book went to press, see Michael MacKenzie, Saskia Scholtes and Paul Davis, 'Wake-up Call for Investors', *Financial Times* (London) 28 July 2007, 1.

[5] International Monetary Fund, *Global Financial Stability Report* (2007) 15.

[6] Takeovers Panel, 'Insider Participation in Control Transactions' *Issue Paper No 19* (2007); see also the final Guidance Note published on 7 June 2007: Takeovers Panel, 'Insider Participation in Control Transactions' *Guidance Note No 19* (2007).

[7] See *Re Netsmart Technologies, Inc Shareholders Litigation* 2007 WL 1576151 (Del. Ch. March 14, 2007) (criticising the failure of the board to solicit a higher bid: at 21); *Re Lear Corporation Shareholders Litigation* 2007 WL 1732588 (Del. Ch. June 15, 2007) (criticizing self-interested dealing by the Chief Executive Officer and mandating disclosure); *Re Topps Co. Shareholders Litigation* 2007 WL 1732586 (Del. Ch. 14 June 2007) (positioning Delaware as court of first instance to generate 'a body of decisional authority': at 7).

[8] Financial Services Authority, 'Private Equity: A Discussion of Risk and Regulatory Engagement' (Discussion Paper 06/06, 2006) 9; see also Financial Services Authority, 'Private Equity, A Discussion of Risk and Regulatory Engagement' (Feedback Statement 07/03, 2007) 7. The Financial Services Authority ('FSA') has established a Financial Crime and Intelligence Division to target market abuse, money laundering and fraud, see FSA, 'New FSA Team to Crack Down on Financial Crime' (Press Release, 22 January 2007). The Chair of the Federal Reserve in the United States has also highlighted the threat of market manipulation, see Ben Bernanke, 'Regulation and Financial Innovation'

by the exercise of unsubtle pressure on providers of core capital and leveraged debt. The superannuation industry has been cautioned against over-investing in illiquid heavily leveraged assets.[9] Within the banking sector the loosening of contractual covenants (making borrowing conditions much more favourable) has been identified as a major contributing factor to systemic threats at each level of control.[10]

Leading private equity practitioners in New York, London and Sydney agree that the global dependency on leverage is highly risky. 'The market that is most overblown and most dangerous and the scariest is the leveraged finance market', remarks John Barber, Managing Partner of Citigroup Private Equity in New York. 'It is those markets silliness that is allowing most of the private equity boom.' The weakening of contractual covenants is, as he puts it, 'the cherry on top of the whipped cream on top of the ice cream' for private equity.[11] Across the Atlantic in London, the Group Communications Director of 3i, one of Europe's largest private equity groups, accepts 'covenants are of variable quality'.[12] Both suggest, however, that it is essential to disaggregate irrational lending from rational borrowing. Moreover, in high growth markets such as Australia, the industry argues less than three per cent of all loans are made to private equity backed-business.[13] This raises a critical question. If the direct risk posed is statistically insignificant, why

---

(Speech delivered at the Financial Markets Conference, Sea Island, Georgia, 15 May 2007) 6.

[9] Peter Costello, 'Opening Address' (Speech delivered at the ASIC Summer School, Sydney, 5 March 2007).

[10] On calls for restraint, see Presidential Working Group and US Agency Principals, *Agreement on Principles and Guidelines Regarding Private Pools of Capital* (2007) 3. Already there are signs that the policy approach is hardening slightly, with a particular focus on the propensity of lenders to provide 'bridge financing' in order to gain access to lucrative underwriting and debt securitisation assignments, see Greg Ip, 'Fed, Other Regulators Turn Attention to Risk in Lenders LBO Lending', *Wall Street Journal* (New York), 18 May 2007, C1; for acceptance of structural imperatives in the marketplace, see FSA, 'Discussion Paper 06/06', above n 8, 60 (suggesting the covenant loosening is linked to the perception that the corporations targeted are much more profitable and thus less likely to default: at 59. The study also found that relationship banking has declined, competitive auctions have increased, a synthesis that reduces meaningful restraints: at 60).

[11] Interview with John Barber (New York, 24 April 2007).

[12] Interview with Patrick Dunne (London, 23 March 2007).

[13] Submission to Senate Standing Committee on Economics, Parliament of Australia, Canberra, 1 May 2007, 4 (Australian Venture Capital and Private Equity Association Limited ('AVCAL')).

has private equity generated such opposition that it has become 'the whipping boy' of wider market forces?[14]

Political salience can be attributed to the size and quality of corporations targeted. Low price to earning ratios, for example, makes large scale capitalised US companies arguably one of the cheapest asset classes available. Even accounting for the present frothiness of the market, with an average price-earnings ratio of 16.9, the S&P index remains 1.9 per cent below a 20 year average (and substantially below the peak of 27.8 encountered at the peak of the dot-com bubble in 2000). Similarly, low levels of corporate debt make Australian corporations particularly attractive, as indeed does large swathes of the Asia-Pacific.[15] At divisional level, global divestiture of non-core assets to generate earnings has disproportionately benefited the private equity industry. Arguably, its leading practitioners have perfected the art of the sale rather than discovered a magic formula to generate longer-term growth.[16]

In part, the problem for the industry is endogenous. Flawed presentation, coupled with the extraordinary personal returns and the transaction fees associated with these deals, inevitably invokes 'the politics of envy'.[17] Proponent confidence in a perceived superior

---

[14] Interview with John Barber, above n 11; see also Douglas Lowenstein (President, Private Equity Council), House Financial Services Committee, United States Congress, Washington DC (16 May 2007) 6–7. The US Treasury Secretary consciously linked problems in the sub-prime mortgage sector to private equity financing, saying both had been marked by 'excess', see MacKensie et al, above n 4.

[15] 'Private Equity Has Eyes on Developing World', *Australian Financial Review* (Sydney), 18 May 2007, 40.

[16] KPMG, 'Increasing Value from Disposal' (Press Release, 28 February 2007), (reporting that 46 per cent of corporate sellers in a global survey of mergers and acquisitions decision-makers felt that they had not maximised value from disposal). Private equity financiers have fared substantially better, most recently. The most glaring example surrounds the sale of Hertz by Ford and its subsequent listing, see below n 57 and accompanying text; see also Geoffrey Newman, 'Airport Sale Nets Macquarie $115m', *The Weekend Australian* (Sydney), 19–20 May 2007, 32 (on Macquarie Airport's sale of its share in Birmingham Airport to the Ontario Teachers Plan Board) after failing to gain a majority shareholding).

[17] Editorial, 'Politics of Envy Alive and Well', *Australian Financial Review* (Sydney), 18 May 2007; see also Leon Gettler, 'In the Politics of Pay, It's up to Us to Show Them the Money', *The Age* (Melbourne), 19 May 2007, 6–7. For the United States, see Kara Scannell, 'House Clears an Executive Pay Measure', *Wall Street Journal* (New York), 21 April 2007, A3 (reporting on the 269 to 134 passage of a Bill that would give shareholders the right to vote on a non-binding resolution on executive compensation); see also House Financial Services Committee, United States Congress, Washington DC, *Private Equity's Effects on Workers and Firms* (16 May 2007).

operating model, linked to a doctrinaire defence of laissez-faire economics, has bordered, at times, on arrogance.[18] Articulating such a narrow vision of utility makes the political establishment nervous. National elections are pending in three of the most important private equity markets — the United States, the United Kingdom and Australia. In such circumstances, conspicuous consumption is not necessarily an advisable public relations strategy.[19] It is not surprising therefore that political defences tend to emanate from those insulated from electoral competition, such as the European Union Commissioner for Internal Markets, Charlie McCreevy.[20]

Paradoxically, the primary virtue associated with private equity, namely its capacity to evade the public disclosure regime, has become a major problem. It has made the industry particularly vulnerable to critiques based on transparency and accountability. While opacity is common to many alternative investment vehicles, including esoteric derivative trading, private equity has a very public face. Moreover, the extent to which iconic (and profitable) corporations are being de-listed and restructured has an immediate market as well as socio-political impact. As such, it has prompted unexpected and forthright criticism from within the financial establishment. Michael Gordon, one of the most influential fund managers in the City of London, caused consternation recently with a scathing rejection of the private equity model:

---

[18] Alan Murray, 'Private Equity's Successes Stir Up a Backlash that May Be Misdirected', *Wall Street Journal* (New York), 9 February 2007, A9 (quoting David Rubinstein of the Carlyle Group saying private equity had done 'an awful job' in public relations terms because of its tendency to 'brag about how much money we make); see also Philip Yea, 'Do We Condemn or Cheer the Flight to Private Equity', *Financial Times* (London), 15 February 2007, 15 (Yea, who is chief executive of 3i, was unapologetic: 'While it may seem unfair that the private equity model has the advantage, that surely is the point of capitalism — that those with the advantage win': at 15).

[19] Stephen Swartzmann, co-founder of the Blackstone Group, held a lavish party in New York to celebrate his 60th birthday, featuring performances by Rod Stewart and Patti LaBelle, see Nelson Schwartz, 'Wall Street's Man of the Moment', *Fortune* (New York), 5 March 2007, 40–3. There is no suggestion whatsoever that the event was in any way inappropriate (eg, Dennis Kozlowski's use of Tyco money to hold a party in Sardinia for his wife). The point is that enhancing visibility in such a manner generates questions about how the money is made.

[20] Charlie McCreevy, 'Private Equity: Getting It Right' (Speech delivered to the All Parliamentary Group, British Venture Capital Association, London, 22 March 2007).

> Institutions and their advisers are choosing to move into a form of investment that provides little real diversification from equities over time; comes with higher risks because of leverage; has far less transparency than a portfolio of listed stocks — and for which the institution has to pay premium fees. Am I the only one struggling to make sense of this.[21]

The intervention undoubtedly serves the entrenched interests of the fund management industry. Pension funds in the United Kingdom are expending proportionately more capital in private equity vehicles. Although this expenditure is within stress levels mandated by specific fund corporate governance protocols, there is concern that trustees lack sufficient knowledge about the products being marketed or appreciate the vast differences in fund performance and management style.[22] Much more significantly, the rise of the leveraged buyout within the City of London has unsettled stable alliances. Leading financiers have attempted to channel political pressure by expressing concern about worker and wider stakeholder rights.[23] In the process, the sedimentary foundations of market capitalism have been disturbed. From London to Canberra (and, to a limited extent, Washington) it has proved impossible to limit discussion of private equity to technocratic analysis.[24] This is not necessarily without normative value.

---

[21] Michael Gordon, Letter to the Editor, *Financial Times* (London), 31 January 2007, 14. Open contestation within the City of London about asset class utility and how to regulate it is not only unusual, it inevitably politicises the issue, see generally Michael Moran, *The British Regulatory State* (2002).

[22] Interview with Michael Gordon (London, 23 March 2007).

[23] Jim Pickard and Peter Smith, 'Myners Warns of Risks from Private Equity', *Financial Times* (London), 20 February 2007, 1 (concern that private equity threatened job security and benefits); for opposition within industrial conglomerates, see Jon Ashworth and Allister Heath, 'The Barbarians Back at the Gate', *The Business* (London), 3 February 2007, 18–20.

[24] House Financial Services Committee, *Private Equity's Effects on Workers and Firms*, above n 17; Senate Standing Committee on Economics, *Inquiry into the Private Equity Investment and Its Effects on Capital Markets and the Australian Economy*, Parliament of Australia, Canberra, 18 March 2007; Treasury Select Committee, *Transparency in Financial Markets and the Structure of UK PLC*, Parliament of the United Kingdom, London, 20 March 2007. The UK inquiry covers 'the effects of the current corporate status of private equity funds, including both their domicile and ownership structure', taxation implications and the wider socio-economic context, terms of reference that were subsequently adopted by its Australian counterpart.

Disputation generates the opportunity to partially reconstruct the social contract governing the corporation and the market in which it is nested.[25] This occurs for three interconnected reasons, sketched here but explored in more detail below. First, the LBO exposes the control limitations of the extant corporate governance paradigm. Positing wealth maximisation for shareholders as the primary purpose of the corporation reduces the capacity of governance to deal with the ideational challenge presented by private equity.[26] Given that most LBOs offer substantial premiums over underlying market prices shareholders are rarely compromised, unless the sale process is itself fundamentally flawed. This suggests the need to rearticulate both the objectives of corporate governance and strategies required to protect stakeholders from the vagaries of what amounts to a financial revolution.

Second, these internal deficiencies are magnified at market level because of transactional dynamics (particularly in sectors or jurisdictions in which one institutional actor has overwhelming presence). This dominance can impoverish the capacity of those providing corporate advisory services to either caution or exercise restraint. More generally, the dynamics of private equity make the efficacy of the gatekeeper function accorded to intermediaries by law or professional norms potentially unsustainable in the longer term. Amelioration of potential excess requires market participants to reach fundamental agreement on the social function of regulation irrespective of whether a rules or principles based approach is adopted.

Third, private equity's continued expansion is predicated on securing an increasing share of pension fund asset allocation. In the Australian context, it is unfortunate that submissions to a Senate Inquiry have adopted an unnecessarily defensive tone.[27] At issue is not the

---

[25] See Frank Easterbrook and Daniel Fischel, *The Economic Structure of Corporate Law* (1991).

[26] Justin O'Brien, 'Managing Conflicts: The Sisyphean Tragedy (and Absurdity) of Corporate Governance and Financial Regulation Reform' (2007) 20 *Australian Journal of Corporate Law* 317.

[27] Submissions to an Australian parliamentary inquiry by the superannuation industry suggested the political fears were unfounded. UniSuper, for example, noted the importance of private equity to asset portfolio balance within appropriate stress levels (2.5–7.5 per cent of total investments), see Submission to Senate Standing Committee on Economics, Parliament of Australia, Canberra, 26 April 2007 (UniSuper) stating it will not 'shun buyout managers, public to private deals, or private equity more generally' but seek 'to manage these risks through sound portfolio construction and manager selection': at 6; see also Submission to Senate Standing Committee on Economics, Parliament of

legitimacy of private equity; rather how the financial and social impact can be managed. A focused dialogue can generate protocols designed to further ultimate societal as well as proximate wealth maximisation goals.

The remainder of the chapter is structured as follows. First, the structural determinants of the private equity market are mapped. Second, the chapter demonstrates how the battle for control of Qantas crystallises the latent and extant risks within and between critical nodes in the corporate governance matrix. Third, it evaluates differential regulatory and jurisprudential responses. In the final section the chapter argues if the LBO offered a true and lasting solution to intrinsic and intractable corporate governance problems, its remarkable renaissance should be uniformly welcomed. In reality, however, the locus of the principal–agent conflict it ostensibly solves is displaced to a largely unregulated arena, which, in turn, exacerbates potential systemic oversight deficiencies. The chapter concludes that the threat to market integrity derives not from the material size of the private equity market but the inculcation of its ideational terms of reference. Unless challenged, these forces of 'creative destruction' risk the sustainability of the asset class.

I A CHRONICLE OF A DEATH FORETOLD

Private equity captured market and public imagination in 2006 and early 2007. The frenetic pace of change is encapsulated in the fact that nine of the ten largest LBOs have taken place in the past 18 months.[28] The record set in the RJR Nabisco takeover stood for 17 years. In 2006, Kohlberg Kravis Roberts broke the record by acquiring HCA, a US-based healthcare corporation, for US$33 billion. Its private equity rival, Blackstone Partners, eclipsed this with the purchase of Equities Office Property Trust for US$38.9 billion (including debt).[29] Now even that looks likely to be surpassed with the planned acquisition of TXU, a Texas utility and the sale by Daimler of Chrysler to Cerberus Capital

---

Australia, Canberra, May 2007 (Australian Institute of Superannuation Trustees), drawing a distinction between positive investment in venture capital and more problematic corporate-raiders, which can be dealt with through corporate governance procedures: at 9.

[28] 'Will Street Pity the Fools', *Wall Street Journal* (New York), 5 January 2007, C14.

[29] Blackstone sold US$22 billion worth of the EOP portfolio within weeks of the purchase, see 'Blackstone Profit is $2bn on Sales', *Chicago Tribune* (Chicago), 14 March 2007 (online edition).

Management, which will involve raising US$65 billion in debt.[30] Key to the deal is a restructuring of pension liabilities. If Cerberus is successful it could put the other Detroit automakers into play and place private equity squarely in the mainstream of corporate finance.[31] Notwithstanding a severe retraction of liquidity in July 2007 causing the postponement of securitised debt offerings, including those advanced to consummate the TXU and Chrsyler deals, the renaissance appeared to confirm a controversial hypothesis first advanced in 1989 that we are witnessing 'the eclipse of the public corporation'[32] Before evaluating the factors that have facilitated the global renaissance of private equity, it is necessary to discuss the industry's *modus operandi*.

(A) *Inside the Alchemist Workshop*

Despite the exponential increase in the number of private equity investment vehicles, the operating structure has remained remarkably homogeneous.[33] The archetypal private equity fund tends to coalesce around a limited liability partnership model.[34] The manner in which

[30] Cerberus Capital Management has US$16.5 billion of assets under management, including ownership of Air Canada. Like many private equity firms it has excellent political connections. Cerberus is chaired by the former Treasury Secretary John Snow. It is perhaps unfortunate that, according to Greek myth, Cerberus was a three-headed dog with a snake for a tail that guarded the gates of Hades.

[31] Gina Chon, Jason Singer and Jeffrey McCracken, 'Chrysler Deal Heralds New Direction for Detroit', *Wall Street Journal* (New York), 15 May 2006, A1.

[32] Jensen, 'Eclipse of the Public Corporation', above n 1; see also Michael Jensen, 'The Modern Industrial Revolution: Exit and the Failure of Internal Control Mechanisms' (1993) 48 *Journal of Finance* 831, 869–70; see also Jensen's contribution in 'Morgan Stanley Roundtable on Private Equity and Its Import for Public Companies' (2006) 18 *Journal of Applied Corporate Finance* 8, 12 (arguing that the risk of failure is minimised by structural barriers to cross subsidisation).

[33] For overview of the industry, see Paul Gompers and Josh Lerner, *The Money of Invention: How Venture Capital Creates New Wealth* (3rd ed, 2004); Josh Lerner, Felda Hardymon and Ann Leamon, *Venture Capital and Private Equity: A Casebook* (3rd ed, 2004). For pen profiles of major institutional actors and their investment philosophies, see Jennifer Hewett, 'Private Lives', *Australian Financial Review Magazine* (Sydney), February 2007, 44–53; Henry Sender, 'Inside the Minds of Kravis, Roberts', *Wall Street Journal* (New York), 3 January 2007, A1; see more generally 'The Uneasy Crown', *Economist* (London), 10 February 2007, 69–71; Katie Benner et al, 'The Power List', *Fortune* (New York), 5 March 2007, 45–50.

[34] Some major holding funds do trade publicly in their own right, for example, the fully listed 3i in the United Kingdom and Onex Partners in Canada. There are however significant differences in operating styles. 3i, for example, invests across the whole range

private equity players in the United States are listing does little to change this dynamic.[35] Each fund has a finite operating lifespan, normally 10 years, which is under the control of a General Partner. The General Partner decides strategic focus and portfolio balance. It conducts due diligence on planned acquisitions, recruits or disposes operational management, and decides divestiture policy. The model precludes the investors, known as limited partners, from exercising any direct decision-making role (as indeed are institutional investors under the public corporation).

Operational discretion is limited only by the size of the capital initially raised, any contractual covenants negotiated by the investors, or subsequently imposed by institutional lenders.[36] Examples of the former include limits on geographic or industry exposure, as well as detailed guidelines on what constitutes due diligence and whether external validation of valuations are required pre-purchase.[37] Post-purchase, a critical governance concern is to prevent controlling interest expropriation through excessive fee charging. Disputes are resolved by recourse to private law. Little or no room for external oversight over freedom to contract is envisaged. In the public sphere, the securities regulator, for example, can demand changes to a company prospectus. By contrast the private equity contract is negotiated almost entirely behind closed doors, with non-disclosure clauses limiting discussion of either terms or investments.

---

of private equity, from venture capital, through 'patient' minority shareholding to LBOs. Unlike many of its competitors, 3i does not engage in club deals nor does it target large-capitalised corporations, factors that have minimised its risk profile: interview with Patrick Dunne, above n 12.

[35] See Dennis Berman, Henry Sender and Gregory Zuckerman, 'Blackstone Aims to Keep Control as Public Entity', *Wall Street Journal* (New York), 23 March 2007, A1 (reporting that shares will be offered in the underlying management vehicle, which will be structured as a limited partnership). In this Blackstone is following the example of Fortress Investment Group, which sought a partial listing in February 2007 and the model already followed by Onex in Canada, which sees its chief executive control the firm through a complex share structure that gives him the right to select 60 per cent of the board while controlling less than 25 per cent of the equity, see Karen Richardson and Jason Singer, 'Private Equity, Public Offerings Have a History', *Wall Street Journal* (New York), 2 April 2007, A1. Private equity firms are not alone in adopting such a strategy. A similar move was associated with the Google IPO in 2004.

[36] See Douglas Cumming and Sofia Johan, 'Is It the Law or the Lawyers? Investment Covenants Around the World' (2006) 12 *European Financial Management* 535, 539–41.

[37] See AVCAL, above n 13, 9.

The Limited Partner commits a specified percentage of capital, which is drawn (on demand) as required. The partnership is structured to minimise liability in the event of an individual corporate failure within the portfolio (for example by capping the percentage of overall capital deployed in single investments and curtailing cross-subsidisation). Management fees are normally pegged at between one and three per cent of the total committed (although they may be front-loaded). The maximum return on investment is normally capped at 80 per cent, net of specific transaction fees, including the purchase of technical legal and accounting advice.[38] Known as 'carried interest', this premium may, however, be subject to the fund exceeding a pre-determined success rate (for example, a certain percentage return).

Initial investment is normally committed within the first five years of the fund. This enhances the maximisation of returns before the fund elapses and capital returned (unless contractually varied). The General Partner has a vested interest to close the fund well in advance of formal closure. Redemption signals higher investment returns, eases subsequent marketing and obviate potential conflicts of interest between competing internal investment funds.

In practice, access to this most illiquid of asset classes is restricted to institutional and accredited investors and a limited number of high net worth individuals.[39] Relative opacity has, however, made the industry vulnerable to criticism. Exemption from public law disclosure obligations in the United States, for example, has been presented as evasion.[40] Recent research suggests increased disclosure could enhance deal flow by making the asset class more attractive to a greater range of risk-averse institutional investors.[41] Conversely, leading private equity funds wish to maintain discretion over either portfolio performance or the mix of investors in each fund to protect proprietary intellectual

---

[38] Joseph Bartlett and W Eric Swan, 'Private Equity Funds: What Counts and What Doesn't' (2001) 26 *Journal of Corporate Law* 393, 398.

[39] An exception is when the private equity management group partially or fully lists. Here, however, the public investor does not have access to the funds under management rather in the profits accruing to the management group itself (net of operating costs).

[40] Steve Hurdle, 'A Blow to Public Investing: Reforming the System of Private Equity Fund Disclosures' (2005) 53 *University of California Los Angeles Law Review* 239, 244–50.

[41] Douglas Cumming and Sofia Johan, 'Regulatory Harmonisation and the Development of Private Equity Markets' (Law and Economics Workshop No 13, University of California, Berkeley, 2006) 28.

capital. Disclosure could also erode the alchemist mystique associated with already (apparently) successful funds, which is used to justify managerial fees. What is also clear, however, is the marked diversity in fund performance. Inordinate focus on increased deal scalability risks misconceiving the private equity market. Size is not necessarily an accurate indicator of performance.[42] Only the top quartile of private equity funds in the United States has outperformed the market, although European funds have fared rather better.[43] Given the statistical evidence of patchy performance, it is necessary to more finely granulate why private equity has captured the ideational zeitgeist.

(B) *Back to the Future: The Return of the LBO*

Earlier periods of sustained merger and acquisition activity tended to be concentrated, corresponding to sector-specific shocks, such as deregulation, privatisation or maturation.[44] Evidence from the LBO boom in United States and the United Kingdom, and, more recently, Australia cannot be so readily explained. Linguistic change underscores the extent of the metamorphosis. The 'corporate raider' has transmogrified into the 'sponsor' of 'portfolio companies'. Chrematistic financial engineering has been transformed into governance arbitrage. Private equity is no longer perceived as the domain of corporate extortionists, a characterisation graphically, if erroneously, depicted in the quintessential account of the chaotic RJR Nabisco takeover battle.[45]

---

[42] Steve Kaplan and Antoinette Schoar, 'Private Equity Performance: Returns, Persistence and Capital Flows' (2005) 60 *Journal of Finance* 1791; Josh Lerner, Antoinette Schoar and Wan Wang, 'Smart Institutions, Foolish Choices: The Limited Partner Performance Puzzle' (Research Paper No 4523–05, Sloan School of Management, Massachusetts Institute of Technology, 2005). For empirical study suggesting major overvaluations linked to calculation based on gross rather than net returns, see Ludovic Pahalippou and Oliver Gottschalg, 'The Performance of Private Equity Funds' (Working Paper, EFA Moscow Meetings 2005, INSEAD, Paris, 2006).

[43] Neil Harper and Antoon Schnneider, 'Private Equity's New Challenge' (2004) *The McKinsey Quarterly* 2.

[44] Mark Mitchell and John Mulherin, 'The Impact of Industry Shocks on Takeover and Restructuring Activity' (1996) 41 *Journal of Financial Economics* 193.

[45] Bryan Burroughs and John Helyar, *Barbarians at the Gates* (1990); Connie Bruck, *The Predators' Ball, The Inside Story of Drexham Burnham and the Rise of the Junk Bond Raiders* (1989); James B Stewart, *Den of Thieves* (1993); see also, however, Michael Jensen and Donald Chew, *US Corporate Governance: Lessons From the 1980s* (1997), available at <http://papers.ssrn.com/abstract=146150> (characterising the rise in LBOs as

Many senior banking and managerial executives have expressed a preference for undertaking consultancy for private equity funds rather than take up board positions with publicly listed corporations.[46] Despite the changed corporate landscape, the narrow normative claim advanced by the industry has remained constant. Now, as then, proponents point to four interlinked advantages associated with (even a temporary) public market exit.

First, the private equity fund recombines equity, knowledge and control. Due diligence undertaken in advance of an acquisition generates superior technical and market intelligence.[47] The key is not simply financial engineering but rather, it is claimed, a superior governance model.[48] Peter Yates, the Chief Executive of Allco Equity Partners used a seminar aimed at retail investors in Sydney in May 2007 to propagate the sector's work ethic. 'Financial engineering', he said, 'does not make a bad deal good; it can make a good deal great.'[49] What he omitted to mention is that the risk is often transferred at an early stage. The private equity fund uses additional debt obligation to rapidly repay part of the initial capital outlay. The banks underwriting the debt issue also reduce their initial exposure, through securitising and on-selling the debt.[50]

---

an overdue attack on entrenched and profligate management which had been deliberately misunderstood by a populist media reporting).

[46] Glenda Korporaal, 'Clarke Lashes Out at Governance Laws', *The Australian* (Sydney), 28 March 2007, 21 (reporting that the founder of Macquarie Bank would not take up any public directorships on his retirement, because he did not think 'the risks and the package are worth it': at 21).

[47] The capacity to generate and evaluate this research is a further reason why investors are drawn to boutique investment houses.

[48] Jensen, 'Morgan Stanley Roundtable', above n 32, 13.

[49] Peter Yates (Speech delivered at the ASX Investor Hour, Australian Shareholder Association, Sydney, 15 May 2007). For evidence that financial engineering plays more significant role than organisational form, see Robert Cressy, Federico Munari and Alessandro Maliero, *Playing to Their Strengths? Evidence that Specialisation in the Private Equity Industry Confers Competitive Advantage* (February 2007), available at <http//ssrn.com/abstract=964367>.

[50] FSA, 'Discussion Paper 06/06', above n 8, 13 (reporting survey evidence from the most active banks operating in London. Equity financing mushroomed from €58 billion to €67.9 billion between June 2005 and July 2006. It also found, however, that the risk was quickly parceled out to other lenders. The evidence suggests that bank exposure is reduced to 19.4 per cent of original investment within 120 days: at 14). Two further factors are apparent In the Asia-Pacific region. Firstly, liquidity has increased dramatically as a consequence of Chinese corporate IPO activity on the Hong Kong and, to a lesser extent, London markets. The additional income cannot be repatriated into China because of inflationary fears. As a result, this capital is put increasingly into

Increasingly, this debt is finding its way onto the retail market through the marketing of unsecured debentures.[51]

A critical refinement to public corporate governance is a simplification of the controlling mechanism. Lines of authority and responsibility are clarified and subject to ongoing review.[52] The fund may accept the operational plan put forward by entrenched management or, more regularly, provide it with syndicated in-house expertise drawn from a burgeoning range of executives recruited to either provide a consulting service or give credibility to future acquisition targets.[53] It is further argued that proximity of the owner to the decision-making process allows for any strategy reformulations to be agreed and implemented quickly.[54] Recent research suggests the most successful deals are informed by constant engagement with operational management, particularly in the first three months.[55] Particularly in cases

---

securitised private equity debt; see Anthony Neoh, 'China's Financial Markets — Growth Opportunity and Challenge' (Speech delivered at the ASIC Summer School, Sydney, 5 March 2007). In addition, China has emerged as a significant investor in private equity management vehicles, most notably through its $3bn investment in the Blackstone Initial Public Offering. This dependency is likely to grow given a sudden increase in risk aversion, see Paul Davies, Lina Saigol, Michael MacKensie and Saskia Scholtes, 'Markets Lose Their Appetites for LBOs', *Financial Times* (London) 28 July 2007, 9.

[51] For regulatory fears associated with retail exposure in the liberal Australian marketplace, see Joanne Gray, 'ASIC Agnostic on Private Equity', *Australian Financial Review* (Sydney), 16 May 2007, 10.

[52] The Australian Venture Capital Association suggests two critical advantages include 'a board less driven by process' and recouping of 'valuable time (up to 20 per cent) that was previously spent representing the company to the investor community,' see AVCAL above n 13, 11.

[53] Erin White and Joann Lublin, 'Private Equity Firms Stock Up on Executives', *Wall Street Journal* (New York), 16 May 2007, B1. When the fund builds up a corporate presence but does not have full control it can use its stake to execute change, see Nick Tabakoff, 'Venture Capital Blamed as PBL Media Bones Eddie McGuire', *The Weekend Australian* (Sydney), 19–20 May 2007, 31 (reporting the departing CEO's claim that he left because he 'didn't want to be an accountant' and focus on 'financial mechanics': at 31).

[54] See Lucinda Schmidt, 'Surviving Private Equity', *Australian Financial Review Boss Magazine* (Sydney), May 2007, 46–51 (emphasising the speed of decision-making in a range of Australian and New Zealand firms acquired by global private equity firms); see also UniSuper, above n 27 (suggesting private equity firms have 'the best and most effective form of governance' but warning that 'strong growth in the size of the private equity market and the dramatic increase in the number of managers and investors in these markets may have led to the information asymmetry arbitrage being eroded': at 3).

[55] Andreas Beroutsos, Andrew Freeman and Conor Kehoe, 'What Public Companies Can Learn from Private Equity' (2007) *McKinsey on Finance* 1–5.?

involving the acquisition of subsidiaries this engagement reduces corporate dependency and, if handled adroitly, energises frontline staff. This perspective is particularly propagated in the retail arena, where sales personnel are often provided with profit-sharing incentives.[56]

Second, linking incentive payments to actual rather than relative performance aligns the interests of both the portfolio client manager and the fund's delegated representative. Generally, the private equity executive's own bonus is tied to the performance of his charge rather than the fund as a whole. Third, the LBO generally allows for a longer term planning process. The industry presents itself as purveyors of 'patient capital; with portfolio companies are held for at least three years before exit through re-listing in an Initial Public Offering or on-sold.[57] This gives temporary relief from earnings management imperatives associated with the public markets and allows for the deployment of investment that could, in the public markets, invoke a credit downgrade

---

[56] Fiona Tyndall and Allan Jury, 'My Store', *Australian Financial Review Boss Magazine* (Sydney), February 2007, 17–20 (reporting the staff had been energised. Rather than viewing the changes with suspicion, they had acted like 'a whole bunch of unshackled horses': at 17). See also Richard Gluyas, 'Myer's Makeover Reaps $1bn', *The Australian* (Sydney), 28 March 2007, 21 (reporting an 84 per cent rise in profits since the acquisition).

[57] If market conditions permit, LBO funds will re-list very quickly. The most glaring example involved the car rental company, Hertz. It was bought in December 2005 by a consortium that included the Carlyle Group and Merrill Lynch Global Private Equity Partners, six months after Ford decided not to proceed with its own IPO. The investors paid a total of US$14 billion for the company, US$2.3 billion in cash, the remainder leveraged. George Tamke, a Clayton Dubilier & Reid partner named Chairman of the Board of Directors opined: 'the company's underlying strengths — an exceptional global brand, premium pricing supported by superior customer service and a history of industry innovation — form a strong platform on which to pursue further growth initiatives', see CD&R (Press Release, 12 September 2005). The LBO group took on a further US$6 billion loan, paid out a US$1 billion dividend and announced an intention to re-float seven months later. The partnership received a further US$500m bonus payment on completion of the offering on 15 November 2006. See generally David Henry and Emily Thornton, 'Buy It, Flip It, then Strip It', *Businessweek* (New York), 7 August 2006, 28–31. Although share prices have been sustained and marginally increased, so too has the level of the market making it difficult to ascertain whether real value has been generated. For overview, see Jerry Cao and Josh Lerner, *The Performance of Reverse Leveraged Buyouts* (15 October 2006), available at <http://ssrn.com/abstract=937801> (using data compiled from 496 RLBOs from 1980–2002. The study found that of the 53 returned to the market with a year all under-performed, providing 'partial support for the claim that "flipping back" does not add value': at 14).

or trigger a share price reduction.[58] Fourth, and most controversially, exiting the public market reduces the regulatory and tax burden. This may make for more effective use of capital. It also has the potential to negatively impact on corporate tax revenue, key areas of concern in the parliamentary deliberations now underway in Canberra, Washington and Westminster.[59]

In narrowly defined financial terms, therefore, the private equity model appears to offer a superior framework. If, however, as noted above, out-performing the market is illusory outside the top quartile of funds, what other factors need to be considered to explain growing infatuation with the asset class. Regulatory flight appears superficially attractive, particularly in the United States.[60] Changes to the US corporate governance regime, including increased compliance costs and legal risk, are said to have made management much more amenable to the advantages of going private.[61] Regulators are under increasing pressure not to exercise instruments of control. Creative enforcement mechanisms, such as mandating governance change in exchange for a decision to stay or drop corporate prosecutions are presented, with partial judicial justification, as the illegitimate exercise of prosecutorial discretion.[62] The cost (generated primarily by the audit profession itself)

---

[58] Blackstone Partners has begun the process of re-listing the online travel business Orbitz Worldwide, which it bought in August 2006. The prospectus discloses 'weaknesses in our material internal controls over financial reporting' as well as an incomplete 'global technology platform', see Bill Barnhart, 'Blackstone Wants to Abort Bumpy Flight on Orbitz', *Chicago Tribune* (Chicago), 11 May 2007 (online edition).

[59] The extent to which tax arbitrage reduces revenue is, of course country specific. In Australia, debt-equity integrity rules were introduced in 2001 to prevent arbitrage lowering the corporate tax base, see Submission to Senate Standing Committee on Economics, *Inquiry into the Private Equity Investment and its Effects on Capital Markets and the Australian Economy*, Parliament of Australia, Canberra, 11 May 2007, 5–6 (Ernst & Young).

[60] See McKinsey Report, *Sustaining New York's and the US' Global Financial Services Leadership* (2007) 83, 87; Committee on Capital Markets Regulation, *Interim Report of the Committee on Capital Markets Regulation* (2006) 116–34.

[61] McKinsey, above n 60, 17; Committee on Capital Markets Regulation, above n 60, xii.

[62] The Securities and Exchange Commission ('SEC') in Washington has adopted a rules-based protocol system, see SEC, *Rules of Practice* (2006). The Financial Services Authority in London frames its enforcement agenda around generic statements of regulatory principles, including efficiency and economy, the role of management, proportionality, international coordination and need to safeguard competition, see FSA, *Principles of Good Regulation* (2006). In essence, the principles differ little from guidance already offered by US counterparts, see in particular US Department of Justice

of validating internal control processes are blamed (on the SEC) for driving business off-market and offshore. On these accounts, the reprise of the LBO is simultaneously presented as a rational response to ill-considered political interference and evidential support for oversight retrenchment.

Some critics go further and complain about the entire governance regime. Among them is Martin Lipton, one of the most influential and respected mergers and acquisitions lawyers in New York: 'The real motivation is dissatisfaction with the public market.'[63] Lipton built his practice on defending boards of management from hostile takeovers. His support for the current wave of takeovers derives primarily from the manner in which the corporate governance agenda has privileged process over strategy. Private equity is viewed as having a more effective governance system and, in the main, provides shareholders with a fair opportunity to exit:

> Most of these deals are fair deals, negotiated at arms length. These are not deals in which somebody is stealing the company. Most involve some kind of auction, or market test for the price and the institutions have been very successful in the UK, Western Europe and here in forcing an increase in price when they think the initial offering is inadequate.[64]

Company directors are much more receptive to private equity entreaties, he argues, because they are 'just fed up with external 'encrustations' that affect their ability to manage the company.'[65] He suggests the assault on board authority from aggressive institutional

---

Principles of Federal Prosecution of Business Organisations (2003). What does differ is the extent to which the default mechanism for securing behavioural change in the United States is enforcement rather than consultation driven, see John Coffee, 'Law and the Market: The Role of Enforcement' (Paper presented at the Dynamics of Capital Market Governance Workshop, Australian National University, 14 March 2007).

[63] Interview with Martin Lipton (New York, 23 April 2007).

[64] Ibid. Lipton made his reputation by designing the so-called 'poison pill' defence in the 1980s. Ratified by the Delaware Court of Chancery, the most important venue for adjudicating corporate disputes in the United States, the strategy imposed such onerous financial penalties that it dampened hostile takeovers for a generation. But for Lipton, two decades later market conditions make it almost impossible to sustain public ownership, especially if the price is reasonable, management agree and the process for managing market exit transparent.

[65] Ibid.

investors has profoundly changed the corporate landscape. Lipton's critique suggests that an enabling system of oversight would better protect the maintenance of the public model. The empirical evidence demonstrates that a light-touch principles-based approach to regulation does not necessarily guarantee the maintenance of public ownership. The City of London, for example, has also witnessed an exponential increase in private equity activity. Funds raised through initial listing were outstripped by market exits in 2006. The result has been a reduction in share availability and concomitant decline in the value of the London market.[66]

Tracing a direct connection with differential regulatory responses to corporate scandal, therefore, offers an incomplete and potentially misleading causal explanation. Its power is further dissipated by the fact that major private equity providers are themselves not only seeking listing but seeking a highly conditional form of it in New York itself. What soul-searching there is in Wall Street about the future of the public corporation serves a much narrower purpose. It is designed solely to pressure regulators into reducing the regulatory burden, thereby protecting its competitive advantage vis-à-vis London. While private equity in the United States is used as a mechanism to cow regulators, across the Atlantic the debate is at once more nuanced and, potentially, more destabilising, precisely because it has disturbed the foundations of market capitalism.

(C) *The Creative Destruction of Private Equity*

One of the most parsimonious heuristic metaphors for describing the impact of private equity comes from the noted mid-20th century economist Joseph Schumpeter. Writing in the midst of a global conflagration, Schumpeter argued that the key public policy challenge facing capitalist society was how to manage its inherent disequilibrium. For Schumpeter, the 'perennial gale' of change 'incessantly revolutionises the economic structure from within, incessantly destroying the old one, incessantly creating a new one. This process of Creative Destruction is the essential fact about capitalism.'[67] Change (potentially but not assuredly) emanates from the impact on the existing order from 'the competition from the new commodity, the new technology, the new

---

[66] See FSA, 'Discussion Paper 06/06', above n 8, 3.

[67] Joseph Schumpeter, *Capitalism, Socialism and Democracy* (1943) 84.

source of supply, the new type of organisation.' This challenge 'strikes not at the margins of the profits and the outputs of the existing firms but at their foundations and their very lives.'[68]

Contrary to its usage by management consultants, who hijacked the term at the turn of the millennium to justify retrenchment, 'creative destruction' in the classic sense is far from unproblematic.[69] Change can weaken loyalty, trust and institutional knowledge. Contemporary ethnographies of the corporation highlight the internal social dislocation and anxiety this process generates for employees (including middle management).[70] 'The divorce between command and accountability', accentuated by what Sennett terms 'a shortened framework of institutional time', can lead to 'social degradation' for those not directly remunerated by implementation.[71] Failure can have much deeper resonance if, irrespective of foundation, the entity to which the individual is attached holds iconic status as the repository of national virtues.[72] Thus, unless change is deemed essential or desirable, it is difficult to neutralise wider political objections.

The private equity industry has proved increasingly adept at managing this process in the United States. The consortium bidding for control of the Texas utility company, TXU, used concern about climate change, for example, to justify a commitment to rescind plans to build 11 new coal-fired power stations. This environmental altruism served an undeclared dual purpose. First, it neutralised the environmental lobby.[73] Second, it justified an immediate retrenchment on capital investment.[74]

---

[68] Ibid.

[69] See, eg, Richard Foster and Sarah Kaplan, *Creative Destruction* (2001). This myopic approach reduces both the range and application of Schumpeterian theory, see Thomas McCraw, *Prophets of Innovation: Joseph Schumpeter and Creative Destruction* (2007) 6; see also Horst Hanusch and Andreas Pyka, 'Principles of Neo-Schumpetarian Economics' (2007) 31 *Cambridge Journal of Economics* 275.

[70] See, eg, Robert Puttnam, *Bowling Alone* (2000); Richard Sennett, *The Corrosion of Character* (1998).

[71] Richard Sennett, *The Culture of the New Capitalism* (2006) 57, 181.

[72] Georgina Born, *Uncertain Vision: Birt, Dyke and the Reinvention of the BBC* (2004).

[73] The proposed deal did cause some infighting among environmentalists after the event but not enough to scupper the initial support, see Rebecca Smith and Jim Carlton, 'Environmentalist Groups Feud Over Terms of TXU Buyout', *Wall Street Journal* (New York), 3 March 2007, A1.

[74] Andrew Ross Sorkin, 'A Buyout Deal that Has Many Shades of Green', *New York Times* (New York), 27 February 2007, B1; see also Editorial, 'The New Greenmail', *Wall Street Journal* (New York), 27 February 2007, A16 (noting the public relations coup in

Likewise, Cerberus Capital Management's planned acquisition of Chrysler is predicated on a sidebar agreement with the United Auto Workers trades union in which both sides accept unless the deal was consummated, the company could file for bankruptcy protection.[75] Absent this cover, private equity is exceptionally vulnerable to not just the politics of envy, but also the politics of fear. Both are likely to increase before this mergers and acquisitions cycle completes precisely because many of the corporations now being targeted are neither in distress nor intrinsically mismanaged, which is why the Qantas deal, to be explored in detail below, proved so problematic.

In a highly-charged editorial, the *Financial Times* noted in December 2005 that 'the private equity "barbarians" are back. Only this time they are not at the gate. They are inside the castle and holding a banquet fit for a king.'[76] A year on, the paper advised the industry to 'exercise discretion'.[77] Even those most bullish about the industry's virtues accept that prudence is advisable. 'People are making a lot of money; secondly they are making a lot of money with clear action', accepts John Barber, managing partner of Citigroup Private Equity in New York.[78] 'Layoffs, taking back working capital, moving headquarters, transferring businesses from Germany to Dallas are the sorts of action that attract attention. People are buying companies now that have impact, that touch upon enough workers, enough customers and touch government.'[79]

While the asset class generates substantial profits for the entrepreneurs leading vehicles, recruited management and those providing capital and advisory services, it forges the creation of powerful counter-coalitions by shifting the location of core value within the regulatory sub-system.[80] In the battle for advantage, entrenched interests

---

enlisting the support of the environmental lobby but pointedly seeing an emergent alliance that could be detrimental to shareholders).

[75] See above n 30–1 and accompanying text.

[76] Editorial, 'While the Sun Shines', *Financial Times* (London), 3 December 2005, 14.

[77] Editorial, 'Private Equity Should Beware its Own Success', *Financial Times* (London), 22 December 2006, 14.

[78] Interview with John Barber, above n 11.

[79] Ibid.

[80] See Paul Sabatier, 'An Advocacy Coalition Framework of Policy Change and the Role of Policy Oriented Learning Therein' (1988) 21 *Policy Sciences* 129 (linking policy change to intersection between relative subsystem and 'external perturbation, i.e. the effects of systemic events- changes in socio-economic conditions, outputs from other

seek to maintain corporate or market dominance by injecting a moral and ethical dimension. 'No social system can work in which everyone is supposed to be guided by nothing except his short-term utilitarian ends', warned Schumpeter when he concluded that 'the stock market is a poor substitute for the Holy Grail.'[81] The lack of transparency provides an opening for fund managers to castigate governance and regulatory arbitrage and deploy ideational resources to support legislative intervention.[82] One senior fund manager in the City of London suggests that the active support of management in private buy-outs simply increases the moral hazard.[83] He describes the market as being in a state of frenzy not seen since the 1980s:

> It is hard to make the comparison because you are older, wiser, perhaps more cynical, but it does feel way worse. What was once the preserve of the landed gentry is now something that someone of thirty-two years of age can aspire to because of the 50 million to 100 million they made over the past two years. Greed will kill this. The greed of the industry will kill this.[84]

While somewhat overblown, the intervention serves to dilute doctrinal faith, blur self-referential boundaries and weaken the conceptual foundations of associational governance.[85] Armed with this global

---

sub-systems and changes in the system wide governing coalition — on the resources and constraints of sub-system actors': at 148).

[81] Schumpeter, above n 67, 137,

[82] Chantal Mouffe, *On The Political* (2005) 17–21.

[83] Interview with Michael Gordon, above n 22; for evidence of downward earnings manipulation pre-purchase, see T W Wu, 'Management Buyouts and Earnings Management' (1997) 12 *Journal of Accounting, Auditing and Finance* 373 (finding evidence of accounting manipulation in 87 MBOs in the United States between 1980–87). See also De-Wai Chou, Michael Gombola and Feng Ying Liu, 'Earnings Management and Stock Performance of Reverse Leveraged Buyouts' (2006) 41 *Journal of Financial and Quantitative Analysis* 407.

[84] Interview with Michael Gordon, above n 22; for Australia, see Peter Weekes, 'Equity, for Fund and Profit', *The Sunday Age* (Melbourne), 20 May 2007 (online edition) (quoting Deutsche Bank Head of Private Wealth: 'I have never in my life seen this much capital chasing deal flows. It considerably exceeds what we saw in 1999, which was obscene, and the whole thing ended in a flash in 2001').

[85] As such, it represents an exogenous force with systemic opportunities (cf Sabatier, above n 80) and risks (cf Schumpeter, above n 67).

overview, we are now in a position to map more closely the interplay of forces on the regulatory debate in Australia itself.

II CHARTING AN ICARIAN FLIGHTPATH

With demand outstripping supply in fund development, subscription and acquisition targets, private equity has expanded beyond the core markets. Australia has become a core beachhead. From outlier, it has become the third biggest private equity arena outside the United States and the United Kingdom. Low levels of corporate debt, a stable legal order, structural changes to the superannuation industry and a vibrant financial services sector have made Australia exceptionally attractive as both a source of targets and of funding. The combined value of planned and executed transactions in 2006 amounted to AUS$27 billion, a significant spike on the previous five-year average of AUS$1.5 billion.[86] This represents a fraction of the overall value of the businesses listed on the Australian Stock Exchange.[87] It is difficult, however, to overstate the impact of private equity on the domestic corporate firmament.

A senior partner in the Sydney office of Ernst & Young captured the mood with a colorful, if mixed, metaphor. The Australian corporate market, he reported, 'is being trawled for fallen angels and there are no sacred cows.'[88] None appeared more so than Qantas, the Australian flag-carrier, which was subjected to a keenly fought arbitrage battle, which, if successful would have amounted to the largest buy-out in aviation history. While many of the Qantas transaction terms were neither unique nor indeed problematic, the putative takeover fused many of the conflicting arguments about private equity's utility. Unlocking the black

---

[86] Reserve Bank of Australia, *Statement on Monetary Policy* (12 February 2007) 45. The trend continued into the first quarter of 2007, see Alan Jury, 'Private Equity Interest Jumps,' *Australian Financial Review* (Sydney), 30 March 2007, 79 (reporting AUS$4.2 billion planned transactions in the first quarter, more than double the previous year).

[87] The Australian Venture Capital Association estimates the total value of private equity transactions to be under 1.54 per cent, of the capitalisation of the Australian Stock Exchange. Moreover, it estimates that even accounting for leverage, its members can only deploy AUS$40 billion, which would buy 2.74 per cent of the ASX, see AVCAL above n 13, 5, 20.

[88] Ernst & Young, 'Mergers and Acquisitions Index' (Press Release, 5 December 2006). Most Australian transactions were strategic realignments in response to regulatory change (Channel 7 and Channel 9) or partial divestiture of non-core business units (the sale of Myer Department Stores by the Coles Group). The single hostile bid saw Kohlberg Kravis Roberts target Coles Group. The bid was rebuffed twice.

box of the Qantas deal helps to illuminate not only why the consortium lost control but also wider accountability dilemmas associated with the perfectly legal privileging of private rights over public duties.

(A) *The Fall to Earth*

The life support system sustaining the most important putative private equity transaction in Australia was turned off at 9.10AM on Thursday 17 May. In a statement to the Australian Stock Exchange, Airline Partners Australia ('APA'), the bidding consortium, conceded 'in the current environment and circumstances a renewed offer on terms acceptable to APA would not be likely to succeed. On that basis APA has decided not to proceed with a renewed offer at this time'.[89] The phrasing is intriguing.

Given the global boom in private equity transactions at the time, it appears, on the face of it, an unduly pessimistic assessment, particularly for a consortium driven by Macquarie, the pre-eminent investment bank in Australia (then trading at a significant premium) and arguably already the largest private equity firm in the world.[90] The reference to 'acceptable terms' adds to the ambiguity. It hints at a subterranean conflict, which partially emerged in the legal argument over whether the consortium had, in fact, secured that mandatory 50 per cent support on the day the offer closed to allow the bid to proceed for a further two weeks.

APA had based its threshold claim on the securing of late acceptances and on short-lived legal argument that highlighted a standard contractual clause foreclosing the splitting of shareholdings. The clause informed potential participants they were deemed to have 'irrevocably accepted' the offer 'in respect of all your Qantas shares despite any difference between that number and the number of Qantas shares shown on the acceptance form.'[91]

Whether and, if so, to what extent the untested contractual provision could be enforced is questionable. Moreover, wresting control in such circumstances was never going to be sufficient to sway the court

---

[89] APA (Press Release, 17 May 2007).
[90] Stuart Washington, 'Winning Formula: Aggression and Persistence', *Sydney Morning Herald* (Sydney), 19 May 2007 (online edition); Elizabeth Knight, 'MacBank Does Have an Achilles Heel', *Sydney Morning Herald* (Sydney), 16 May 2007 (online edition).
[91] *APA Bidders Statement* (2007) cl 7.3(f)(i).

of public or political opinion (or indeed inure the consortium to the market). As John Durie noted sardonically in the *Australian Financial Review*, the clause 'was not designed as a trap for careless hedge funds.'[92]

While no direct causal connection can be traced, the withdrawal of APA's bid coincided with ministerial questioning over whether Qantas had managed the share registry to ensure foreign ownership was kept within legal boundaries. APA retreated in the face of rising political contestation. The consortium, which had dominated the Australian media agenda for months, sought to paint defeat as a moral victory and a demonstration of responsible corporate stewardship.

> Given the amount of time it would take were the issue to be litigated, and the consequent uncertainty for both Qantas and its shareholders, APA has decided not to pursue arguments that it did achieve voting power in excess of 50 per cent by the offer deadline of 4 May 2007.[93]

The statement deflected responsibility for failure but it could not disguise the scale of the loss.

By Friday 4 May, despite a concerted campaign that focused on increasingly shrill claims that failure to consummate the deal threatened an immediate collapse in the Qantas share price, the consortium struggled to reach even the minimum 50 per cent required to prompt a two-week statutory extension. At 8.30PM APA conceded market rejection.[94] APA intimated that the deal had 'apparently' failed because it had secured only a 45.66 per cent acceptance rate.

A number of hours later a further economic interest of 4.96 per cent was extracted from a US-based hedge fund. This late acceptance formed the basis for the APA's application to the Takeovers Panel. It argued that a technical failure to reach the threshold constituted 'unacceptable circumstances'.[95] No credible explanation was offered as

---

[92] See Steve Creedy, 'Qantas Takeover Farce May End in Court', *The Australian* (Sydney), 8 May 2007, 1; John Durie, 'Bid for Qantas Looks a Goner', *The Australian Financial Review* (Sydney), 11 May 2007, 64.

[93] APA (Press Release, 8 May 2007).

[94] APA (Press Release, 4 May 2007).

[95] *Corporations Act 2001* (Cth) s 657A(1)–(3). There is, however, no definition of what constitutes 'unacceptable circumstances'. The Takeovers Panel has to adjudicate this by reference to an 'efficient, competitive and informed markets' (s 602) and its

to why the deadline had been missed beyond miscalculation. The Takeovers Panel was unimpressed.[96] APA, it argued, had made it clear that the bid would lapse at 7.00PM on 4 May. From the panel's perspective, the 'truth in takeovers' principle meant absent compelling evidence to the contrary, the deadline must hold. APA launched an appeal and simultaneously pressed the Australian Securities and Investments Commission ('ASIC') to intervene. The approach was rebuffed.[97]

Much media comment has focused on the allegedly errant behaviour of one US hedge fund.[98] The broader question of why the consortium failed to lock-in sufficient acceptances in advance repays considered attention. Institutional investors appeared to have committed the smallest proportion of their shares. This was a rational trading strategy to maximise potential profits during the mandatory two week extension should the threshold have been reached. At its most fundamental, judgment is reducible to trust and the market did not trust the consortium's claims that the bid was on a knife-edge.

Market unease intensified over the weekend as APA exhausted market and regulatory approaches. Investment banking sources in Sydney suggest privately that the approach adopted by the consortium was counter-productive, adding, perhaps erroneously, to perceptions of hubris and arrogance in equal measure. Somewhat remarkably, the APA legal submission to the Takeovers Panel blamed failure on media misrepresentation. As a consequence, it claimed, 'the market was

---

consideration of 'the national interest': Takeovers Panel 'Unacceptable Circumstances' *Guidance Note No 1* (28 September 2004) 3. The Panel articulates the latter as the need to 'consider wider issues such as: what signals its decision to make, or not to make, a declaration of unacceptable circumstances in individual cases, will send to the market and the wider investing community': at 5.

[96] Takeovers Panel, 'Qantas Airways Limited 02 — Receipt of Application and Decision' (Press Release, 6 May 2007); for full decision see *In the Matter of Qantas 02R* (2007) ATP 07.

[97] ASIC, 'Statement on Qantas' (Press Release, 7 May 2007).

[98] Scott Rochfort, 'Qantas Farce: Heads Will Roll', *Sydney Morning Herald* (Sydney), 7 May 2007, 1; Matthew Murphy, 'Qantas Admits Takeover Bid Dead', *The Age* (Melbourne), 7 May 2007, 1; James Hall, 'Credibility at Stake at Every Corner', *Australian Financial Review* (Sydney), 7 May 2007, 19; Jennifer Hewett, 'Crash: Private Equity Falls Back to Earth', *The Weekend Australian* (Sydney), 5–6 May 2007, 33; Katrina Nicholas, 'MacBank Runs into Flak as Blame Games Takes Off', *Australian Financial Review* (Sydney), 12–13 May, 2007, 26–7; Alan Kohler, 'In the End APA Lacked Bottle', *Sydney Morning Herald* (Sydney), 12–13 May 2007, 45.

misinformed as to the prospects of the bid succeeding and … it was this misinformation that induced Qantas shareholders into a false sense that they would have more time to accept the Offer than they actually did.'[99]

At a broader political level, there could be no mistaking the federal government's frustration with the turn of events. As the lawyers conferred, the government made a very public request to Qantas to verify whether its share registrar was in compliance with legal requirements to ensure a dominance of domestic ownership.[100] Somewhat lamely, the Qantas board replied that it was conducting an urgent reconciliation.

At its first board meeting after the market rejection of the biggest attempted aviation buyout, Margaret Jackson tendered her resignation, but only after it became clear that an increasingly desperate attempt to retain the position was doomed to fail.[101] Despite overseeing a process that unlocked significant latent value within the airline, her open support for the deal made her position untenable. Jackson was deemed to have supported a bid that significantly undervalued the corporation. The chief executive of Qantas, Geoff Dixon, remained silent, as he had throughout the process, a silence that ensured the maintenance of his position.

The market rejected the deal on price, not principle, making it possible that the issues raised could reemerge should debt markets stabilise. Although there is merit in the suggestion by the Treasurer, Peter Costello, that the regulatory 'system has worked well',[102] retracing the tortuous flight path of the Qantas bid reveals a multitude of weak points in the governance of LBOs in Australia, particularly those involving entrenched insiders. The true significance of the Qantas deal rests not on its iconic status, but the extent to which its backers placed deal consummation imperatives over restraint. As such, it simultaneously demonstrates the increased reach and overreach of private equity.

---

[99] *In the Matter of Qantas 02R* (2007) ATP 07, 5.

[100] *Qantas Sale Act 1992* (Cth) s 7(1)(g); Steve Creedy and Glenda Korporaal, 'Canberra to Order Qantas Sell-Off', *The Australian* (Sydney), 8 May 2007, 21.

[101] Katrina Nicholas and Vesna Poljak, 'Jackson to Quit in Qantas Fallout', *Australian Financial Review* (Sydney), 18 May 2007, 1. Margaret Jackson had earlier claimed that those who rejected the bid without recognising that it would have a material downward impact on the share price had 'a mental problem with the operation of the market'. The statement served to transfer a recommendation into active lobbying. For the lobbying to retain her position, see Kate Askew, 'Mental as Anything', *Sydney Morning Herald* (Sydney), 12–13 May 2007, 41.

[102] 'Offer Over, Its Back to the Board', *The Australian* (Sydney), 8 May 2007, 26.

(B) *The Deal Structure*

Qantas is one of the most profitable airlines in the world. It operates within a domestic duopoly and enjoys a virtual stranglehold on lucrative trans-Pacific routes ensured high passenger yields. Although vulnerable to exogenous forces, such as an outbreak of SARS or a future terrorist attack using commercial airlines, the corporation had devised and partially implemented an ambitious growth strategy. This was based on the exponential growth of Jetstar, the group's low-cost subsidiary. Despite the opportunities, the stock languished on the Australian Stock Exchange, its legally mandated primary domicile.[103] It was not surprisingly that the board would countenance a private equity approach. Rebuffed by the Qantas board when it first offered AUS$5.35 a share, APA returned with a marginally improved offer the following day.[104] Predictably enough, the bid fell within the fair price range calculated by independent advisors retained after the board endorsed the buy-out.[105]

The bid was predicated on APA gaining a 90 per cent economic interest, which would allow for a compulsory purchase. It also involved the airline accruing AUS$8 billion dollars in debt. The proposed market exit of an (albeit privatised) island economy icon was always going to satisfy a national interest objection, the sole subjective criterion on which the government could block the sale. The first imperative for the consortium was to get clearance from Canberra.

The consortium was carefully calibrated to allay political sensitivities. First, the retention of the existing senior management along with their strategy provided continuity. Second, private equity financing was presented as offering quantitative and qualitative benefits simply not attainable through public ownership. Potential conflicts, such as Macquarie's management role in Sydney Airport (which could limit landing slots to competitors) were presented as synergies.

Equally Allco Finance's core aircraft leasing business was presented as evidence of airline experience. Second, the consortium voluntarily (if belatedly) submitted to a Foreign Investment Review Board adjudication to demonstrate good faith (while protesting that it

---

[103] *Qantas Sale Act 1992* (Cth) s 7(1)(k).

[104] 14 December 2006. The offer represented a 60 per cent premium above the average of Qantas shares prior to rumours of a takeover bid were confirmed on 22 November 2006: see *APA Bidders Statement*, above n 91, 15.

[105] Qantas, *Target's Statement*, 9 February 2007, 39.

was unnecessary). The economic and voting interests were carefully aligned to avoid triggering formal regulatory or political scrutiny (see Table 1).[106]

Table 1. The Qantas Control Play.

Partner	Equity Provision (AUS $m)	Economic Interest	Voting Interest
Allco Equity Partners	956.1	26.9	35.4
Allco Finance	300	8.4	11.1
Macquarie Bank	525.5	14.7	14.7
Texas Pacific Group	891	25	14.9
Onex Partners	445.5	12.5	9
Institutional Investors	409.9	11.5	14.9
Senior Management		—	1
Total Australian		51.0	61.2
Total Foreign		49.0	38.8

Tough talking by the Treasurer, Peter Costello, that the government would ensure that the bid satisfied all legal requirements, was, however, just that. The cleverness of the deal lay in the fact that it backed the government into an ideological corner just months before a federal election. To thwart a legally compliant offer, which provided shareholders with a 60 per cent premium, would leave the government vulnerable to criticism that it had reneged on principle.[107] While the

[106] Allco Equity Partners subsequently changed its own constitution, mirroring that imposed on Qantas, by limiting foreign ownership in both absolute and aggregate terms, see Allco Equity Partners (Press Release, 6 March 2007).

[107] A view endorsed in some sections of the international business press, see Editorial, 'Qantas and the Markets', *Wall Street Journal* (New York), 23 March 2007 (online edition).

approach represented a logical extension of principle not to intervene in the operation of the market, the government claimed the consortium had acquiesced to additional restraints through a formal enforceable undertaking:

> The Minister for Transport and Regional Services and I have negotiated and received a legally enforceable Deed from APA. The Deed has been provided voluntarily by APA and does not involve any commitments from the Commonwealth. In the event of a possible breach, the Commonwealth will be able to have the Deed enforced. The Deed will apply until APA no longer has a controlling interest in Qantas under the *Corporations Act 2001* or has sold all, or substantially all, of its airline business.[108]

The undertaking was presented as the most detailed secured from a corporation in Australian history. In reality it was an exercise in political symbolism, totally devoid of substance.[109] The requirement to retain jobs, regional services and maintenance facilities were all subject to 'market conditions'. The restrictions only applied to the consortium and there was no mechanism to extend even symbolic political control to subsequent owners.[110]

Just as the government was neutralized, so too was the Federal Australian Labor Party. In its sole contribution to the debate, Labor promised to subject the document to extensive legal analysis, a promise that was not publicly followed through. Keen to demonstrate its pro-business credentials, the ALP was remarkably reticent about being seen to be too close to the union movement, which used the Qantas transaction to press its case for reform to labor relations laws.

The presentation of the consortium's strategy attracted more searching analysis from the Takeovers Panel, which ruled 'a number of

---

[108] Peter Costello (Treasurer) and Mark Vaile (Deputy Prime Minister and Minister for Transport and Regional Services) 'Qantas Airways Ltd' (Joint Press Release, 6 March 2007), available at <http://www.treasurer.gov.au/tsr/content/pressreleases/2007/009.asp>. Similarly, Costello promised to ensure tax base would be protected, see Katrina Nicholas and Leonore Taylor, 'Costello Puts Private Equity on Tax Alert', *Australian Financial Review* (Sydney), 10 April 2007, 1.

[109] See David Crowe, 'Promises Aplenty, but Hard to Enforce,' *Australian Financial Review* (Sydney), 7 March 2007, 11.

[110] See Laura Tingle, 'Political Nightmare in the Baggage Hold', *Australian Financial Review* (Sydney), 7 March 2007, 9.

statements in, and omissions from the bidders statement 'were sufficiently misleading to give rise to unacceptable circumstances.'[111] These related to Texas Pacific Group's ('TPG') track record in the airline industry. The carefully worded decision upheld a compliant from the Australian and International Pilots Association that the original bidders statement did not accurately reflect TPG's investment strategy. The bidder statement gave the impression that TPG's involvement was crucial to the resurgence of Continental and the exponential growth in the European low-cost carrier, Ryanair. It omitted to mention the speed with which TPG sold out its investment. The panel held:

> If the APA ownership consortium had no commitment from TPG to remain in the consortium while the consortium owns or controls Qantas, reference to TPG's experience in the airline industry had the potential to mislead unless it was clearly qualified by disclosure that TPG retains the ability to sell down its entire investment in APA at any time from the completion of the APA offer.[112]

What is surprising is that it took a union complaint to get this matter onto the agenda. With the opposition silent and the government hamstrung, adjudication passed to the market itself. A Melbourne-based fund manager controlling four per cent of Qantas attained celebrity status by rejecting the bid (on price not principle).[113] The rejection was sufficient to scupper any chance of compulsory purchase. With APA unable to gain sufficient support, the leveraging terms were renegotiated to enable the consortium gain majority shareholding of what would

---

[111] Takeovers Panel, 'Qantas Airways Limited — Panel Decision' (Press Release, 20 March 2007).
[112] Ibid.
[113] Katrina Nicholas, 'The Man Who Said No', *Australian Financial Review* (Sydney), 31 March 2007, 22–3 (Andrew Sissons, Managing Director of Balanced Asset Management, alleged that market pressure for the deal to proceed meant that his investment strategy, based on a three year value cycle was subjected to a 'continuous stream of deliberate misinformation': at 22. He also rejected accusations that he was merely looking for a higher price. 'Our game is relative, and theirs is absolute … We understand their rules, but we don't want to play by them': at 23). UBS Global Asset Management, which held six per cent of the airline also held out, without publicly declaring its hand (despite the fact that the parent investment banking arm of the business stood to gain AUS$40m in transaction fees); in the United States, public rejection rates are rising, particularly when management is retained, see Gretchen Morgensen, 'Just Say No to Lowball Buyout Offers', *New York Times* (New York), 20 May 2007 (online edition).

remain a publicly listed corporation. The covenants were so weak that one investment banker described them as non-existent. The debt was secured in stock rather than assets.[114] In effect, the banks offered one of the largest bridging finance deals ever seen, precisely the kind of transaction that has so worried the Federal Reserve in Washington.[115]

The revised strategy, disclosed to the stock exchange, indicated that AUS$4 billion would be returned to the new owners through a combination of earnings and increased debt. The disclosure made manifest the theoretical returns associated with the financial engineering, embarrassing both the government and just as significantly the banks providing the financing. Investment banking sources in Sydney suggest privately that proceeding with the deal at that stage was both a tactical and strategic mistake. The covenant-lite strategy sent an unmistakable message that risk management systems were predicated on maintaining access to underwriting assignments. More problematically, it served to fuel criticism. Media coverage turned hostile.[116] In addition, any remaining political capital was squandered. In such circumstances, it was inevitable that when the deal ran into trouble that no intervention would be forthcoming.

The financial stakes, the lauded political skills associated with Macquarie and the technical nature of the deadline breach gave the consortium an arguable case for proceeding. The hybrid nature of the Australian regulatory system, based on an admixture of rules and principles, gave flexibility to the Takeovers Panel to adopt a responsive reading of unacceptable circumstances. By rejecting the claim on literal grounds, the Takeovers Panel sent an unambiguous signal back to the

---

[114] See Malcolm Maiden, 'Bankers Are Being Very Brave', *Sydney Morning Herald* (Sydney), 13 April 2007, 19 (a 'global precedent for aggression in private equity bid funding'); see also Elizabeth Knight, 'It's the Mother of All Margin Loans', *Sydney Morning Herald* (Sydney), 13 April 2007, 19. It also demonstrated the growing importance of hybrid markets, which mirrors the 'stub equity' financing now introduced in the United States, see Dennis Berman, 'Unusual Buyout Offers a Piece to Shareholders', *Wall Street Journal* (New York), 27 April 2007, A1, A12.

[115] See above n 10 and accompanying text.

[116] See Scott Rochfort, 'Raiders to Gouge $4 b from Qantas', *Sydney Morning Herald* (Sydney), 13 April 2007, 1; Scott Rochfort, 'Qantas Raiders May Share Spoils', *Sydney Morning Herald* (Sydney), 13 April 2007, 19; Steve Creedy, 'APA to Rip $4bn out of Qantas', *The Australian* (Sydney), 13 April 2007, 19; Kate Askew and Scott Rochfort, 'Bigger Debt Could Undo Qantas', *Sydney Morning Herald* (Sydney), 14 April 2007, 39.

business community.[117] The Australian Securities and Investments Commission reinforced this.

Amid speculation that it was targeting British Airways, APA withdrew and pulled down its website. Macquarie released operating profits of AUS$1.5 billion that the chief executive argued provided 'a very convincing measure of our reputation'.[118] The Qantas failure was blamed on tactical misjudgment by a 'number of key investors', partial recognition that the sole focus on Samuel Heyman's hedge fund operation is misplaced. Moss sought, however, to apportion blame to the activities of hedge funds more generally, which had been encouraged to enter the share registry precisely because they were likely to sell.[119] A second embarrassment, involving the failure to gain control of Alinta was also blithely cast aside.[120] As the Bank changed 'from being an Australian institution growing internationally to a global institution headquartered in Australia … our business is way bigger than two transactions in one country.'[121]

With significant opportunities occurring offshore, there is a reduced imperative to foster domestic relations or exercise restraint. The insouciance suggests that Macquarie growth model centres solely on financial returns. It is undoubtedly successful but the very complexity makes it exceptionally vulnerable to changes in investor risk appetite, as the sharp fall in its share value in July attests.

III ALIGNING AND CONFLICTING INTERESTS

Market exit reduces public oversight. It allows the de-listed corporation to bypass the elaborate corporate governance, financial reporting and disclosure obligations imposed after the collapse of Enron and other corporations in both the United States and here in Australia. The transformative potential (and risk) occurs at a number of levels. As noted above these include, but are not limited to: the impact of entreaties on the

---

[117] *In the Matter of Qantas 02R* (2007) ATP 07, 2.

[118] Eric Johnston, 'Global MacBank Roars to Record $1.5bn Profit', *Australian Financial Review* (Sydney), 16 May 2007, 1 (58 per cent of total income was attributed to the takeover boom, with the profits rising by 78 per cent).

[119] See Danny John, Lisa Murray and Kate Askew, 'Up, Up and Away', *Sydney Morning Herald* (Sydney), 19–20 May 2007, 41, 45.

[120] See below n 143–4 and accompanying text.

[121] Johnston, above n 120 (reporting that Macquarie carried out 240 transactions valued at AUS$160 billion globally).

governance of target corporations; the efficacy of fiduciary duty, conflicts of interest management systems and codes of conduct as restraining forces on financial intermediary self-dealing; and the danger of market manipulation and wider macroeconomic instability.[122] These challenges pertain irrespective of whether the regulatory regime adopted is primarily mandatory (US), enabling (UK), or combined (Australia). As the debate over private equity intensifies, so to does the contestation over the efficacy of control mechanisms at each node in the overarching matrix.[123] The discussion below centres primarily on the Australian legal and regulatory framework in the aftermath of the Qantas failure.

(A) *The Limits of Directorial Discretion*

For the senior management of the corporation and its professional advisors the pre-contract stage is the most problematic. How each node manages the potential conflict with existing shareholders or their delegated authority, the board of directors, over what constitutes the long-term interests of the corporation determines the integrity of the wider corporate governance architecture. Insofar as the strategic decisions are taken in good faith and with reasonable diligence, the business judgment default applies.[124] Directors have a statutory obligation to disclose any potential conflict of interest.[125] They also have a common law obligation to 'identify clearly the perceived conflict and to suggest a course of action to limit the possible damage.'[126] The boom in LBOs involving entrenched management makes this process exceptionally difficult to manage.[127]

The pre-eminent obligation on the board is to ascertain whether the sale of the corporation is in its best interest. This is determined by reference to both procedural fairness and price. Guidance recently

---

[122] See above n 5–10 and accompanying text.
[123] For a measured summation of the contours of this battle, see Editorial, 'Barbarians Back in the Dock, *Economist* (London), 1 March 2007, 10 (arguing that while many of the claims made against private equity, particularly asset stripping are easily refuted the fees charged for asset management are largely warranted).
[124] *Corporations Act 2001* (Cth) ss 201, 180(1), 180(2) respectively.
[125] *Corporations Act 2001* (Cth) s 191.
[126] *Fitzsimons v R* (1997) 15 ACLC 666, 668.
[127] The failure to manage these conflicts has sparked open criticism from Don Argus, Chairman of BHP Billiton, see Andrew Cornell, 'Boards Out of Step with Takeover Frenzy: Argus', *Australian Financial Review* (Sydney), 15 May 2007, 1.

provided by the Takeovers Panel is designed to articulate what both mean in practice. Participating insiders should disclose the proposed buy-out approach to the board prior to the provision of non-public information.[128] In addition, this information should only be disclosed with board consent.[129] On immediate notification of a potential bid, the board is advised to establish protocols to distance the corporation from the conflicted managers.

While noting the absence of a legal requirement to launch a full auction, the Takeovers Panel argues that financial information should be made freely available to trigger (at the very least) a rival bid. Failure by a target company board to do so would, it is suggested, be viewed with suspicion.[130] Both the draft and final versions of the guidance ostensibly reject a prescriptive approach. They resolve potential incommensurability problems by requiring significantly more robust systems of control.[131] It remains to be seen, however, whether the guidance will change corporate practice. Significantly, while the chief executive of the utility company Alinta resigned because of the potential conflict, his counterpart in Qantas remained in place, oblivious (or dismissive) of the Takeovers Panel deliberations. While the Qantas board designed its own protocols in advance of the draft guidance, it is certainly arguable that the bid would have had much more credibility if

---

[128] Takeovers Panel, 'Insider Participation in Control Transactions' *Draft Guidance Note No 19* (2007) [12]; Takeovers Panel, *Guidance Note No 19*, above n 6, [19];

[129] Takeovers Panel, *Guidance Note No 19*, above n 6, [19(b)(i)].

[130] Ibid [25].

[131] Takeovers Panel, *Issue Paper No 19*, above n 6, [18]. The protocols include determination that control over the bid rests with non-executive directors through an Independent Board Committee ('IBC'). IBC representatives should attend all meetings between participating management and bidder, ensure all communication between the bidder and participating management goes through IBC, consider whether to require participating management to (temporarily) resign from executive or board positions and secure confirmation from participating management that no non-public information has been disclosed. The final version of the guidance makes clear that these were illustrative rather than a de facto standard, see Takeovers Panel, *Insider Participation in Control Transactions* (Public Consultation Response Statement, 7 June 2007) 5. See also Takeovers Panel, *Guidance Note No 19*, above n 6, [18–19] (highlighting the fact that participating insiders should only 'in appropriate circumstances, stand aside or resign from their management/board positions in order to pursue the proposed bid (recognising that certain legal and equitable obligations, including with respect to confidentiality and use of information may continue notwithstanding such resignation and subject to the board's ongoing right to require assistance from those insiders during any leave of absence': at [19(b)(ii)])

Geoff Dixon and the other conflicted managers had considering stepping aside once the Takeovers Panel had intervened. Although there was no legal requirement for this, it would have demonstrated a commitment to the bid. Moreover, such signaling may have made investors much more wary of holding onto Qantas stock, thus positioning APA as the only credible alternative.

(B) *Investing in Conflict*

The transformation of investment banks from passive provider of capital or advisory services to active fund managers represents a significant recalibration of the integrated banking model.[132] The surge in Macquarie Bank's profits was inextricably linked to its global private equity operation. Goldman Sachs recently announced plans to launch a US$19 billion superfund. Merrill Lynch Global Private Equity Partners already controls one of the top ten private equity funds. Both saw overall profits increase dramatically last year.[133] Merrill Lynch's unit reported a 300 per cent increase in profits for the second quarter in 2006, in part because of the profits accruing from the Hertz 'flip back'.[134] The contribution these units make to group profits demonstrates their critical importance. One Capital Partners, the private equity arm of J P Morgan, contributed US$550 million of the US$3.5 billion profit announced in 2006.

The situation is exacerbated by debate over at what precise stage investment banks owe fiduciary duties to their clients and whether these restrictions can or should be contracted out by sidebar arrangements.[135] Recent market practice calls into question the limits of internally policed

---

[132] Innovation, however, does not guarantee success, as the failure of the Qantas bid demonstrates, see Jennifer Hewett and Glenda Korporaal, 'It's Red Faces at MacBank', *The Australian* (Sydney), 8 May 2007, 27.

[133] Heidi Moore, 'Revenue Gap Widens', *Financial News Online*, 26 February 2007 (Goldman profits increased by 52 per cent; Merrill Lynch 37 per cent).

[134] On the Hertz deal, see above n 57 and accompanying text.

[135] See Andrew Tuch, 'Investment Banks as Fiduciaries: Implications for Conflicts of Interests' (2005) 29 *Melbourne University Law Review* 478. The Federal Court denied jurisdictional authority on the grounds that contractual terms can exclude fiduciary duty, see *ASIC v Citigroup* NSD 651 of 2006 ((28 June 2007) [266-281] ('Whether a party is subject to fiduciary obligations, and the scope of any fiduciary obligations, is to be determined by construing the contract as a whole in the light of the surrounding circumstances known to the parties and the purpose and object of the transaction: at [281]).

and validated codes of conduct in dealing with this problem.[136] Macquarie Bank, for example, found itself in an overt conflict in the machinations surrounding a MBO at Alinta. When the potential conflict was initially reported, both Macquarie and Alinta proclaimed that their actions were within legal boundaries. The Bank sought to clarify its position but not before it had been very publicly sacked and the chief executive officer resigned.[137]

A critical part of the regulatory infrastructure to curtail insider trading and market manipulation among financial intermediaries has been to foster the creation and maintenance of 'Chinese Walls'. These impose a structural separation between corporate 'insiders' (for example, those advising external corporations on mergers and acquisitions or running private equity funds) and 'outsiders' (for example, those trading on behalf of clients or the bank's own account on the basis of publicly available information).[138]

Within the private equity context, the rise in proprietary trading raises significant questions about the quality of the oversight process, in particular whether informational barriers prevent the trading of non-public information. While regulators in Australia have been careful not to become embroiled in deal specific private equity controversies, there can be no mistaking unease. This concern was particularly apparent in

---

[136] Whether compliance is an adequate framework is highly questionable. For a spectacular case involving its failure, see Randall Smith, Kara Scannell and Paul Davies, 'A Brazen Insider Scheme Revealed', *Wall Street Journal* (New York), 2 March 2007, C1 (reporting an insider trading case involving a lawyer working for the compliance department of Morgan Stanley relaying information to an analyst at UBS who, in turn, forwarded it to a hedge fund manager at Bear Stearns).

[137] 'Alinta Boss Quits over Management Buy-Out Row', *Australian Financial Review* (Sydney), 12 January 2007, 1. This is a problem that crosses jurisdictions. In the United Kingdom, for example, Goldman Sachs was involved in the buy-out of British Airports Authority just months after providing its board with strategic advice on how to rebuff such an approach. In the event, a subsequent bid by Macquarie for control of Alinta was rebuffed, see Brett Clegg, 'No Patsies around this Time to Subsidise the Fee Factory', *Australian Financial Review* (Sydney), 31 March 2007, 12–13.

[138] The leading authority in the United Kingdom accepts that while Chinese Walls can have a place, unless it can be demonstrated that controls work, there is an assumption that information will travel within the firm, see *Prince Jefri Bolkiah v KPMG* [1999] 2 WLR 215, 235 (Millett LJ); in Australia the regulator faced an embarrassing setback when a high profile case against Citigroup was dismissed on the facts pleaded. The court ruled, however, that on the same facts 'Chinese Walls may not be as solid as the name implied, see *ASIC v Citigroup*, NSD651 of 2006 (28 June 2007) [604].

draft guidelines offered by the Takeovers Panel over the integrity questions posed by the integrated investment banking model:

> The Panel does not intend to impede normal business transaction or relationships, which are not relevant in the context of a control transaction. However, the Panel will be concerned if professional and other advisors who, by reason of their previous association with a target company have come into possession on non-public information seek to become part of an actual or potential bidding vehicle or bidding consortium.[139]

The actions of both the senior management and Macquarie in the Alinta case, for example, would appear to trigger regulatory concern identified above.

IV THE DYNAMICS OF REGULATORY REFORM

Mapping how ideational discourse is calibrated requires detailed analysis across a number of key stages, including control over the agenda, implementation and evaluation.[140] How are different constituencies organising and mobilising themselves. How is change in one jurisdiction experienced elsewhere? How are pressures to reform regulatory practice transmitted from one jurisdiction to another, and by which methods? What is the mediating impact of intervening variables, such as national structures, institutions, political preferences and societal interests? Within the scope of this chapter it is only possible to sketch the outlines of this process, in large part because we are at such an early stage in the private equity cycle.

The preference for self-regulation is particularly evident in the private equity firmament. What has also become clear is that the industry has become increasingly cognisant of the need to enlist support or at least

[139] Takeovers Panel, *Issue Paper No 19*, above n 6, [11]. The final version resiles from this absolute position, see Takeovers Panel, *Guidance Note No 19*, above n 6. ('An entity which has such information through its role as an adviser to the target will not be regarded as an "insider" for the purposes of this Guidance Note where it is acting in a different capacity in relation to a bid or potential bid, if there are appropriate and effective Chinese walls in place and the significant non-public information is quarantined from that part of the entity which is so acting': at [11].)

[140] Tony Porter and Karsten Ronit, 'Self-Regulation as Policy Process: The Multiple and Criss-Crossing Stages of Private Rule Making' (2006) 39 *Policy Sciences* 41.

nullify external criticism.[141] The creation of a Private Equity Council in Washington on 26 December 2006 by the premier funds — including Blackstone, KKR and Carlyle — is an indication of just how important it has become to pro-actively manage the policy process, even in the United States.[142] Signaling over tax issues, in particular whether 'carried interest' represented capital gains has spooked the industry. Private equity spokespersons gave a particularly desultory performance at the Westminster Treasury Select Committee recently. Their performance was not helped by the quip by a senior practitioner that cleaners pay more tax.[143] Likewise, in the United States, former Treasury Secretary Robert Rubin, now Vice Chairman at Citigroup, has maintained that the case exists to look at the private equity tax base. Private equity funds have also sought to influence the wider debate through a series of funded research initiatives and the establishment of extensive lobbying networks.[144]

A comparison of the debate in London and New York highlights differential political priorities and ideational referents. In the United States, the debate is still carried out at a rather technical level in which wider socio-political considerations are deemed irrelevant. The takeover of failing car company Chrysler illustrates differences in attitude between New York and London. As noted above, it is indicative of private equity's growth that it secured control with relatively little opposition. Moreover, the restructuring, redesign and re-engineering however brutal, is seen as a necessary corrective to the problems of public market bureaucracy. 'There is a reason why Toyota is the number

---

[141] Lionel Barber and Peter Smith, 'Permira Accepts Need to Be More Open', *Financial Times* (London), 22 February 2007, 1.

[142] Carlyle Group, 'Private Equity Council is Formed to Provide Research and Information' (Press Release, 26 December 2006) available at <http://www.carlyle.com/eng/news/l5-news3673.html>; see also Lowenstein, above n 14 and accompanying text.

[143] 'Taken to the Cleaners', *The Economist* (London), 12 June 2007 (online edition). As The Economist notes, however, the danger is that changing tax structures will simply encourage private equity firms to relocate to more favorable regimes,

[144] Private equity funds announced a two million dollar research project at the World Economic Forum in Davos. It will be coordinated by the Dean of Columbia Business School, Glenn Hubbard. Here in Australia, the Australian Private Equity and Venture Capital Association has retained professional consultants to provide research demonstrating added value. Its submission to the Senate Inquiry prominently displays a favourable quote from the FSA on the utility of private equity on its cover sheet.

one car company in the United States at least in terms of profitability', says John Barber of Citigroup Private Equity in New York.[145]

> It is because for 35 years the unions thought short-term about how many people they thought should be employed, what they should make, and the work rules, and for that reason they have driven Detroit into ruin. When private equity firms come in they are making companies which are going to be much more competitive long term in the global economy than the companies they takeover.[146]

This rationale has been widely accepted within political discourse in the United States. Notwithstanding the House Financial Services Committee Hearings, with the potential exception of tax, change is much more likely to emanate from the global export of initiatives now under way in the United Kingdom, which offers a mediation between European rejection and American embrace.

Oppositional rhetoric in the United Kingdom has not quite descended to that heard in Germany, where private equity funds have been castigated as 'locusts', but it has come close. The leading private equity fund Permira has been subject to a virulent campaign of abuse. This included parading a camel outside a church service attended by its chief executive, Damon Buffini.[147] Substantial job losses at high-profile acquisitions in the United Kingdom such as at the Automobile Association, National Car Parks and Birds Eye, have galvanised union opposition, according to the General Secretary of the Trades Union Congress ('TUC'), the peak movement for organised labor.

> In all of those cases there have been issues of union recognition or job cuts in ways that are seen as simply not acceptable. The ultimate owners are not seen as people who can be engaged or properly held accountable for the decisions that they are ultimately responsible for.[148]

---

[145] Interview with John Barber, above n 11.

[146] Ibid.

[147] The insult relates to a Bible parable that it is easier for a camel to pass through the eye of a needle than get into heaven, see 'Damon Buffini', *Profile, Money Week* (London), 23 February 2007, 40.

[148] Interview with Brendan Barber (London, 23 March 2007).

As with Australia, union membership and influence went into precipitous decline in the United Kingdom. Paradoxically, private equity has reversed that process. The TUC has now emerged as potentially the most effective alternative voice within the European Union. It has done so not by strike action but by embarrassing both the government and the private equity movement through adopting the language of governance and transparency.

The bombastic way in which private equity has presented leverage as tax efficient has undermined somewhat the credibility of its claims of responsible corporate citizenship. By raising the issue now, the unions raise an inevitable corollary: why hasn't New Labour stepped in? The departure of Tony Blair has forced contenders for the New Labour leadership to attend much more closely to underpinning ideological principles. The political changing of the guard thus provided a time-limited opportunity for the unions to influence the direction of policy. In a recent speech, Barber likened the private equity funds to 'amoral asset strippers after a quick buck.'[149]

Despite the rhetoric, Barber has also recognised that engagement rather than confrontation is more likely to generate results. The key leverage device has been the 300 billion under asset management with trades union pension funds. 'We have in the TUC a network of a 1000 trustees and we are working on a briefing note for that network. It will not be saying just pull out of private equity. That would be naïve.'[150] Instead the unions are working on a draft set of protocols governing how the pension funds intermediate with private equity.

Paradoxically, the global private equity boom has been driven by the injection of capital from the very source that the reinvigorated corporate governance paradigm posits as exercising the necessary control over managerial excess. Across the capital markets public pension funds have made a strategic decision to invest heavily in private equity but done little to agitate for stronger contractual covenants.[151] Just as

---

[149] Christopher Adams and Peter Smith, 'TUC Chief Attacks Private Equity Industry', *Financial Times* (London), 20 February 2007, 1. Barber further claimed the industry was 'pretty much allowed to operate with impunity': ibid.

[150] Ibid.

[151] Alan Murray, 'How Labor's Pension Funds Are Playing Private Equity Two Ways', *Wall Street Journal* (New York), 28 February 2007, A10 (quoting research that 22 per cent of all new money raised for private equity funding in the United States in 2005 derived from labor superannuation schemes). Sometimes the dialectic between disclosure and privacy can pertain within the one investor. Contrast, for example, the shareholder

problematically, notwithstanding claims of ethical investment, there is reduced emphasis on potential costs to current members.[152] According to the TUC General Secretary, the aim in starting a dialogue with the trustees is strategic: 'It will be asking them to encourage them to consider the kinds of businesses and the approach to business that private equity takes.'[153] The first step is the development of key protocols that are capable of monitoring and enforcement..

> The challenge is for us to identify in more precise terms than we have done to date what are the principles that we expect the private sector to live up to. We have to think through how that can be articulated. We have to think through both the principles and some mechanism of securing compliance, otherwise the principles themselves can be pretty vacuous.[154]

Having re-found its voice, the trades union movement is unlikely to accept entreaties by either the industry or Treasury to leave the governance of private equity to a technocratic elite. In so doing it may be providing a scarce public good. In this regard, the defensive and narrow approach adopted by the Australian superannuation industry to the Senate Inquiry is not only shortsighted. It is also arguably an abdication of responsibility. The creative destruction of private equity forces may reduce the degree of public oversight. It also enhances the degree to which private equity owners – including the pension funds – must take responsibility for stakeholders whose voice has been silenced.

CONCLUSION

As this chapter has demonstrated, the expansion of private equity poses a series of interconnected risks to both the corporate governance paradigm and to the regulation of the markets. Whether individual corporations

---

activism displayed by California Public Employees Pension Fund within the corporate governance arena generally with its resistance to the release of information relating to its own private equity investments: see Hurdle, above n 40, 255–7.

[152] A case in point is the Qantas superannuation fund, which declined to mandate the voting interests of the three investment managers with delegated authority over its stake in the airline: see 'Qantas Staff Fund Won't OK Takeover', *The Australian* (Sydney), 8 February 2007, 23.

[153] Interview with Brendan Barber, above n 148.

[154] Ibid.

undertake novel financing arrangements or acquiesce to excessive debt levels are, of course risk appetite decisions best left to the business itself. In that regard, for example, the federal government's decision to allow the Qantas sale to proceed, given that it did not breach legal restraints, was both rational and, in the circumstances, justified. What the takeover boom has also demonstrated, however, is the paucity of guidance to ensure that appropriate checks and balances are in place to limit managerial incentives to de-list.

The policy advice provided by the Takeovers Panel here in Australia is a credible attempt to close down some of the loopholes. It also highlights the critical importance of linking abstract principles to granular articulations of what these principles mean in practice. This goes some way to ensuring that potential directorial abuses are minimised and that shareholder interests will be protected. This does not solve, however, the wider question of the impact of private equity on the wider corporate governance paradigm. Restoring faith in market forces requires participants to pay much greater attention to the interwoven relationship between the market, legal restraints and the political process. Public listing provides a mechanism to reinforce the softer conceptions of governance associated with stakeholder rights, if only because there are opportunities to hold the company to account. An expansion of private equity may also lead to an erosion of conceptions of corporate social responsibility not least because success is measured on strictly financial terms.

A more difficult regulatory challenge is how to link acceptance of market risk with the development of more sophisticated mechanisms to ensure it is carried out within acceptable levels of probity. The transaction fees involved certainly raise at least the prospect that internal restraining mechanisms may not be powerful enough to ensure effective due diligence. This problem pertains throughout the investment cycle, from provision of strategic advice to rebuff or acquiesce in a leverage buy-out, through to the IPO allocation when private equity seeks to dispose of the asset.

The increasing involvement of investment banking in the management of private equity funds reinforces the potential problems. The difficulties are magnified precisely because regulators have been placed increasingly on the defensive over the limits of regulatory authority. Just as private equity providers have only themselves to blame for poor media management of their personal lives, strategic miscalculations on the part of the regulator can lead to seepage of media and political support.

Private equity does offer many benefits, not least the possibility of energising tired corporate models. It also poses substantial risks. How it should be regulated is a matter of profound public concern. What is required is sustained engagement between regulators, the professions and market participants. This debate is a vital component of the due diligence necessary to moderate the forces of creative destruction unleashed across global financial markets.

Chapter 12

Institutions, Integrity Systems and Market Actors

Seumas Miller

As is well-known, the collapse of the US corporation, Enron, had a devastating effect on shareholders and employees.[1] And in its wake came the revelations of a litany of unethical practices, including conflicts of interests, such as that of CFO Andrew Fastow, auditing failures, corrupt (if not necessarily unlawful) practices, such as the creation of so-called Special Purpose Entities calculated to mislead shareholders in relation to actual performance, and so on.[2] Moreover, the Enron collapse was only one among a number of recent corporate corruption scandals, including WorldCom and the giant accounting firm Arthur Andersen and, in the Australian context, One.Tel and HIH. The HIH Royal Commission found that, as the company lurched towards collapse, it engaged in corporate excesses involving travel, entertainment, charitable donations, and executive gifts.[3] These excesses stripped over AUS$32 million out of its assets. Staff were given gold watches, and a tip of AUS$700 was paid at

---

[1] Peter C Fusaro and Ross M Miller, *What Went Wrong at Enron* (2002).

[2] See Seumas Miller, 'Corruption' in *Stanford Encyclopedia of Philosophy* (Winter, 2005), for an account of corruption and its divergence (at times) from illegality.

[3] 'HIH Regulator Deceived', *The Australian* (Sydney), 24 January 2003; Farid Varess, 'The Buck Will Stop at the Board? An Examination of Directors' (and Others) Duties in Light of the HIH Collapse' (2002) 16 *Commercial Law Quarterly* 12.

a dinner attended by the CEO and HIH executives at Port Douglas.[4] Just weeks before the collapse, AUS$180 000 was paid to a Melbourne football club which was in some financial difficulty. The HIH collapse has sparked a lively debate into the ethical responsibility of company directors and the role of corporate regulators. The Australian Prudential Regulation Authority, among other corporate regulators, claims that it was profoundly misled by HIH, and thus it, in turn, had inadvertently misled the government about the seriousness of the crisis facing the company. The federal opposition has questioned how the collapse was not anticipated by the regulatory authorities, given the amount of material showing that HIH was in trouble up to two years before the collapse.

The corporate collapses and corruption scandals of the late 1990s and early 2000s in the US, Australia and elsewhere appear to be part of a recurring cycle.[5] Recall the corporate scandals of the 1980s in the US and elsewhere.[6] That period was notable for a stock market crash, a junk bond collapse, the bankruptcy of numerous highly-leveraged clients, the prevalence of the unlawful practice of insider trading, and the fining and imprisonment of the likes of Michael Milken and Ivan Boesky. Milken paid fines in excess of US$600 million, Boesky over US$100 million.[7] Self-evidently, these corporate collapses were extraordinarily damaging economically, but apparently they might also be ongoing; perhaps the question is not whether there will be a recurrence, but rather when it will take place. If so, then these corporate collapses and corruption scandals might not be aberrations, but rather symptoms of underlying systemic deficiencies in corporate law and regulation, and perhaps of structural deficiencies in the corporate sector itself, notably in the financial services area. Perhaps, therefore, it is worth trying to take a bird's-eye view of the contours of the macro-institutional setting in which particular corporate collapses and corruption scandals have taken place, and doing so from an ethical perspective.

In this chapter I focus on the ethical, as opposed to legal, financial or political, dimensions of this problem and, in particular, on

---

[4] Port Douglas is an expensive tropical resort some 1500 miles away from Sydney, where HIH was based.

[5] Frank Clarke, Graeme Dean and Kyle Oliver argue as much in *Corporate Collapse: Accounting, Regulatory and Ethical Failure* (revised ed, 2003).

[6] See, eg, Trevor Sykes, *The Bold Riders* (1984).

[7] James B Stewart, *Den of Thieves* (1992) 20.

ethics at the macro-institutional level. In the first section I sketch a normative theoretical account of social institutions; in the second section I outline some of the key features of what I will refer to as an integrity system for institutions; and in the third and final section, in light of my accounts of social institutions and integrity systems, I offer some speculations concerning some of the ethical problems confronting the corporate sector in general, and the financial services sector in particular.

In this chapter I argue that the basic normative question that needs to be asked of a business corporation, or financial market, is the same as for any other social institution, namely: What collective good(s) does it exist to provide? I further argue that, normatively speaking, social institutions including business corporations and markets exist for ultimate — and not merely proximate — purposes or ends, namely, to provide collective goods, for example material goods, the coordination of buyers and sellers of material goods. Here Adam Smith's invisible hand mechanism is salient. The outcome of the workings of the invisible hand is the ultimate purpose of this institutional mechanism: the pursuit of financial gain, the proximate end. Finally, I argue that in the case of the financial services sector, in particular, the prior fundamental ethical question as to the ultimate institutional ends of this sector remains unanswered. Yet without an answer to this question, an integrity system for the financial services sector — and a regulatory system insofar as it is concerned with institutional (ethical) integrity, as it surely must be — is quite literally without one of its basic purposes: it does not know what ethical ends it is seeking to embed in its target institution, ie in the financial services sector.

But we are getting ahead of ourselves. Our first task is the provision of an account of social institutions. In fact, the term, 'social institution', is somewhat unclear both in ordinary language and in the philosophical literature. However, contemporary sociology is rather more consistent in its use of the term. Typically, contemporary sociologists use the term to refer to complex social forms that reproduce themselves, such as governments, universities, hospitals, business corporations, markets and legal systems. A typical definition is that proffered by Jonathan Turner: 'a complex of positions, roles, norms and values lodged in particular types of social structures and organising relatively stable patterns of human activity with respect to fundamental problems in producing life-sustaining viable societal structures within a given environment'.[8] Again, Anthony Giddens says: 'Institutions by definition are the more enduring features of social life'.[9] He goes on to list as institutional orders modes of discourse, political institutions, economic institutions and legal institutions.[10]

At this point it might be asked why a theory of social institutions in general, and a theory of market institutions in particular, has, or ought to have, any philosophical interest; why not simply leave such theorising to the sociologists and/or the economists? One important reason stems from the normative concerns of philosophers: concerns about what ought to be, as opposed to what is, or has been. Here I note that what ought to be is not a fanciful notion, but rather a partial extrapolation from what is and, ultimately, a statement of what realistically could be. Philosophers, such as John Rawls,[11] have developed elaborate normative theories concerning the principles of justice that ought to govern social institutions. Famously, Rawls argued that social institutions ought to be structured in such a way as to benefit the least well-off. Advocates of free market economics have argued that this is just what deregulated markets do, and have pointed to the freeing up of the Chinese and Indian economies as evidence of this. Whatever the truth of such claims, my point is that even the most staunch free-marketeers have normative or ethical commitments: they are committed, in particular, to the ethical value of the social institution of private property, the moral force of contractual obligations, and the human right of individual freedom. Viewed from this perspective, the disputes between free-marketeers and social democrats are normative disputes concerning, for example, the circumstances under which considerations of social justice or overall social benefit (the public good) ought to limit the freedom of individuals or organisations to contract or engage in economic transactions. Consider in this connection the arguments in favour of and against the recent global surge in private equity mergers and acquisitions. Note also that in the contemporary setting of a rapidly globalising world, including the development of a wide range of global institutions, the parameters of social justice concerns and of the public good can no longer simply be taken to be national boundaries. The

---

[8] Jonathan Turner, *The Institutional Order* (1997) 6.

[9] Anthony Giddens, *Constitution of Society: Outline of the Theory of Structuration* (1984) 31.

[10] Ibid.

[11] John Rawls, *Theory of Justice* (1972).

public good of global institutions, such as the global economic and financial systems, includes the well-being of those living in the impoverished nations of the world.[12]

In addition to normative theorising in relation to principles of distributive justice and the like at the macro-institutional level, philosophers in the area of business ethics have addressed specific ethical failures, such as bribery, conflicts of interest, and so on. Remarkably, most of this normative theorising, including by Rawls, has been done in the absence of a developed (general) theory of the nature and point of the very entities (social institutions) to which the principles of justice in question are supposed to apply, and, in particular, in the absence of developed theories (special theories) of the nature and point of business corporations, and financial and other markets.[13] (I take it that advocates of corporate social responsibility are not offering a worked out normative theory, so much as giving expression to (doubtless, reasonable) ethical concerns.[14]) Surely the adequacy of one's normative account of the justice or otherwise, of any given social institution, or system of social institutions, will depend at least in part on the nature and point of that social institution or system. Moreover, such theorising is highly germane even to specific ethical questions in business or finance ethics. For example, it is difficult to determine whether or not some alleged conflict of interest is ethically acceptable or

---

[12] For an account of global economic justice in sympathy with the kind of view being propounded in this chapter, see Joseph Stiglitz, *Globalisation and Its Discontents* (2002).

[13] Rawls' theory principally applies to a set of institutions that comprise a society. However, there are transnational institutions. Moreover, it may be that his principles of justice are acceptable at the level of a set of societal institutions but not (say) at the level of a type of social institution, eg the university. My concern in this chapter is principally with the normative theory of types of social institution and, specifically, with market institutions.

[14] Nor is so-called 'stakeholder theory' a theory in the required sense; rather it first identifies an indeterminate set of groups with financial interests in, or who otherwise might be affected by, corporations, eg shareholders, employees, customers, etc. Second, it assumes that such 'stakeholders' ought, to some extent, or in some respect, have their interests taken into account in decision-making by, or in relation to, the corporation; ie, stakeholder 'theory' gestures at an indeterminate set of moral claims that 'stakeholders' might make in relation to corporations. However, such an indeterminate list and associated vague moral claims do not qualify as a theory; at best they constitute raw data that itself stands in need of normative theorising. Certainly, 'stakeholder theory' is no substitute for a normative theory of the nature and point of the corporation. For an account of stakeholder theory, see Kenneth E Goodpaster, 'Business Ethics and Stakeholder Analysis' (1991) 1 *Business Ethics Quarterly* 53.

not, independent of a normative theoretical account of the nature and point of the relevant social institutions and/or of their constitutive institutional roles. An auditor auditing a company's accounts has a conflict of interest if the auditor has shares in the company he or she is auditing; but this would not necessarily be so for a plumber contracted to unblock the company's drains and who also happens to hold shares in the company. How so? To answer this question the nature and point of the institutional role of the auditor in the context of the corporate sector needs to be specified.

I SOCIAL INSTITUTIONS

Social institutions need to be distinguished from less complex social forms such as conventions, social norms, roles and rituals. The latter are among the constitutive elements of institutions.[15] Social institutions also need to be distinguished from more complex and more complete social entities, such as societies, polities or cultures, of which any given institution is typically a constitutive element. A society or polity, for example, is more complete than an institution since a society — at least as traditionally understood — is more or less self-sufficient in terms of human resources, whereas an institution is not. Thus, arguably, for an entity to be a society it must sexually reproduce its membership, have its own language and educational system, provide for itself economically and — at least in principle — be politically independent.

Social institutions are often organisations. Moreover, many institutions are *systems* of organisations. For example, capitalism is a particular kind of economic institution, and in modern times capitalism consists in large part in specific organisational forms — including multinational corporations — organised into a system. Further, some institutions are *meta-institutions*: they are institutions (organisations) that organise other institutions (including systems of organisations). For example, governments are meta-institutions. The institutional end or function of a government consists in large part in organising other institutions (both individually and collectively); thus governments regulate and coordinate economic systems largely by way of (enforceable) legislation. Note that in the modern world many global

---

[15] The following teleological model of social institutions is elaborated in more detail in Seumas Miller, *Social Action: A Teleological Account* (2001). See also Seumas Miller, 'Social Institutions' in *Stanford Encylopedia of Philosophy* (Winter, 2006).

social institutions transcend in various respects the boundaries and jurisdictional and/or enforcement reach of the meta-institutions, for example governments, that regulate and coordinate their activities. Consider here the jurisdictional problems of holding Union Carbide to account in respect of the Bhopal Gas Disaster of 1984 in which over 20000 nearby slum-dwellers lost their lives and over 100000 suffered permanent, severe ill-health as a consequence of inadequate safety measures at Union Carbide's plant.[16]

Having informally marked-off social institutions from other social forms, let us turn to a consideration of some general properties of social institutions. Here there are four salient properties, namely, function, structure, culture and sanctions.

Roughly speaking, an institution that is an organisation or system of organisations consists of an embodied (occupied by human persons) structure of differentiated roles. These roles are defined in terms of tasks and rules regulating the performance of those tasks. Moreover, there is a degree of interdependence between these roles, such that the performance of the constitutive tasks of one role cannot be undertaken, or cannot be undertaken except with great difficulty, unless the tasks constitutive of some other role or roles in the structure have been undertaken or are being undertaken. Further, these roles are often related to one another hierarchically, and hence involve different levels of status and degrees of authority. Importantly, these roles are related to one another, in part in virtue of their contribution to (respectively) the *end(s)* or *function(s)* of the institution; and the realisation of these ends or functions normally involves interaction between the institutional actors in question and external actors. These ends or functions are diverse. An overarching end of the criminal justice system, for example, is the administration of justice, and a particular end of the professional role of auditor is the provision of true and fair financial records.[17]

---

[16] Amnesty International, *Clouds of Injustice: Bhopal Disaster 20 Years On* (2004). While Bhopal was a case of negligence rather than intent to do harm, in terms of actual loss of life and damage to health this was a much worse disaster than 9/11, eg 3000 died in the attack on the Twin Towers. However, the response to the Bhopal disaster on the part of US authorities, in particular, was far from adequate.

[17] This claim might be regarded as controversial. However, normatively speaking, it is difficult to see what the end of auditing could be, if not to provide a true and fair record: see, eg, Tom Campbell, 'True and Fair to Whom: A Philosophical Approach to Auditing' in Tom Campbell and Keith Houghton (eds), *Ethics and Auditing* (2005) ch 5. At any rate, if this is rejected as the normatively appropriate end or purpose of auditing, then, let

The constitutive roles of an institution and their relations to one another can be referred to as the *structure* of the institution. Institutions in this sense are dynamic, evolving entities; as such, they have a history, the diachronic structure of a narrative, and (usually) a partially open-ended future. Moreover, institutions interact with one another, competitively (eg competing firms in the same industry), cooperatively (eg police organisations, law courts and prisons), and, in some cases, by virtue of a relationship of authority (eg business firms and law courts). In some instances, institutions need to be structured so as have a degree of independence in the context of interaction, for example, law courts and corporations. Inevitably, interaction brings with it relationships of influence, if not power, and not simply one-way relations from the formal institutional authority, for example law courts, to the formal institutional subordinate, for example a business corporation.[18]

Aside from the formal and usually explicitly stated, or defined, tasks and rules, there is an important implicit and informal dimension of an institution, roughly describable as institutional *culture*. This notion comprises the informal attitudes, values, norms, and ethos or 'spirit' that pervades an institution. Culture in this sense determines much of the activity of the members of that institution, or at least the manner in which that activity is undertaken. So while the explicitly determined rules and tasks might say nothing about bending or breaking the rules — or even forbid such activity — or about being driven by the need to generate favourable quarterly reports, these attitudes and practices might in fact be pervasive; they might be part of the culture (as appears in fact to have been the case at Enron). Naturally, there can be competing cultures within a single organisation: the culture comprised of attitudes and norms that is aligned to the formal and official complex of tasks and rules might compete with an informal and 'unofficial' culture that is adhered to by a substantial sub-element of the organisation's membership.

In addition to structure, function and culture, social institutions necessarily involve sanctions of various kinds. Social institutions involve *informal* sanctions, such as moral disapproval following on non-conformity to institutional norms. However, formal sanctions, such as punishment, are also a feature of institutions.[19]

---

some other preferred purpose be substituted. Either way my point in relation to institutional and occupational ends, purposes or functions will be unaffected.

[18] See Lauren B Edelman, 'Overlapping Fields and Constructed Legalities', in this book.

[19] Jon Elster, *Cement of Society* (1989) ch XV.

Social institutions have a multifaceted normative dimension. Moral categories that are deeply implicated in social institutions include human rights and duties, contract-based rights and obligations, and rights and duties derived from the production and consumption of collective goods. Take police institutions. Police are typically engaged in protecting people from being deprived of, for example, their human right to security of the person or their institutional right to property. Now consider business. Most business organisations do not have the protection of human rights as a purpose; nor should they. On the other hand, moral rights are an important *side constraint* on business activity. Business organisations should not engage in activities that violate the human rights of workers or other members of the community: for example, clothing manufacturers should not exploit children as underpaid workers in underdeveloped countries.

A further point about markets and business organisations is that, normatively speaking, they have both *proximate* ends and *ultimate* ends. The proximate end of market actors might be to maximise their financial self-interest or the firm's profits or shareholder value — the means to these ends being the production of goods for consumption or the provision of services. However, such proximate goals are not the ultimate ends of markets or of the social institution of the modern corporation. Qua social institutions, markets and corporations ought to (and in fact do, albeit imperfectly) serve larger purposes than this, such as to contribute to the material well-being of human societies. Whether this larger purpose is the material betterment of the least well-off (as Rawls suggests) or to maximise the overall benefit (as utilitarians suggest) is a matter for reasoned argument. Moreover, the fact that some prior institution existing outside the market is privatised, indeed legally incorporated, would not undermine this fundamental proposition concerning social institutions. A prison, for example, does not cease to have as an ultimate end the deterrence of criminality and protection of ordinary citizens from dangerous persons merely because it becomes privatised. Rather — again, normatively speaking — a proximate end, for example maximising shareholder value or making a profit, has in effect been (rightly or wrongly) 'designed-in' to a pre-existing institution as a means to better realise its ultimate purpose. To claim that the ultimate purpose of the institution of the modern corporation — a product, if ever there was one, of institutional design — is, for example, simply and only to maximise profits or shareholder value, is (on this ends-based, ie *teleological*, account of social institutions) to confuse proximate with ultimate purposes.[20] Thus the proximate end of corporate financial service providers in capital markets might be to maximise shareholder value, but the ultimate purpose is something beyond this, for example to make capital available at reduced costs to productive firms.[21]

Let us now focus on institutional moral rights. There are at least two species of institutional (moral) rights. There are *individual* institutional (moral) rights and there are *joint* (institutional) moral rights. Joint moral rights are moral rights that attach to individual persons, but do so jointly. For example, in the context of the social institution of property rights, the joint owners of a piece of land might have a joint right to exclude would-be trespassers, and one single owner of a piece of land might have a right to exclude would-be trespassers, but only on condition that another single owner of a second piece of land likewise had such an exclusion right. Joint rights need to be distinguished from universal individual human rights (as opposed to individual *institutional* rights). The right to life is an example of a universal individual human right. Each human being has an individual human right to life. However, since one's possession of the right to life is wholly dependent on properties one possesses as an individual, it is not the case that one's possession of the right to life is dependent on someone else's possession of that right.

Sometimes the end realised in joint action is not merely a collective end, it is also a collective *good*. (By *collective* good I simply mean that the good is collectively or jointly produced; I do not mean to imply that it is collectively or jointly consumed — it might be, and often is, individually consumed.) If so, then a joint right may well be generated. What is the relationship between joint moral rights and collective goods? The good is a realised collective end; and the participants in realising that collective end, ie the contributors to the production of that good, possess a joint right to this collective good. It is easy to see why these persons, and not some other persons, would have a right to such a good: they are the ones responsible for its existence, or

---

[20] For an historically informed account of the purposes of corporations and, in particular, regulation of corporations see Melvin J Dubnick, '*Sarbanes-Oxley* and the Search for Accountable Corporate Governance' in this book.

[21] John Coffee suggests as much in his paper, 'Law and the Market: The Role of Enforcement' (Paper presented at the Dynamics of Capital Market Governance Forum, Australian National University, Canberra, 14 March 2007).

continued existence. In this connection consider the shareholders, members of the board of directors, managers and workers (shareholders, officers and employees) in a factory that produces cars that are sold for profit. Board members, managers, shareholders and workers in the factory have a joint right to be remunerated from the sales of the cars that they have jointly produced. It is also clear that if one participating agent has a right to the good, then — other things being equal — so do the others. That is, there is interdependence of rights with respect to the good. Now notice that the board members, managers, shareholders and workers — and indeed the car company itself — depend for their skills, knowledge, security, transport and so on, on other social institutions, including educational and policing institutions, legal and political institutions, transport and communication infrastructure, etc. Accordingly, the moral rights to the collective goods produced by the car company include rights that attach to members of the wider society; this moral fact is reflected in tax regimes, including corporate tax, albeit often inadequately. Evidently, many corporations often pay less tax than is fair or reasonable by virtue of 'creative accounting' and/or their ability to exploit offshore tax havens, for example in poor countries desperate to attract investment. Notice further that these joint moral rights are not equivalent to, or reducible to, moral rights based on legal contracts. A contract might or might not reflect a person's contribution to the production of a collective good, depending on a host of contingencies (notably relationships of power). Consider in this connection the extraordinarily generous executive compensation packages on offer in some corporations.

Social institutions are in part defined in terms of their collective ends. Moreover, as we have just seen, when such collective ends are also collective goods then this gives rise to joint moral rights to those goods. That is, 'functional' properties (collective ends) give rise to deontic properties (joint rights) under certain conditions — especially the condition that the collective end in question is also a good.

Let me now give more detailed attention to the moral duties or obligations that attach to institutional roles, and the sources of such institutional obligations. Obligations, like rights, are deontic properties. In our above example of a factory, workers and manager obviously have duties, including moral duties that go hand-in-hand with their rights, for example a worker's moral duty to do a reasonable day's work or a manager's (director) fiduciary duties to shareholders not recklessly to put at risk their money. But shareholders also have duties and responsibilities, and not simply rights. For example, they have responsibilities not to invest their money in corporations that are generating profits by bribing public officials to gain lucrative contracts, instead of by virtue of a superior economic performance.

Just as is the case with rights, the obligations attached to institutional roles flow in part from the purposes or ends of the institution. Moreover, the purposes or ends of the institution themselves derive — ultimately — from social needs (and not simply aggregated individual desires). Consider the individual human and society-wide needs for adequate food, clothing, shelter, health, and so on. No single member of a social group could provide for any of these needs, but if they act jointly they can do so. But needs, as opposed to desires, generate moral obligations. So the various needs of social groups that can only be adequately met by the joint action of members of the same or other groups generate collective responsibilities on the part of these groups to jointly so act. Moreover, where such collective responsibilities can most effectively be discharged by establishing institutions and institutional roles (whose institutional duties consist of providing for these needs), such as agricultural, clothing, building, and pharmaceutical industries (and associated institutional roles), then members of the social group who have the collective responsibility, also have a derivative responsibility to establish such institutions and see to it that they realise their institutional purposes. For example, governments have a responsibility (where required) to establish such institutions and to regulate such institutions (once they are established) to ensure that they are realising their institutional purposes. When institutions and their constitutive roles have been established on some adequate moral basis, such as, say, the social need for adequate housing, or (derivatively) the need for housing loans, then those who undertake these roles necessarily put themselves under obligations of various kinds — obligations that attach to, and are in part constitutive of, those roles. Let us consider three different categories of such role obligations.

Perhaps there are professional roles that anyone can undertake if he or she so wishes. Presumably the role of professional writer is one of these. On the other hand, it would be morally outrageous for someone to set up as a surgeon without any proper training. Whether or not it is morally acceptable for someone to undertake a professional role without demonstrable competence in that role turns partly on the purpose of the role (how important is it to discharge the role), and partly on the extent of the harm an incompetent professional in the role is likely to do to clients or customers. Obviously anyone who holds a senior position in a large institution, such as a corporation, a bank, or a university, is capable of doing great good, but also of inflicting enormous harm on people who entrust their careers, money or whatever to that organisation. Arguably, therefore, it is a serious moral fault to undertake such a role without demonstrable competence. Most role obligations presuppose competence. Accordingly, many breaches of role obligations are not instances in which the role occupant lacks competence. It is possible for someone who is, say, a competent banker, nevertheless to be negligent in the giving and approving of loans and in the monitoring of various banking activities for which he or she is responsible. The claim here would not be that bankers were incompetent to undertake the roles they undertook, but rather that they did not exercise that competence when in those roles. Similar points can be made in respect of lawyers, auditors, doctors, and so on.

Once again, the moral significance of recklessness and negligence will vary from one professional context to another. It is no doubt foolish, but it is not morally wrong, for a gambler to be reckless or negligent with his or her own money. But the question that needs to be asked is whether or not ongoing recklessness and negligence is morally problematic — as opposed to being merely foolish — for a banker. The answer is presumably that it is. Just as an inability competently to undertake the professional role of a doctor, welfare worker, lawyer, director, banker, and so on is likely to cause enormous harm to patients, clients, depositors, shareholders, so recklessness in the provision of medical services, auditing services, legal advice, or loans, is likely to cause enormous harm to these people. The point here is that these professional obligations are also moral obligations. They are moral obligations in part by virtue of the institutional purpose served by the professional role in question. They are also moral obligations in part by virtue of the magnitude of the harm to clients that is likely to ensue if these professional obligations are not properly discharged in the overall context of the institution of the bank having been established, persons having entrusted their savings to these banks, and so on.

A final issue here concerns the ascription of responsibility within an institutional framework. As we have seen, in an institutional framework outcomes are typically the result of many actions by many people. Accordingly, there is a tendency for individuals to fail to see themselves as responsible for the outcomes of the collective activity of the institution. This tendency is especially prevalent in a professional context of negligence, incompetence and non-adherence to established procedures. These responsibilities —which, as we have seen, are moral as well as professional — do not cease to be real merely because they are ignored. In the first place, each individual member of a collective entity, such as a committee or board of directors, has a responsibility to follow established procedures. For example, an individual banker ought not to approve large loans without the appropriate supporting documentation. In the second place, the notion of collective responsibility entails that the decisions of the collective as a whole are the responsibility of each individual member, whether that member in fact influenced those decisions or not. For example, if the driving force behind a dubious loan proposal is some individual member of a board of directors, this does not absolve other members of the board of responsibility for the outcome of the loan being approved. In the third place, no individual member of a collective such as a committee or board of directors is absolved of his or her moral responsibilities merely because those around him or her are failing to discharge theirs. If there is the possibility of individual members opposing irresponsible conduct or resigning, then those individuals who choose not to take either of these courses of action are morally responsible for the actions of the collective.

We can conclude that the ethical dimension is quite central to 'normal' professional practice. The professions are not simply activities that are driven by the possibility of financial and other rewards to those individuals who engage in them, they are also activities in part governed by professional responsibilities that are also moral responsibilities. In light of the above discussion, we are entitled to conclude that there are multiple sources of deontic properties, such as rights and obligations, and that they include the following ones.

Firstly, as we have just seen, collective ends — that are also collective goods — generate joint moral rights and duties under certain conditions. So the normative dimension of institutions involves more than deontic properties, and some deontic properties are presupposed by this normative dimension. Specifically, it involves the ethical or moral worth of the ends or purposes of institutions, ie the kinds of human goods that institutions produce or fail to produce. Accordingly, the definition of an institution will typically include a description of the human good that it purports to produce. For example, universities purport to produce knowledge and understanding, economic systems ought to produce material well-being, and so on. Secondly, institutional structures, including hierarchical structures, give rise to rights and duties, for example, a CEO instructs a subordinate to undertake a financial task. Thirdly, promises generate obligations to perform the promised actions. This is relevant to institutional actors insofar as they enter into contracts, undertake oaths of office, and the like. Moreover, part of the moral and/or legal basis of some institutions, such as corporations and governments, might consist in part in contracts or quasi-contracts, for example the so-called social contract between an elected government and its citizens or between regulators and those they regulate. Fourth, various natural properties that persons have, for example, human needs, generate moral rights, namely human rights and correlative duties. Typically, human rights act as side constraints on the actions of institutional actors.

This multiplicity of sources of deontic properties suggests a pluralist explanatory account of the deontic properties of institutional actors, including market actors. Moreover, on a teleological account of social institutions, participants in an institution pursue a collective good, and this gives rise to deontic properties (rights and duties). However, this (normative) teleological explanation of deontic properties needs to be supplemented by recourse to the other above-mentioned sources of deontic properties, for example promises (including contracts), and human rights. The two points to be stressed here are as follows. Firstly, normatively speaking, social institutions including business corporations and markets exist for ultimate — and not merely proximate — purposes or ends, namely, to provide collective goods, for example material goods, the coordination of buyers and sellers of material goods. As mentioned above, here Adam Smith's invisible hand mechanism is salient. The outcome of the workings of the invisible hand is the ultimate purpose of this institutional mechanism; the pursuit of financial gain, the proximate end. Secondly, again normatively speaking, the rights and duties of institutional actors, including CEOs, directors, managers, shareholders, employees, derive in part from the collective ends, ie collective goods, that are the raison d'être for the existence of that social institution.

So the fundamental normative question that needs to be asked of a business corporation, or financial market, is the same as for any other social institution, namely: What collective good(s) does it exist to provide? Once an acceptable answer to this question is provided then a host of subsidiary normative questions arise including the following ones: Who is possessed of a jointly held right to this good and on what moral basis? What are the duties of these rights bearers?

II INTEGRITY SYSTEMS

While regulatory frameworks and integrity systems typically overlap — and ought to be mutually reinforcing — they are not identical notions, theoretically speaking; albeit regulatory systems are often understood as including what I am referring to as integrity systems.[22] A regulatory framework is a structured set of explicit laws, rules or regulations governing behaviour, issued by some institutional authority and backed by sanctions. It often serves to ensure compliance with minimum ethical standards (namely those enshrined in a law, rule or regulation), but this is not its only purpose. There are many laws, rules and regulations that have little or nothing to do with ethics. An integrity system, by contrast — at least as I am using the term — is an assemblage of institutional entities, roles, mechanisms and procedures, the purpose of which is to ensure compliance with minimum *ethical* standards and promote the pursuit of *ethical* goals. Nevertheless, integrity systems obviously heavily rely on regulations and laws.

In practice, integrity 'systems' are a messy assemblage of formal and informal devices, processes and roles, and they operate in often indeterminate and unpredictable ways. The term 'integrity', as used in the expression 'integrity system', is also problematic in that it appropriates a moral notion normally used to describe individual human agents and applies it to organisations and other large groups of individuals. Roughly speaking, individual human persons have integrity if: (1) they possess the full array of central moral virtues, such as honesty, loyalty, and trustworthiness, and (2) they exercise rational and morally informed judgment in their adherence to the virtues, including when their self-interest might dictate otherwise. By contrast with the notion of an individual person's integrity, integrity used in the context in

---

[22] See, eg, Christine Parker, *The Open Corporation* (2002).

which we are employing it here (of an 'integrity system' for institutions) applies to the members of organisations and occupations, and also to the structure, function and culture of organisations.[23] The integrity of an organisation or occupational group is in large part dependent upon the individual integrity of its members, and therefore an integrity system is in large part focused on developing and maintaining the individual integrity of these members. Nevertheless, these organisations and groups are not simply the sum of their members, and so determining the integrity levels of an organisation or group is not simply a matter of summing the levels of integrity of the individuals who happen to be its members at a particular time.

In the first place, the individuals who comprise institutions, including the so-called professions, are role occupants, and the responsibilities and virtues required of them are somewhat different from, and in some respects greater than, those required of ordinary individual persons not occupying such roles. So, for instance, scrupulous attention to numerical detail might be a constitutive virtue of the role of an accountant, but not of the role of a husband.[24] Moreover, what counts as a professional responsibility or virtue, both in terms of technical and ethical competencies, varies greatly across different professional and occupational groups. While, arguably, the 'zealous advocacy of one's clients' interests' might be a critical virtue to the role of a lawyer or barrister in an adversarial legal system, it is not a critical virtue for the engineer. One important task, then, for any specific profession is to determine what precisely the constitutive virtues of the individual role occupant are, and devise strategies to ensure that these virtues are developed and maintained in the members of that profession.

In the second place, the integrity of an institution is not simply a matter of the integrity of the individual role occupants who comprise it. For the integrity of an institution is partly a matter of the structure, function and culture of the institution. Consider structure, both legal and administrative. In an institution possessed of integrity the administrative processes and procedures in relation to, for example, promotion or complaints and discipline, would embody relevant ethical principles of

[23] For an elaboration of an integrity system for occupational groups, see Andrew Alexandra et al, *Professionalisation, Ethics and Integrity*, Report for the Professional Standards Council (2006).

[24] On the role of auditors, and on recent shortcomings, see Tom Campbell and Keith Houghton (eds), *Ethics and Auditing* (2005).

fairness, procedural justice, transparency, and the like. Now consider function or ends. In an institution possessed of integrity the organisational goals actually being pursued would align closely with the morally legitimate (including ultimate) functions of the institution, such as, for example, the promotion of public safety for an engineering firm, or of the financial health of audited corporations for an auditing firm, rather than purely commercial and other proximate goals, such as profit.

Moreover, in the case of markets and business corporations more generally, realising the ultimate, as opposed to proximate, institutional purposes is a fundamental ethical concern. Here there is a need to address an array of questions including the contribution of the business, market or industry to human material well-being. For example, the 'contribution' to human health of the tobacco industry is self-evident, but so is the international pharmaceutical industry's if, as appears to be the case, it is neglecting the development of drugs for poverty related diseases afflicting millions in favour of drugs for the minor ailments of much smaller numbers of the relatively rich. Again, the real costs, for example environmental costs, of specific industries need to be factored into institutional cost–benefit analyses of the extent of the realisation of proximate and ultimate ends. In the case of the financial services sector in particular, there appears to be a prior fundamental ethical question in need of an answer: namely, what are, ie what ought to be, the ultimate institutional ends of this sector? Is it to provide capital to any person or organisation that will maximise shareholder value? Arguably this is (again) to confuse proximate with ultimate ends. At any rate, without an answer to this question, an integrity system — and a regulatory system insofar as it is concerned with institutional (ethical) integrity, as it surely must be — is quite literally without one of its basic purposes: it does not know what ethical ends it is seeking to embed in the target institution(s). I return to this theme in the next section. Finally, consider culture. In an institution possessed of integrity, the pervasive ethos or spirit, ie the culture, would be one that was, for example, conducive to high performance, both technically and ethically, and supportive in times of need, but intolerant of serious incompetence or misconduct.

Integrity systems exist to promote institutional ethical integrity and combat institutional corruption. In order to succeed they first need to identify the nature and causes of the ethical failures, including at the levels of structure, function and culture. Second, it is necessary to devise institutional mechanisms, if they do not already exist, to identify the loci of what will be taken to be individual and collective moral responsibility. This amounts to institutionalising ethical responsibility. Importantly, this process does not necessarily involve identifying a pre-existing source of ethical responsibility; it can, and often does, involve creating a locus of institutional responsibility to deal with an identified ethical problem. Perhaps initially, no one was aware of conflicts of interest problems in some corporations, for example, lawyers in incorporated legal practices. However, once the problem is identified, some institution or institutional role occupant (or occupant), for example a solicitor-director, needs to be created to deal with this issue. That person or persons can now be held institutionally responsible for this ethical problem. Here it is important to note the possibility of collective moral responsibility, ie of a number of persons (the members of the board of directors, the managers, the employees, the shareholders, the members of an external regulatory agency) being held to be jointly ethically (and institutionally) responsible. Notice that the person or persons in question are now not only institutionally, but also ethically, responsible. Third, given that the loci of individual and collective ethical responsibility have thus been identified, if not created, the matter of accountability then arises in relation to the ones with ethical (and institutional) responsibility. Such accountability can take the form of a set of rules, mechanisms of compliance and processes for adjudication of alleged non-compliance, and, if necessary, processes for punishment. However, ethical failure does not necessarily translate into legal or even administrative liability. Whether or not it does so is a matter or the seriousness of the infraction, the efficacy of such liability, and so on. This is one of the reasons an integrity system does not necessarily mirror a regulatory system, even an internal institutional self-regulatory system.

In looking at options to promote integrity and combat ethico-professional failures, it is very easy to leap to a particular kind of solution, for example, rule-based or principle-based systems of regulation, even a single 'magic bullet' solution (like increasing penalties or giving more intrusive powers to investigative agencies), and doing so without considering the full array of implications, including the demonstrable (as opposed to hoped for) benefits (which of these measures has been tested and, as a consequence, is *known* to work?), and the costs in terms of resources, damage to ethico-professional ethos, and so on. Enforcement mechanisms, for example, are important, especially in relation to ethical offences that are sufficiently serious to be also criminal offences. However, enforcement is only one part of the solution to ethical problems, ie one component of an integrity system. Again in relation to enforced requirements, rules need to work hand-in-glove with principles. Yet for some problems in some areas, for example conflicts of interest, the emphasis might need to be on principles in the context of procedural requirements, such as an internal but independent mechanism for determination of any putative conflict of interest. In other areas such as disclosure requirements, principles and rules might both need to be met, for example, an auditor's report must be both a true and fair record and comply with technical rules.[25]

Moreover, 'magic bullet' solutions in particular are sometimes offered in relative ignorance of both the actual nature and causes of the problems they are supposed to address. The truth is sometimes in the detail. For example, in attempting to determine the causes of unethical practices in a given profession there are a number of preliminary questions that need to be addressed. One set of questions pertains to the precise nature of the unethical practice at issue, and the context in which it occurs. Consider legal practitioners operating in the context of incorporated, multidisciplinary legal practices. Are there, for example, some compelling practical facts that explain the unethical practice of conflicts of interest or breaches of confidentiality in this context? What pressures and opportunities might there be for the unethical practice in question? Another set of questions concerns the extent of the corruption or unethical practice: Is it sporadic or continuing, restricted to a few 'rotten apples', or widespread within the area? In answering these questions, what is called for is the provision of evidence-based conclusions.

At other times one cannot see the wood for the trees. In the case of the global financial sector, integrity assurance is in the hands of national governments. However, national governments — and their regulatory agencies — are not simply umpires, they are also players in the financial 'game'. Governments, for example, seek to assist their own industries and businesses at the expense of ones from other countries, for example in relation to 'level playing fields' in trade and other markets. Consider the restrictive trade practices of the EU and US in regard to agricultural products and the consequent harmful effect on African economies in particular.

---

[25] Clarke, Dean and Oliver, above n 5, 320.

Even when the answers to the above-mentioned questions have been provided, there will arise further questions in relation to any remedies proposed. For example, any contemplation of mechanisms to redress ethico-professional misconduct that will require the expenditure of energy and resources needs to be justified in terms of the seriousness and extent of the misconduct to be successfully combated. Consider here the claims that the post-Enron regulation in the US, the *Sarbanes-Oxley Act of 2002*,[26] has had costs that are greater than the benefits it has provided — and, of course, the counter-claims. More importantly, such remedies need to be efficacious, and efficacious over the longer term. Pious rhetoric accompanied by tough regulation does not necessarily deliver the required long-term results. Nevertheless, if *Sarbanes-Oxley* is working, then surely the costs that it imposes in terms of reporting and disclosure requirements, audit committees with financial experts and independent directors etc, are justified. Certainly, the costs of an *effective* regulatory system in relation to corporate malfeasance would have to be enormous if they were to outweigh the benefits. Understanding the causes of ethico-professional misconduct and failures and the tailoring of remedies to address them will involve considering and distinguishing between three sorts of motivation for compliance with moral principles and ethical ends.

One reason for compliance is the fear of punishment; hence the use, or threatened use, of the so-called 'big stick'. So, for example, person A does not defraud organisation B because A fears that he or she will get caught and locked up. A second reason for compliance arises from the benefit to oneself. Hence the possible utility of the so-called 'carrot' approach. So, for example, B pays B's workers reasonable wages because by doing so the workers are healthy, work productively, and B makes good profits. These two reasons are essentially appeals to self-interest. Taken in combination, they constitute the 'stick–carrot' approach much loved by many contemporary economists. However, there is a third reason for compliance. This is moral belief or desire to do what is right. A refrains from fraud because A believes that it is morally wrong to steal.

There are also important connections to be highlighted and promoted between 'self-interest' and 'moral belief and sentiment', so that these conceptions are more in balance and integrated and less at

---

[26] Pub L No 107–204, 116 Stat 745 (2002) ('*Sarbanes-Oxley*').

odds. First, of course, the appeal to moral sentiment must be balanced by the appeal to self-interest. If, for example, it is at great cost to one's self to be honest or fair, then one may have sufficient reason not to be honest or fair. Indeed, the reason need not be purely self-interested, but also count as moral. Suppose that, faced with retrenchment, an employee commits fraud in order to provide for his family, his reasons here include ones from both prudence and morality.

It is evident that widespread and ongoing compliance typically requires appeals to self-interest (sticks and carrots) but also appeals to moral beliefs. Ideally, integrity systems should have penalties for those who do not comply, should enable benefits to flow to those who do comply, and should resonate with the moral beliefs of the people thus regulated. For example, laws and regulations should be widely thought to be fair and reasonable. Thus, an institutional design that proceeds on the assumption that self-interest is the only human motivation worth considering, fails. It fails because it overlooks the centrality of moral beliefs in human life, and therefore does not mobilise moral sentiment. On the other hand, an institutional design that proceeds on the assumption that self-interest can be ignored, and that a sense of moral duty on its own will suffice, also fails; it fails because self-interest is an ineradicable and pervasive feature of all human groups. Moreover, deserved reputation has a pivotal role to play in the convergence of self-interest and ethical concerns. Here I am not so much speaking of reputation for performance (including economic performance) as of reputation for ethical integrity, albeit performance and integrity are connected and to some extent overlap.

Let me explain what might be referred to as a virtuous triangle. High reputation is much sought after by occupational groups and firms alike, and a low one to be avoided at all costs. Consider the collapse of the giant accounting Arthur Andersen following on their loss of reputation. Accordingly, there is an opportunity to mobilise this reputational desire in the service of promoting ethical standards. Here the aim is to ensure that organisational and professional reputation aligns with actual ethical practice, ie that an organisation, group or individual's high or low reputation is deserved. The way to achieve this is by designing appropriate integrity systems. Key elements of an integrity system track compliance with rules such as accountability. The additional thought here is that key elements of an integrity system should track features of organisation and occupational groups that determine or should determine reputation. Most explicitly, reputational indexes could be constructed whereby an ethics audit awards scores in relation to specific ethical standards. Deserved reputation represents an important nexus between self-interest and concern about others, and so, for our purposes here, between the self-interest of firms and occupational groups and concern about consumers, clients or the public generally. Here there are three elements in play: (1) reputation; (2) self-interest; (3) ethical requirements, such as particular ethico-institutional standards, but also more general desiderata such as client/consumer protection. Hence my reference to a virtuous triangle. The idea is that these three elements need to interlock in the following way.

First, reputation is linked to self-interest; this is obviously already the case — individuals, groups and organisations desire high reputation and benefit materially and in other ways from it. Second, reputation needs to be linked to ethics in that reputation ought to be deserved; as already mentioned, the integrity systems are the means to achieve this. Third, and as a consequence of the two already mentioned links, self-interest is linked to ethics; given robust integrity systems that mobilise reputational concerns, it is in the self-interest of individuals, groups and firms to comply with ethico-institutional standards. I should also reassert that self-interest is not the only or ultimate motivation for human action; the desire to do the right thing is also a powerful motivator for many, if not most, people. Accordingly, the triangle is further strengthened by the motivation to do right.

Integrity systems can be thought of as being either predominantly reactive or predominantly preventive.[27] Naturally, the distinction is somewhat artificial, since there is a need for both reactive elements, eg, a complaints and discipline system, as well as preventive elements, eg, codes of practice, ethics training and transparency of processes, in any adequate integrity system. Integrity-building strategies involve reactive systems as well as preventive systems. Within preventive systems there are mechanisms that promote ethical behaviour, there are corporate governance mechanisms with, for example, anti-fraud or corruption functions, and there are various transparency and disclosure mechanisms.

Moreover, it seems clear that an adequate integrity system cannot afford to do without reactive as well as preventive systems; and

[27] Derived in part from Seumas Miller, Peter Roberts and Ed Spence, *Corruption and Anti-Corruption* (2005) ch 7.

that preventive systems need to have all the elements detailed above. This suggests that there are two important issues. The first is the adequacy of each of the elements of the above systems, for example how adequate are the complaints and discipline processes including the investigative capacity? Or, how effective are the mechanisms of disclosure? The second issue pertains to the level of integration and complementarity between the reactive and the preventive systems; to what extent do they act together to mutually reinforce one another? We should therefore think of (better) integrity systems as holistic in character, and conceive of specific integrity-building mechanisms as elements of a unified, integrated, holistic integrity system the elements of which reinforce, rather than conflict with, one another.

III CORPORATIONS, FINANCIAL MARKETS AND MARKET ACTORS

Notwithstanding the general features of integrity systems for institutions adumbrated above, any given integrity system for an institution must be tailored to the needs of that particular institution. Arguably market actors, including financial service providers, present a number of relatively distinct problems when it comes to devising integrity systems to ensure ethical practice and the pursuit of ethical ends. At any rate, this assumption is a source of the following speculations concerning the integrity system or systems for these groups.

In the first place, and as noted above, market actors do not have an ethical purpose as their proximate end; rather they have some commercial end, such as profit maximisation. The ultimate end is one provided for by the invisible hand. Market actors pursue (individual and collective) self-interest and — by virtue of the workings of the invisible hand — the material well-being of the society is provided for. In this respect market actors are unlike, say, doctors or hospitals. The latter can reasonably be required to have the promotion of life and health at the forefront of their concerns, ie as their proximate as well as ultimate (professional and institutional) ends. Economic self-interest, especially when linked to social status and power, is a powerful driver, and establishing markets in previously non-market economies and deregulating previously heavily regulated market economies, has unleashed a great deal of hitherto dormant human energy. Moreover, the modern corporation as an institution, and the development of global financial markets, has enabled the mobilisation of vast capital sums in the service of this human energy. (They have, of course, in turn relied heavily on scientific and technological developments.) One only has to visit Shanghai today and remember what it was like 20 years ago to appreciate the power of market forces (especially government-assisted market forces).

However, from an ethical point of view, the *institutionally structured* self-interested orientation of market actors — including corporations — may well give rise to an immediate problem. How is this institutionally structured impetus and habit of pursuing economic self-interest to be contained within reasonable limits and channeled in appropriate directions? Presumably, this is in part to be achieved by means of some mix of self-regulation and external regulation. However, it is also predicated on the guiding ethico-conceptual frameworks (as opposed to prevailing ideologies) and related self-understandings of these market actors. At any rate, this brings us to a second set of problems.

It is one of the principal tasks of those who design and oversee the market system, including governments and — under the direction of governments — regulators, to ensure that the ultimate purposes of markets (and, therefore, market actors) are in fact achieved, ie to contain and channel the pursuit of economic self-interest. Perhaps there is a lack of clarity in the collective minds of governments and regulators in relation to their role in this regard. Politicians these days sometimes talk as if the market is an intrinsic good, ie good in itself and independently of its outcomes in terms of human material well-being. But on the view elaborated above, markets need to be conceived in purely instrumentalist terms; they are simply a means to an (ultimate) end (even if this is not the end to be pursued by the market actors themselves).

Moreover, if one looks, for example, at the objectives of many regulators one typically finds only limited aims, for example to reduce crime and protect consumers, and procedural concerns, for example to promote competition and efficiency.[28] There is little or no reference to what I have been referring to as the ultimate ends of markets, ie the

[28] Eg, the Australian Competition and Consumer Commission is concerned among other things with the traditional professions but appears to have little or no focus on the distinctive ethical ends of the traditional professions, such as legal practitioners, as compared with other occupational groups: see Alexandra et al, above n 23. Incidentally, I am not here blaming regulators; they can only carry out the tasks governments give them.

outcome the invisible hand is supposed to bring about. Rather, the image of regulation is one in which regulators are umpires whose sole job is to impartially enforce the rules of the game. But in games, the pleasure of playing aside, there is only one end, namely winning, and this is an end pursued by the players, not the umpires. But here the analogy between markets and games breaks down: markets, unlike games, have an end beyond 'winning'; they have ultimate, as opposed to proximate, ends. In the case of markets, 'winning', for example making a profit, is only a proximate end, and, as such, a means to a further and larger purpose, namely the material well-being of the society (both national and, in the case of international financial markets, global).

Further, there is the problem mentioned above of the ambiguous role of national governments and regulators when it comes to global markets, including global financial markets. National governments and their regulators are to some extent partisan, and (understandably) seek to look after the economic interests of their own industries and businesses, including their financial service providers. Moreover, in the absence of a uniform set of global regulations and a single global regulator with real authority, regulators operating at a national level can be played off against one another by multinational corporations. In the case of the global financial sector, regulation and integrity assurance are ultimately in the hands of national governments. However, national governments — and their regulatory authorities — are not simply umpires, they are also players in the financial — and, more generally, corporate — 'game'. For example, the UK government – and its financial regulator (the Financial Services Authority) — cannot be expected to regulate entirely impartially in the interests of ethical ends and principles, given the substantial interest the UK government has in ensuring that the UK corporate and financial sector retains and increases the benefits accruing to it from global financial markets.

A third set of problems confronting the establishment of an integrity system or systems for some market actors, perhaps especially corporations and financial service providers, pertains to the professions. Lawyers and accountants have important roles to play in the integrity systems of corporations, including financial service providers. For example, auditors conduct audits in order to determine financial propriety and performance, and enable disclosure thereof to regulators and shareholders. However, in many cases auditors and auditing firms appear to have become themselves predominantly market actors, driven principally by the proximate goal of economic self-interest. Arguably, they have (perhaps unconsciously) sought to mask this — and limit their exposure to civil litigation — by taking refuge in compliance with technical procedural requirements, such the accounting rules, in preference to a moral commitment to substantive ethical principles, such as true and fair record.[29] At any rate, the status of auditors as independent professional adjudicators of, for example, financial health has been significantly compromised. To this extent an important element in the integrity system for corporations has been weakened.[30]

Perhaps there is a fourth problem pertaining to various specific unethical practices, such as insider trading and conflicts of interest; one that derives in part from the de-coupling of ultimate ethical purposes from the self-understanding of market actors, and from the regulation of market actors by governments and their regulatory agencies. The unethical practices in question are not *mala in se* — they are not bad in themselves. Consider insider trading. Insider trading is not bad in itself as, for example, murder is bad in itself. Rather insider trading is only morally problematic in a particular institutional context. Now assume that one holds the view, putting it crudely, that markets exist only to further the self-interest of market actors, for example to maximise profit or return to shareholders. Why not, then, engage in some insider trading, given that it is in one's self-interest, ie it is financially very rewarding and it is not easily detected. It might be replied that one should not do so because one is breaking the rules, indeed the law. But unlike murder, insider trading is not morally wrong in itself. Compliance with the law is reinforced by strong moral sentiment, but equally compliance is reduced in the absence of strong moral sentiment. And so, if the practice is not bad in itself, the attitude may take hold; if one can get away with it, why not do it?

Perhaps fair competition is the ethical issue here? But competition in the corporate sector is inevitably unfair; appeals to fairness may (reasonably enough) carry little moral weight. Rather the substantive moral objection to insider trading is presumably that in the long run if enough people practice it, then it undercuts the ultimate, not

---

[29] Clarke, Dean and Oliver, above n 5, 319.

[30] In addition, it might be that auditors are not well-prepared to detect fraud: see Nicholas M Hodson, 'Why Auditors Don't Find Fraud', in this book.

simply the proximate, ends of the corporate sector.[31] Without compliance with a set of rules or laws that promote competition, the market will not deliver the outcomes promised by the invisible hand. However, this ultimate purpose of markets is not in the forefront of the minds of market actors, preoccupied as they are, and need to be, with the proximate ends of generating profit or maximising shareholder value.[32] This is perhaps especially the case in the financial services sector. For this sector is arguably at a double remove from the ultimate purposes of the market as a whole. In accordance with the invisible hand it seeks to provide finance to firms that in turn — and again in accordance with the invisible hand — generate the products actually required for the material well-being of the wider society. But if this ultimate purpose is lost sight of — in the self-understanding of market actors and in the policy making of/regulation by governments and regulators — then perhaps insider trading is bound to be viewed by market actors as much less serious an ethical (as opposed to legal) offence than in reality it is.

A fifth set of issues arise from various perverse incentives that can exist in local and global markets, including financial markets. Competition, including competitive markets, can and do provide discipline to market actors. However, this is not necessarily or always the case. Consider the so-called tragedy of the commons in which everyone pursuing their self-interest destroys the environment. Again consider bribery. It might be the case that, for most corporations in some sector, bribing officials is necessary in order to be competitive, given that even a small number of other corporations will engage in this practice. Compliance with a legally enforced ethical principle might be in a market actor's self-interest, but only if the enforcement mechanisms are such that everyone (or most) complies. Similarly, there might be competitive pressure to invest in unethical corporations, given the highly lucrative returns, and given that one's competitors are doing so. Again, when liability does not appropriately track ethical responsibility this can lead to perverse incentives. An incentive structure, for example,

[31] In fact some have argued that insider trading should not be a legal offence, since if it was allowed it would not have harmful consequences.

[32] On the other hand, I do not accept the proposition that market actors need not have any understanding nor pay any heed to the larger ultimate purposes of markets. The latter attitudes on the part of market actors can lead to an attitude of, for example, breaking the law if one can get away with it.

in which market actors are allowed, indeed encouraged, to take great financial risks with other people's money in order to achieve enormous financial benefits for themselves (and not simply for the investors and shareholders), yet can do so without commensurate legal and financial liability attaching to themselves in the case of things going wrong, is surely tailor-made for corruption. Accordingly, there is a need for institutional re-design of a kind that either decreases the potential financial benefits to such market actors, or increases their liability, or introduces some mixture of both.

More generally, the collective responsibilities of industries to realise their institutional purposes, including the collective responsibilities of financial service providers in capital markets, typically consist of highly dispersed individual responsibilities that attach to individual persons within firms, individual firms within the industry, institutions without the industry, and so on and so forth. The collective responsibility, for example, to lower the cost of capital is not one that can be discharged by any one, or even a small group, of market actors within a given capital market. Given the diffuse character of such collective responsibilities — and its attendant incentive structure — many industries, financial service providers included, will not discharge these collective responsibilities and, as a consequence, these industries will not adequately realise their institutional purposes. Hence the need (and resultant responsibility) on the part of governments in particular to intervene to adjust these incentive structures and, if necessary, to design-in appropriate institutions or sub-elements thereof.

Perverse incentive structures can be addressed by recourse to interventions that reconfigure the incentive structures.[33] Such interventions can take the form of solving jurisdictional problems in global settings, and increasing enforcement options and/or the intensity of enforcement. Thus Joseph Stiglitz suggests that:

> Any country in which the corporation (or the substantial owners of the corporation) has assets should provide a venue in which suits can be brought or in which enforcement actions to ensure payment of liabilities can be undertaken. The corporation may incorporate where it wants, but this should

[33] See Susan Rose-Ackerman, *Corruption and Government: Causes, Consequences and Reform* (1999), for a variety of types of prescription, including adjusting incentive structures, in relation to corruption.

> not make it any less accountable for its actions in other jurisdictions.[34]

In addition, he suggests global widening of the possibility of class action in relation to corporate price-fixing. While obviously of great importance, these jurisdictional and enforcement methods are not always sufficient. Other options are themselves market-based, for example reducing supply of a product or service by factoring in real costs (and requiring that they be paid), reducing demand for a product by high sales tax or limiting availability. Some of these options involve ambitious innovations to the market system itself, including the global financial system. For example, Stiglitz has proposed a radical extension of the concept of Special Drawing Rights to create a new global reserve currency that would help stabilise financial markets and also make reserves available for wealth creation projects in impoverished countries, increasing literacy, reducing poverty-related diseases, addressing global warming and other 'ultimate' market ends.[35] Still other options are based on the importance of reputation to the self-interest of market actors, for example, ethics reputational indices might be established to seek to draw attention to their unethical practices or orientations. Here, as elsewhere, it might be useful to recall the possible utility of the above-described triangle of virtue with its strategy of mobilising a set of interlocking ethical and self-interested motivations.

A sixth and final cluster of problems derives in part from the foregoing ones, and pertains to education, ethos and ideology. If the prevailing ethos or culture of an organisation, and perhaps even ideology of central elements of a sector, downplays ethical considerations in favour of self-interest, then it should hardly surprise when self-interest overrides compliance with ethical principles, even ones enshrined in the law. This is no doubt especially the case in a context of high temptation and opportunity on the one hand, and low risk of detection and conviction on the other, for example insider trading in some corporate settings. The point here is not that the majority of individuals themselves engage in corrupt or unethical practices, but rather that in certain cultural or ideological contexts they may well refrain from reporting or otherwise preventing a minority from doing so.

---

[34] Joseph Stiglitz, *Making Globalization Work: The Next Steps to Global Justice* (2006) 206–8. Stiglitz has other suggestions in this regard.
[35] Ibid ch 9.

Many key elements of integrity systems such as ethics codes, codes of practice, education programs, and the like, do not exist, for the most part, directly to prevent or deter the few people who are wrongdoers from doing wrong, but rather to ensure that the many are intolerant of the wrongdoing of the few. In this context it is perhaps worth pointing out that most fraudsters are detected and convicted as a consequence of the disclosures of their colleagues.

Bibliography

1 Books/Articles/Reports

Abrahamson, Eric, 'Managerial Fashion' (1996) 21 *Academy of Management Review* 254

Aguilera, Ruth V, 'Corporate Governance and Director Accountability: An Institutional Comparative Perspective' (2005) 16 *British Journal of Management* S39

Aguilera, Ruth, et al, 'Corporate Governance and Social Responsibility: A Comparative Analysis of the UK and the US' (2006) 14 *Corporate Governance: An International Review* 147

Albiston, Catherine, 'The Rule of Law and the Litigation Process: The Paradox of Losing by Winning' (1999) 33 *Law and Society Review* 869

Albiston, Catherine R, 'Bargaining in the Shadow of Social Institutions: Competing Discourses and Social Change in Workplace Mobilization of Civil Rights' (2005) 39 *Law and Society Review* 11

Alexandra, Andrew, et al, *Professionalisation, Ethics and Integrity Systems: The Promotion of Professional Ethical Standards, and the Protection of Clients and Consumers, Report for the Professional Standards Council* (2006)

Alva, Curtis, 'Delaware and the Market for Corporate Charters: History and Agency' (1990) 15 *Delaware Journal of Corporate Law* 885

Amnesty International, *Clouds of Injustice: Bhopal Disaster 20 Years On* (2004)

Anabtawi, Iman, 'Secret Compensation' (2004) 82 *North Carolina Law Review* 835

Anabtawi, Iman, 'Some Skepticism about Increasing Shareholder Power' (2006) 53 *University of California Los Angeles Law Review* 561

APA, *Bidders Statement* (2007).

Armour, John and Skeel, David A, 'Who Writes the Rules for Hostile Takeovers, and Why? The Peculiar Divergence of US and UK Takeover Regulation' (2007) *Georgetown Law Journal* (forthcoming)

Asare, Stephen K, Cunningham, Lawrence A and Wright, Arnold, 'The *Sarbanes-Oxley Act*: Legal Implications and Research Opportunities' (2007) 19 *Research in Accounting Regulation* 81

Austin, John L, *How to Do Things with Words* (1975)

Austin, Robert P, *Company Directors and Corporate Social Responsibility: UK and Australian Perspectives* (2007)

Australian Government, *Rethinking Regulation: Report of the Taskforce on Reducing Regulatory Burdens on Business: Australian Government's Interim Response* (April 2006)

Australian Government, *Rethinking Regulation: Report of the Taskforce on Reducing Regulatory Burdens on Business: Australian Government's Response* (August 2006)

Australian Securities and Investment Commission, *Working for Australia: ASIC Annual Report 2005–06* (2006)

Australian Securities and Investment Commission, 'ASIC Commences Proceedings against Citigroup for Conflicts and Insider Trading Breaches' (Press Release, 31 March 2006)

Australian Securities and Investment Commission, 'ASIC v Citigroup' (Press Release, 17 July 2007)

Australian Securities and Investment Commission, 'Further Amended Statement of Claim' (26 March 2007), available at <http://www.asic.gov.au/asic/asic.nsf/byheadline/ASIC+v+Citigroup?openDocument>

Avi-Yonah, Reuven S, 'The Cyclical Transformations of the Corporate Form: A Historical Perspective on Corporate Social Responsibility' (2005) 30 *Delaware Journal of Corporate Law* 767

Ayres, Ian and Braithwaite, John, *Responsive Regulation, Transcending the Deregulation Debate* (1992).

Babbitt, Susan, 'Personal Integrity, Politics and Moral Imagination' in Brennan, Samantha, et al (eds), *A Question of Values: New Canadian Perspectives on Ethics and Political Philosophy* (1997) 107

Bainbridge, Stephen M, 'Director Primacy and Shareholder Disempowerment' (2006) 119 *Harvard Law Review* 1735

Baldwin, Robert, 'The New Punitive Regulation' (2004) 67 *Modern Law Review* 351

Bamberger, Kenneth, 'Regulation as Delegation: Private Firms, Decisionmaking, and Accountability in the Administrative State' (2006) 56 *Duke Law Journal* 377

Bank for International Settlements, *69th Annual Report* (1999)

Barabosi, Albert-Laszlo, *Linked: The New Science of Networks* (2002)

Baron, James N, Dobbin, Frank R and Jennings, P Deveraux, 'War and Peace: The Evolution of Modern Personnel Administration in US Industry' (1986) 92 *American Journal of Sociology* 350

Bartlett, Joseph and Swan, W Eric, 'Private Equity Funds: What Counts and What Doesn't' (2001) 26 *Journal of Corporate Law* 393

Baxt, Robert, Black, Ashley and Hanrahan, Pamela, *Securities and Financial Services Law* (6th ed, 2003)

Baynes, Leonard M, 'Just Pucker and Blow? An Analysis of Corporate Whistleblowers, the Duty of Care, the Duty of Loyalty, and the *Sarbanes-Oxley Act*' (2002) 76 *St John's Law Review* 875

Beattie, Vivien and Thomson, Sarah Jane, 'Intangibles and the OFR' (2005) *Financial Management* 29

Bebchuk, Lucian, 'The Case for Shareholder Access to the Ballot' (2003) 59 *Business Lawyer* 43

Bebchuk, Lucian, 'The Case for Increasing Shareholder Power' (2005) 118 *Harvard Law Review* 833

Bebchuk, Lucian, 'Letting Shareholders Set the Rules' (2006) 119 *Harvard Law Review* 1784

Beetham, David, *The Legitimation of Power* (1991)

Berle, Adolph A and Means, Gardiner C, *The Modern Corporation and Private Property* (1932)

Berman, Harold J, *Law and Revolution: The Formation of the Western Legal Tradition* (1983)

Beroutsos, Andreas, Freeman, Andrew and Kehoe, Conor, 'What Public Companies Can Learn from Private Equity' (2007) *McKinsey on Finance* 1

Bird, Joanna and Hill, Jennifer, 'Regulatory Rooms in Australian Corporate Law' (1999) 25 *Brooklyn Journal of International Law* 555

Bisom-Rapp, Susan, 'Scripting Reality in the Legal Workplace: Women Lawyers, Litigation Prevention Measures, and the Limits of Anti-Discrimination Law' (1996) 6 *Columbia Journal of Gender and Law* 323

Bisom-Rapp, Susan, 'Bulletproofing the Workplace: Symbol and Substance in Employment Discrimination Law Practice' (1999) 26 *Florida State University Law Review* 959

Bisom-Rapp, Susan, 'Exceeding Our Boundaries: Transnational Employment Law Practice and the Export of American Lawyering Styles to the Global Workforce' (2004) 25 *Comparative Labor Law and Policy Journal* 257

Black, Julia, 'Critical Reflections on Regulation' (2002) 27 *Australian Journal of Legal Philosophy* 1

Black, Julia, 'The Emergence of Risk Based Regulation and the New Public Management in the UK' (2005) *Public Law* 512

Blumberg, Phillip I, 'The Corporate Personality in American Law: A Summary Review' (1990) 38 *American Journal of Comparative Law* 49

Blumrosen, Alfred, *Modern Law: The Law Transmission System and Equal Employment Opportunity* (1993)

Bolton, Patrick, Scheinkman, Jose A and Xiong, Wei, 'Executive Compensation and Short-Termist Behavior in Speculative Markets' (2006) 73 *Review of Economic Studies* 577

Born, Georgina, *Uncertain Vision: Birt, Dyke and the Reinvention of the BBC* (2004)

Bovens, Mark, *The Quest for Responsibility: Accountability and Citizenship in Complex Organisations* (1998)

Braithwaite, John, *Corporate Crime in the Pharmaceutical Industry* (1984)

Braithwaite, John B, 'Rules and Principles: A Theory of Legal Certainty' (2002) 27 *Australian Journal of Legal Philosophy* 47

Bratton, William W, 'The New Economic Theory of the Firm: Critical Perspectives from History' (1989) 41 *Stanford Law Review* 1471

Bratton, William W and McCahery, Joseph A, 'Comparative Corporate Governance and the Theory of the Firm: The Case against Global Cross Reference' (1999) 38 *Columbia Journal of Transnational Law* 213

Bratton, William W, 'Enron, *Sarbanes-Oxley* and Accounting: Rules versus Principles versus Rents' (2003) 48 *Villanova Law Review* 1023

Brint, Steven and Karabel, Jerome, 'Institutional Origins and Transformations: The Case of American Community Colleges' in Powell, Walter W and DiMaggio, Paul J (eds), *The New Institutionalism in Organizational Analysis* (1991) 337

British Venture Capital Association, *The Economic Impact of Private Equity in the UK* (2006)

Britnell, R H, 'English Markets and Royal Administration before 1200' (1978) 31 *Economic History Review* 183

Brown, J Robert, 'Criticizing the Critics: *Sarbanes-Oxley* and Quack Corporate Governance' (2006) 90 *Marquette Law Review* 309

Bruck, Connie, *The Predators' Ball: The Inside Story of Drexham Burnham and the Rise of the Junk Bond Raiders* (1989)

Bryan, Penelope, 'Killing Us Softly: Divorce Mediation and the Politics of Power' (1992) 40 *Buffalo Law Review* 441

Bryan, Penelope, 'Reclaiming Professionalism: The Lawyer's Role in Divorce Mediation' (1994) 28 *Family Law Quarterly* 177

Bryde, David, 'Methods for Managing Different Perspectives of Project Success' (2005) 16 *British Journal of Management* 119

BT, Social Report (1999)

Bumiller, Kristin, 'Victims in the Shadow of the Law: A Critique of the Model of Legal Protection' (1987) 12 *Signs* 421

Bumiller, Kristin, The Civil Rights Society: The Social Construction of Victims (1988)

Burawoy, Michael, Manufacturing Consent: Changes in the Labor Process under Monopoly Capitalism (1979)

Burroughs, Bryan and Helyar, John, *Barbarians at the Gates* (1990)

Bush, Robert A B, 'Defining Quality in Dispute Resolution: Taxonomies and Anti-Taxonomies of Quality Arguments' (1989) 66 *Denver University Law Review* 335

Bush, Robert A B and Folger, Joseph P, *The Promise of Mediation: Responding to Conflict through Empowerment and Recognition* (1994)

Business Council of Australia, *Business Regulation Action Plan for Future Prosperity* (2005)

Business in the Community, Insight Investment and FTSE Group, *Rewarding Virtue: Effective Board Action on Corporate Responsibility* (2005)

Cahill, Mia L, *The Social Construction of Sexual Harassment Law: The Role of the National, Organizational, and Individual Context* (2001)

Campbell, John L, 'Mechanisms of Evolutionary Change in Economic Governance: Interaction, Interpretation, and Bricolage' in Magnusson, Lars and Ottosson, Jan (eds), *Evolutionary Economics and Path Dependence* (1997) 10

Campbell, Tom, 'True and Fair to Whom: A Philosophical Approach to Auditing' in Campbell, Tom and Houghton, Keith (eds), *Ethics and Auditing* (2005) ch 5

Cao, Jerry and Lerner, Josh, *The Performance of Reverse Leveraged Buyouts* (15 October 2006), available at <http://ssrn.com/abstract=937801>

Carlin, Jerome E, *Lawyer's Ethics: A Survey of the New York City Bar* (1966)

Carney, William J, 'The Costs of Being Public after *Sarbanes-Oxley*: The Irony of "Going Private"' (2006) 55 *Emory Law Journal* 141

Carroll, Archie B, 'The Pyramid of Corporate Social Responsibility: Toward the Moral Management of Organizational Stakeholders' (1991) 34 *Business Horizons* 39

Carroll, Archie B, 'Corporate Social Responsibility: Evolution of a Definitional Construct' (1999) 38 *Business and Society* 268

Carver, Jeremy P, 'The Role of the Lawyers: Hired Guns or Public Servants' in O'Brien, Justin (ed), *Governing the Corporation: Regulation and Corporate Governance in an Age Of Scandal and Global Markets* (2005) 223

Cary, William L, 'Federalism and Corporate Law: Reflections upon Delaware' (1974) 83 *Yale Law Journal* 663

Chambliss, Elizabeth, *Title VII as Displacement of Conflict* (1996) (unpublished manuscript)

Chandler, Alfred D, Strategy and Structure: Chapters in the History of the American Industrial Enterprise (1962)

Chandler, Alfred D, *The Visible Hand: The Managerial Revolution in American Business* (1977)

Chandler, William B and Strine, Leo E, 'The New Federalism of the American Corporate Governance System: Preliminary Reflections of Two Residents of One Small State' (2003) 152 *University of Pennsylvania Law Review* 953

Chapple, Larelle and Christensen, Blake, 'The Non-Binding Vote on Executive Pay: A Review of the *CLERP 9* Reform' (2005) 18 *Australian Journal of Corporate Law* 263

Charny, David, 'The Politics of Corporate Convergence' in Gordon, Jeffrey N and Roe, Mark J (eds), *Convergence and Persistence in Corporate Governance* (2004) 293

Chayes, Abram and Chayes, Antonia H, 'Corporate Counsel and the Elite Law Firm' (1985) 37 *Stanford Law Review* 277

Cheek, James H, 'Approaches to Market Regulation' in Oditah, Fidelis (ed), *The Future for the Global Securities Market* (1996) 243

Cheffins, Brian R, 'Does Law Matter? The Separation of Ownership and Control in the United Kingdom' (2001) 30 *Journal of Legal Studies* 459

Chou, De-Wai, Gombola, Michael and Liu, Feng Ying, 'Earnings Management and Stock Performance of Reverse Leveraged Buyouts' (2006) 41 *Journal of Financial and Quantitative Analysis* 407

Clark, Michael E, 'Hamstrung or Properly Calibrated? Federalism and the Appropriate Role of Government in the Post-*Sarbanes-Oxley* World' (2004) 1 *International Journal of Disclosure and Governance* 385

Clarke, Frank, Dean, Graeme and Oliver, Kyle, *Corporate Collapse: Accounting, Regulatory and Ethical Failure* (revised ed, 2003)

Clemens, Elisabeth S, 'Organizational Repertoires and Institutional Change: Women's Groups and the Transformation of US Politics, 1890–1920' (1993) 98 *American Journal of Sociology* 755

Clemens, Elisabeth S, *The People's Lobby: Organizational Innovation and the Rise of Interest Group Politics in the United States, 1890–1925* (1997)

Clune, William H, 'A Political Model of Implementation and the Implications of the Model for Public Policy, Research, and the Changing Role of Lawyers' (1983) 69 *Iowa Law Review* 47

Cocking, Dean and Oakley, Justin, 'Indirect Consequentialism, Friendship and the Problem of Alienation' (1995) *Ethics* 86

Coffee, John C '"No Soul to Damn: No Body to Kick": An Unscandalized Inquiry into the Problem of Corporate Punishment' (1981) 79 *Michigan Law Review* 386.

Coffee, John C, 'The Future as History: The Prospects for Global Convergence of Corporate Governance and its Implications' (1999) 93 *Northwestern University Law Review* 641

Coffee, John C, 'Do Norms Matter? A Cross-Country Evaluation' (2001) 149 *University of Pennsylvania Law Review* 2151

Coffee, John C, 'Understanding Enron: "It's about the Gatekeepers, Stupid"' (2002) 57 *Business Lawyer* 1403

Coffee, John C, 'Racing towards the Top? The Impact of Cross-Listings and Stock Market Competition on International Corporate Governance' (2002) 102 *Columbia Law Review* 1757

Coffee, John C, 'The Attorney as Gatekeeper: An Agenda for the SEC' (2003) 103 *Columbia Law Review* 1293

Coffee, John C, 'Gatekeeper Failure and Reform: The Challenge of Fashioning Relevant Reforms' (2004) 84 *Boston University Law Review* 301

Coffee, John C, 'What Caused Enron? A Capsule Social and Economic History of the 1990s' (2004) 89 *Cornell Law Review* 269

Coffee, John C, *Gatekeepers: The Professions and Corporate Governance* (2006)

Coglianese, Cary, 'Legitimacy and Corporate Governance' (2007) 32 *Delaware Journal of Corporate Law* 159

Cohen, Ira J, *Structuration Theory: Anthony Giddens and the Constitution of Social Life* (1989)

Committee on Capital Markets Regulation, *Interim Report of the Committee on Capital Markets Regulation* (2006)

Companies and Securities Advisory Committee, *Shareholder Participation in the Modern Listed Public Company: Final Report* (2000)

Conrad, Charles, 'The Illusion of Reform: Corporate Discourse and Agenda Denial in the 2002 "Corporate Meltdown"' (2004) 7 *Rhetoric and Public Affairs* 311

Co-operative Bank, *Ethical Consumerism Report* (2006), available at <http://www.co-operativebank.co.uk>

Corporations and Markets Advisory Committee, *Corporate Social Responsibility: Discussion Paper* (2005)

Corporations and Markets Advisory Committee, *The Social Responsibility of Corporations: Report* (2006)

Coustan, Harvey, et al, '*Sarbanes-Oxley*: What It Means to the Marketplace' (2004) 197 *Journal of Accountancy* 43

Cressy, Robert, Munari, Federico and Maliero, Alessandro, *Playing to Their Strengths? Evidence that Specialisation in the Private Equity Industry Confers Competitive Advantage* (February 2007), available at <http//ssrn.com/abstract=964367>

Cumming, Douglas and Johan, Sofia, 'Is It the Law or the Lawyers? Investment Covenants Around the World' (2006) 12 *European Financial Management* 535

Cunningham, Lawrence A, 'The *Sarbanes-Oxley* Yawn: Heavy Rhetoric, Light Reform (and It Might Just Work)' (2003) 36 *University of Connecticut Law Review* 915

Cunningham, Lawrence A, 'A Prescription to Retire the Rhetoric of "Principles-Based Systems" in Corporate Law, Securities Regulation and Accounting' (2007) *Vanderbilt Law Review* (forthcoming), available at <http://papers.ssrn.com/sol3/papers.cfm?abstract_id=970646>

Dalton, Dan R and Dalton, Catherine M, '*Sarbanes-Oxley* Legislation and the Private Company: If Not a Marriage, Then Certainly an Engagement' (2005) 26 *Journal of Business Strategy* 8

Davies, Paul and Hopt, Klaus, 'Control Transactions' in Kraakman, Reinier, et al (eds), *The Anatomy of Corporate Law: A Comparative and Functional Approach* (2004) 157

Davis, Gerald F and Thompson, Tracy A, 'A Social Movement Perspective on Corporate Control' (1994) 39 *Administrative Science Quarterly* 141

Davis, Kenneth B, 'Judicial Review of Fiduciary Decision-Making — Some Theoretical Perspectives (1985) 80 *Northwestern University Law Review* 1

Defoe, Daniel, The Anatomy of Exchange Alley or a System of Stock-Jobbing (1719)

Deiser, George F, 'The Juristic Person — I' (1908) 57 *University of Pennsylvania Law Review and American Law Register* 131

Deiser, George F, 'The Juristic Person — II' (1909) 57 *University of Pennsylvania Law Review and American Law Register* 216

Deiser, George F, 'The Juristic Person — III' (1909) 57 *University of Pennsylvania Law Review and American Law Register* 300

Delgado, Richard, et al, 'Fairness and Formality: Minimizing the Risk of Prejudice in Alternative Dispute Resolution' (1985) *Wisconsin Law Review* 1359

Dewey, John, 'The Historic Background of Corporate Legal Personality' (1926) 35 *Yale Law Journal* 655

DiMaggio, Paul J and Powell, Walter W, 'The Iron Cage Revisited: Institutional Isomorphism and Collective Rationality in Organizational Fields' (1983) 48 *American Sociological Review* 147

Dixon, John, Kouzmin, Alexander and Korac-Kakabdse, Nada, 'Managerialism — Something Old, Something Borrowed, Little New: Economic Prescription versus Effective Organizational Change in Public Agencies' (1998) 11 *International Journal of Public Sector Management* 164

Dobbin, Frank, et al, 'Equal Employment Opportunity Law and the Construction of Internal Labor Markets' (1993) 99 *American Journal of Sociology* 396

Dorf, Michael, 'Legal Indeterminacy and Institutional Design' (2003) 78 *New York Law Review* 875

Douglas, David C, 'A Charter of Enfeoffment under William the Conqueror' (1927) 42 *English Historical Review* 245

Dubnick, Melvin J, *Seeking Salvation for Accountability* (2002)

Dubnick, Melvin J, 'Accountability and Ethics: Reconsidering the Relationships' (2003) 6 *International Journal of Organization and Organization Theory and Behavior* 405

Dubnick, Melvin J, 'Accountability and the Promise of Performance: In Search of the Mechanisms' (2005) 27 *Public Performance and Management Review* 376

Dubnick, Melvin J, *Situating Accountability* (2007)

Dunn, Edwina, 'James Hardie: No Soul to be Damned and No Body to be Kicked' (2005) 27 *Sydney Law Review* 339

Easterbrook, Frank and Fischel, Daniel, *The Economic Structure of Corporate Law* (1991)

Eatwell, Roger, *The 1945–1951 Labour Governments* (1979)

Edelman, Lauren B, 'Legal Environments and Organizational Governance: The Expansion of Due Process in the Workplace' (1990) 95 *American Journal of Sociology* 1401

Edelman, Lauren B, 'Legal Ambiguity and Symbolic Structures: Organizational Mediation of Civil Rights Law' (1992) 97 *American Journal of Sociology* 1531

Edelman, Lauren B, Abraham, Steven E and Erlanger, Howard S, 'Professional Construction of the Legal Environment: The Inflated Threat of Wrongful Discharge Doctrine' (1992) 26 *Law and Society Review* 47

Edelman, Lauren B, Erlanger, Howard S and Lande, John, 'Internal Dispute Resolution: The Transformation of Civil Rights in the Workplace' (1993) 27 *Law and Society Review* 497

Edelman, Lauren B and Suchman, Mark C, 'The Legal Environments of Organizations' (1997) 23 *Annual Review of Sociology* 479

Edelman, Lauren B and Cahill, Mia L, 'How Law Matters in Disputing and Dispute Processing (or, the Contingency of Legal Matter in Alternative Dispute Resolution)' in Bryant, Garth and Sarat, Austin (eds), *How Law Matters* (1998) 15

Edelman, Lauren B and Petterson, Stephen, 'Symbols and Substance in Organizational Response to Civil Rights Law' (1999) 17 *Research in Social Stratification and Mobility* 107

Edelman, Lauren B, Uggen, Christopher and Erlanger, Howard S, 'The Endogeneity of Legal Regulation: Grievance Procedures as Rational Myth' (1999) 105 *American Journal of Sociology* 406

Edelman, Lauren B and Suchman, Mark C, 'When the Haves Hold Court: Speculations on the Organizational Internalization of Law' (1999) 33 *Law and Society Review* 941

Edelman, Lauren B, Fuller, Sally Riggs and Mara-Drita, Iona, 'Diversity Rhetoric and the Managerialization of Law' (2001) 106 *American Journal of Sociology* 1589

Edelman, Lauren B, 'Law at Work: The Endogenous Construction of Civil Rights' in Nielsen, Laura Beth, and Nelson, Robert L (eds), *Handbook of Employment Discrimination Research: Rights and Realities* (2005) 337

Edelman, Murray J, *The Symbolic Uses of Politics* (1964)

Edelman, Murray, *Politics as Symbolic Action: Mass Arousal and Quiesence* (1971)

Editorial, 'Incorporation by Implication under the *Sherman Act*' (1917) 30 *Harvard Law Review* 263

Eisenstein, Ilana H, 'Keeping Charity in Charitable Trust Law: The Barnes Foundation and the Case for Consideration of Public Interest in Administration of Charitable Trusts' (2003) 151 *University of Pennsylvania Law Review* 1747

Elster, Jon, *Cement of Society* (1989)

Enriques, Luca, 'Bad Apples, Bad Oranges: A Comment from Old Europe on Post-Enron Corporate Governance Reforms' (2003) 38 *Wake Forest Law Review* 911

Evans, Frank, 'The Evolution of the English Joint-Stock Limited Trading Company: VII. Trading Companies Incorporated under General Act of Parliament' (1908) 8 *Columbia Law Review* 461

Evans, Frank, 'The Evolution of the English Joint-Stock Limited Trading Company' (1908) *Columbia Law Review* 339

Ewick, Patricia and Silbey, Susan S, The Common Place of Law: Stories from Everyday Life (1988)

Farber, David B, 'Restoring Trust after Fraud: Does Corporate Governance Matter?' (2005) 80 *Accounting Review* 539

Fearnley, Stella and Hines, Tony, 'The Regulatory Framework for Financial Reporting and Auditing in the United Kingdom: The Present Position and Impending Changes' (2003) 38 *International Journal of Accounting* 215

Felstiner, William L F, Abel, Richard L and Sarat, Austin, 'The Emergence and Transformation of Disputes: Naming Blaming, Claiming …' (1981) 15 *Law and Society Review* 631

Financial Reporting Council, *The Turnbull Guidance as an Evaluation Framework for the Purposes of Section 404(a) of the* Sarbanes-Oxley Act (2004), available at <http://www.frc.org.uk/corporate>

Financial Reporting Council, *Internal Control: Revised Guidance for Directors on the* Combined Code (2005), available at <http://www.frc.org.uk/corporate/internalcontrol.cfm>

Financial Services Authority, *Reasonable Expectations: Regulation in a Non-Zero Failure World* (2003)

Financial Services Authority, *Enforcement Process Review: Report and Recommendations* (2005), available at <http://www.fsa.gov.uk/pubs/other/enf_process_review_report.pdf>

Financial Services Authority, *FSA Business Plan 2006/2007* (2006)

Financial Services Authority, *FSA Simplification Plan* (2006)

Financial Services Authority, *Principles-Based Regulation: Focusing on the Outcomes that Matter* (2007)

Fineman, Martha, 'Dominant Discourse, Professional Language, and Legal Change in Child Custody Decisionmaking' (1988) 101 *Harvard Law Review* 727

Finn, Paul, *Fiduciary Obligations* (1977)

Fisher, Roger and Ury, William, *Getting to Yes: Negotiating Agreement without Giving in* (1981)

Fiss, Owen M, 'Against Settlement' (1984) 93 *Yale Law Journal* 1073

Fisse, Brent and Dellit, Chris, 'Civil Liability under Australian Securities Regulation: The Possibility of Strategic Enforcement' in Walker, Gordon and Fisse, Brent (eds), *Securities Regulation in Australia and New Zealand* (1994) 570

Fligstein, Neil, *The Transformation of Corporate Control* (1990)

Fligstein, Neil, 'The Structural Transformation of American Industry: An Institutional Account of the Causes of Diversification in the Largest Firms, 1919–1979' in Powell, Walter W and DiMaggio, Paul J (eds), *The New Institutionalism in Organizational Analysis* (1991) 311

Fligstein, Neil, *The Architecture of Markets: An Economic Sociology of Twenty-First Century Capitalist Societies* (2001)

Flint, David, *A True and Fair View in Company Accounts* (1982), available at <http://www.icas.org.uk>

Ford, Christie L, 'New Governance, Compliance and Principles-Based Securities Regulation' (2007) *American Business Law Journal* (forthcoming), available at <http://ssrn.com/abstract=970130>

Foster, Richard and Kaplan, Sarah, *Creative Destruction* (2001)

Foucault, Michel, 'Governmentality' in Burchell, Graham, Gordon, Colin and Miller, Peter (eds), *The Foucault Effect: Studies in Governmentality: With Two Lectures by and an Interview With Michel Foucault* (1991) 87

Fowles, A J, 'Changing Notions of Accountability: A Social Policy View' (1993) 6 *Accounting, Auditing and Accountability Journal* 97

Freeman, Alan, 'Antidiscrimination Law: The View from 1989' in Kairys, David (ed), *The Politics of Law: A Progressive Critique* (1990) 121

Freeman, Jody, 'Collaborative Governance in the Administrative State' (1997) 45 *University of California Los Angeles Law Review* 1

Freeman, Jody, 'Extending Public Law Norms through Privatization' (2003) 116 *Harvard Law Review* 1285

Friedland, Roger, and Alford, Robert R, 'Bringing Society Back In: Symbols, Practices, and Institutional Contradictions' in Powell, Walter W and DiMaggio, Paul J (eds), *The New Institutionalism in Organizational Analysis* (1991) 232

Friedman, Judith J and DiTomaso, Nancy, 'Myths about Diversity: What Managers Need to Know about Changes in the US Labor Force' (1996) 38 *California Management Review* 54

Friedman, Lawrence M, *A History of American Law* (1973)

Fuller, Sally Riggs, Edelman, Lauren B and Matusik, Sharon F, 'Legal Readings: Employee Interpretation and Mobilization of Law' (2000) 25 *Academy of Management Review* 200

Fusaro, Peter C and Miller, Ross M, *What Went Wrong at Enron* (2002)

Gabilondo, Jose, 'Financial Moral Panic! *Sarbanes-Oxley*, Financier Folk Devils, and Off-Balance-Sheet Arrangements' (2006) 36 *Seton Hall Law Review* 781

Gagne, Margaret L, Gavin, Joanne H and Tully, Gregory J, 'Assessing the Costs and Benefits of Ethics: Exploring a Framework' (2005) 110 *Business and Society Review* 181

Galanter, Marc, 'Why the 'Haves' Come Out Ahead: Speculations on the Limits of Legal Change' (1974) 9 *Law and Society Review* 95

Gates, Megan N, 'The *Sarbanes-Oxley Act* and non-US issuers: Considerations for international companies' (2003) 10 *Journal of Commercial Biotechnology* 40

Geiger, Marshall N and Taylor, Porcher L, 'CEO and CFO Certifications of Financial Information' (2003) 17 *Accounting Horizons* 357

Giddens, Anthony, *The Constitution of Society, Outline of the Theory of Structuration* (1984)

Gierke, Otto F V, *Political Theories of the Middle Age* (1958)

Gillon, Steven M, *That's Not What We Meant to Do: Reform and Its Unintended Consequences in Twentieth-Century America* (2000)

Gilson, Ronald J, 'Globalizing Corporate Governance: Convergence of Form or Function' in Gordon, Jeffrey N and Roe, Mark J (eds), *Convergence and Persistence in Corporate Governance* (2004) 128

Global Public Policy Symposium, *Global Capital Markets and the Global Economy: A Vision From the CEOs of the International Audit Networks* (2006)

Gompers, Paul and Lerner, Josh, *The Money of Invention: How Venture Capital Creates New Wealth* (3rd ed, 2004)

Goodpaster, Kenneth E, 'Business Ethics and Stakeholder Analysis' (1991) 1 *Business Ethics Quarterly* 53

Gordon, Jeffrey N, 'What Enron Means for the Management and Control of the Modern Business Corporation: Some Initial Reflections', (2002) 69 *University of Chicago Law Review* 1233

Gordon, Jeffrey N and Roe, Mark J (eds), *Convergence and Persistence in Corporate Governance* (2004)

Gray, Joanna, 'The Legislative Basis of Systemic Review and Compensation for the Mis-Selling of Retail Financial Services and Products' (2004) 25 *Statute Law Review* 196

Gray, Joanna and Hamilton, Jenny, *Implementing Financial Regulation* (2006) 28

Hampton Review, *Reducing Administrative Burdens: Effective Inspection and Enforcement*, March 2005, available at <http://www.hm-treasury.gov.uk/budget/budget_05/other_documents/bud_bud05_hampton.cfm>

Hancher, Leigh and Moran, Michael, 'Organizing Regulatory Space' in Hancher, Leigh and Moran, Michael (eds), *Capitalism, Culture, and Economic Regulation* (1989) 271

Hansmann, Henry and Kraakman, Reinier, 'The End of History for Corporate Law' (2001) 89 *Georgetown Law Journal* 439

Hanusch, Horst and Pyka, Andreas, 'Principles of Neo-Schumpetarian Economics' (2007) 31 *Cambridge Journal of Economics* 275

Harper, Neil and Schnneider, Antoon, 'Private Equity's New Challenge' (2004) *The McKinsey Quarterly* 2

Hart, Oliver, 'Corporate Governance: Some Theory and Implications' (1995) 105 *Economic Journal* 678

Hawkins, Keith, Environment and Enforcement: Regulation and the Social Definition of Pollution (1984)

Heimer, Carol, 'Competing Institutions: Law, Medicine and Family in Neonatal Intensive Care' (1999) 33 *Law and Society Review* 17

Hein, Leonard W, 'The British Business Company: Its Origins and Its Control' (1963) 15 *University of Toronto Law Journal* 134

Heinz, John P and Laumann, Edward O, *Chicago Lawyers: The Social Structure of the Bar* (1977)

Henderson Global Investors, *Tax, Risk and Corporate Governance: Findings from a Survey of the FTSE350* (2005)

Her Majesty's Revenue and Customs, *Modernising Powers, Deterrents and Safeguards: A Consultation on the Developing Programme of Work* (2006)

Her Majesty's Treasury, *The Green Book: Appraisal and Evaluation in Central Government* (2007)

Herman, Edward S, *Corporate Control, Corporate Power* (1981)

Hertig, Gerard, 'Convergence of Substantive Law and Convergence of Enforcement: A Comparison' in Gordon, Jeffrey N and Roe, Mark J (eds), *Convergence and Persistence in Corporate Governance* (2004) 328

Hessen, Robert, 'The Modern Corporation and Private Property: A Reappraisal' (1983) 26 *Journal of Law and Economics* 273

Higgs, Derek, Report to the UK Department of Trade and Industry, *Review of the Role and Effectiveness of Non-Executive Directors* (2003)

Hill, Jennifer G, 'Regulatory Responses to Global Corporate Scandals' (2005) 23 *Wisconsin International Law Journal* 367

Hill, Jennifer G, 'The Persistent Debate about Convergence in Comparative Corporate Governance' (2005) 27 *Sydney Law Review* 743

Hill, Jennifer G, 'Regulating Executive Remuneration: International Developments in the Post-Scandal Era' (2006) 3 *European Company Law* 64

Hoffmann, Elizabeth A, 'Confrontations and Compromise: Dispute Resolution at a Worker Cooperative Coal Mine' (2001) 26 *Law and Social Inquiry* 555

Hollander, Charles and Salzedo, Simon, *Conflicts of Interest and Chinese Walls* (2nd ed, 2004)

Hollister, Huddson T, '"Shock Therapy" for *Aktiengesellschaften*: Can the *Sarbanes-Oxley* Certification Requirements Transform German Corporate Culture, Practice and Prospects?' (2005) 25 *Northwestern Journal of International Law and Business* 453

House of Commons Journals (1875)

Hurdle, Steve, 'A Blow to Public Investing: Reforming the System of Private Equity Fund Disclosures' (2005) 53 *University of California Los Angeles Law Review* 239

Hurst, James Willard, Law and Economic Growth: The Legal History of the Lumber Industry in Wisconsin 1836–1915 (1964)

Hutton, Will, *The State We're In* (1995)

Ingham, Geoffrey, *Capitalism Divided? The City and Industry in British Social Development* (1984)

Inland Revenue, *A General Anti-Avoidance Rule for Direct Taxes* (1998)

Institute of Chartered Accountants of Scotland, *Principles Not Rules: A Question of Judgement* (2006), available at <http://www.icas.org.uk>

International Monetary Fund, *Global Financial Stability Report* (2007)

International Organisation of Securities Commissions, *Objectives and Principles of Securities Regulation* (2003)

Iwai, Katsuhito, 'The Nature of the Business Corporation: Its Legal Structure and Economic Functions' (2002) 53 *Japanese Economic Review* 243

Jacoby, Sanford M, *Employing Bureaucracy: Managers, Unions, and the Transformation of Work in American Industry, 1900–1945* (1985)

Jensen, Michael, 'Eclipse of the Public Corporation' (1989) 67 *Harvard Business Review* 61

Jensen, Michael, 'The Modern Industrial Revolution: Exit and the Failure of Internal Control Mechanisms' (1993) 48 *Journal of Finance* 831

Jensen, Michael, 'Morgan Stanley Roundtable on Private Equity and its Import for Public Companies' (2006) 18 *Journal of Applied Corporate Finance* 8

Jensen, Michael and Chew, Donald, *US Corporate Governance: Lessons From the 1980s* (1997), available at <http://papers.ssrn.com/abstract=146150>

Johnston, William B and Packer, Arnold E, *Workforce 2000: Work and Workers for the 21st Century* (1987)

Jordan, Cally, 'The Conundrum of Corporate Governance' (2005) 30 *Brooklyn Journal of International Law* 983

Jordan, Cally, 'The Chameleon Effect: Beyond the Bonding Hypothesis for Cross-Listed Securities' (2007) *New York University Journal of Law & Business* (forthcoming), available at <http://ssrn.com/abstract=907130>

Kahan, Marcel, 'Jurisprudential and Transactions Developments in Takeovers' in Hopt, Klaus, et al (eds), *Comparative Corporate Governance* (1998) 683

Kahn-Freund, O, 'On Uses and Misuses of Comparative Law' (1974) 37 *Modern Law Review* 1

Kaplan, Robert, *Adversarial Legalism: The American Way of Law* (2003)

Kaplan, Steve and Schoar, Antoinette, 'Private Equity Performance: Returns, Persistence and Capital Flows' (2005) 60 *Journal of Finance* 1791

Karmel, Roberta S, 'Should a Duty to the Corporation Be Imposed on Institutional Shareholders?' (2004) 60 *Business Lawyer* 1

Kaufman, Herbert, *The Forest Ranger: A Study in Administrative Behavior* (1967)

Kaufman, Herbert, Administrative Feedback: Monitoring Subordinates' Behavior (1973)

Keenan, Jack, 'Corporate Governance in UK/USA Boardrooms' (2004) 12 *Corporate Governance* 172

Kennedy, Duncan, 'Form and Substance in Private Law Adjudication' (1976) 89 *Harvard Law Review* 1685

Kennedy, Duncan, 'Toward an Historical Understanding of Legal Consciousness: The Case of Classical Legal Thought in America, 1850–1940' (1980) 3 *Research in Law and Sociology* 3

Kershaw, David, 'Evading Enron: Taking Principles Too Seriously in Accounting Regulation' (2005) 68 *Modern Law Review* 594

Kitagawa, Tokusuke, 'Some Reflections on the Corporate Theory, Including a Japanese Perspective' (1960) *Duke Law Journal* 535

Kleinman, Daniel Lee and Vallas, Steven, 'Science, Capitalism, and the Rise of the "Knowledge Worker": The Changing Structure of Knowledge Production in the United States' (2001) 30 *Theory and Society* 451

Klick, Jonathon and Mitchell, Gregory, 'Government Regulation of Irrationality: Moral and Cognitive Hazards' (2006) 90 *Minnesota Law Review* 1620

Klonoski, Richard J, 'Foundational Considerations in the Corporate Social Responsibility Debate' (1991) 34 *Business Horizons* 9

Komoroski, Jennifer L, 'The Hershey Trust's Quest to Diversify: Redefining the State Attorney General's Role When Charitable Trusts Wish to Diversify' (2004) 45 *William and Mary Law Review* 1769

Konrad, Alison M and Linnehan, Frank, 'Formalized HRM Structures: Coordinating Equal Employment Opportunity or Concealing Organizational Practices?' (1995) 38 *The Academy of Management Journal* 787

Kostiner, Idit, 'Evaluating Legality: Toward a Cultural Approach to the Study of Law and Social Change' (2003) 27 *Law and Society Review* 328

Kraakman, Reinier, et al (eds), *The Anatomy of Corporate Law: A Comparative and Functional Approach* (2004)

Krawiec, Kimberly, 'Cosmetic Compliance and the Failure of Negotiated Governance' (2003) 81 *Washington University Law Q*uarterly 487

Krieger, Linda, 'Civil Rights Perestroika: Intergroup Relations after Affirmative Action' (1998) 86 *California Law Review* 1251

La Porta, Rafael, et al, 'Law and Finance' (1998) 106 *Journal of Political Economy* 1113

La Porta, Rafael, Lopez-de-Silanes, Florencio and Shleifer, Andrei, 'Corporate Ownership around the World' (1999) 54 *Journal of Finance* 471

La Porta, Rafael, et al, 'Investor Protection and Corporate Governance' (2000) 58 *Journal of Financial Economics* 3

La Porta, Rafael, et al, 'Investor Protection and Corporate Valuation' (2002) 57 *Journal of Finance* 1147

Lamba, Asjeet S and Stapledon, Geoffrey P 'The Determinants of Corporate Ownership Structure: Australian Evidence' (Public Law Research Paper No 20, Faculty of Law, University of Melbourne, 2001), available at <http://ssrn.com/abstract=279015>

Langbein, John H, 'The Contractarian Basis of the Law of Trusts' (1995) 105 *Yale Law Journal* 625

Langevoort, Donald C, 'The Social Construction of *Sarbanes-Oxley*' (2006) *Michigan Law Review* (forthcoming), available at <http://papers.ssrn.com/sol3/papers.cfm?abstract_id=930642>

Larson, Magali Sarfatti, The Rise of Professionalism: A Sociological Analysis (1977)

Le Grand, Julian, 'Knights, Knaves or Pawns? Human Behaviour and Social Policy' (1997) 26 *Journal of Social Policy* 149

Leavitt, Harold J, Dill, William R and Eyring, Henry B, 'Rulemakers and Referees' in Ermann, M David and Lundman, Richard J (eds), *Corporate and Governmental Deviance* (1978) 259

Leblebici, Huseyin, and Salancik, Gerald R, 'Stability in Interorganizational Exchanges: Rulemaking Processes of the Chicago Board of Trade' (1982) 27 *Administrative Science Quarterly* 227

Lerner, Josh, Hardymon, Felda and Leamon, Ann, *Venture Capital and Private Equity: A Casebook* (3rd ed, 2004)

Lessig, Lawrence, 'Open Code and Open Societies: Values of Internet Governance' (1998–2000) 74 *Chicago–Kent Law Review* 1405

Lessig, Lawrence, *Code and Other Laws of Cyberspace* (1999)

Levi, Michael, Regulating Fraud, White Collar Crime and the Criminal Process (1987)

Licht, Amir N, 'Cross-Listing and Corporate Governance: Bonding or Avoiding?' (2003) 4 *Chicago Journal of International Law* 141

Licht, Amir N, 'Legal Plug-ins: Cultural Distance, Cross-Listing, and Corporate Governance Reform' (2004) 22 *Berkeley Journal of International Law* 195

Linck, James S, Netter, Jeffry M and Yang, Tina, 'The Effects and Unintended Consequences of the *Sarbanes-Oxley Act*, and Its Era, on the Supply and Demand for Directors' (2007), available at <http://papers.ssrn.com/sol3/papers.cfm?abstract_id=902665>

Linsley, Colin, 'Auditing, Risk Management and a Post *Sarbanes-Oxley* World' (2003) 24 *Review of Business* 21

Lloyd, Trevor O, *Empire to Welfare State* (1970)

Lobel, Orly, 'The Renew Deal: The Fall of Regulation and the Rise of Governance in Contemporary Legal Thought' (2004) 89 *Minnesota Law Review* 342

Lounsbury, Mark, Ventresca, Marc and Hirsch, Paul, 'Social Movements, Field Frames, and Industry Emergence: A Cultural–Political Perspective on US Recycling' (2003) 1 *Socio-Economic Review* 71

Lyons, M, 'The Impact of Managerialism on Social Policy: The Case of Social Services' (1998) 21 *Public Productivity and Management Review* 419

MacIver, Robert M, *The Modern State* (1926)

MacNeil, Iain, 'FSA 1986: Does s 62 Provide an Effective Remedy for Breaches of Conduct of Business Rules?' (1994) 15 *Company Lawyer* 172

MacNeil, Iain and Lau, Alex, 'International Corporate Regulation: Listing Rules and Overseas Companies' (2001) 50 *International and Comparative Law Quarterly* 787

MacNeil, Iain, 'Shareholders' Pre-Emptive Rights' (2002) *Journal of Business Law* 78

MacNeil, Iain, *An Introduction to the Law on Financial Investment* (2005)

MacNeil, Iain and Li, Xiao, 'Comply or Explain: Market Discipline and Non-Compliance with the *Combined Code*' (2006) 14 *Corporate Governance: An International Review* 486

Macrory Report, *Regulatory Justice: Making Sanctions Effective* (2006), available at <http://www.cabinetoffice.gov.uk/REGULATION/news/2006/060522.asp>

Maitland, F R W I, 'Corporation Sole' (1900) 16 *Law Quarterly Review* 335

Majone, Giandomenico, 'Regulation in Comparative Perspective' (1999) 1 *Journal of Comparative Policy Analysis* 309

Marshall, Anna Maria, 'Idle Rights: Employees' Legal Consciousness and the Construction of Sexual Harassment Policies' (2005) 39 *Law and Society Review* 83

Mason, E S, 'The Apologetics of "Managerialism"' (1958) 31 *Journal of Business* 1

McAdam, Doug, and Scott, W Richard, 'Organizations and Movements' in Davis, Gerald F, et al (eds), *Social Movements and Organization Theory: Building Bridges* (2004) 4

McBarnet, Doreen and Whelan, Christopher, 'The Elusive Spirit of the Law: Formalism and the Struggle for Legal Control' (1991) 54 *Modern Law Review* 848

McBarnet, Doreen and Whelan, Christopher, *Creative Accounting and the Cross-Eyed Javelin Thrower* (1999)

McBarnet, Doreen, 'After Enron: Corporate Governance, Creative Compliance and the Uses of Corporate Social Responsibility' in O'Brien, Justin (ed), *Governing the Corporation: Regulation and Corporate Governance in an Age of Scandal and Global Markets* (2005) 205

McBarnet, Doreen, 'After Enron Will "Whiter than White Collar Crime" Still Wash?' (2006) 46 *British Journal of Criminology* 1091

McBarnet, Doreen, 'Corporate Social Responsibility beyond Law, through Law, for Law: The New Corporate Accountability' in McBarnet, Doreen, Voiculescu, Aurora and Campbell, Tom (eds), *The New Corporate Accountability: Corporate Social Responsibility and the Law* (2007) 9

McBarnet, Doreen, *The New Corporate Accountability: CSR and the Law* (2007)

McClendon, Janice K, 'Bringing the Bulls to Bear: Regulating Executive Compensation to Realign Management and Shareholders' Interests and Promote Corporate Long-Term Productivity' (2004) 39 *Wake Forest Law Review* 971

McConvill, James and Bagaric, Mirko, 'Towards Mandatory Shareholder Committees in Australian Companies' (2004) 28 *Melbourne University Law Review* 125

McCraw, Thomas, *Prophets of Innovation: Joseph Schumpeter and Creative Destruction* (2007)

McDonough, William, 'Accountability in the Age of Global Markets', in O'Brien, Justin (ed), *Governing the Corporation: Regulation and Corporate Governance in an Age of Scandal and Global Markets* (2005) 47

McGhee, John, *Snell's Equity* (30th ed, 2000)

McKinsey Report, *Sustaining New York's and the US' Global Financial Services Leadership* (2007)

McLean, Janet, 'Personality and Public Law Doctrine' (1999) 49 *University of Toronto Law Journal* 123

McRae, Hamish and Cairncross, Frances, *Capital City, London as a Financial Centre* (1985)

McVea, Harry, 'Financial Services Regulation under the Financial Services Authority: A Reassertion of the Market Failure Thesis' (2005) 64 *Cambridge Law Journal* 413

Meagher, R P, Heydon, J D and Leeming, M J, *Meagher, Gummow & Lehane's Equity: Doctrines & Remedies* (4th ed, 2002)

Menkel-Meadow, Carrie, 'Toward Another View of Legal Negotiation: The Structure of Problem-Solving' (1984) 31 *University of California Los Angeles Law Review* 754

Meyer, Heinz-Dieter, 'The New Managerialism in Education Management: Corporatization or Organizational Learning?' (2002) 40 *Journal of Educational Administration* 534

Meyer, John W and Rowan, Brian, 'Institutionalized Organizations: Formal Structure as Myth and Ceremony' in Powell, Walter W and DiMaggio, Paul J (eds), *The New Institutionalism in Organizational Analysis* (1991) 41

Micklethwait, John and Wooldridge, Adrian, *The Company: A Short History of a Revolutionary Idea* (2003)

Milhaupt, Curtis J, 'Property Rights in Firms' in Gordon, Jeffrey N and Roe, Mark J (eds), *Convergence and Persistence in Corporate Governance* (2004) 210

Miller, Richard E and Sarat, Austin, 'Grievances, Claims and Disputes: Assessing the Adversary Culture' (1981) 15 *Law and Society Review* 525

Miller, Seumas, *Social Action: A Teleological Account* (2001)

Miller, Seumas, 'Corruption' *Stanford Encyclopedia of Philosophy* (Winter, 2005)

Miller, Seumas, Roberts, Peter and Spence, Ed, *Corruption and Anti-Corruption* (2005)

Miller, Seumas, 'Social Institutions' *Stanford Encylopedia of Philosophy* (Winter, 2006)

Minow, Martha, 'Interpreting Rights: An Essay for Robert Cover' (1987) 96 *Yale Law Journal* 1860

Mirvis, Theodore N, Savarese, John F and Miller, Carol, 'The New Regulatory and Enforcement Environment' (2005) *Securities Reporter* 10

Mitchell, Lawrence E, 'The Death of Fiduciary Duty in Close Corporations' (1990) 138 *University of Pennsylvania Law Review* 1675

Mitchell, Lawrence E, 'Fairness and Trust in Corporate Law' (1993) 43 *Duke Law Journal* 425

Mitchell, Lawrence E, The *Sarbanes-Oxley Act* and the Reinvention of Corporate Governance?' (2003) 48 *Villanova Law Review* 1189

Mitchell, Mark and Mulherin, John, 'The Impact of Industry Shocks on Takeover and Restructuring Activity' (1996) 41 *Journal of Financial Economics* 193

Mitchell, Timothy, 'The Limits of the State: Beyond Statist Approaches and Their Critics' (1991) 85 *American Political Science Review* 77

Moore, Christopher W, The Mediation Process: Practical Strategies for Resolving Conflict (1986)

Moran, Michael, *The British Regulatory State* (2002)

Morgan, Bronwen, 'Technocratic v Convivial Accountability' in Dowdle, Michael (ed), *Public Accountability, Designs, Dilemma and Experiences* (2006) 243

Morgan, Edward V and Thomas, William A, *The Stock Exchange — Its History and Functions* (1962)

Mouffe, Chantal, *On The Political* (2005)

Needham, Charles W, 'Franchises' (1915) 15 *Columbia Law Review* 97

Nelson, Robert L, 'The Future of American Lawyers: A Demographic Profile of a Changing Profession in a Changing Society' (1994) 44 *Case Western Reserve Law Review* 345

Nelson, Robert L and Bridges, William, *Legalizing Gender Inequality: Courts, Markets and Unequal Pay for Women* (1999)

Nelson, Robert L, and Nielsen, Laura Beth, 'Cops, Counsel, or Entrepreneurs: The Shifting Roles of Lawyers in Large Business Corporations' (2000) 34 *Law and Society Review* 457

Nielsen, Laura Beth, 'Situating Legal Consciousness: Experiences and Attitudes of Ordinary Citizens about Law and Street Harassment' (2000) 34 *Law and Society Review* 1055

North, Douglass C, 'Comment on Stigler and Friedland, "The Literature of Economics: The Case of Berle and Means"' (1983) 26 *Journal of Law and Economics* 269

O'Brien, Justin, 'Securing Corporate Accountability or Bypassing Justice? The Efficacy and Pitfalls of Pre-Trial Diversion' (2006) 19 *Australian Journal of Corporate Law* 161

O'Brien, Justin, 'The Politics of Symbolism: *Sarbanes-Oxley* in Context' in Ali, Paul U and Gregoriou, Greg N (eds), *International Corporate Governance after* Sarbanes-Oxley (2006)

O'Brien, Justin, 'Managing Conflicts: The Sisyphean Tragedy (and Absurdity) of Corporate Governance and Financial Regulation Reform' (2007) 20 *Australian Journal of Corporate Law* 317

O'Brien, Justin, Redesigning Financial Regulation: The Politics of Enforcement (2007)

O'Donnell, Cyril, 'Origins of the Corporate Executive' (1952) 26 *Bulletin of the Business Historical Society* 55

Office of Best Practice Regulation, *Best Practice Regulation Handbook* (2006)

Oliver, Christine, 'Strategic Responses to Institutional Processes' (1991) 16 *Academy of Management Review* 145

Organisation for Economic Cooperation and Development, *The OECD Guidelines for Multinational Enterprises* (2000)

Orloff, Ann Shola, and Skocpol, Theda, 'Why Not Equal Protection? Explaining the Politics of Public Social Spending in Britain, 1900–1911, and the United States, 1880s–1920' (1984) 49 *American Sociological Review* 726

Packer, Herbert L, The Limits of the Criminal Sanction (1968)

Page, Stephen, 'Measuring Accountability for Results in Interagency Collaboratives' (2004) 64 *Public Administration Review* 591

Page, Stephen, 'The Web of Managerial Accountability: The Impact of Reinventing Government' (2006) 38 *Administration and Society* 166

Paredes, Troy A, 'A Systems Approach to Corporate Governance Reform: Why Importing US Corporate Law Isn't the Answer' (2004) 45 *William and Mary Law Review* 1055

Parker, Christine, *The Open Corporation* (2002)

Parker, Christine, et al, 'Introduction' in Parker, Christine, et al (eds), *Regulating Law* (2004)

Parker, Christine E, 'Meta-Regulation: Legal Accountability for Corporate Social Responsibility', in McBarnet, Doreen, Voiculescu, A and Campbell, Tom (eds), *The New Corporate Accountability: Corporate Social Responsibility and the Law* (2007)

Patterson, Margaret and Reiffen, David, 'The Effect of the *Bubble Act* on the Market for Joint Stock Shares' (1990) 50 *Journal of Economic History* 163

Pensions Investment Research Consultants, *Corporate Governance Annual Review 2004* (2004)

Penzance, Lord, London Stock Exchange Commission, *Report of the Commissioners* (1878)

Perino, Michael A, 'Enron's Legislative Aftermath: Some Reflections on the Deterrence Aspects of the *Sarbanes-Oxley Act of 2002*' (2002) 76 *St John's Law Review* 671

Pettit, Philip, A Theory of Freedom: From the Psychology to the Politics of Agency (2001)

Pinto, Arthur R, 'Globalization and the Study of Comparative Corporate Governance' (2005) 23 *Wisconsin International Law Journal* 477

Piotroski, Joseph D and Srinivasan, Suraj, 'The *Sarbanes-Oxley* Act and the Flow of International Listings' (2007), available at <http://ssrn.com/abstract=956987>

Pistor, Katharina, et al, 'The Evolution of Corporate Law: A Cross-Country Comparison', (2002) 23 *University of Pennsylvania Journal of International Economic Law* 791

Pistor, Katharina and Xu, Chenggang, 'Incomplete Law' (2003) 35 *New York University Journal of International Law and Policy* 931

Poole, D L, et al, 'Evaluating Performance Measurement Systems in Nonprofit Agencies: The Program Accountability Quality Scale (PAQS)' (2000) 21 *American Journal of Evaluation* 15

Porter, Tony and Ronit, Karsten, 'Self-Regulation as Policy Process: The Multiple and Criss-Crossing Stages of Private Rule Making' (2006) 39 *Policy Sciences* 41

Presidential Working Group and US Agency Principals, *Agreement on Principles and Guidelines Regarding Private Pools of Capital* (2007)

Preston, Lee E and Post, James E, 'The Third Managerial Revolution' (1974) 17 *Academy of Management Journal* 476

Prosser, Tony, 'Regulation and Social Solidarity' (2006) 33 *Journal of Law and Society* 364

Public Company Accounting Oversight Board, *Observations on Board's Implementation of PCAOB Standards Relating to Auditors' Responsibilities with Respect to Fraud* (Release No 2007–001, 22 January 2007), available at <http://www.pcaobus.org/News_and_Events/News/2007/01-22.aspx>

Puttnam, Robert, *Bowling Alone* (2000)

Rao, Hayagreeva, Morrill, Calvin and Zald, Meyer, 'Power Plays: How Social Movements and Collective Action Create New Organizational Forms' (2000) 22 *Research in Organizational Behavior* 237

Rappaport, Steve, 'Social structure and mobility in sixteenth century London: I' (1983) IX *The London Journa*l 107

Rappaport, Steve, 'Social structure and mobility in sixteenth century London: II' (1984) X *The London Journal* 107

Rawls, John, *Theory of Justice* (1972)

Raymond, Robert L, 'The Genesis of the Corporation' (1906) 19 *Harvard Law Review* 350

Redfield, James M, 'The Development of the Market in Archaic Greece' in Anderson, B L and Latham, A J H (eds), *The Market In History* (1986) 29

Reichman, Nancy, 'Moving Backstage: Uncovering the Role of Compliance Practices in Shaping Regulatory Policy' in Schlegel, Kip and Weisburd, David (eds), *White-Collar Crime Reconsidered* (1992) 244

Reserve Bank of Australia, *Statement on Monetary Policy*, 12 February 2007

Ribstein, Larry E, 'Market vs Regulatory Responses to Corporate Fraud: A Critique of the *Sarbanes-Oxley Act of 2002*' (2002) 28 *Journal of Corporation Law* 1

Ribstein, Larry E, '*Sarbanes-Oxley* after Three Years' (University of Illinois Law and Economics Research Paper, University of Illinois College of Law, 2005)

Richardson, Gary, 'Guilds, Laws, and Markets for Manufactured Merchandise in Late-Medieval England' (2004) 41 *Explorations in Economic History* 1

Rider, Barry A K, Abrams, Charles and Ferran, Eilis, *Guide to the* Financial Services Act 1986 (2nd ed, 1989)

Robb, George, *White-Collar Crime in Modern England, Financial Fraud and Business Morality, 1845-1929* (1992)

Roberts, John, 'Trust and Control in Anglo-American Systems of Corporate Governance: The Individualizing and Socializing Effects of Processes of Accountability' (2001) 54 *Human Relations* 1547

Rockness, Howard and Rockness, Joanne, 'Legislated Ethics: From Enron to *Sarbanes-Oxley*, the Impact on Corporate America' (2005) 57 *Journal of Business Ethics* 31

Roe, Mark J, 'Path Dependence, Political Options, and Governance Systems', in Hopt, Klaus and Wymeersch, Eddy (eds), *Comparative Corporate Governance: Essays and Materials* (1997)

Roe, Mark J 'Delaware's Competition' (2003) 117 *Harvard Law Review* 588

Romano, Roberta, 'Quack Corporate Governance' (2005) 28 *Regulation* 36

Romano, Roberta, 'The *Sarbanes-Oxley Act* and the Making of Quack Corporate Governance' (2005) 114 *Yale Law Journal* 1521

Rose, Carol M, 'Crystals and Mud in Property Law' (1988) 40 *Stanford Law Review* 577

Rose, Nikolas and Miller, Peter, 'Political Power beyond the State: Problematics of Government' (1992) 43 *British Journal of Sociology* 173

Rose, Nikolas S, *Powers of Freedom: Reframing Political Thought* (1999)

Rose, Nikolas, 'Government and Control' (2000) 40 *British Journal of Criminology* 321

Rose-Ackerman, Susan, *Corruption and Government: Causes, Consequences and Reform* (1999)

Rosen, Robert E, 'The Inside Counsel Movement, Professional Judgement and Organizational Representation' (1989) 64 *Indiana Law Journal* 479

Rosenberg, Gerald N, The Hollow Hope: Can Courts Bring About Social Change? (1991)

Rosenbloom, David H, *Administrative Law for Public Managers* (2003)

Ryan, Lori V, 'Corporate Governance and Business Ethics in North America: The State of the Art' (2005) 44 *Business and Society* 40

Sabatier, Paul, 'An Advocacy Coalition Framework of Policy Change and the Role of Policy Oriented Learning Therein' (1988) 21 *Policy Sciences* 129

Sampson, Anthony, *The Changing Anatomy of Britain* (1982)

Sanders, Joseph, Hamilton, V Lee and Yuasa, Toshikyuki, 'The Institutionalization of Sanctions for Wrongdoing Inside Organizations: Public Judgements in Japan, Russia, and the United States' (1998) 32 *Law and Society Review* 871

Schmidt, Reinhard H and Spindler, Gerald, 'Path Dependence and Complementarity in Corporate Governance' in Gordon, Jeffrey N and Roe, Mark J (eds), *Convergence and Persistence in Corporate Governance* (2004) 114

Schmitthoff, M, 'The Origin of the Joint-Stock Company' (1939) 3 *University of Toronto Law Journal* 74

Schneiberg, Marc, 'Organizational Heterogeneity and the Production of New Forms: Politics, Social Movements, and Mutual Companies in American Fire Insurance, 1899–1930' (2002) 19 *Sociology of Organizations* 39

Schneiberg, Marc and Clemens, Elisabeth, 'The Typical Tools for the Job: Research Strategies in Institutional Analysis' (2006) 24 *Sociological Theory* 195

Schneiberg, Marc and Soule, Sarah, 'Institutionalization as a Contested, Multi-Level Process: The Case of Rate Regulation in American Fire Insurance' in Davis, Gerald F, et al (eds), *Social Movements and Organization Theory: Building Bridges* (2004) 122

Schultz, Vicki, 'Telling Stories about Women and Work: Judicial Interpretations of Sex Segregation in the Workplace in Title VII Cases Raising the Lack of Interest Argument' (1990) 103 *Harvard Law Review* 1749

Schumpeter, Joseph, *Capitalism, Socialism and Democracy* (1943)

Schwarzkopf, David L and Miller, Hugh M, 'Early Evidence of How *Sarbanes-Oxley* Implementation Affects Individuals and Their Workplace Relationships' (2005) 110 *Business and Society Review* 21

Scott, Austin W, 'The Fiduciary Principle' (1949) 37 *California Law Review* 539

Scott, James C, *Seeing Like a State: How Certain Schemes to Improve the Human Condition Have Failed* (1998)

Scott, Marvin B and Lyman, Stanford M, 'Accounts' (1968) 33 *American Sociological Review* 46

Scott, W Richard, 'Unpacking Institutional Arguments' in Powell, Walter W and DiMaggio, Paul J (eds), *The New Institutionalism in Organizational Analysis* (1991) 164

Scott, W Richard, *Institutions and Organizations* (2nd ed, 2002)

Scott, W Richard, Organizations: Rational, Natural, and Open Systems (5th ed, 2005)
Scott, W Richard and Meyer, John W, 'The Organization of Societal Sectors: Propositions and Early Evidence' in Powell, Walter W and DiMaggio, Paul J (eds), *The New Institutionalism in Organizational Analysis* (1991) 108
Scott, W Richard, et al, *Institutional Change and Health Care Organizations: From Professional Dominance to Managed Care* (2000)
Searle, John R, 'Meaning and Speech Acts' (1962) 71 *Philosophical Review* 423
Searle, John R, *Speech Acts: An Essay in the Philosophy of Language* (1969)
Searle, John R, 'How Performatives Work' (1989) 12 *Linguistics and Philosophy* 535
Selznick, Philip, *Law, Society and Industrial Justice* (1969)
Selznick, Philip, *TVA and the Grass Roots* (1989)
Sennett, Richard, *The Corrosion of Character* (1998)
Sennett, Richard, *The Culture of the New Capitalism* (2006)
Sesonske, Alexander, *Jean Renoir: the French Films, 1924–1939* (1980)
Shapiro, Susan P, 'Collaring the Crime, Not the Criminal: Reconsidering the Concept of White-Collar Crime' (1990) 55 *American Sociological Review* 346
Shaw, George Bernard, *The Doctor's Dilemma* (1911)
Shearing, Clifford, 'A Constitutive Conception of Regulation' in Braithwaite, John and Grabosky, Peter (eds), *Business Regulation and Australia's Future* (1993) 67
Sherman, John F, 'Human Rights Implications of the 2004 Amendments to the US Sentencing Guidelines for Organizational Defendants' (2007) *International Commission of Jurists* (forthcoming)
Shleifer, Andrei, and Vishny, Robert W, 'A Survey of Corporate Governance' (1997) 52 *Journal of Finance* 737
Silbey, Susan and Sarat, Austin,'Dispute Processing in Law and Legal Scholarship: From Institutional Critique to the Reconstruction of the Juridical Subject' (1989) 66 *Denver University Law Review* 437
Skeel, David A, 'Corporate Anatomy Lessons' (2004) 113 *Yale Law Journal* 1519
Skrentny, John, *The Ironies of Affirmative Action: Politics, Culture, and Justice in America* (1996)
Slater & Gordon, *Prospectus* (13 April 2007), available at <http://www.slatergordon.com.au/docs/prospectus/Prospectus.pdf>
Smith, Adam, *The Wealth of Nations* (1776)
Smith, Bryant, 'Legal Personality' (1928) 37 *Yale Law Journal* 283
Smith, Thomas A, 'The Efficient Norm for Corporate Law: A Neotraditional Interpretation of Fiduciary Duty' (1999) 98 *Michigan Law Review* 214
Solomon, Jill and Solomon, Aris, *Corporate Governance and Accountability* (2004)
Spurr, John, 'A Profane History of Early Modern Oaths' (2001) 11 *Transactions of the Royal Historical Society* 37
Stephens, David O, 'The *Sarbanes-Oxley Act*: Records Management Implications' (2005) 15 *Records Management Journal* 98
Stewart, James B, *Den of Thieves* (1992)

Stewart, James B, *Den of Thieves* (1993)

Stigler, George J and Friedland, Claire, 'The Literature of Economics: The Case of Berle and Means' (1983) 26 *Journal of Law and Economics* 237

Stiglitz, Joseph, *Globalisation and Its Discontents* (2002)

Stiglitz, Joseph, Making Globalization Work: The Next Steps to Global Justice (2006)

Stinchcombe, Arthur L, When Formality Works: Authority and Abstraction in the Law and Organizations (2001)

Stone, Christopher D, Where the Law Ends: The Social Control of Corporate Behavior (1975)

Strawson, P F, 'Intention and Convention in Speech Acts' (1964) 73 *Philosophical Review* 439

Strine, Leo E, 'Toward a True Corporate Republic: A Traditionalist Response to Bebchuk's Solution for Improving Corporate America' (2006) 119 *Harvard Law Review* 1759

Stryker, Robin, 'Legitimacy Processes as Institutional Politics: Implications for Theory and Research in the Sociology of Organizations' (2000) 17 *Research in the Sociology of Organizations* 179

Stryker, Robin, Scarpellino, Martha and Holtzman, Mellisa, 'Political Culture Wars 1990s Style: The Drum Beat of Quotas in Media Framing of the *Civil Rights Act of 1991*' (1999) 17 *Social Stratification and Mobility* 33

Sturm, Susan, 'Second Generation Employment Discrimination: A Structural Approach' (2001) 101 *Columbia Law Review* 458

Sullivan, Kathleen M, 'The Supreme Court 1991 Term — Foreword: The Justices of Rules and Standards' (1992) 106 *Harvard Law Review* 22

Sunstein, Cass, After the Rights Revolution: Re-Conceiving the Regulatory State (1990)

Sunstein, Cass R, 'Problems with Rules' (1995) 83 *California Law Review* 953

SustainAbility, Taxing Issues — Responsible Business and Tax (2006)

Sutton, John R, et al, 'Legalization of the Workplace' (1994) 99 *American Journal of Sociology* 944

Swift, Jonathan, *Gulliver's Travels* (1726)

Sykes, Trevor, *The Bold Riders* (1984)

Tackett, James A, Wolf, Fran and Claypool, Gregory A, '*Sarbanes-Oxley* and Audit Failure: A Critical Examination' (2004) 19 *Managerial Auditing Journal* 340

Tackett, James A, Wolf, Fran and Claypool, Gregory A, 'Internal Control under *Sarbanes-Oxley*: A Critical Examination' (2006) 21 *Managerial Auditing Journal* 317

Tax Justice Network, (2005) 1(1) *Tax Justice Focus Newsletter* 8

Teubner, Gunther, 'Legal Irritants: Good Faith in British Law or How Unifying Law Ends Up in New Divergences' (1998) 61 *Modern Law Review* 11

Thompson, Robert B, 'Corporate Governance after Enron' (2004) 40 *Houston Law Review* 99

Tilly, Charles, 'Reasons Why' (2004) 22 *Sociological Theory* 445

Tilly, Charles, *Why?* (2006)

Tolbert, Pamela S and Zucker, Lynne G, 'Institutional Sources of Change in the Formal Structure of Orgnaizations: The Diffusion of Civil Service Reform, 1880–1935' (1983) 28 *Administrative Science Quarterly* 22

Toms, Steven and Wright, Mike, 'Divergence and Convergence within Anglo-American Corporate Governance Systems: Evidence from the US and UK, 1950–2000' (2005) 47 *Business History* 267

Tuch, Andrew, 'Investment Banks as Fiduciaries: Implications for Conflicts of Interests' (2005) 29 *Melbourne University Law Review* 478

Turner, Jonathan, *The Institutional Order* (1997)

Tushnet, Mark, 'An Essay on Rights' (1984) 62 *Texas Law Review* 1363

UK Department of Trade and Industry and the Treasury, Coordinating Group on Audit and Accounting Issues, *Final Report* (2003)

US Department of Justice, *Enron Task Force Agreement with Merrill Lynch on Deferred Prosecution* (2003)

US Department of Justice, *Principles of Federal Prosecution of Business Organisations* (2003)

US Department of Justice, *Re KPMG: Deferred Prosecution Agreement* (2005)

US General Accounting Office, *Employment Discrimination: Most Private Sector Employers Use Alternative Dispute Resolution, Report to Congress* (1995)

US General Accounting Office, *Long Term Capital Management — Regulators Need to Focus Greater Attention on Systemic Risk* (1999)

US Securities and Exchange Commission, *Review of the Proxy Process Regarding the Nomination and Election of Directors* (2003)

US Securities and Exchange Commission, *Rules of Practice* (2006)

Vagts, Detlev F, 'Extraterritoriality and the Corporate Governance Law' (2003) 97 *American Journal of International Law* 289

Varess, Farid, 'The Buck Will Stop at the Board? An Examination of Directors' (and Others) Duties in Light of the HIH Collapse' (2002) 16 *Commercial Law Quarterly* 12

Visentini, Gustavo, 'Compatibility and Competition between European and American Corporate Governance: Which Model of Capitalism?' (1998) 23 *Brooklyn Journal of International Law* 833

Vogel, David, *The Market for Virtue: The Potential and Limits of Corporate Social Responsibility* (2005)

Vogel, Steven, 'Why Freer Markets Need More Rules' in Candy, Marc, Levin, Martin and Shapiro, Martin (eds), *Creating Competitive Markets* (2006) 25

von Dornum, Deirdre D, 'The Straight and the Crooked: Legal Accountability in Ancient Greece' (1997) 97 *Columbia Law Review* 1483

von Nessen, Paul, 'Corporate Governance in Australia: Converging with International Developments' (2003) 15 *Australian Journal of Corporate Law* 1

Waldron, Jeremy, *Law and Disagreement* (1999)

Westin, Alan F and Feliu, Alfred G, 'Resolving Employment Disputes without Litigation' (1988)

Wexler, Stephen, 'Practicing Law for Poor People' (1970) 79 *Yale Law Journal* 1049

Whincop, Michael, 'Another Side of Accountability: The Fiduciary Concept and Rent-Seeking in the Governance of Government Corporations' (2002) 25 *University of New South Wales Law Journal* 379

Whittaker, MA, 'Tackling Systemic Risk on Markets: Barings and Beyond' in Fidelis Oditah (ed), *The Future for the Global Securities Market* (1996) 257

Williams, Cynthia A and Conley, John M, 'An Emerging Third Way? The Erosion of the Anglo-American Shareholder Value Construct' (2005) 38 *Cornell International Law Journal* 493

Williams, Patricia, 'Alchemical Notes: Reconstructing Ideals from Deconstructed Rights' (1987) 22 *Harvard Civil Rights–Civil Liberties Law Review* 401

Wormald, Patrick, 'Engla Lond: the Making of an Allegiance' (1994) 7 *Journal of Historical Sociology* 1

Wu, T W, 'Management Buyouts and Earnings Management' (1997) 12 *Journal of Accounting, Auditing and Finance* 373

Wymeersch, Eddy, 'Implementation of the Corporate Governance Codes' in Hopt, Klaus, et al (eds), *Corporate Governance in Context: Corporations, States and Markets in Europe, Japan, and the US* (2005)

Yablon, Charles M and Hill, Jennifer G, 'Timing Corporate Disclosures to Maximize Performance-Based Remuneration: A Case of Misaligned Incentives?' (2000) 35 *Wake Forest Law Review* 83

2 Cases

Abramson v University of Hawaii, 594 F 2d 202 (9th Cir, 1979)

Aequitas v Sparad No 100 Limited (2001) 19 ACLC 1006

Alexander v Gardner-Denver Co, 415 US 36 (1974)

Anderson v Methodist Evangelical Hospital, Inc, 464 F 2d 723 (CA6 1972)

Australian Securities and Investments Commission v Citigroup Global Markets Australia Pty Ltd (No 4) [2007] FCA 963

Brisentine v Stone & Webster Engineering (11th Cir, 21 July 1997) (No 96–6866)

Bristol & West Building Society v Mothew [1998] Ch 1

Brown v Board of Education, 347 US 483 (1954)

Burlington Industries v Ellerth, 524 US 742 (1998)

Caparo Industries Plc v Dickman [1990] 2 AC 605

Cole v Burns Intern Sec Services, 133 (DC Cir, 11 Feb 1997) (No 96-7042)

Consul Developments Pty Ltd v DPC Estates Ltd (1975) 132 CLR 373

Cotran v Rollins Hudig Hall International, Inc, 17 Cal 4th 93 (1998)

D&J Constructions Pty Limited v Head (1987) 9 NSWLR 118

Daly v The Sydney Stock Exchange Limited (1986) 160 CLR 371

Delgado v Lehman, 665 F Supp 460 (1987)
Faragher v City of Boca Raton, 118 S Ct 1115 (1998)
Fitzsimons v R (1997) 15 ACLC 666
Furniss v Dawson [1984] AC 474
Gilmer v Interstate/Johnson Lane Corp, 111 S Ct 1647 (1991)
Giordano v William Patterson College, 804 F Supp 637 (D NJ, 1992)
Goodman Fileder Incorporated (No 2) (2003) ATP 5
Hadid v Lengest Communications Inc [1999] FCA 1798
Hospital Products Limited v United States Surgical Corporation (1984) 156 CLR 41
Hunter v Allis-Chalmers, 797 F 2d 1417 (1986)
In the Matter of Qantas 02R (2007) ATP 07
Kelly v Cooper [1993] AC 205
Leopold v Baccarat, Inc, 82 Fair Empl Prac Cas (BNA) 105, SDNY, 14 February 2000
Mago v Shearson Lehman Hutton, Inc, 956 F 2d 932 (9th Cir, 1992)
Meinhard v Salmon (1928) 164 NE 545
Meritor Savings Bank v Vinson, 106 S Ct 2399 (1981)
Miller v Bank of America, 600 F 2d 211 (1971))
Munford v Barnes & Co, 441 F Supp 459 (1977)
Prince Jefri Bolkiah v KPMG [1999] 2 WLR 215
R (ex parte Fleurose) v Securities and Futures Authority [2002] IRLR 297
Ramsay (WT) Ltd v IRC [1982] AC 300
Re Caremark International Inc Derivative Litig, 698 A 2d 959, 970 (Del Ch, 1996)
Re Netsmart Technologies, Inc Shareholders Litigation, Del CA 2573 VCS
Re SS&C Technologies, Del CA 1525 VCL
Waltman v International Paper Co, 875 F 2d 468 (1989)
Yates v Avco Corp, 819 F 2d 630 (1987)

3 Legislation And Treaties

Act to Restrain the Number and Practice of Brokers and Stock-Jobbers 1697 (UK)
Alien Tort Statute of 1789, 28 USC 1350 (US)
Americans with Disabilities Act of 1990 42 USC § 12112 (1990) (US)
Australian Securities and Investments Commission Act 2001 (Cth) (AUS)
Bank of England Act 1946 (UK) c 27
Barnard's Act 1734 (UK)
Bubble Act 1720 (UK)
Civil Rights Act of 1964, 42 USC § 2000e–2 (2000) (US)
Combined Code on Corporate Governance 2003 (UK)
Companies (Audit, Investigations and Community Enterprise) Act 2004 (UK) c 27
Companies Act 1985 (UK) c 6
Companies Act 2006 (UK) c 46
Company Directors Disqualification Act 1986 (UK) c 46

Convention for the Protection of Human Rights and Fundamental Freedoms, opened for signature 4 November 1950, CETS No 005 (entered into force 3 September 1953)
Corporate Law Economic Reform Program (Audit Reform and Corporate Disclosure) Act 2004 (Cth) (AUS)
Corporations Act (2001) (Cth) (AUS)
Criminal Justice Act 1987 (UK) c 38
Explanatory Memorandum, Corporate Law Economic Reform Program (Audit Reform and Corporate Disclosure) Bill 2003 (Cth)
Explanatory Memorandum, Exposure Draft, Corporations Amendment Bill (No 2) 2005 (Cth)
Federal Arbitration Act, 9 USC §§ 1–16 (US)
Financial Services Act 1986 (UK) c 60
Financial Services and Markets Act 2000 (UK) c 8
Human Rights Act 1998 (UK) c 42
Joint Stock Companies Act 1844 (UK)
Leeman's Act 1867 (UK)
Property, Stock and Business Agents Act 2002 (NSW) (AUS)
Public Company Accounting Reform and Investor Protection Act of 2002, Pub L No 107-204, 116 Stat 745 (2002) (US)
Public Service Act 1999 (Cth) (AUS)
Qantas Sale Act 1992 (Cth) (AUS)
The Companies (Defective Accounts) (Authorised Persons) Order 2005 (SI 2005/699) (UK)
The Directors' Remuneration Report Regulations 2002 (SI 2002/1986) (UK)
The Financial Services and Markets Act 2000 (Right of Action) Regulations 2001 (SI 2001/2256) (UK)
The Prospectus Regulations 2005 (SI 2005/1433) (UK)
The Supervision of Accounts and Reports (Prescribed Body) Order 2005 (SI 2005/715) (UK)
Trade Practices Act 1974 (Cth) (AUS)

4 OTHER MATERIALS

Adams, Christopher and Smith, Peter, 'TUC Chief Attacks Private Equity Industry', *Financial Times* (London), 20 February 2007, 1
Airline Partners Australia (Press Release, 4 May 2007)
Airline Partners Australia (Press Release, 8 May 2007)
Airline Partners Australia (Press Release, 17 May 2007)
'Alinta Boss Quits over Management Buy-Out Row', *Australian Financial Review* (Sydney), 12 January 2007, 1
Allco Equity Partners (Press Release, 6 March 2007)

Anderson, Jenny, 'US Financial Sector Is Losing Its Edge, Report Says', *New York Times* (New York), 22 January 2007, 3

Arcot, Sridhar, Bruno, Valentina and Grimaud, Antoine, 'Corporate Governance in the UK: Is the Comply-or-Explain Approach Working?' <http://fmg.lse.ac.uk/upload_file/496_1st%20Dec%20paper.pdf>

Asare, Stephen K, Cunningham, Lawrence A and Wright, Arnold, 'The *Sarbanes-Oxley* Act: Legal Implications and Research Opportunities' (Research Paper No 122, Boston College Law School, 2006), available at <http://ssrn.com/abstract=947356>

Ashworth, Jon and Heath, Allister, 'The Barbarians Back at the Gate', *The Business* (London), 3 February 2007, 18

Askew, Kate, 'Mental as Anything', *Sydney Morning Herald* (Sydney), 12–13 May 2007, 41

Askew, Kate and Rochfort, Scott, 'Bigger Debt Could undo Qantas', *Sydney Morning Herald* (Sydney), 14 April 2007, 39

ASX Corporate Governance Council, Principles of Good Corporate Governance and Best Practice Recommendations (2003), available at <http://www.shareholder.com/visitors/dynamicdoc/document.cfm?documentid=364&companyid=ASX>

ASX Corporate Governance Council, Response to the Implementation Review Group Report (2004)

ASX Corporate Governance Council, *Explanatory Paper and Consultation Paper* (2006)

ASX Corporate Governance Council Implementation Review Group, Principles of Good Corporate Governance and Best Practice Recommendations: Report to the ASX Corporate Governance Council (2004)

ASX Corporate Governance Council Implementation Review Group, *Second Report to the ASX Corporate Governance Council* (2005), available at <http://www.asx.com.au/about/pdf/Second_IRG_report_final.pdf>

Australian Securities and Investment Commission, 'Statement on Qantas' (Press Release, 7 May 2007)

Banks, Gary, 'Reducing the Regulatory Burden: The Way Ahead' (Speech delivered at the Monash Centre for Regulatory Studies, Melbourne, 17 May 2006)

Barber, Lionel and Smith, Peter, 'Permira Accepts Need to Be More Open', *Financial Times* (London), 22 February 2007, 1

Barnhart, Bill, 'Blackstone Wants to Abort Bumpy Flight on Orbitz', *Chicago Tribune* (Chicago), 11 May 2007 (online edition)

Bartholomeusz, Stephen, 'How Greedy Hedge Funds Wrecked Qantas Deal', *The Age* (Melbourne), 8 May 2007 (online edition)

Benner Katie, et al, 'The Power List', *Fortune* (New York), 5 March 2007, 45

Berman, Dennis, Sender, Henry and Zuckerman, Gregory, 'Blackstone Aims to Keep Control as Public Entity', *Wall Street Journal* (New York), 23 March 2007, A1

Berman, Dennis, 'Unusual Buyout Offers a Piece to Shareholders', *Wall Street Journal* (New York), 27 April 2007, A1

Bernanke, Ben, 'Regulation and Financial Innovation' (Speech delivered at the Financial Markets Conference, Sea Island, Georgia, 15 May 2007)

'Bernanke Calls for UK-Style Regulation', *Financial Times* (London), 15 May 2007

Bernasek, Anna, 'Why Let the IRS See What the SEC Doesn't?', *New York Times* (New York), 5 February 2006

Better Regulation Commission, *Risk, Responsibility and Regulation, Whose Risk Is It anyway?* <http://www.brc.gov.uk>

Black, Julia, *Mapping the Contours of Contemporary Financial Services Regulation* (CARR Discussion Paper No 17, 2003), available at <http://www.lse.ac.uk/collections/CARR>

'Blackstone Profit Is $2bn on Sales', *Chicago Tribune* (Chicago), 14 March 2007 (online edition)

Briault, Clive, 'Treating Customers Fairly and More Principles-based Regulation' (Speech delivered at FSA Summer School, Cambridge, 24 July 2006), available at <http://www.fsa.gov.uk/pages/Library/Communication/Speeches/2006/0724_cb.shtml>

Broshko, Erinn B and Li, Kai, 'Corporate Governance Requirements in Canada and the United States: A Legal and Empirical Comparison of the Principles-Based and the Rules-Based Approaches' (Working Paper, Sauder School of Business, University of British Columbia, 2006), available at <http://papers.ssrn.com/sol3/papers.cfm?abstract_id=892708>

Bruce, Robert, 'Transatlantic Squabbles over "True and Fair"', Financial Times (London), 1 March 2007

Buffini, Fiona, 'AWB Scandal Erodes Line in Sand Hopes', *Australian Financial Review* (Sydney), 16 February 2006, 12

Carlyle Group, 'Private Equity Council Is Formed to Provide Research and Information' (Press Release, 26 December 2006)

Chon, Gina, Singer, Jason and McCracken, Jeffrey, 'Chrysler Deal Heralds New Direction for Detroit', *Wall Street Journal* (New York), 15 May 2006, A1

'Citigroup's Brazen Bond Bet Pays Off: But Sooner or Later There Will Be a Casualty', *Guardian Unlimited* (London), 11 August 2004

Citizens for Tax Justice, 'Less than Zero: Enron's Income Tax Payments, 1996–2000' (2002) <http://www.ctj.org/html/enron.htm>

Clayton Dubilier & Reid (Press Release, 12 September 2005)

Clegg, Brett, 'No Patsies around this Time to Subsidise the Fee Factory', *Australian Financial Review* (Sydney), 31 March 2007, 12

Coffee, John C, 'A Theory of Corporate Scandals: Why the US and Europe Differ', (Working Paper No 274, Centre for Law and Economic Studies, Columbia University School of Law, 2005)

Coffee, John C, 'Law and the Market: The Impact of Enforcement' (Working Paper No 304, Centre for Law and Economic Studies, Columbia University School of Law, 2007)

Coffee, John, 'Law and the Market: The Role of Enforcement' (Paper presented at the Dynamics of Capital Market Governance Workshop, Australian National University, 14 March 2007)

Cole, Margaret, 'FSA Investigations & Enforcement 2007: A Practitioner's Guide for Regulated Firms' (Speech delivered at the City and Financial Conference, 24 January 2007)

Cole, Margaret, 'Insider Dealing in the City' (Speech delivered at the London School of Economics, 17 March 2007)

Committee on Finance Hearing 108–371, United States Senate, Washington DC *Tax Shelters: Who's Buying, Who's Selling, and What's the Government Doing About It?* (21 October 2007).

Commonwealth, HIH Royal Commission, *The Failure of HIH Insurance* (2003)

Cornell, Andrew, 'The Year of Easy Money', *Weekend Australian Financial Review* (Sydney), 27 December 2006, 20

Cornell, Andrew, 'Boards Out of Step with Takeover Frenzy: Argus', *Australian Financial Review* (Sydney), 15 May 2007, 1

Corporate Law Economic Reform Program (1998) Commonwealth of Australia <http://www.treasury.gov.au/documents/264/PDF/clerp.pdf>

Corporate Watch, *The Business Case for CSR* <www.corporatewatch.org/?lid=2680>

Costello, Peter, 'Opening Address' (Speech delivered at the ASIC Summer School, Sydney, 5 March 2007)

Costello, Peter (Treasurer) and Vaile, Mark (Deputy Prime Minister and Minister for Transport and Regional Services) 'Qantas Airways Ltd' (Joint Press Release, 6 March 2007), available at <http://www.treasurer.gov.au/tsr/content/pressreleases/2007/009.asp>

Creedy, Steve, 'Qantas Takeover Farce May End in Court', *The Australian* (Sydney), 8 May 2007, 1

Creedy, Steve and Korporaal, Glenda, 'Canberra to Order Qantas Sell-Off', *The Australian* (Sydney), 8 May 2007, 21

Creedy, Steve, 'APA to Rip $4bn out of Qantas', *The Australian* (Sydney), 13 April 2007, 19

Crowe, David, 'Promises Aplenty, but Hard to Enforce,' *Australian Financial Review* (Sydney), 7 March 2007, 11

Cumming, Douglas and Johan, Sofia, 'Regulatory Harmonisation and the Development of Private Equity Markets' (Law and Economics Workshop No 13, University of California, Berkeley, 2006)

Cutler, Stephen, 'Tone at the Top: Getting It Right' (Speech delivered at the Second Annual General Counsel Roundtable, Washington DC, 3 December 2004)

Davidoff, Steven M, 'Regulating Listings in a Global Market' (Research Paper No 07–02, Wayne State University Law School, 2007), available at <http://ssrn.com/abstract=964704>

Donaldson, William, 'US Capital Markets in the Post-*Sarbanes-Oxley* World: Why Our Markets Should Matter to Foreign Issuers' (Speech delivered at the London School of Economics, London, 25 January 2005)

Dubnick, Melvin J, 'Orders of Accountability' (Speech delivered at World Ethics Forum: Leadership, Ethics and Integrity in Public Life, Oxford, 2006)

Durie, John, 'ASIC Treads Fine Line on Hardie', *Australian Financial Review* (Sydney), 16 February 2007, 84

Durie, John, 'Bid for Qantas Looks a Goner', *Australian Financial Review* (Sydney), 11 May 2007, 64

Editorial, 'Politics of Envy Alive and Well', *Australian Financial Review* (Sydney), 18 May 2007

Editorial, 'Barbarians Back in the Dock, *Economist* (London), 1 March 2007, 10

Editorial, 'While the Sun Shines', *Financial Times* (London), 3 December 2005, 14

Editorial, 'Private Equity Should Beware its Own Success', *Financial Times* (London), 22 December 2006, 14

Editorial, 'The New Greenmail', *Wall Street Journal* (New York), 27 February 2007, A16

Editorial, 'Qantas and the Markets', *Wall Street Journal* (New York), 23 March 2007 (online edition)

Enforcement Strategy Policy Document (2006) Companies House <http://www.companieshouse.gov.uk/about/policyDocuments/enforcementStrategy.pdf>

Ernst & Young, 'Mergers and Acquisitions Index' (Press Release, 5 December 2006)

Evans, Simon, 'KKR Wins inside Running in $21bn Two-Horse Race', *Australian Financial Review* (Sydney), 12–13 May 2007, 3

Farrelly, P, 'Regulators in Wonderland', *The Observer, Business Section*, 25 May 1997, 7

Ferran, Eilis, 'Company Law Reform in the UK: A Progress Report' (Working Paper No 27/2005, European Corporate Governance Institute, Cambridge, 2005)

Financial Reporting Council, *Memorandum of Understanding between the Financial Reporting Review Panel and the Financial Services Authority* (2005) <http://www.frc.org.uk/images/uploaded/documents/300305%20-%20FSA-FRRP%20Memorandum%20of%20Understanding%20_Final_1.pdf>

Financial Reporting Review Panel, *Financial Reporting Review Panel Operating Procedures* <http://www.frc.org.uk/frrp/how/procedures.cfm>

Financial Services Arrangement, 'Senior Management Arrangements, Systems and Controls' (Consultation Paper 35, 1999)

Financial Services Authority, 'The Regulation of Approved Persons' (Consultation Paper 26, 1999)

Financial Services Authority, *An Ethical Framework for Financial Services* (Discussion Paper No 18, 2002)

Financial Services Authority, *Final Notice to the 'Shell' Transport and Trading Company plc* (2004) <http://www.fsa.gov.uk/pubs/final/shell_24aug04.pdf>

Financial Services Authority, 'FSA Fines Citigroup £13.9 million (€20.9mn) for Eurobond Trades' (Press Release, 28 June 2005), available at <http://www.fsa.gov.uk/pages/Library/Communication/PR/2005/072.shtml>

Financial Services Authority, 'FSA Closes Enquiries into Shell Individuals' (Press Release, 9 November 2005)

Financial Services Authority, *Principles of Good Regulation* (2006)

Financial Services Authority, *Final Notice to David John Maslen* (2006) <http://www.fsa.gov.uk/pubs/final/maslen.pdf>

Financial Services Authority, 'FSA Fines Deutsche Bank £6.3 million and Mr David Maslen £350,000 for Market Conduct' (Press Release, 11 April 2006), available at <http://www.fsa.gov.uk/pages/Library/Communication/PR/2006/036.shtml>

Financial Services Authority, 'Measuring Market Cleanliness' (Occasional Paper 23, 2006)

Financial Services Authority, 'Private Equity: A Discussion of Risk and Regulatory Engagement' (Discussion Paper 06/06, 2006)

Financial Services Authority, 'Private Equity, A Discussion of Risk and Regulatory Engagement' (Feedback Statement 07/03, 2007)

Financial Services Authority, 'New FSA Team to Crack Down on Financial Crime' (Press Release, 22 January 2007)

Financial Services Authority, 'Updated Measurement of Market Cleanliness' (Occasional Paper 25 2007)

Financial Services Authority, *Facts and Figures* <http://www.fsa.gov.uk/Pages/About/Media/Facts/index.shtml>

Financial Services Lawyers Association, 'Principles-Based Regulation: Can It Work?' (Inauguration Forum: Ethics in Financial Services Law, 7 June 2007), available at <http://www.FSLA.org.uk>

Friedman, Milton, 'The Social Responsibility of Business Is to Increase Its Profits', *New York Times Magazine* (New York), 13 September 1970, 32

'FSA Regulation Move to Cost City £50m', *Financial Times* (London), 7 February 2007, 4

Furse, Clara, 'Comment: SOX Is Not to Blame — London Is Just Better as a Market', *Financial Times* (London), 18 September 2006, 19

Gadziala, Mary Ann, 'Rebuilding Ethics and Compliance in the Securities Industry' (Speech delivered at the NYSE Regulation First Annual Securities Conference, Securities and Exchange Commission, New York, 23 June 2005)

Galanter, Marc and Rogers, Joel, 'A Transformation of American Business Disputing? Some Preliminary Observations' (Working Paper, Institute for Legal Studies, Madison, 1991)

Gettler, Leon, 'In the Politics of Pay, It's up to Us to Show Them the Money', *The Age* (Melbourne), 19 May 2007, 6

Gettler, Leon, 'IFSA Censures States over 100-Member Rule', *Sydney Morning Herald* (Sydney), 21 June 2006, 37

Glassman, Cynthia, 'Remarks: Priorities and Concerns at the SEC' (Speech delivered at the 10th Annual Corporate Counsel Compliance Institute, Washington DC, 9 March 2006)

Gluyas, Richard, 'Meyer's Makeover Reaps $1bn', *The Australian* (Sydney), 28 March 2007, 21

Gordon, Michael, Letter to the Editor, *Financial Times* (London), 31 January 2007, 14

Gray, Joanne, 'ASIC Agnostic on Private Equity', *Australian Financial Review* (Sydney), 16 May 2007, 10

Green, John, 'Heroes for More than One Day', *Australian Financial Review* (Sydney), 11 April 2007, 62

Hall, James, 'Credibility at Stake at Every Corner', *Australian Financial Review* (Sydney), 7 May 2007, 19

Henry, David and Thornton, Emily, 'Buy It, Flip It, then Strip It', *Businessweek* (New York), 7 August 2006, 28

Hewett, Jennifer, 'Crash: Private Equity Falls Back to Earth', *The Weekend Australian* (Sydney), 5–6 May 2007, 33

Hewett, Jennifer, 'Private Lives', *Australian Financial Review Magazine* (Sydney), February 2007, 44

Hewett, Jennifer and Korporeal, Glenda, 'It's Red Faces at MacBank', *The Australian* (Sydney), 8 May 2007, 27

Hewitt, Conrad, 'Remarks' (Speech delivered at Baruch College, New York, 3 May 2007)

Hewitt, Conrad, 'Remarks' (Speech delivered at the Practising Law Institute's SEC Speaks Series, Washington DC, 9 February 2007)

'HIH Regulator Deceived', *The Australian* (Sydney), 24 January 2003

Hill, Andrew, *Lombard Column*, *Financial Times* (London), 7 February 2007

Houlder, Vanessa, 'Tax Avoidance as a Morality Tale', *Financial Times* (London), 22 November 2004

House Financial Services Committee, *Private Equity's Effects on Workers and Firms*, United States Congress, Washington DC, 16 May 2007

Huertas, Thomas F, FSA Director Wholesale Firms Division and Banking Sector Leader, 'Counting on Compliance: The Implications of More Principles-Based Regulation' (Speech delivered at the Fourth Annual Complinet Compliance Conference, 31 January 2007)

Huertas, Thomas, 'Regulating the Relationship: Banks, Firms and the FSA' (Speech delivered at the Joint AFB and ACT Conference, 8 February 2005), available at <http://www.fsa.gov.uk/Pages/Library/Communication/Speeches/2005/sp226.shtml>

Humphry, Richard, 'If Not, Why Not?' (Speech delivered at Australian Institute of Company Directors Forum, Sydney, 2 April 2003)

Hutter, Bridget M, 'The Attractions of Risk-based Regulation: Accounting for the Emergence of Risk Ideas in Regulation' (Discussion Paper No 33, Centre for Analysis of Risk and Regulation, London School of Economics, 2005), available at <http://www.lse.ac.uk/collections/CARR>

Ichimura, Hidehiko and Taber, Christopher R, 'Direct Estimation of Policy Impacts' (Working Paper, National Bureau of Economic Research, Cambridge, Massachusetts, 2000)

Interview with Christopher Wray, 'The Justice Department's Rational Approach to Deterring Corporate Crime', *The Metropolitan Corporate Counsel* (New Jersey), July 2005, 35, available at <http://www.metrocorpcounsel.com/pdf/2005/July/35,53.pdf>

Interview with David Hartnett, *Accountancy Age*, October 2005

Ip, Greg, 'Fed, Other Regulators Turn Attention to Risk in Lenders LBO Lending', *Wall Street Journal* (New York), 18 May 2007, C1

John, Danny, Murray, Lisa and Askew, Kate, 'Up, Up and Away', *Sydney Morning Herald* (Sydney), 19–20 May 2007, 41

Johnston, Eric, 'Global MacBank Roars to Record $1.5bn Profit', *Australian Financial Review* (Sydney), 16 May 2007, 1

Johnston, Ian, 'The New Financial Services Reform Disclosure Regime, Likely Impacts on our Industry' (Speech delivered at the Financial Planning Association Conference, Gold Coast, 10 May 2002)

Jury, Alan, 'Private Equity Interest Jumps,' *Australian Financial Review* (Sydney), 30 March 2007, 79

Kaplow, Louis, 'Rules versus Principles: An Economic Analysis' (1992) 42 *Duke Law Journal* 557

Klinger, Scott and Sklar, Holly, 'Titans of the Enron Economy', *The Nation*, 5 August 2002

Knight, Elizabeth, 'It's the Mother of All Margin Loans', *Sydney Morning Herald* (Sydney), 13 April 2007, 19

Knight, Elizabeth, 'MacBank Does Have an Achilles Heel', *Sydney Morning Herald* (Sydney), 16 May 2007 (online edition)

Knott, David, 'Changing Dynamics of the Superannuation Industry' (Speech delivered at the Association of Superannuation Funds of Australia Ltd Luncheon, Sydney, 25 September 2002)

Kohler, Alan, 'In the End APA Lacked Bottle', *Sydney Morning Herald* (Sydney), 12–13 May 2007, 45

Korporaal, Glenda, 'Clarke Lashes Out at Governance Laws', *The Australian* (Sydney), 28 March 2007, 21

KPMG, *Tax in the Boardroom* (Discussion Paper, 2004)

KPMG, 'Increasing Value from Disposal' (Press Release, 28 February 2007)

Kroeker, James, 'Remarks' (Speech delivered at the Conference on Principles-Based Accounting and the Challenges of Implementation, New York, 4 April 2007)

La Porta, Rafael, et al, 'Investor Protection: Origins, Consequences and Reform' (Financial Sector Discussion Paper, World Bank, 1999)

Labaton, Stephen, 'Officials Reject More Oversight of Hedge Funds', *New York Times* (New York), 23 February 2007, 1

Lerner, Josh, Schoar, Antoinette and Wang, Wan, 'Smart Institutions, Foolish Choices: The Limited Partner Performance Puzzle' (Research Paper No 4523–05, Sloan School of Management, Massachusetts Institute of Technology, 2005)

Lew, Nicholas and Ramsay, Ian 'Corporate Governance Law Reform and Delisting in Australia' (Research Paper No 202, Centre for Corporate Law and Securities Law Regulation, University of Melbourne, 2006)

'London Issues Guidelines for Foreign Listings', *Financial Times* (London), 9 May 2007, 43

Lowenstein, Douglas, House Financial Services Committee, United States Congress, Washington DC (16 May 2007)

Maiden, Malcolm, 'Bankers Are Being Very Brave', *Sydney Morning Herald* (Sydney), 13 April 2007, 19

Maitland, Alison, 'BT Chairman Criticises US Governance', *Financial Times* (Sydney), 23 November 2004, 22

McCarthy, Sir Callum, 'Risk Based Regulation: The FSA's Experience' (Speech delivered at ASIC Summer School, Sydney, 13 February 2006

McCarthy, Sir Callum, 'Financial Regulation: Myth and Reality' (Speech delivered at the British American Business London Insight Series and Financial Services Forum, 13 February 2007)

McCreevy, Charlie, 'Private Equity: Getting It Right' (Speech delivered to All Parliamentary Group, British Venture Capital Association, London, 22 March 2007)

Moore, Heidi, 'Revenue Gap Widens', *Financial News Online*, 26 February 2007

Morgenson, Gretchen, 'Just Say No to Lowball Buyout Offers', *New York Times* (New York), 20 May 2007 (online edition)

Morgenson, Gretchen, 'Investors Get Voice on Pay at Verizon', *New York Times* (New York), 19 May 2007, 1

Morgenson, Gretchen, 'Whispers of Mergers Set Off Suspicious Trading', *New York Times* (New York), 27 August 2006, A1

Murphy, Matthew, 'Qantas Admits Takeover Bid Dead', *The Age* (Melbourne), 7 May 2007, 1

Murray, Alan, 'Private Equity's Successes Stir Up a Backlash that May Be Misdirected', *Wall Street Journal* (New York), 9 February 2007, A9

Murray, Alan, 'How Labor's Pension Funds Are Playing Private Equity Two Ways', *Wall Street Journal* (New York), 28 February 2007, A10

Neoh, Anthony, 'China's Financial Markets — Growth Opportunity and Challenge' (Speech delivered at ASIC the Summer School, Sydney, 5 March 2007)

Newman, Geoffrey, 'Airport Sale Nets Macquarie $115m', *The Weekend Australian* (Sydney), 19–20 May 2007, 32

Nicholas, Katrina and Taylor, Leonore, 'Costello Puts Private Equity on Tax Alert', *Australian Financial Review* (Sydney), 10 April 2007, 1

Nicholas, Katrina, 'The Man Who Said No', *Australian Financial Review* (Sydney), 31 March 2007, 22

Nicholas, Katrina, 'MacBank Runs into Flak as Blame Games Takes Off', *Australian Financial Review* (Sydney), 12–13 May, 2007, 26

Nicholas, Katrina and Poljak, Vesna, 'Jackson to Quit in Qantas Fallout', *Australian Financial Review* (Sydney), 18 May 2007, 1

O'Brien, Justin, Interview with John Barber (New York, 24 April 2007)

O'Brien, Justin, Interview with Patrick Dunne (London, 23 March 2007)

O'Brien, Justin, Interview with Michael Gordon (London, 23 March 2007)

O'Brien, Justin, Interview with Martin Lipton (New York, 23 April 2007)

'Offer Over, Its Back to the Board', *The Australian* (Sydney), 8 May 2007, 26

Pahalippou, Ludovic and Gottschalg, Oliver, 'The Performance of Private Equity Funds' (Working Paper, EFA Moscow Meetings 2005, INSEAD, Paris, 2006)

Parliamentary Joint Committee on Corporations and Financial Services, *Corporate Responsibility: Managing Risk and Creating Value*, Parliament of Australia, Canberra, 2006

Paulson, Henry, 'Opening Remarks' (Speech delivered at the Treasury's Capital Markets Competitive Conference, Georgetown University, 13 March 2007)

Paulson, Henry, 'Remarks: Competitiveness of US Capital Markets' (Speech delivered at the Economic Club of New York, New York, 20 November 2006)

Pearce, Chris, 'Government consults on proposed corporate governance reforms' (Press Release, 7 February 2005)

Pearce, Chris, 'Key Corporate Governance Reforms in Jeopardy' (Press Release, 27 July 2007)

Pickard, Jim and Smith, Peter, 'Myners Warns of Risks from Private Equity', *Financial Times* (London), 20 February 2007, 1

Pitt, Harvey, 'Remarks' (Speech delivered at the Annual Meeting of the American Bar Association's Business Law Section, Washington DC, 12 August 2002)

Plender, John, 'Western crony capitalism', *Financial Times* (London), 3-4 October 1998, 10

Power, Michael, 'Organizations and Auditability: A Theory' (Paper presented at *SCORE Conference*, Stockholm, 2005)

Priest, Marcus and Skulley, M, 'ASIC Seeks Bans for Hardie Asbestos Directors', *Australian Financial Review* (Sydney), 16 February2007, 1

Priest, Marcus, 'Lawyers Float a Multi-Billion Dollar Idea', *Australian Financial Review* (Sydney), 18 May 2007, 1

'Private Equity Has Eyes on Developing World', *Australian Financial Review* (Sydney), 18 May 2007, 40

Profile, 'Damon Buffini', *Money Week* (London), 23 February 2007, 40

Qantas, *Target's Statement*, 9 February 2007

'Qantas Staff Fund Won't OK Takeover', *The Australian* (Sydney), 8 February 2007, 23

Rhodes, William, 'A Market Correction Is Coming, This Time for Real', *Financial Times* (London), 29 March 2007, 11

Richardson, Karen and Singer, Jason, 'Private Equity, Public Offerings Have a History', *Wall Street Journal* (New York), 2 April 2007, A1

Rochfort, Scott 'Qantas Raiders May Share Spoils', *Sydney Morning Herald* (Sydney), 13 April 2007

Rochfort, Scott, 'Raiders to Gouge $4 b from Qantas', *Sydney Morning Herald* (Sydney), 13 April 2007, 1

Rochfort, Scott, 'Qantas Farce: Heads Will Roll', *Sydney Morning Herald* (Sydney), 7 May 2007, 1

Romano, Roberta, 'The *Sarbanes-Oxley Act* and the Making of Quack Corporate Governance' (Working Paper No 04-37, ICF Yale University, 2004), available at <http://ssrn.com/abstract=596101>

Ross Sorkin, Andrew, 'A Buyout Deal that Has Many Shades of Green', *New York Times* (New York), 27 February 2007, B1

Rutenberg, Jim, 'Bush Tells Wall St to Rethink Pay Practices', *New York Times* (New York), 1 February 2007, 11

Scannell, Kara and Hughes, Siobhan, 'House Clears an Executive-Pay Measure', *Wall Street Journal* (New York), 21 April 2007, A3

Scannell, Kara, 'House Clears an Executive Pay Measure', *Wall Street Journal* (New York), 21 April 2007, A3

Scannell, Kara, 'Insider Trading: It's Back with a Vengeance', *Wall Street Journal* (New York), 5 May 2007, B1

Schmidt, Lucinda, 'Surviving Private Equity', *Australian Financial Review Boss Magazine*, May 2007, 46

Schwartz, Nelson, 'Wall Street's Man of the Moment', *Fortune* (New York), 5 March 2007, 40

Senate Select Committee to Study Governmental Operations with Respect to Intelligence Activities, United States Senate, Washington DC (1975–6)

Senate Standing Committee on Economics, Inquiry into the Private Equity Investment and its Effects on Capital Markets and the Australian Economy, Parliament of Australia, Canberra, 18 March 2007

Senator Fred Thompson, Committee on Homeland Security and Governmental Affairs Hearing, United States Senate, Washington DC, *The Fall of Enron: How Could It Have Happened?* (24 January 2002)

Sender, Henry, 'Inside the Minds of Kravis, Roberts', *Wall Street Journal* (New York), 3 January 2007, A1

Smith, Philip, *Negligence Claims Could Reach New Height with Litigation Funding Trend* (15 February 2007) Accountancy Age <http://www.accountancyage.com/best-practice/analysis/2183554/negligence-claims-reach-heights>

Smith, Randall, Scannell, Kara and Davies, Paul, 'A Brazen Insider Scheme Revealed', *Wall Street Journal* (New York), 2 March 2007, C1

Smith, Rebecca and Carlton, Jim, 'Environmentalist Groups Feud Over Terms of TXU Buyout', *Wall Street Journal* (New York), 3 March 2007, A1

Social Funds, *Newsroom* <http://www.socialfunds.com/news>

Solomon, Deborah, 'Treasury Targets Financial Fixes', *Wall Street Journal* (New York), 18 May 2007, C1

'Strengthening Corporate Governance', UK, Parliamentary Debates, House of Commons, 29 January 2003 (Patricia Hewitt)

Submission to Senate Standing Committee on Economics, Parliament of Australia, Canberra, May 2007 (Australian Institute of Superannuation Trustees)

Submission to Senate Standing Committee on Economics, Parliament of Australia, Canberra, 1 May 2007 (Australian Venture Capital and Private Equity Association Limited)

Submission to Senate Standing Committee on Economics, *Inquiry into the Private Equity Investment and its Effects on Capital Markets and the Australian Economy*, Parliament of Australia, Canberra, 11 May 2007 (Ernst & Young)

Submission to Senate Standing Committee on Economics, Parliament of Australia, Canberra, 26 April 2007 (UniSuper)

Swan, Wayne, 'Speech to ASFA: Building Prosperity for the Next Decade' (Speech delivered at the Association of Superannuation Funds Australia Ltd Lunch, Westin Hotel, Sydney, 15 March 2007)

Tabakoff, Nick, 'Venture Capital Blamed as PBL Media Bones Eddie McGuire', *The Weekend Australian* (Sydney), 19–20 May 2007, 31

Takeovers Panel, 'Insider Participation in Control Transactions' *Issue Paper No 19* (2007)

Takeovers Panel, 'Unacceptable Circumstances' *Guidance Note 1* (28 September 2004)

Takeovers Panel, 'Insider Participation in Control Transactions' *Draft Guidance Note No 19* (2007)

Takeovers Panel, 'Insider Participation in Control Transactions' *Guidance Note No 19* (2007)

Takeovers Panel, *Insider Participation in Control Transactions* (Public Consultation Response Statement, 7 June 2007)

Takeovers Panel, 'Qantas Airways Limited — Panel Decision' (Press Release, 20 March 2007)

Takeovers Panel, 'Qantas Airways Limited 02 — Receipt of Application and Decision' (Press Release, 6 May 2007)

Taskforce on Reducing Regulatory Burdens on Business, Parliament of Australia, *Rethinking Regulation: Report of the Taskforce on Reducing Regulatory Burdens on Business* (January 2006)

The Berne Declaration, *First 'Public Eye Awards' for Irresponsible Corporate Behaviour* (11 January 2005) <http://www.evb.ch/en/p25003365.html>

'The Uneasy Crown', *Economist* (London), 10 February 2007, 69

Tiner, John, 'Principles-Based Regulation and What It Means for Insurers' (Speech delivered at Insurance Sector Conference, 20 March 2006), available at <http://www.fsa.gov.uk/pages/Library/Communication/Speeches/2006/1013_jt.shtml>

Tiner, John, 'Principles Based Regulation: The EU Context' (Speech delivered at APCIMS Annual Conference, Barcelona, 13 October 2006)

Tiner, John, 'Keynote Address' (Speech delivered at the FSA Conference on More Principles-Based Regulation, 23 April 2007)

Tiner, John, 'Harnessing the Market through Principles and Disclosure' (Speech delivered at the Association of Corporate Treasurers, 24 April 2007)

Tingle, Laura, 'Political Nightmare in the Baggage Hold', *Australian Financial Review* (Sydney), 7 March 2007, 9

Treasury Select Committee, *Transparency in Financial Markets and the Structure of UK PLC*, Parliament of the United Kingdom, London, 20 March 2007

Tyndall, Fiona and Jury, Allan, 'My Store', *Australian Financial Review Boss Magazine* (Sydney), February 2007, 17

UK Department of Trade and Industry, 'Bill to Save Business Millions Receives Royal Assent' (Press release, 8 November 2007)

US Securities and Exchange Commission, *Standards Relating to Listed Company Audit Committees*, Final Rule (9 April 2003) available at <http://www.sec.gov/rules/final/33-8220.htm>

US Securities and Exchange Commission, 'SEC Votes to Propose Changes to Disclosure Requirements Concerning Executive Compensation and Related Matters' (Press release, 17 January 2006)

Washington, Stuart, 'Winning Formula: Aggression and Persistence', *Sydney Morning Herald* (Sydney), 19 May 2007 (online edition)

Waters, Dan, 'Implementing Principles-Based Regulation' (Speech delivered at the Association of British Insurers Conference, London, 7 December 2006), available at <http://www.fsa.gov.uk/pages/Library/Communication/Speeches/2006/1207_dw.shtml>

Waters, Dan, 'NEWCOB and More Principles-Based Regulation' (Speech delivered at NEWCOB Briefings, January/February 2007)

Weekes, Peter, *The Sunday Age* (Melbourne), 20 May 2007 (online edition)

White, Erin and Patrick, Aaron O, 'Shareholders push for vote on executive pay', *Wall Street Journal* (New York), 26 February 2007, B1

White, Erin and Lublin, Joann, 'Private Equity Firms Stock Up on Executives', *Wall Street Journal* (New York), 16 May 2007, B1

Whittaker, Andrew, 'Professional and Financial Regulation — Conflict or Convergence?' (Speech delivered at Fountain Court Chambers Conference, 31 January 2006), available at <http://www.fsa.gov.uk/pages/Library/Communication/Speeches/2006/0131_aw.shtml>

'Will Street Pity the Fools', *Wall Street Journal* (New York), 5 January 2007, C14

Wilson, Sarah, 'Supervision in a Principles-Based World' (Speech delivered at the FSA Retail Firms Division Conference, London, 27 February, 2007

Wolff, Martin, 'New Revolution as Unfettered Finance Reshapes the Global Economy', *The Australian* (Sydney), 25 June 2007, 33

Wray, Christopher, 'Remarks' (Speech delivered at American Bar Association White Collar Crime Luncheon, University Club, Washington DC, 25 February 2005)

Yates, Peter, (Speech delivered at the ASX Investor Hour, Australian Shareholder Association, Sydney, 15 May 2007)

Yea, Philip, 'Do We Condemn or Cheer the Flight to Private Equity', *Financial Times* (London), 15 February 2007, 15